From the Foreword to *Movies with Stanley Cavell in Mind*

Stanley Cavell matters to us all because he explains film's affinity to philosophy, not in a traditional, academic sense, but in our everyday lives: philosophy responds to the desire that drives us to film in the first place. He matters, in this sense, not only for the study of film, but way beyond it—since film is an essential part of our contemporary form of life. Cavell is, to my mind, the best thinker for helping us account for the power of the film experience, and the fourteen chapters collected here provide ample reason for understanding the importance of Cavell for the study of film. All of the contributors to this wonderful, collective enterprise—brought together by David LaRocca—have in a similar way encountered him and his work. Whether they are revisiting films Cavell loved or taking up the invitation to explore new films, they reveal the importance of Cavell's writing and method.

SANDRA LAUGIER, Professor of Philosophy, Université Paris 1 Panthéon-Sorbonne, France

Praise for *The Thought of Stanley Cavell and Cinema: Turning Anew to the Ontology of Film a Half-Century after* The World Viewed

A brilliant collection of original essays by major figures in the field. The genius of Cavell's writings on film is in sharp focus throughout—likewise the continued provocation of *The World Viewed* and its successor books and essays.

MICHAEL FRIED, J. R. Herbert Boone Emeritus Professor of Humanities and the History of Art, Johns Hopkins University, USA

Stanley Cavell argued that film exists in a state of philosophy. Part of what he meant by this was that thinking about a film is a way of doing philosophy. That has been his influential and most controversial claim. The authors in this collection explore what he might have meant in ways more variegated, thoughtful, original and illuminating than anything I have seen before. *The Thought of Stanley Cavell and Cinema*, exemplary in its clarity and carefulness, is a watershed both in our understanding of Cavell and of film itself.

ROBERT PIPPIN, Evelyn Stefansson Nef Distinguished Service Professor, University of Chicago, USA

Now for a new audience comes David LaRocca's edited collection *The Thought of Stanley Cavell and Cinema*. [...] The expertise of its contributors speaks for itself, and it will undoubtedly become [...] the definitive record of the scholars of Cavell and what they had to say about *The World Viewed* at the time of Cavell's death. [...T]he collection will serve as further evidence of the canonization of *The World Viewed* and its centrality to the discipline of film-philosophy or the philosophy of film (*Screening the Past*, no. 45).

> REX BUTLER, Professor of Art History & Theory, Monash University, Australia

Praise for *Inheriting Stanley Cavell: Memories, Dreams, Reflections*

Inheriting Stanley Cavell, beautifully edited by David LaRocca, is so much more than a gathering of reminiscences and testimonials. So many of the pieces in the volume prove gripping, and they cumulatively transformed my sense of what Cavell had accomplished. This volume makes a strong case for the revolution that Cavell's extraordinary philosophic sensibility, powerful presence as a teacher, and wide-range of concerns brought about in North American philosophy. For many of the contributors, Cavell not only revived their faith in philosophy, but showed them what it meant to be alive in their feelings and thinking. He demonstrated, not only in *The Claim of Reason* but in his astonishing exploration of films, Shakespearean tragedies, and Wittgenstein, Emerson, and Thoreau, that the road back to ordinary language criticism was open, and our best hope for restoring value to humanistic study. The collection is also impressive for its decision to include dissenting voices.

> GEORGE TOLES, Distinguished Professor of English, Theatre, Film & Media, University of Manitoba, Canada

In moods ranging from the elegiac to the exuberant to the contentious, the essays collected here remember Cavell and his work, put it to further use, and engage with it critically. Together their authors compose a conversation that amounts to what Cavell once described philosophy as being—an education for grownups—in which accomplished, mature thinkers continually seek their better selves, amidst the plights and possibilities of culture.

> RICHARD ELDRIDGE, Charles and Harriett Cox McDowell Professor of Philosophy, Swarthmore College, USA

The welcoming tone rightly identified by the editor as one genius of Stanley Cavell's exacting style has demonstrably been answered by this timely volume—and in just the right blend of reminiscence, reflection, and fresh testing. The intellectual heritage proposed, and so luminously proven, across these pages—convening a lineage of distinguished readers in their role, as always, of interlocutors—honors the balance of intimacy and reach in Cavell's influential philosophical writing: a style of thought inseparable from the searching prose that gave, that gives, it shape.

GARRETT STEWART, James O. Freedman Professor of Letters, University of Iowa, USA

The voices gathered in this collection, each finding a different balance between the claims of memory, sympathy, and critique, together illuminate the relation between Stanley Cavell's life and his writings, and disclose an unattained but attainable future for philosophy to which we all might be attracted.

STEPHEN MULHALL, Fellow and Tutor in Philosophy, New College, University of Oxford, UK

David LaRocca has gathered together some of the world's foremost scholars of Stanley Cavell's work for this terrific volume of essays responding to Cavell's philosophy. Collating reprints of groundbreaking essays and original contributions, the book offers wonderful insight into the breadth and depth of Cavell's influence and features a beautifully detailed and lucid introduction by LaRocca that interweaves the various strands of Cavell's philosophy and their legacies. This is without doubt a definitive body of responses to Cavell's work: a must-read for anyone interested in Cavell's work, whatever discipline they are approaching from, and whatever their level of specialism.

CATHERINE WHEATLEY, Reader in Film Studies, King's College London, UK

AUTHORED, EDITED, OR COEDITED BOOKS BY DAVID LaROCCA

On Emerson

Emerson's Transcendental Etudes by Stanley Cavell

The Philosophy of Charlie Kaufman

Estimating Emerson: An Anthology of Criticism from Carlyle to Cavell

Emerson's English Traits and the Natural History of Metaphor

The Philosophy of War Films

A Power to Translate the World: New Essays on Emerson and International Culture

The Bloomsbury Anthology of Transcendental Thought: From Antiquity to the Anthropocene

The Philosophy of Documentary Film: Image, Sound, Fiction, Truth

The Thought of Stanley Cavell and Cinema: Turning Anew to the Ontology of Film a Half-Century after The World Viewed

Inheriting Stanley Cavell: Memories, Dreams, Reflections

Movies with Stanley Cavell in Mind

Metacinema: The Form and Content of Filmic Reference and Reflexivity

The Geschlecht Complex: Addressing Untranslatable Aspects of Gender, Genre, and Ontology

Television with Stanley Cavell in Mind

GUEST EDITED

Conversations: The Journal of Cavellian Studies
  No. 7: *Acknowledging Stanley Cavell*

Movies with Stanley Cavell in Mind

Edited by
David LaRocca

BLOOMSBURY ACADEMIC
NEW YORK • LONDON • OXFORD • NEW DELHI • SYDNEY

BLOOMSBURY ACADEMIC
Bloomsbury Publishing Inc
1385 Broadway, New York, NY 10018, USA
50 Bedford Square, London, WC1B 3DP, UK
29 Earlsfort Terrace, Dublin 2, Ireland

BLOOMSBURY, BLOOMSBURY ACADEMIC and the Diana logo are
trademarks of Bloomsbury Publishing Plc

First published in the United States of America 2021
Paperback edition published in 2023

Volume Editor's Part of the Work © David LaRocca, 2021

Each chapter © of Contributors

For legal purposes the Acknowledgments on p. 319 constitute an extension
of this copyright page.

Cover design: Jason Anscomb / rawshock design

All rights reserved. No part of this publication may be reproduced or transmitted
in any form or by any means, electronic or mechanical, including photocopying,
recording, or any information storage or retrieval system, without prior
permission in writing from the publishers.

Bloomsbury Publishing Inc does not have any control over, or responsibility for,
any third-party websites referred to or in this book. All internet addresses given in
this book were correct at the time of going to press. The author and publisher
regret any inconvenience caused if addresses have changed or sites have ceased
to exist, but can accept no responsibility for any such changes.

A catalog record for this book is available from the Library of Congress.

ISBN: HB: 978-1-5013-5191-4
PB: 978-1-5013-8016-7
ePDF: 978-1-5013-5912-1
eBook: 978-1-5013-5193-8

Typeset by Deanta Global Publishing Services, Chennai, India

To find out more about our authors and books visit www.bloomsbury.com and sign
up for our newsletters.

[T]O TAKE AN INTEREST IN AN OBJECT *is to take an interest in one's experience of the object, so that to examine and defend my interest in these films is to examine and defend my interest in my own experience, in the moments and passages of my life I have spent with them. [. . .]*

Checking one's experience is a rubric an American, or a spiritual American, might give to the empiricism practiced by Emerson and by Thoreau. I mean the rubric to capture the sense at the same time of consulting one's experience and of subjecting it to examination, and beyond these, of momentarily stopping, *turning yourself away from whatever your preoccupation and turning your experience away from its expected, habitual track, to find itself, its own track: coming to attention. The moral of this practice is to educate your experience sufficiently so that it is worthy of trust. The philosophical catch would then be that the education cannot be achieved in advance of the trusting.*

—STANLEY CAVELL, Pursuits of Happiness

CONTENTS

Foreword: The Importance of Stanley Cavell for
   the Study of Film
      SANDRA LAUGIER   xiii

Introduction: The Seriousness of Film Sustained
      DAVID LaROCCA   1

I The Companionship of Film and Philosophy   31

   1 Love and Class in Douglas Sirk's *All That
      Heaven Allows*
         ROBERT B. PIPPIN   33

   2 Lévinas, Cavell, and the Films of the Dardenne
      Brothers
         WILLIAM ROTHMAN   57

   3 The Specter of the Electronic Screen:
      Bruno Varela's Reception of Stanley Cavell
         BYRON DAVIES   72

II Recollecting and Remembering   91

   4 The Pertinence of the Stars: Achieving
      Mortality in *Little Did I Know* and
      Only Angels Have Wings
         STEVEN G. AFFELDT   93

5   In Praise of Cinema: Cavell, Arnaud Desplechin,
    and Telling What Counts in *Trois souvenirs
    de ma jeunesse*
       JOSEPH MAI   112

III Rethinking Remarriage   129

   6   Morality and Recognition: A Cavellian Reading
       of Elaine May's *A New Leaf*
          PAUL SCHOFIELD   131

   7   Remarriage Comedy, the Next Generation:
       In Bold Pursuit of Happiness
          K. L. EVANS   148

IV The Female Voice Heard Anew   173

   8   Passionate Utterances: Cavell, Film, and
       the Female Voice
          CATHERINE WHEATLEY   175

   9   Cavell, Altman, Cassavetes: The Melodrama
       of the Unknown Woman in *A Woman Under
       the Influence* and *Nashville*
          CHARLES WARREN   191

V Contending with Conditions, Human and Otherwise   199

   10 Stanley Kubrick and Stanley Cavell: Cinematic
       Syntax, Avoidance, and Acknowledgment
          DAVID MIKICS   201

   11 The Use and Abuse of Documentary Confessionals:
       Cavell, Žižek, and the Possibility of Justice in
       The Unknown Known and *The Act of Killing*
          AMIR KHAN   221

12 Pursuits of Happiness in the Time of War: On
    Borhane Alaouié's *Beirut: The Encounter*
        DANIELE RUGO   235

VI Visibility, Audibility, and Intelligibility   251

    13 Chantal Akerman and Stanley Cavell: Viewing
        in *La Captive* and Reviewing in Moral
        Perfectionism
            KATE RENNEBOHM   253

    14 Contemplating the Sounds of Contemplative
        Cinema: Stanley Cavell and Kelly Reichardt
            DAVID LAROCCA   274

Acknowledgments   319
Contributors   322
Index   328

FOREWORD

The Importance of Stanley Cavell for the Study of Film

SANDRA LAUGIER

STANLEY CAVELL'S TEACHING AND WRITING have been on my mind nearly every day since I first entered one of his classes on film, when I arrived as a visiting student from Paris at the Department of Philosophy at Harvard University in 1984. The timing of my arrival explains why I am particularly fond of movies (and television shows) from the 1980s, even though Cavell's classes were on classic Hollywood melodramas and comedies. Little did I know that, in time, I would end up translating most of Stanley's books into French, and dedicating most of my scholarly labor to understanding, presenting, and discussing his work. Back then, I just happened to walk into one of his classes, and "he had me." I imagine something of the same effect can happen to anyone today, and it may be a reason for picking up *Movies with Stanley Cavell in Mind*. I felt so lucky to discover a philosophy that took entirely seriously not merely film, but the power of the experience of film and its importance in one's life. For me, the encounter was a turning point: Cavell's work, and Cavell on film, became the most important thing in my intellectual life, giving it continuity and me strength. The fourteen chapters collected here provide ample reason for understanding the importance of Stanley Cavell for the study of film.

All of the contributors to this wonderful, collective enterprise—brought together by David LaRocca—have in a similar way encountered him and his work. Whether they are revisiting films Cavell loved or taking up the invitation to explore new films, they reveal the importance of Cavell's writing and method. Indeed, by teaching each of us what importance *is*, that is, what matters to us (to me, to you, hence, to everyone), Cavell taught us how to learn from ourselves what is important—and, more particularly, how film matters. The revelation of one's own relevance, of the possibility and the necessity of *making use of who one is*, is something that all of Cavell's readers and students owe him, and to his conception of film. Moreover, such lessons are evident to the ordinary viewer, so one need not be a professional philosopher or a publishing film critic to appreciate their implications. The chapters to follow—and the helpfully orienting Introduction—exemplify the availability of philosophy for the study of film, and the many ways that Cavell's work can be profitably taken up to manifest it.

Since memory for Cavell, and for all of us, is so intimately connected to our experience of movies, it is not surprising that, looking back now, I realize the importance of the publication of *Pursuits of Happiness* (1981; in French, 1993, Editions des Cahiers du cinéma)—one of those intellectual events that invisibly transforms the intellectual and moviegoing lives of so many people. It was one of the first works by Cavell made accessible to the French-speaking public (even before his landmark, *The Claim of Reason*) and an instant classic in France: a guide to viewing Hollywood film as well as an always welcome, and once read, irreverent, wedding present.

In the mix of the chapters to follow, one must be struck by the fact of Cavell's presence on the European continent and especially in francophone Europe, the birthplace of film criticism. His ideas, and even his own words, are explicitly present in the works of the French filmmaker Arnaud Desplechin, who quotes directly from *Pursuits of Happiness* at the end of *Comment je me suis disputé . . . (ma vie sexuelle)* (*My Sex Life . . . or How I Got into an Argument*, 1996); and the final scene of *Les fantômes d'Ismaël* (*Ismael's Ghosts*, 2017) has Marion Cotillard deliver a long passage lifted straight from the end of Cavell's memoir, *Little Did I Know*. Cavell has made a similar and striking impression on the Belgian filmmaking duo, the Dardenne brothers, Jean-Pierre and Luc, in, among other places, their film *La fille inconnue* (*The Unknown Girl*, 2016). Translating Cavell's English to French, with my friend Christian Fournier—*Pursuits of Happiness* and *The World Viewed*, as well as so many of Cavell's essays on film—has been an extraordinarily rewarding experience and kindled a lifelong wonder. Of course, I am not alone—as the contributors in what follows make clear. In France, a country where Hollywood cinema has been historically beloved by film critics, filmmakers, and the public since the 1950s, the strength of support for Cavell's work—in *Cahiers du cinéma*, *Trafic*, *Positif*, and publications devoted to film—has been steady and remains so. A recent, new edition of *A la recherche du Bonheur* (*Pursuits of Happiness*) in a *poche* (i.e., a small format paperback edition) was an unexpected bestseller, and a great help to the publisher during the coronavirus pandemic.

How could Cavell's remarks on film in the 1970s and early 1980s about films from the 1930s and 1940s be a hit—and hit the heart and mind—in the 2020s? In part, I think, because the study of film, as conceived by Cavell, is about heeding a trust in one's experience. In *Pursuits of Happiness*, for example, he examines the act of "checking one's experience," which is to say, of examining one's own experience, of "let[ting] the object or the work of your interest teach you how to consider it."¹ To educate one's experience so as to be made educable by it. To be interested in film *as* thought means to be interested in, and rely on, our experience in order to find the right words to describe and express it. This task is "a conceptual as much as an experiential undertaking; it is a commitment to being guided by our experience but not dictated to by it."² What is unique, in Cavell's reading of film as a medium, is his interpretive anchoring in the works themselves—in individual films— and his way of showing how the film (the whole film, including actors and production and cinematography and dialogue) brings its own intelligence to its making, that this intelligence itself educates us. Hence Cavell's take on the ontology of film where "the question what becomes of objects when they are filmed and screened—like the question what becomes of particular people, and specific locales, and subjects and motifs when they are filmed by individual makers of film—has only one source of data for its answer, namely the appearance and significance of just those objects and people that are in fact to be found in the succession of films, or passages of films, that matter to us."³

* * * *

The importance of film lies in its power to make *what matters* emerge: "to magnify the feeling and meaning of a moment."⁴ So the experience of film is what cultivates in us a specific ability to see the too often invisible importance of things and moments, and emphasizes the covering-over or invisibility of importance in our lives, of what matters to us, *what we mind*. For importance, ironically enough, is essentially what can be *missed*, what remains unseen until later, or possibly, forever.

The pedagogy of film is that while it amplifies the significance of moments, it also reveals the "inherent *concealment* of significance."⁵ As Cavell writes,

> If it is part of the grain of film to magnify the feeling and meaning of a moment, it is equally part of it to counter this tendency, and instead to acknowledge the fateful fact of a human life that the significance of its moments is ordinarily not given with the moments as they are lived, so that to determine the significant crossroads of a life may be the work of a lifetime.⁶

What Cavell describes here is something else than mere attentiveness or inattentiveness or carelessness: it is a fundamental structure of experience, again, "an inherent *concealment* of significance, as much as its revelation."⁷ Human experience reveals itself as defined by our cinephilic capacity for seeing detail, reading expressions. In turn, expression articulates the concealment *and* the revelation of importance—ultimately becoming the texture of our life form, uncannily shared by film.

Yet, expression is not easily forthcoming; this is the difficulty that Cavell describes when he speaks of the temptation of inexpressiveness and of isolation, and shows the essential vulnerability of human experience. We experience "the appearance and significance" of things (places, faces, patterns, words), but only, as it were, afterward, after words. So it is that we discover importance not only through accurate and refined perceptions, but also through our suffering and misperceptions, in other words, through our failures to perceive. Because "missing the evanescence of the subject" is constitutive of our ordinary lives, and for Cavell at the core of philosophy—and of the difficulty of philosophy.[8]

Cavell matters to us all because he explains film's affinity to philosophy, not in a traditional, academic sense, but in our everyday lives: philosophy responds to the desire that drives us to film in the first place. He matters, in this sense, not only for the study of film, but way beyond it—since film is an essential part of our contemporary form of life. Films, passages of films, or movie characters that matter to us are "[l]ike childhood memories whose treasure no one else appreciates, whose content is nothing compared to their unspeakable importance for me."[9] Cavell is, to my mind, the best thinker for helping us account for the power of the film experience: the way in which our life is, for instance, also made up of fragments of cinema, which are then part of our experience in the same way as dreams or memories that haunt us. Because cinema presents these important moments to us, they become important moments in our lives. Such moments, lived in real time and in the time of film, are often unassailable and indeterminate; their meaning is not given to us while we are living them, hence the importance of reflecting on film, as if on a memory or a dream.

As Cavell puts it as early as *The World Viewed*, "We involve the movies in us. They become further fragments of what happens to me, further cards in the shuffle of my memory, with no telling what place in the future."[10] In *Little Did I Know*, Cavell's final work, he confesses the autobiographical and nostalgic hold of popular cinema on him. But his work on film is obviously, for all of us here, reunited thanks to this late, last book, the discovery and implementation of unprecedented and infinite capacities to appreciate the most diverse films—and even now and increasingly, television series; of those weak links that come from the sharing of fleeting yet deeply inscribed shared experiences. At present and in the time to come, Stanley Cavell's work stands as a reliable resource and a constant source for having new experiences and new insights. The following chapters provide occasions for thinking about how the pursuit of cinema—whatever happens to us and to the world—means the pursuit of happiness. And for thinking about the importance of Stanley Cavell and the importance of film, inseparably together.

Notes

1 Stanley Cavell, "Words for a Conversation," in *Pursuits of Happiness: The Hollywood Comedy of Remarriage* (Cambridge: Harvard University Press, 1981), 12, 10.
2 Ibid., 10.
3 Stanley Cavell, "What Becomes of Things on Film," in *Themes Out of School: Effects and Causes* (San Francisco: North Point Press, 1984), 182–83.
4 Stanley Cavell, "The Thought of Movies," *Themes Out of School*, 11. For more on these passages, see my "The Importance of Being Alive," in *Inheriting Stanley Cavell: Memories, Dreams, Reflections*, ed. David LaRocca (New York: Bloomsbury, 2020), 231–42.
5 Ibid., italics in original.
6 Ibid.
7 Ibid., italics in original.
8 Ibid., 14.
9 Stanley Cavell, "The Acknowledgment of Silence," in *The World Viewed: Reflections on the Ontology of Film* (Cambridge: Harvard University Press, 1971, Enlarged Edition, 1979), 154.
10 Ibid.

INTRODUCTION

The Seriousness of Film Sustained

David LaRocca

IN AMERICA, HALF A CENTURY AGO, Stanley Cavell almost single-handedly gave credence to the philosophical study of film. The legitimacy of the act was familiar to scattered European theorists, who had begun practicing a criticism of films that treated them with a reverence formerly reserved for the fine arts; on American turf, though, the study of philosophy had become a rarefied component of the academy and thus situated very far from everyday life defined, in part, by the experience of the decidedly popular art form known as "the movies." Indeed, it was Cavell's attention to the medium—to the ontology of film—that laid the groundwork for consecrating the enterprise more generally: where, for example, writing about Charlie Chaplin and Buster Keaton might be deemed worthy of speculation in the same breath as the "monsters of fame" who dominated the philosophical pantheon.[1] Quite consequentially, around the same time, Cavell would also transform who would inhabit that rarefied strata by making a case for the likes of Ralph Waldo Emerson and Henry David Thoreau. In turn, those nineteenth-century American philosophers would underwrite an unlikely partnership with J. L. Austin and Ludwig Wittgenstein that culminated in Cavell's innovation of Emersonian moral perfectionism, an outlook that fundamentally changed the philosophical study of popular culture in its incarnation as the movies.

Cavell's contribution to rethinking film's status as an art, and his tandem enterprise to shuffle and expand the philosophical canon, unsettled the potential for an emerging and auspicious domain for thought. He created the conditions for taking cinema seriously as a subject worthy of philosophical criticism. "Philosophers, it seemed," Cavell recalled, "had almost without exception left the field alone. Should this be taken for granted? Or oughtn't the fact of this neglect itself inspire suspicion?"[2] While inheritors of logical empiricism, such as Willard Van Orman Quine, shared the hallway with Cavell and other luminaries (Robert Nozick, Hilary Putnam, and John Rawls) presided nearby, Cavell capably, and with unmatched nerve and grace, published essay after essay and book after book about how film was if made for philosophy.[3] "Given my restiveness with philosophy's treatment, or avoidance, or stylization, of human experience," Cavell asked, "what better way to challenge the avoidance than through the worldwide phenomenon of cinema?"[4] Instead of treating film like an anachronism—coming much too late for philosophy to care about, or believing it unworthy of philosophy's indelible questions and vaunted aspirations—Cavell regarded cinema as a discovery of world-historic significance for philosophical insight. The philosophical study of film was not capricious, esoteric, or frivolous, but strikingly essential. Though we have, by now, become accustomed to film-philosophy as a robust and respected field of its own, such a quick historical sketch displaces the notion that the intellectual climate was always congenial to such valuations, or as promiscuously and productively interdisciplinary as it is now.

Cavell, however, didn't just take *film* seriously (as noted, lots of critics—cinéastes—were passionate about the celluloid creations of auteurs, avant-gardists, and experimentalists), he turned our attention to the "screwball" comedies and melodramas ("weepies," "women's pictures") of the 1930s and 1940s. In *these* films, in *Hollywood*, Cavell found philosophy. We were told, for example, that Cary Grant's C. K. Dexter Haven in *The Philadelphia Story* (1940, dir. George Cukor) was none other than a philosopher! We were shown that the silly, madcap, and zany can embody great art—not kitsch but a compelling dispatch to the highfalutin. Needless to say, thinking of *Mr. Deeds Goes to Town* (1936, dir. Frank Capra), Cavell admitted and anticipated resistance: "Some will be unwilling to grant this degree of seriousness to Mr. Deeds's courtroom lecture on silliness and thinking, and they may wish to protect their sense of the serious by suggesting that Deeds's words are at best a parody of philosophy, not the thing of philosophy itself."[5] And yet, as Cavell shows time and again, comedies—even mainstream comedies with no pretensions to contributing to our knowledge of the film medium (much less the history of philosophy)—become vectors for "giving significance to the possibilities of film" and the possibilities of philosophy (indeed, even as parody).[6] Through such savvy interpretations, heeding the beckoning intelligence of the art that populates and animates everyday life in the twentieth and twenty-first centuries, Cavell made possible for us (authored and authorized in one seamless coupling) the ongoing project of taking film seriously, and whether such instances arrive from Hollywood or elsewhere. Almost at once and then for decades to follow, his remarks on film became exemplary for the ways in which he treated film *philosophically*—as a medium and an aesthetic dimension in which to consider what is of importance, what achieves significance.

Thinking Through Film: Stanley Cavell and the Writing of Film-Philosophy

As Cavell tells it, early on he "found little charm in analytical aesthetics."[7] He remembers "[i]ndividual works in the arts never seemed for my taste to talk back sufficiently to philosophy, to find their footing within philosophy, to make philosophy look at its own limitations, its own dependence on literary conditions."[8] At mid-century, philosophy was in competition with science, physics, linguistics, logic, and mathematics to give an account of itself; in this respect, with its radical commitment to verificationism, it was largely turned away from the arts and humanities (including moral philosophy and religion)—seeking either to once-and-for-all offload troublesome ethical and metaphysical conundrums (labeling them "nonsense"), or, barring that, translate them into some more scientifically reliable form. But Cavell, in this context and against its grain, was sensible to the accomplishments of literary critics—T. S. Eliot, William Empson, I. A. Richards, Kenneth Burke, R. P. Blackmur, Robert Penn Warren, Paul Goodman—and decided "I wanted philosophy to take on such criticism, perhaps be taken on by it."[9] (One thinks of how F. R. Leavis has been described as wanting to introduce "seriousness" into the act and art of literary criticism.[10] For Cavell, though, J. L. Austin's interest in the serious was more prominent and proximate.[11])

As part of Cavell's desire to, as it were, turn philosophy toward cinema, he had a realization: "I came to the idea of experimenting with what could be said about film."[12] Though there were prodigious stirrings beforehand, such experiments began in force in 1971 with *The World Viewed: Reflections on the Ontology of Film*, a book that he substantively expanded in 1979. The ambitions of the work and the context of its appearance have prompted Jennifer Fay to describe the book (admiringly) as "a preposterous work of film theory and philosophy."[13] The arresting assessment conjures a picture of the work's professional incongruity, which in turn may have invited ridicule, yet the etymology of the word gets at the crux of the book's existence "in the wrong order"—at once after itself (*posterus*) and before itself (*prae*): *The World Viewed* is simultaneously a belated report from Cavell's life with movies between 1935 and 1960 (a duration in which, he says, "[m]emories of movies are strand over strand with memories of my life"[14]) and anticipatory of what could be done when that intimacy and enthusiasm is channeled through a passionate interest in an eclectic range of literary and philosophical texts. Noël Carroll, also reflecting on the seminal event of the book's first appearance, muses that "Cavell's work provided both inspiration and legitimatization to younger philosophers who grew up movie-mad and aspired to unite their love of film with their love of philosophy."[15] Taking stock of present circumstances, Robert Pippin observes that "[t]he idea that films could have a bearing on philosophy, and especially that there could be a form of cinematic, reflective thought that deserved the name of philosophy itself, remains quite a controversial one."[16] Of course, Pippin adds, when Cavell began to treat film as a philosophical medium in the early 1960s, "it was even more controversial. Indeed, the very idea was outrageous." Cavell himself confessed: "There was, I do not deny, a certain pleasurable indecorousness in the idea of taking film into a philosophy classroom, anyway in the English-speaking dispensation of the subject."[17] Since those days, Cavell's wager has turned him from an iconoclast into part of the pantheon.

To take seriously what appears to be, for many, an unserious medium (viz., film, or in demotic lingo, "the movies"), and at that, some of its most playful-seeming instances—comedies, romances, romantic comedies, the decidedly self-mocking genre, "screwballs," as well as the most melodramatic of melodramas—becomes one of the more conspicuous gifts of Cavell's peerless approach to philosophizing. For many people, movies are a major source of entertainment (as now and increasingly, the heirs of theatrically released cinema—the on-demand stand-alones and serials that populate digital platforms, traveling under the quaintly generic name "television"); yet, it would be a stretch for such audiences to articulate how films do work—"how films think"—much less how they might think philosophically. A significant part of Cavell's wide-ranging legacy must be that so many of us not only have found a way of seeing and hearing how film and philosophy are correlated enterprises, but also how we, as individual viewers, might go about making films work for us philosophically. For one thing, a deliberate reencounter with the photographic nature of film will suggest that "we have forgotten how mysterious these things are"—these moving pictures of people, places, and events from another time, along with the sounds they make—and "this is in fact something movies teach us."[18] The interaction between the flickering audiovisual dispatches and our own minds remains a first point of the medium's uncanny provocations and instructions. Film, then, would appear to be a medium replete with content worthy of extended, indefinite contemplation, especially when philosophy is defined this way, as it is by Cavell:

> I understand [philosophy] as a willingness to think not about something other than what ordinary human beings think about, but rather to learn to think undistractedly about things that ordinary human beings cannot help thinking about, or anyway cannot help having occur to them, sometimes in fantasy, sometimes as a flash across a landscape; such things, for example, as whether we can know the world as it is in itself, or whether others really know the nature of one's own experiences, or whether good and bad are relative, or whether we might not now be dreaming that we are awake [. . .]. Such thoughts are instances of that characteristic human willingness to allow questions for itself which it cannot answer

with satisfaction. [. . . P]hilosophers after my heart will rather wish to convey the thought that while there may be no satisfying answers to such questions *in certain forms*, there are, so to speak, directions to answers, *ways to think*, that are worth the time of your life to discover.[19]

To think of philosophy in these terms would make one necessarily receptive to the fact and features of cinema—with its status as something one "cannot help having occur" and as something "ordinary human beings think about." Thus, ordinary language philosophy (or criticism) should find in movies philosophy in and of the ordinary.

Given the prominence of Cavell's writing on cinema since the 1970s, including its conspicuous and continually spreading impact on generations of scholars (e.g., excerpts from *The World Viewed* that appeared in *Film Theory and Criticism* in 1974 may be considered one such important vector for the dissemination of Cavell's writing on film[20]), we may refer, for lack of a better phrase, to "Cavell's films"—especially those two cycles of films he anointed and theorized as genres: the comedy of remarriage (in *Pursuits of Happiness*, 1981) and the melodrama of the unknown woman (in *Contesting Tears*, 1996).[21] The mandate for the present volume is to think *with* Cavell about Hollywood yet also *beyond* his familiar roster of films and novel thematics. Though films of the 1930s and 1940s (again Cavell's films) must form the textual and contextual background for an endeavor such as this book, the greater balance of films written about in this collection are films Cavell himself never wrote about—and maybe never saw. Thus, there is a double sense to our titular phrase "movies with Stanley Cavell in mind": in which we are not solely exploring, as it were, Cavell's movies, but also other, different, newer movies—beyond Cavell's geographical and temporal range. These "other films," in turn, help us think anew about Cavell's own, established work on "his films," and the genres he generated to account for their achievements; and at the same time, the fresh examples liberate his writing on that highly conscribed set of movies so they may become profitable for a much more expansive scope of films and media types (e.g., television, experimental and avant-garde works, animation, digital), now and into the future. Indeed, there is even a palpable third sense to the title, namely, that Cavell's influence extends to filmmakers who have Cavell in mind when they make films, famously Terrence Malick,[22] but also, as contributors to this volume attest to and examine, Arnaud Desplechin, the Dardenne brothers, and Bruno Varela. Thinking with Cavell, in these several, layered respects, is both retrospective and prospective—looking back so we can also look ahead. It is a marvel and measure of the depth and perspicacity of Cavell's writing that it can provide entrée not only into the films he loved and artfully analyzed, but also into movies he didn't experience or reflect upon—and for added measure, inspire filmmakers too. Rare among film critics and philosophers of his generation (and perhaps rarer still since), Cavell blended traits of distinctive acumen, ecumenical interest, eloquent diction, and a recognizable voice to confirm that his writings on films from the 1930s and 1940s would hold up under the scrutiny, irony, and media-saturated landscapes we inhabit in the 2020s and appear destined for in the 2030s and 2040s. We are, then, still in the early stages of accounting for Cavell's accomplishments as a writer, thinker, and tutor in the philosophical study of cinema.

While we are indebted to Cavell's accomplishments, and undertake to articulate how and why we are, we also strive to build upon—and beyond— them. Indeed, part of the "beyond" takes us beyond Hollywood. This volume features close readings and the critical reception of many French films; films made in Belgium, Lebanon, Indonesia, and Mexico; mainstream American comedies of the 1960s and 1990s; contemporary dramas; documentaries (made in America and elsewhere); works of avant-garde, experimental, and contemplative cinema; and more. Yet, this broad labor, conducted in a Cavellian mood, is predicated on having first taken *Hollywood* seriously. To seek, to find meaning of the sort these analysts have achieved means to have been already touched, moved, transformed by Cavell's particular brand and style of taking words seriously, of taking cinema seriously, and most controversially and uniquely, of taking the sounds and images of Hollywood cinema seriously. So, let it be a measure of Cavell's success as a reader of Hollywood, and his influence on the very nature of viable contemporary philosophical critique, that our authors have here found ways of drawing his work *out of* Hollywood—exporting it and thereupon applying its inspirations in such disparate, global, and otherwise non-Hollywood contexts.

While some critics declare that Cavell's writing on genre is "limited to a small corpus of films from a single national cinema,"[23] and, thereby, situate it for easier dismissal, there are robust countervailing efforts, among them scores of articles and scattered chapters as well as representative edited collections and monographs, such as Catherine Wheatley's *Stanley Cavell and Film: Scepticism and Self-Reliance at the Cinema*, Daniel Shaw's *Stanley Cavell and the Magic of Hollywood Movies*, Rex Butler's *Stanley Cavell and the Arts: Philosophy and Popular Culture*, Stephen Mulhall's *Stanley Cavell: Philosophy's Recounting of the Ordinary*, D. N. Rodowick's *Philosophy's Artful Conversation*, Andrew Klevan's *Disclosure of the Everyday*, Rupert Read and Jerry Goodenough's *Film as Philosophy*, Andrew Taylor and Áine Kelly's *Stanley Cavell, Literature, and Film*, Garry L. Hagberg's *Stanley Cavell on Aesthetic Understanding*, Amir Khan's *Comedies of Nihilism*, Daniele Rugo's *Philosophy and the Patience of Film in Cavell and Nancy*, Sianne Ngai's *Our Aesthetic Categories*, Charles Warren's *Beyond Document*, Paola Marrati's *Understanding Cavell, Understanding Modernism*, Robert B. Pippin's *Filmed Thought*, Lawrence F. Rhu's *Stanley Cavell's American Dream*, William Rothman's *Must We Kill the Thing We Love?*; a recent run of contributions in *The Thought of Stanley Cavell and Cinema* and *Inheriting Stanley Cavell*; and revelatory remembrances gathered in a commemorative issue of *Conversations: The Journal of Cavellian Studies*.[24] An au courant double issue of *Discourse*, edited by Jennifer Fay and Daniel Morgan, "Cinema, Modernism, and the Perplexing Methods of Stanley Cavell," continues the trend to revisit Cavell's influential, now canonical work, while also marking out new and propitious pathways from it.[25]

In the course of the fourteen chapters collected here, anchored by an astute Foreword, what we find are scholars trying to acknowledge, contend with, and extend Cavell's work—helping us appreciate its ongoing pertinence (often in surprising places), while also coming to terms with the occasional limits, oversights, or distortions that stand in need of correction, adjustment, or supplement. Such activities are highly productive for continuing to inherit Cavell's work, especially now, after his death in 2018, since we have moved into a space of assessing his legacy. Some chapters show authors exploring Cavell's thinking in the context of new film instances, while other contributors aim for the realignment or refinement of standard bearers—thereby productively reformulating the terms of the debate he offered. Either way, we are privy to recondite readings of Cavell's prose and the many films that are drawn in for closer inspection. Both moves befit inheritors who are eager to put the movies that matter to them into conversation with a philosophical approach to cinema that has elevated the standards for criticism.

As Andrew Klevan said of V. F. Perkins, we can say of Cavell: "He justifies the serious study of film."[26] Cavell inspires such study in us, those gathered here to think with him about film, and those who are dispersed elsewhere but writing in a similar vein. As Cavell may be said to have (also) legitimated the serious study of Ralph Waldo Emerson and Henry David Thoreau for generations of philosophers (yet another landmark contribution to philosophy[27]), so too has he made the serious—call it, in part, philosophical—study of film a natural, presumed aspect of the contemporary climate of cultural interpretation. Indeed, at a time when "motion pictures" (and the sounds that accompany them) are fracturing in ever-more dynamic ways (from streaming serials to video game narratives, from AR/MR/VR to myriad online platforms; contending with CGI, deepfakes, and generative adversarial networks [GANs]; and viewed on screens that range from the digital smartphone to IMAX), we may at once feel liberated to probe these vertiginous new terrains and daunted by our sense of cinema's receding relevance. The closing of movie theaters during the coronavirus pandemic has challenged Hollywood's hegemony on the design and meaning of the moviegoing experience like nothing else before it—and we are left to wonder what awaits. What better way, then, to bear the times and the transition it hastens than by drawing a line of continuity between techniques and traditions, by inventively emulating models of serious analysis? After all, didn't Cavell take comfort and gain confidence from reading James Agee, André Bazin, and Robert Warshow as he began writing about film—and music, opera,

American Transcendentalists, Freud, and Shakespeare—from within the precincts of high-Anglo-analytic philosophy? He did.[28] And so can we read Cavell in a similar spirit of communion.

Film, Seriously

The superlative-laden appreciations and the fulsome encomia of Cavell's work generally—though his approach to film analysis stands out in its gathering of praise—often hide deeper resources. When George Steiner says, "[a]t its best, his play of thought, his 'wordings of the world' have music, a stroke of wonder rare in current philosophical argument" and in his writing we find "a harvest truly of the American grain and prodigality,"[29] we are gratifyingly compelled to acknowledge strains of singularity in his contributions to the history of philosophy. Likewise, when Hilary Putnam observed of Cavell that he is "one of the great minds of our time, but he is not the founder of movements or a coiner of slogans or a trader in '-isms,'"[30] we are given a pace for accessing his thought and a clue that our encounter will progress without quick, digested terms and conditions. (Similar things were said of Emerson,[31] some of them by Cavell, who—at the zenith of logical empiricism's dominance—boldly claimed to be "finding in Emerson the founding of American thinking," "a philosophical writer, in principle imaginable as founding philosophy for a nation still finding itself."[32]) Rather than receiving a decoder ring for, or handbook to, Cavell's thought, we are invited to dwell for long stretches in his fecund writing, to inhabit the space of his inimitable prose, and to see where it has taken the contributors. Cavell's intellectual curiosity was cosmopolitan and expeditionary: he found interest in many things and goes a good distance to find them; when he does, whether they be Romantic poetry or Transcendental essay, Golden Age film or opera libretto, Shakespeare play or psychanalytic study, treatise on ordinary language or instances of modernist art, they seem to speak to one another logically, naturally, and convincingly, owing to his startling capacities as a translator of culture.

On another occasion, Putnam described Cavell as "a writer who always speaks to *individuals*—and that means, one at a time."[33] Consequently: "To read Cavell as he should be read is to enter into a conversation with him, one in which your entire sensibility and his are involved, and not only your mind and his mind."[34] But we may add: your heart and soul, or whatever categories and tropes can be deployed to capture the total attributes of a human life. In this collection, taking a cue from Putnam's appreciation of his longtime colleague, we can say that the spirit of the volume aims to sustain such companionability, indeed, to make Cavell's experience of cinema—and the "accounts of films" which he calls "readings"[35]—present for us. And not just for the movies he cared about, but also for the ones that move us—that keep us thinking, that drive us to laughter and tears, that haunt us and live on within us, as if they were personal memories preciously held. In this way, this collection of remarks by able and attuned critics of film culture are instances when each sought to "enter into a conversation with him," to watch movies with him in mind, and thereafter to report on the insights afforded by these intimacies. Another Harvard colleague, Richard Moran, has spoken of Cavell's "concept-determining role" in his "access to the idea of philosophy as such."[36] For Moran, encountering "writing of that depth of responsiveness, serious down to its very syllables" made all the difference.[37]

Thomas Elsaesser once remarked, "Hollywood is truly the world's only global cinema"—meaning that it is the cinema that we, as a global community, share. And with some pleasure, it doesn't announce its Americanness in the title, though the provenance is implied. But, of course, we know there *are* robust movie industries and traditions in countries around the world (from France to Nigeria, India to England, Mexico to Australia, and so on). Thus, as we are speaking of "Hollywood" in this volume, we take it as a sign of *global* culture (not an exclusionary and rarefied precinct of Los Angeles, California, USA). In this way, "Hollywood" denotes itself, of course, but also functions as a handy euphemism or cipher for film of whatever form and geographical origin—that is, as a way of saying "what film makes possible." Though we know from his books on film that Cavell dwelled mainly on works of the American studio system of the 1930s and 1940s, his first book on film, *The World Viewed* (appearing between his first book, *Must We Mean What We Say?* [1969] and his first book on American philosophy, *The Senses of Walden* [1972]), showed that taking *Hollywood* seriously may be the hardest thing for people, for scholars and academics, to do—especially in the 1960s and 1970s, but also, in many cases still, in the present day. How much harder, then, to intentionally and systematically explore more truly global cinemas as well as those films that do not live on the surface of culture, promoted by the juggernaut of a Hollywood marketing campaign?

As a quick scan of the Contents shows, the films and filmmakers brought into conversation with Cavell's reading and understanding of film are very far from the sun-drenched back-lots and gilded studio sound stages of the dream factory, regardless of vintage: *The Act of Killing* (Joshua Oppenheimer), *The Unknown Known* (Errol Morris), *Beirut: The Encounter* (Borhane Alaouié), *A Woman Under the Influence* (John Cassavetes), *Nashville* (Robert Altman), the work of Stanley Kubrick, Arnaud Desplechin, the Dardenne brothers, Bruno Varela, Chantal Akerman, and Kelly Reichardt. Indeed, given the scope of films Cavell tended to write about, a reader may ask, "Where *are* the Hollywood films?" They are here, to be sure (*A New Leaf* and *Galaxy Quest* are conspicuous, as are works contemporaneous with Cavell's films, such as *Only Angels Have Wings*, and those that appear a bit later, such as *All That Heaven Allows*), but such a question highlights something special about Cavell's treatment of Hollywood movies and how he inspired his readers to deviate and to roam—in short, to follow their interests. "What attracts my attention shall have it," wrote Emerson: "It is enough that these particulars speak to me."[38]

As noted, Cavell focused principally on two genres of his own invention and appellation—the comedy of remarriage and the melodrama of the unknown woman; the films that comprise the canon emerged from the classical Hollywood studio systems of the 1930s and 1940s, launching just after the Hays Code had taken effect (*It Happened One Night* [1934, dir. Frank Capra] is the earliest and the only film in Cavell's catalog of comedies to appear before the code was in place; *Blonde Venus* [1932, dir. Josef von Sternberg] is its counterpart among the melodramas).[39] Yet, in the half-century since we have been reading Cavell on film, it is abundantly clear that for Cavell these films are representative and thus indelible. And for that reason, we can watch them on their own terms, for their own virtues, and also think with them beyond the limited realm and timeframe of their creation. One of the presumptions of this collection—indeed, an invitation extended to authors, and now held out to you, the reader of their reflections—involves assessing what Cavell's thinking on film (generally) and film genres and films (specifically) may illuminate for our consideration of movies he did not write about and may have never seen. According to this logic, it is perfectly reasonable and fitting to investigate the range of films we have gathered here to consider, namely, those that exist well beyond Cavell's own library of authorized instances.

Serious Down to Its Very Syllables

Among the lessons we may be said to have learned from Stanley Cavell many involve the nature of seriousness—first, in the art of filmmaking and also in its exhibition as edited art: "We have, as viewers," he writes in thinking about what *His Girl Friday* (1940, dir. Howard Hawks) teaches us by way of its camerawork, actor behavior, and dialogue, "by now received instruction from the film about where we are as well, I mean about where it places us, which means, as it does in each of our other films [in the genre of remarriage comedy], how it places its own images, accounts for their provenance and their presentation";[40] and, secondly, in trusting our instincts to follow things that are of interest to us—as if we cannot, at the start, always or ever say what it is that draws us to them: "My advice is not to ignore them, but also not to let them prevent your imagination from being released by an imaginative work."[41] Cavell's layered commendation, even five decades after *The World Viewed* transformed the study of film from illicit act to professional sanction, can feel like a license to attempt reading film with literary nuance and philosophical precision.[42] In short, such seriousness is defined first by noticing what is happening in the projected world (in or on film) and second, by noticing what that projection occasions in oneself, in the moment one inhabits (and holding firm in one's conviction about the experience).

Such thoughts appear to percolate through literary modernism. One thinks of Lily Briscoe, in Virginia Woolf's *To the Lighthouse*: "Such she often felt herself—struggling against terrific odds to maintain her courage; to say, 'But this is what I see; this is what I see,' and so to clasp some miserable remnant of her vision to her breast, which a thousand forces did their best to pluck from her."[43] Or we can marvel at the aptness of Henry James's advice, which coalesces Cavell's entwined or twinned observation: "Try to be one of the people on whom nothing is lost!"[44] Which is to say that by acts of cultivated attention—or, in James Wood's phrase, "serious noticing"—we put ourselves in a position to find or create something worthwhile.[45] As Cavell showed us, as Emerson before him, criticism is creative; so it should be that the standards and burdens of writing about films are as high as those involved in making them. While Emerson believes "[t]here is something of poverty in our criticism," he counsels a change in outlook: "'Tis the good reader that makes the good book; a good head cannot read amiss, in every book he finds passages which seem confidences or asides hidden from all else and unmistakably meant for his ear."[46] Film criticism at its best is generative even as it relies upon consumption.

A typical, mainstream film review can often seem to be a bit of gossip—a mixture of journalistic fragments about actors, directors, productions, themes, social relevance, the cultural climate in which the film is made and subsequently released, and authorial anecdotes that seldom transform our understanding of the work of art under consideration—unlike Cavell's approach, which so often involves studying and marveling at words and sentences, inflections and innuendos, puns and allusions, the way ordinary language is a performance of philosophy, and the personal stakes of one's individual human life made manifest *in relation* to the projected filmic representations flickering before one's eyes. This is serious noticing "down to the very syllables" of speech—and not just those discrete elements, but also the parts and portions of the mise-en-scène: a film's representations, frame-to-frame, frame-by-frame. Hence the grammar of the everyday in cinema. Interpretation, then, must be analytical, intertextual—in a word, midrashic. With such a method, the syntax of sounds and syllables, framed-images and sequences of moving pictures may all be laden with significance, each one a point of departure for advances in human understanding (or as the case may be, the persistence of stubborn confusions calling out for further illumination). Moreover, bestowing such reserves of interest in our lives—the discrete elements that somehow coalesce to form what we describe as experience—underscores the project, and process of, deliberating on what is serious and what is silly in our lives (the two often uncannily overlapping or trading places); in this lucky labor, arbitrating what matters—becoming perspicuous about the meaning of our ordinary experience—may deliver unanticipated results, among them that what appear to be trivialities and ephemera can take on substantive, transformative import.

As a clinic on his eclecticism and ecumenism, consider how Cavell finds in Cary Grant (or, better, C. K. Dexter Haven) an Emersonian sage. Not just Cavell's frames of reference (here, *The Philadelphia Story* and essayist Ralph Waldo Emerson), but also his mode of addressing and being addressed by film stand out as distinctive. Marshall Cohen, who, with Leo Braudy, anthologized Cavell's writing in *Film Theory and Criticism*, has written about Cavell's philosophical approach to film—his propensity, his capacity to find remarkable things in works of art that occupy the space of the everyday:

> Some [readers, and especially philosophers] are also allergic to the craving for profundity [Cavell] frequently exhibits. (Austin regarded this impulse as the mortal enemy of philosophy.) Is it helpful or simply pretentious to invoke Kant's metaphysics in explicating the barrier screen in *It Happened One Night* (1934)?[47]

Are those our only two options? Or, if we bracket the charge of pretentiousness, how can we understand what Cohen allows as the possible advantageousness of Cavell's approach to what he calls "reading a film"?[48] Who better than Cavell to reply to Cohen's apprehension? "I am not insensitive, whatever defenses I may deploy," Cavell once wrote (decades before Cohen's quandary), addressing the seriousness with which he takes movies, "of an avenue of outrageousness in considering Hollywood films in the light, from time to time, of major works of thought."[49] In a similar spirit of agitation and commendation, Cavell noted that "movies would then have to be accepted as speaking to our common lives with a depth, as well as an immediacy, no different in principle from the depth of Shakespeare or Dickens or Verdi or Manet."[50] Observations such as these, written forty or so years ago, leave us to wonder—and adjudicate—if that dare, that scandal remains in the present day (e.g., of treating films in the company of major works of thought and also *as* major works of thought in their own rights)—and, if so, where. For instance, would *Pursuits of Happiness* be considered a major, viable, and vital contribution to philosophy if it were published within an academic department of philosophy today? Have contributions to the study of film from philosophy become normalized to such an extent that authorial defensiveness, along with an audience's "sense of offense" at the act, are now moments of intellectual history?[51] These are not questions to settle, but rather to inquire after continually, and from whatever intellectual precinct one finds oneself within (as academic insider or outsider). "Such work necessarily contests disciplinary boundaries," Cavell claims, "sometimes by behaving as if they did not exist, sometimes by asking undivided attention to them."[52] Perhaps the scene of the scandal (and attendant defensiveness and outrageousness) has moved court, or perhaps it has evolved to be inherent in the dialogue between the study of philosophy and the study of film.

The analogy of "reading a film" is apt, since it reminds us that Cavell, like many philosophers, and not a few moviegoers, are deeply literate—they have read philosophy, literature, poetry, criticism, history, psychology, anthropology, religious tracts, political theory, and studied art history—so why not imagine that the way a character like C. K. Dexter Haven *becomes* a philosopher is related to the fact that we have philosophers (at least one, but perhaps more than one) in mind as we watch *The Philadelphia Story*? Sounds helpful to me. Indeed, Cavell was decidedly ambivalent to the pedigrees that would divide one kind of art from another; in *The Claim of Reason*, for example, he wrote: "A measure of the quality of a new text is the quality of the texts it arouses."[53] If *It Happened One Night* summons Kant, so be it—so much the better for both of those texts and for us.

Because we watch movies (these selected movies and many others) with *Cavell* in mind (our philosopher, as it were, for the present proceedings), we are privy not only to the fact that he watched movies with the unlikely constellation of Plato, Shakespeare, Kant, Freud, and Emerson in mind, but that in inheriting Cavell's work on film, we necessarily take on the mantle and privilege of watching films philosophically, that is, in the company of philosophers and the written testaments they left behind. Cavell's patrimony, in part, suggests that watching movies should be taken seriously because the art of film should be taken seriously. In this way, a philosophical appreciation of film's ontology (as we find it in *The World Viewed*) underwrites the intellectual ambition of subsequent investigations into, say, genre (as we receive them in *Pursuits of Happiness* and *Contesting Tears*).

Cavell wrote philosophical criticism of film where the moments—all moments in the life of a film, like our own lives—may become the condition for doing and making philosophy. But he did this at a time in culture, in American civilization, when seriousness itself was under attack (as today we may speak of expertise being undermined and marginalized). Looking back over her career from 1996, Susan Sontag wrote in "Thirty Years Later":

> What I didn't understand (I was surely not the right person to understand this) was that seriousness itself was in the early stages of losing credibility in the culture at large [...]. Thirty years later, the undermining of standards of seriousness is almost complete, with the ascendancy of a culture whose most intelligible, persuasive values are drawn from the entertainment industries. Now, the very idea of the serious (and the honorable) seems quaint, "unrealistic," to most people.[54]

Cavell appears to be one of the "right" people to understand the credibility issue Sontag diagnoses. Quite consequentially, we see him turning *toward* the "entertainment industries" of an earlier era to discover or apply seriousness. One's take on Cavell's serious study of film will depend, in some measure, then, on one's points of reference. From the writerly, readerly cinéastes of the Nouvelle Vague (Chabrol, Godard, Resnais, Rivette, Rohmer, Truffaut, Varda, et al.), he would have been a welcome voice speaking a vernacular of familiar obsessions; from the halls of hardcore Anglo-analytic philosophy at mid-century, by contrast, he would have seemed alien, as if lost on campus; by now, from our vantage, Cavell's achievement may be obscured by the integration and thus normalizing of his treatment of films. That is, if we are receptive to Cavell's writing on film, we will already, in some significant proportion, have a penchant for taking cinema seriously, or wanting to. Such a taste or talent will doubtless find encouragement in what follows, since, in Cavell's absence, we are poised to carry on—at once to learn from Cavell's tuitions and to explore our own intuitions.

In a very literal and dramatic way, the work of the authors in this collection, it seems quite plausible, would not have been possible *in this way* without Cavell's intervention into the philosophical treatment of film. Indeed, that film should even be a thing philosophers care about, and thus can preoccupy themselves with. We are, in this sense, his heirs (whatever we write about film), and for that reason alone indebted to his intellectual bravery. Each contributor takes up, in his or her own manner, replies to the question: What does it mean, in our time, to still take movies seriously? The question demands a perpetual holding of what Cavell meant by seriousness—what he made of the appellation and its application to cinema; in large measure, the present volume constitutes a series of vignettes, each of which illumines and kindles ways of thinking with Cavell about cinema, often in modes he might recognize as kindred to his own indelible exemplification of the practice.

Time and again, we are reminded how the very notion of seriousness was a leitmotif of Cavell's broader philosophical project, of which the study of film was a constitutive and thus indispensable part. We discover in Cavell's work the importance of *seriousness* and the seriousness of *importance*. Both of these terms are master-registers in which Cavell undertook his inquiries: what calls and sustains our attention (hence what is important) and what we can say about it (hence what can be done to convey its seriousness). If one feels that a given film is important, can one manage to articulate and defend its seriousness (as a work of art, as a contribution to philosophy, etc.)? The contributors, here gathered, have intrepidly and cannily made their attestations; we are, then, invited to read their attempts and thereafter to recurrently reply in our words: mounting trials, essaying our way forward in the serious art of film criticism.

A Modernist Sensibility for the Art of Film

Since Cavell has identified cinema from the position or perspective of a modernist, that is, as an art defined by "incessant and explicit self-reflection," it is not surprising that he would be taken aback by Wittgenstein's *Philosophical*

Investigations as a writerly version of a modernist inquiry "unlike the self-consciousness of any other undoubted work of philosophy I knew."[55] Since "modern philosophy, in our tradition at any rate, [...] associates intellectual seriousness with science," Cavell became preoccupied with the conditions of and criteria for seriousness. Indeed, he characterized some of his inquiries as befitting and epitomizing a "study of seriousness."[56] For example, in *The World Viewed*, Cavell dwells on the relationship between modernism and the fate of cinema, wondering how film, unlike other modern art forms, "can have been taken seriously without having assumed the burden of seriousness."[57] Able inheritors, such as Gordon C. F. Bearn and Lisa Trahair, have echoed the same preoccupation with meditations such as "Sounding Serious: Cavell and Derrida" and "Serious Film: Cavell, Automatism and Michael Haneke's *Caché*."[58] In fact, whether Cavell is considering his relationship to Derrida's work, his interpretation of Wittgenstein's texts, or our understanding of skepticism (including its tethering to cinema as in: "Film is a moving image of skepticism"[59]), Cavell wants to say: "Be serious. Don't trade your interest in being born on earth for messy theory. Persist in your birthright."[60] Even Cavell's way of saying such things feels serious. We are meant to fathom the weight of our existence—its particularity—as part of our patrimony; and also to remain responsive to the lambency of the ordinary and uneventful. Cavell remembers: "My father admired serious men."[61] So it appears we too should admire and emulate them.

"Taking something seriously" may not sound like much of a provocation, much less a scandal, but it shows its potency when we consider *what* is being treated this way. For it is often not just the way Cavell writes about something that bespeaks his seriousness (say, his capacity to sustain an active attentiveness to details that reveals remarkable things in a work of art), but what he chooses as objects of that attention, and often praise. Take a Hollywood movie. Take, for instance, what you might say about Frank Capra's comedy *Mr. Deed's Goes to Town* (1936). Would that film—with its themes and characters, with its tone—seem like a candidate for philosophical investigation, that is, presuming that it is redundant to say such an investigation is serious? For Cavell, the film is "as extreme an expression of Emersonian perfectionism as I have found on film."[62] Serious, indeed. And Cavell's reasons and reasoning for such seriousness provide a crucial intervention not just on the nature of art (popular and otherwise), what should count as a worthy subject of philosophical investigation, but also what criticism (on film or something else) might amount to:

> I would say, indeed, that it is a principal object of Emerson's thinking to urge a reconsideration of the relation ("the" relation?) of soul and society, especially as regards the sense of priority of one over the other. I take seriously, that is, Emerson's various formulations of the idea that, as he words it in "The American Scholar," "The deeper [the scholar] dives

into his privatest, secretest presentiment, to his wonder he finds this is the most acceptable, most public, and universally true." By taking it seriously I mean I find it intuitively valuable enough that I am moved to work with it in making it plainer. It bears directly on what I have called the arrogance of philosophy, its claim to speak universally, to discover the bases of existence as such.[63]

Here we have an account of interlacing phenomena, since we can identify the nature of criticism (such as we are laboring to achieve in this volume) as a negotiation between "soul and society"—what we say when we see and hear things on film, for example. And, to be sure, there is a "sense of priority" in such matters, call this the authority of convention (what Emerson regularly names "conformity"), and the authority of our own judgment (what Emerson anoints "genius"). Cavell is interested, as he says, in how this "relation" or relationship (is it one or many?) is conducted; to my eye, the relationship—whatever its kind or number—is one of the most essential modes in which a citizen or thinker or film scholar (assuming this trinity may also be a unity) can take seriously a work of art that she feels roused to respond to. Thus, to say that *Mr. Deeds Goes to Town* does *anything* for philosophy takes courage; the coupling itself forces one to front the charge of being "preposterous" or "pretentious."[64] And, since bravery needs an accomplice, we look for a rare cast of mind to *translate* that instinct for taking seriously a silly Hollywood comedy by finding words for it in the realm of criticism. In these ways, Cavell provides us with a veritable account of what such serious criticism can amount to, or at least aspire to, namely: to find oneself "moved to work with [something—a text, a film, a media object] in making it plainer." When someone asks about our work here, "what does it mean to 'take cinema seriously,'" we can reply that we have been moved to make something we saw or felt or thought—in our own, private heart and head—available to society, subject to a community of inquiry.

Antithetical to obscure theory writing, such as the humanities of the postwar period has often been accused of creating (e.g., structuralism, deconstruction, hermeneutics, phenomenology, critical theory, etc.—"postmodernism," generally), Cavell's ordinary language philosophy or ordinary language criticism propels us forward, in each case, in each step, to make things plainer.[65] Not that such writing will be easy to understand, but that its obscurity, if any, is (however paradoxical it may sound) in the service of clarity.[66] Trying to "say in hard words" what one is "moved" to say requires invention and stamina, and the results are not always readily apparent, much less transparent. Thus, the work of interpretation continues with the criticism we receive from others, such as the criticism we have been gifted by Cavell himself. So it is in the pages to come that we have been "watching movies with Cavell in mind," meaning precisely that we have been thinking of films (and much else—not just theater and television and opera and music, but also ancient Greek philosophy, post-Kantian Romanticism, American Transcendentalism, and contemporary trends in theory) in affiliation with the tonality of his prose, the temperament of his arguments, and his emotional and intellectual commitment to the worthiness of such an endeavor. In this way, the vitality of his instinct to create criticism (where others might just shrug and neglect) is productively infectious. Reading Cavell on film makes one not only appreciate a film more (and better), but also conveys the Emersonian whisper that we too may be in possession of ideas that would be, could be, in the service of others. Such, at least, are the intentions of a collection such as the present one: to think with Cavell in order to think after him, to keep taking film seriously, to allow ourselves to remain receptive to the way film moves us and motivates us to make its meanings plainer.

Taking movies seriously—as art, as philosophy—takes some commitment, since, after all, there are a lot of bad movies out there. Do we need to take those movies seriously too? It is not just that the quantity of bad movies exceeds our limited time and analytical resources, but that the quality of such works may undermine the tacit assumption of what William Rothman has called a "philosophical perspective" on film.[67] We can analogize and say that art criticism of paintings makes it plausible to separate the good works from the bad, but then we find moments when so-called "outsider" or "folk" art goes mainstream; or when popular art is dreadful and embarrassing. In the first case, art that is not part of the "art world" is suddenly part of it, institutionalized, given a market; in the second case, art that has a market should be denied one. So, let us take another tack, namely, to say that not only should bad movies be viable in the conversation of how (and why) we take movies seriously, but on occasion, it is a bad movie that provides orientation to good cinema (e.g., provides criteria for exploring what *makes* it good); and that ends up serving to convey, indeed confess, attributes we had not seen on the first or even fifth viewing (e.g., elapsed time will reveal structures of class, race, gender, and culture that were largely invisible but take on an outsized presence when watched twenty-five or fifty or a hundred years later).[68] Moreover, newfound attunement to elements of content is often met with a fresh appreciation of formal qualities—whether they be nascent innovations that are now part of the familiar language of film (continuity editing, use of voiceover, etc.) or indicative of technologies or techniques no longer in wide circulation (black-and-white cinematography, etc.).

Cavell saw the split between high/low, mainstream/art house, "the common, shared, democratic run of movies" and what I am referring to just above as good/bad, and observed that "it is generally true that you do not really like the highest instances unless you also like the typical ones. You don't even know what the highest are instances of unless you know the typical as well."[69] Moreover, as a lesson of the comedy of remarriage is the making or cultivating of humility—the cutting down and re-education of snobs and scolds—so too is the critic's approach to films-as-such, no matter their provenance. Thus, while we, in this collection, use terms like "importance" and "seriousness" in a Cavellian vein, we do so knowing that such ordinary words may arrive on some ears as portentous, pretentious, or both (as indicated by Cohen's consternation above). As a gird, then, we can freely admit (or I will here) that the appeal to—and appeal of—the seriousness of film, and/or of taking films seriously, lies precisely in acts of careful attention to shared texts. In essence, this is what I mean to convey (again, in a Cavellian mood) by the notion that films have "philosophical importance"; or by what Mark Greif glosses as their "impulse to philosophy": namely, that they can bear up under the weight of scrutiny, just as written, philosophical texts can.[70] Since films would appear to summon us to perform such analysis upon them, we should be glad to reciprocate, in kind, with our reflections.

Reflections on Reflections

Stanley Cavell's work in film theory, film history, and film criticism is unique—truly one-of-a-kind—in contemporary philosophy and film studies; and more than being novel, it also appears to be at once enduring and timely—and, for that, compulsively appealing. In what follows, we the gathered authors, aim to continue our collective thinking about Cavell's contribution to cinema studies and philosophy while making something of our own bid to address these interrelated domains of thought. The announced mandate for this collection began with an invitation (no doubt a Cavellian gesture) addressed to seasoned readers of Cavell, as well as capable emerging scholars of his thought, to reengage with Cavell's wide expanse of work on film, this time from the cutting edge of a diversity of fields, subfields, and evolving disciplinary developments (likewise, an approach befitting Cavell's own capacious, roving scholarly habits). Mindful of his other writings on topics such as American Romanticism and Transcendentalism, psychoanalysis, autobiography, and skepticism, contributors have inventively agitated for ways of understanding these more overtly philosophical and literary problematics in the context of our experience of cinematic works. While attentive to Cavell's seminal and sui generis accomplishments, this book, however, is neither a festschrift-after-the-fact nor a gloss of existing primary or secondary literature, and still less is it a repetition of old saws rehearsed by "the experts." Rather, formidable intellects have responded to the invitation—summoned themselves is more like it—to think with boldness, vitality, and dynamic inventiveness on the continued relevance of Cavell's work, aiming to set his achievements in the context of close readings of issues and texts central to philosophy and film. In the sequence of chapters that comprise this group of ambitious interventions into the ways Cavell has significantly impacted at least two major fields—philosophy and film studies—the chapters proceed along a spectrum of texts and questions.

One sort of approach adopted by our authors helps us understand what Cavell is up to in his several books on film (principally *The World Viewed*, *Pursuits of Happiness*, and *Contesting Tears*, but also in the conspicuous achievement of consolidating lessons from those earlier works, *Cities of Words*) as well as highly representative articles and book chapters, such as we find in *Themes Out of School*, *Cavell on Film*, and *Philosophy the Day after Tomorrow*. The contributions by our authors blend the best of review-style readings of Cavell's canonical works—providing entrée for a variety of prospective readers, arriving from a range of disciplines—with pioneering engagements with theories, histories, film catalogs, and other cultural elements that complement Cavell's project or correct it, as the case may be. As Andrew Klevan has remarked, Cavell's "best film criticism [. . .] does not simply reveal the depths—much good criticism does that—but somehow remains faithful to the lambency, to the flickering, to the glow."[71] Such illumination seems fitting for any obsessive interest in the cinematic arts, and we endeavor to show Cavell's achievements, while also indicating what they make possible for us as we face the continuing arrival of new works of film and the manifold heirs of movie traditions. Along these lines, the present volume may be a clear and compelling choice for classroom adoption—for a course on Cavell, or a course that aims to draw inspiration from his writing—since the chapters could become a go-to resource for the student, research scholar, and instructor alike (familiar with Cavell or not), who wishes to get a bearing on what Cavell is talking about in a given book or selected piece: what is at stake in it, and why we should continue to care about the claims Cavell makes.

A related, but different, approach involves attentiveness to the claims of Cavellian "readings" of film with an eye toward addressing specific films, or relevant media or cultural creations, that for whatever reason were beyond Cavell's direct attention. For example, while we have in hand accomplished re-readings and re-thinkings of classical works of Cavell's cinematic catalog—say, *The Philadelphia Story* or *Gaslight* (1944, dir. George Cukor)—we also find our critics looking to any number of films (contemporary and not; mainstream and not; narrative as well as experimental and avant-garde; television-based and animated)—that may benefit from a reading with, alongside, and even in opposition to Cavell's work. In short, the films Cavell has written about are positioned to help us think about films Cavell has not written about. If we are turning to a film for the first time, or returning to it after many viewings (including in the company of Cavell's criticism), we should see this as a movement familiar to Cavellian aspirations, as Klevan put it: "So often in Cavell's work there seems to be the desire not to pin things down, but rather to keep things open. Hence a desire, a compulsion perhaps, to keep returning to the same films and moments. For example, he discusses the closing moments of *Now, Voyager* in at least six different books and essays."[72] Despite the return and the repetition, or perhaps because of such thoughtful compulsions, new things are revealed, time and again—as Cavell writes in *Pursuits of Happiness*: "words [and we might add still images, moving images, sounds, and elements of varied media] that on one viewing pass, without notice, as unnoticeably trivial, on another resonate and declare their implication in a network of significance."[73] (Indeed, Cavell himself insisted that he didn't write on a film again unless he had something new to say about it.)

So it is that Cavell commends us to "a mode of philosophical attention in which you are prepared to be taken by surprise, stopped, thrown back as it were."[74] Such revelations happen, so it seems, especially when reading closely, slowly, attentively, since "a text worth reading carefully, or perpetually, is inexhaustible."[75] As Klevan said on another occasion,"[i]f it is true to say that Cavell was interested in how we *approach* the work, then it is also true to say there is no one way of approaching."[76] We are not, then, going over the same ground Cavell covered with such delicacy and wit (how could we?), but are viewing and reviewing in a spirit of discovery and re-discovery, asking "what remains to be seen and heard?" How might I return to familiar ground under a new aspect; how might I approach new texts with familiar ones in hand? Film, perhaps premiere among the plastic arts, is fit for repetition. As such, the chapters gathered here should not only become a repository of some of the finest contemporary engagements with the application (and reassessment) of Cavell's thoughts about film, they should also stand as a series of useful models that other film students and scholars may use as points of reference and inspiration as they begin or continue their own Cavellian investigations into the reading of cinematic and related works.

And yet—and here we can take a full breath—there may be an abiding or percolating worry. I hear something of it in a reasonable concern that Cavell has given us several compelling models or formulas that we can use to understand new works of cinema. In this way, the intellectual moves that let us know what a Marxian or Freudian, feminist or deconstructionist, interpretation of a given piece of art might be are also applicable to Cavell; that is to say, we are welcome to generate various "Cavellian readings" of whatever artworks come our way. The worry, then, and well founded, is that the theory interferes in the art, that the theory is "inserted" and does not emerge naturally from the art itself (that is, as evidenced by what the work shows). The theory is, in a word, *applied* to the art rather than something we (can) find endogenously present. In this disquieting frame of mind, a film does not stand as art-that-reveals-itself to us (by turns, and by returns), but as a kind of beast of burden, there to carry one's theory from one spot to another in the academic discourse. Or perhaps it is the *theory* that is the beast that we use to carry the film. Either way.

While *The Thought of Stanley Cavell and Cinema* was directed mainly to the ontology of the film medium, *Movies with Stanley Cavell in Mind* addresses kinds of cinematic companionship—first, with Cavell's writing on film (and the films he admired), but also with the specific films that command our attention now. From either mode of engagement, these proceedings elucidate how we may learn from Cavell about the inseparable, if still uncanny, companionship of film and philosophy. Some authors have digested Cavell's work over the course of decades—writing in parallel to him, interacting with him as a contemporary; Robert Pippin, for example, who commences the proceedings with meditations on Douglas Sirk, is a signature instance, since his reference to Cavell is often allusive, even unstated, left uncited because presumed by informed readers. On the other end of the spectrum, we find emerging scholars who are in a position to survey the entirety of Cavell's oeuvre at a glance, retrospectively—and thus are poised to seek and find patterns from *Must We Mean What We Say?* (1969) to *Little Did I Know* (2010); on this end of the spectrum, the exchange with Cavell is more heavily and explicitly citational, or thinking of Emerson, "quotational." In this way, new (or newer) films find partnership with "old" films (namely, those familiar to the Cavell canon).

Among the purposes and affordances of this volume, as it was for *The Thought of Stanley Cavell and Cinema*, is not just the welcoming of complication, correction, even controversy, but finding such frisson productive—that is, admitting that the lively, continuing inheritance of Cavell's work does not proceed by way of adherence to a uniform, settled orthodoxy, but instead through a clear-eyed, full-hearted willingness to hear what successive and succeeding generations find reason to say. Our ability to benefit most from Cavell's once and ongoing legacy may depend on our capacity to take his work to task. As we amiably heed Cavell's own sense that "[a] measure of the quality of a new text is the quality of the texts it arouses," and "a text worth reading carefully, or perpetually, is inexhaustible," we are given a chance not only to scrutinize Cavell's achievements but also to assess how we may amplify or modify them as the case may be.[77] To this end, some contributors introduce us to the kinds of controversies we may be pleased to take seriously, despite the disruption; they push us beyond our comfort zone with respect to some received wisdom on the Cavellian corpus and the understanding of its interpreters. In heterodox offerings, they exemplify a vital present while signaling promising ways forward. Still others draw up what amount to invitations for fresh encounters with Cavell's texts, articulating points that have not, until now, been broached but should be of contemporary and ongoing significance to Cavellian studies and film-philosophy. In these ways, however much we are indebted, we have aimed to be unjustifiably beholden neither to Cavell's texts, nor to the impressive library of secondary literature on his work (some of it written by our own contributors!), but cheerfully and gratefully take them both for granted as a beneficial community of able and abiding interlocutors.

After Sandra Laugier's stimulating Foreword, in which we are given reason to remember, or consider for the first time, how "the experience of film is what cultivates in us a specific ability to see the too often invisible importance of things and moments, and emphasizes the covering-over or invisibility of importance in our lives, of what matters to us, *what we mind*,"[78] Part I provides glimpses of the diversity of approaches to Cavell and cinema. Robert B. Pippin looks to Douglas Sirk's *All That Heaven Allows* (1955) in the light of what Sirk, a German émigré to Hollywood, sees in Thoreau (and Emerson)—a study that cannot help but take for granted Cavell's earlier depositions on the American Transcendentalists and his sense of the significance of melodramas featuring a woman struggling to know and be known by those who surround her.[79] William Rothman, whose several books on Cavell have immensely helped the inheritance of Cavell's relationship to film and thinking about film, shares his impressions of how the Belgian filmmakers Jean-Pierre (b. 1951) and Luc (b. 1954) Dardenne have been sensible to Cavell's writing, and furthermore, how this Belgian uptake of the American philosopher (working within a francophone context) has not only informed the films they have made but is complemented by the thought of Emmanuel Lévinas. Rounding out this initial series of what might be called kinds of Cavellian companionship with cinema, Byron Davies supplies a dispatch from Mexico, where he catches up with the experimental filmmaker Bruno Varela (b. 1971) to analyze—and translate—the filmmaker's appreciation of Cavell for the making of films and a variety of media projects. In this encounter, we gain renewed purchase on the vitality of television studies for thinking about cinema, indeed, that they are, or may be, kindred enterprises; animation, and its variants, also make an advantageous cameo. Moreover, since as Davies notes, "[r]eflecting on the past of a medium at just the moment in which it is undergoing major changes is a central feature of Cavell's writing," so it is that, at present, we, like Cavell before us, occupy an era of radical media disruption—when, among other developments, film and television commingle, reversals in prestige and cultural impact are prevalent, and a wholesale stock-taking about the nature of audiovisual media is underway.

Part II finds Steven G. Affeldt and Joseph Mai exploring the human relationship to one's memory and how cinema can be expressive of this feature of our condition. Affeldt takes interpretive flight from Cavell's mention of *Only Angels Have Wings* in his memoir, *Little Did I Know: Excerpts from Memory*. In this engagement with Howard Hawks's 1939 film, Cavell "not only declares his conviction in the existentially orienting power of Hollywood films and their stars but reveals the deepest philosophical ambition of *Little Did I Know* as a whole." Joseph Mai turns his ear to a conversation between Cavell and the French filmmaker Arnaud Desplechin

(b. 1960), where he discovers "Cavellian themes that [Desplenchin] identifies as important to his work" and how these themes become apparent in an analysis of *Trois souvenirs de ma jeunesse* (*Three Memories of My Youth*; or *My Golden Days*, 2015). So far, then, we do not just have cases of *watching* movies with Cavell in mind (e.g., drawing from his readings of films to help us understand those same films, or others), but also *making* movies with Cavell in mind (as with the Dardenne brothers, Desplechin, and Varela). Thus, if we are mindful, in Pippin's phrasing, that Cavell supplies the "idea that films could have a bearing on philosophy," we have evidence that such influence travels the other way too: that philosophy can have a bearing on filmmaking.[80]

Part III reminds us that among the defining gestures of Cavell's work on comedy and melodrama is the contention that moral perfectionism stands apart from traditional morality, such as deontology and utilitarianism, and also the notion that conversation between the principal pair is decisive for the pursuit of happiness (or, when it falters, the presence of undo, if otherwise avoidable, suffering). Paul Schofield and K. L. Evans offer new takes on these fortified aspects of Cavell's writing beginning with, among other things, providing new film texts for us to read—two American comedies: Schofield draws our attention to Elaine May's (b. 1932) *A New Leaf* (1971), created by a female screenwriter, director, and star; Evans looks to Dean Parisot's (b. 1952) *Galaxy Quest* (1999), a metacinematic comedy. Schofield contends that *A New Leaf* presents a vision of perfectionism in a Cavellian key even as it also helps to make a case that perfectionist impulses lie at the heart of traditional, that is, presumably contrasting moral outlooks, such as Kantianism and utilitarianism. Evans, in a similar spirit of reappraisal, considers the startling possibility that although conversation is at the center of *Galaxy Quest*, talking may not be the most advantageous mode by which a romantic couple finds its way to mutual understanding and thus, reconciliation, or as Cavell puts it, "*back* together, together *again*."[81]

Part IV opens a space for studying the female voice as we hear it on screen (or do not), especially as it is tested, contested, or denied in various melodramas. Catherine Wheatley mounts a multivalent investigation into the reception of Cavell's work by some of his female readers, indeed, revealing in the process that it is *Cavell's* voice that may be at issue. In the diverse mix of extended interpretations of Cavell's work by, among others, Amanda Anderson, Elizabeth Anker, Nancy Bauer, Sarah Beckwith, Alice Crary, Michelle Devereaux, Cora Diamond, Élise Domenach, Jennifer Fay, Shoshana Felman, Rita Felski, Juliet Floyd, Karen Hanson, Marian Keane, Kathleen Kelley, Rosalind Krauss, Áine (Kelly) Mahon, Rachel Malkin, Paola Marrati, Tania Modleski, Toril Moi, Danièle Moyal-Sharrock, Susan Neiman, Elisa New, Sianne Ngai, Yi-Ping Ong, Naoko Saito, Naomi Scheman, Judith Shklar, Lisa Trahair, and Wheatley herself (along with other contributors to this volume: K. L. Evans, Sandra Laugier, and Kate

Rennebohm), it may be highly advantageous not just to hear from doubters and dissenters, but also to learn how both Cavell and Wheatley navigate troubled terrain. Since a single person cannot please everyone and cannot say everything, it is helpful to be reminded how to move forward in one's own particularity and limitedness—and yet also how to venture, now and again, representativeness (to "speak," as Emerson exhorted, "what you think now in hard words").[82] In a chapter complementary to Wheatley's critical survey, Charles Warren revisits two marquee features of seventies cinema, *A Woman Under the Influence* (1974) and *Nashville* (1975). In the milieu of two American filmmakers keenly preoccupied with the cinematic registration of the female voice, Warren cultivates our interest in the ways these films by John Cassavetes (1929–89) and Robert Altman (1925–2006) are in natural conversation with Cavell's enterprise, even if *avant la lettre*. So much the better, since part of Warren's discovery lies in what appears to be a shared generational interest in the woman's voice.

Part V presents studies of the human condition as it encounters inhuman ones (such as war, torture, and similar trials and deprivations), nonhuman ones (such as artificial intelligence), or antihuman ones (such as cults that deface individual identity, or behavior that fractures the logic of waking life and nightmares). David Mikics undertakes a thoroughgoing study of Stanley Kubrick (1928–99) to articulate some of the ways his celebrated films bear relation to Cavell. Amir Khan shifts our attention from the often-violent auteur feature films of Kubrick to challenging nonfiction films by contemporary documentarians Errol Morris (b. 1948) and Joshua Oppenheimer (b. 1974), seeking to apply Cavell (and as a foil, Slavoj Žižek) to better understand the misuse—or "abuse"—of documentary confessionals. Daniele Rugo takes us well beyond the Cavellian catalog to watch Lebanese director Borhane Alaouié's (b. 1941) *Beirut: The Encounter* (*Beyroutou el lika*, 1981) with an interpretation of how romantic conversation functions during wartime: how a "war couple" navigates intimacy and distance, and is forced to adopt new modes of communication while under duress.

In Part VI, the concluding section, Kate Rennebohm and I explore the interrelated themes of audibility, visibility, and intelligibility as they function in the films of Belgian filmmaker Chantal Akerman (1950–2015) and American filmmaker Kelly Reichardt (b. 1964). Though Cavell and Akerman shared a campus for a time, Rennebohm liaises a fresh introduction. Then she articulates the nature of viewing and reviewing for our evolving appreciation of skepticism and moral perfectionism—and quite crucially, what new things may be learned about Cavell's decades-long discourse on these topics from Akerman's *La Captive* (*The Captive*, 2000). I also pursue an introduction, this one between Cavell and Kelly Reichardt, in an effort to bring some of the salient attributes of her films into conversation with features of his philosophical writings on film, among them—and here we come full circle, back to Pippin's inaugurating investigation—what it means for a person to be known (or remain unknown) to herself and others, and how such knowledge and acknowledgment involves the reception or sounds (listening) or the projection of sounds. We have become accustomed to the role of the voice (in speech, through the articulation of everyday thoughts in ordinary language), but are perhaps less attuned to the bypassing or suppressing of such sonic emissions—in characters who avoid, diminish, or defeat conversation, fall silent, or await words, and thereby cede the screen to moving images that are coupled instead with spare music, random man-made noises, and the ambient sounds of nature.

* * * *

One of the distinctive facts of Stanley Cavell's discovery or invention of genres—namely, the comedy of remarriage and the melodrama of the unknown woman—is the way, time and again, he provides a reading of what he sees and hears to substantiate a proposal that the *film* is expressive of philosophy, that is, of meaningful claims, of consecutive thought. If his familiarity with films of the 1930s and 1940s (a familiarity borne of repeated screenings) enabled Cavell to notice content in specific films and patterns across a range of them such that he could propose a defensible genre (or cycle), we contemporaries may be tempted to do the same. For example, to see a new film and say, "it fits into the genre." False positives may lurk, as when the Coen brothers' *Intolerable Cruelty* (2003) was released and Cavell seemed reluctant, despite its pedigree of influences, to confirm that it marked a further instance of the genre; we can take this as a cautionary tale of trying to trace a legacy, and, perhaps in that effort, demand of a work something it cannot bear.

In the present context, searching out and debating criteria for membership in a genre (or cycle) *can* be productive, especially if Cavell's remarks on specific films (and groups of films) help us become attuned to certain topical or thematic aspects—heeding specific lines of dialogue, the performances and gestures of actors, elements of mise-en-scène, etc. Yet, it may be more advantageous, more productive for insight into a given film (and its correlates) to think less in terms of specific traits and more in terms of our relationship with the film itself. As William Rothman and Marian Keane put it: "The kind of understanding Cavell seeks by reading a film is not only an understanding about the film, but an understanding, we might say, with the film—an understanding that acknowledges the film's understanding of itself. We cannot understand a film's worth, its meaning, by applying a theory that dictates what we are to say, but only by entering into a conversation with the film [. . .]."[83]

There is no theorem, formula, or syllogism in Cavell's writing that one might extract and test. Rather, as Thoreau said about books (that they must be "read as deliberately and reservedly as they were written"), so we can say the same about films: only—and quite consequentially—an ongoing practice of such discerning investigation will do.[84] Our project is not so much to aptly "apply Cavell" to each and every film we interpret (as if affixing some kind of conceptual label; or, as if following a recipe, adding an intellectual spice to achieve a specific result), but rather to watch and listen attentively, taking film seriously in each new moment (frame by frame, syllable by syllable). This mood, and posture of regard, may be recognized as an indication of what it means to watch and listen to movies with Stanley Cavell in mind. There may be defensible ways of speaking of "a Cavellian film" (especially those that comprise the cinematic exemplars he dwelled upon in classroom conversations and the written works that followed, that is, in those cases already compellingly argued for by Cavell as well as his accomplices); yet there may be even more reason to consider the advent of a Cavellian way of writing about film. In the pages that follow, there is room, of course, for both of these senses—though there is doubtless more latitude for experimentation afforded by the second approach, which stirs us to ask: What films should we be thinking of in the light of Cavell's discourse on cinema? Not just, what films that Cavell cared about should we be rethinking, but also, what films should we turn to with serious philosophical interest, perhaps for the first time? Though many of the films Cavell thought worthy of repeated reflection over the course of his more than half a century of critical engagement with them do appear in the reports here forthcoming, what is more especially our mandate on this occasion is thinking through instances of cinematic art—whatever their temporal origin, authorial stamp, genre type, or geographical location—in company and companionship with Cavell, that is, with his many works on film, which are themselves representatives and repositories of his sensibility for reading film philosophically.

Notes

1. See Lawrence F. Rhu, "Monsters and Felicities: Vernacular Transformations of the Five-Foot Shelf," in *Inheriting Stanley Cavell: Memories, Dreams, Reflections*, ed. David LaRocca (New York: Bloomsbury, 2020), 161–78.
2. Stanley Cavell, *Little Did I Know: Excerpts from Memory* (Stanford: Stanford University Press, 2010), 423.
3. Stanley Cavell, Preface, *Contesting Tears: The Hollywood Melodrama of the Unknown Woman* (Chicago: The University of Chicago Press, 1996), xii.
4. Cavell, *Little Did I Know*, 423.
5. Stanley Cavell, "Mr. Deeds Goes to Town," in *Cities of Words: Pedagogical Letters on a Register of the Moral Life* (Cambridge: The Belknap Press of Harvard University Press, 2004), 201.
6. Stanley Cavell, *The World Viewed: Reflections on the Ontology of Film* (Cambridge: Harvard University Press, 1971, Enlarged Edition, 1979), 60–61. See also ibid.
7. Cavell, *Little Did I Know*, 422–23.

8   Ibid.
9   Ibid.
10 For example, according to Leavis, "Literary criticism, then, is concerned with more than literature. [. . .] A serious interest in literature cannot be merely literary." R. P. Bilan, *The Literary Criticism of F. R. Leavis* (Cambridge: Cambridge University Press, 1979), 3.
11 See, for example, Hent de Vries, "Must We (NOT) Mean What We Say?" in *The Rhetoric of Sincerity*, ed. Ernst van Alphen, Mieke Bal, and Carel E. Smith (Stanford: Stanford University Press, 2009).
12 Cavell, *Little Did I Know*, 423.
13 Jennifer Fay, "Must We Mean What We Film? Stanley Cavell and the Candid Camera," *Discourse*, "Cinema, Modernism, and the Perplexing Methods of Stanley Cavell," 42, nos. 1–2 (2020): 112.
14 Cavell, Preface, *The World Viewed*, xix.
15 Noël Carroll, "Introduction," in *The Palgrave Handbook of the Philosophy of Film and Motion Pictures*, ed. Noël Carroll, Laura T. Di Summa, and Shawn Loht (New York: Palgrave Macmillan, 2019), xxv.
16 Robert B. Pippin, "The Idea that Films Could Have a Bearing on Philosophy," *Inheriting Stanley Cavell*, 181–86.
17 Cavell, *Little Did I Know*, 424.
18 Cavell, "Sights and Sounds," *The World Viewed*, 19.
19 Stanley Cavell, "The Thought of Movies," in *Themes Out of School: Effects and Causes* (San Francisco: North Point Press, 1984), 9; italics in original. See also how Stephen Mulhall draws "three morals from this conception of philosophy's essence" in "Ways of Thinking: A Response to [Nathan] Andersen and [Julian] Baggini," *Film-Philosophy* 7, no. 25 (August 2003).
20 See *Film Theory and Criticism*, ed. Leo Braudy and Marshall Cohen (Oxford: Oxford University Press, 1974; eighth edition, 2016). Is it a function of fame that Cavell's founding contributions to the volume do not appear in its latest incarnation? Those thinkers deeply and openly indebted to Cavell's work, however, are present—including William Rothman and D. N. Rodowick.
21 See Cavell, "Types; Cycles as Genres," *The World Viewed*, 29–37. See also in this volume, chapter 14, n.20 and n.21.
22 See my "Thinking of Film: What Is Cavellian about Malick's Movies?," in *A Critical Companion to Terrence Malick*, ed. Joshua Sikora (Lanham: Lexington Books of Rowman & Littlefield, 2020), 3–19.
23 Lisa Downing and Libby Saxton, *Film and Ethics: Foreclosed Encounters* (New York: Routledge, 2010), 13–14. See also Catherine Wheatley, *Stanley Cavell and Film: Scepticism and Self-Reliance at the Cinema* (London: Bloomsbury), 189–90.
24 See *Conversations*, no. 7 (June 19, 2019): *Acknowleding Stanley Cavell*.
25 Jennifer Fay and Daniel Morgan, eds., "Cinema, Modernism, and the Perplexing Methods of Stanley Cavell," *Discourse* 42, nos. 1–2 (2020): 3–240.

26 Andrew Klevan, *Disclosure of the Everyday: Undramatic Achievement in Narrative Film* (Trowbridge: Flicks Books, 2000), viii.

27 For a handy digest of Cavell's philosophical recovery of Emerson and Thoreau, see his *Emerson's Transcendental Etudes*, ed. David Justin Hodge (Stanford: Stanford University Press, 2003).

28 In such a list, Cavell also includes Manny Farber, Pauline Kael, Parker Tyler, and Andrew Sarris. See Cavell, "An Autobiography of Companions," *The World Viewed*, 13.

29 George Steiner, "Wording Our World," *The New Yorker* (June 19, 1989), 99.

30 Hilary Putnam, "Philosophy as the Education of Grownups: Stanley Cavell and Skepticism," in *Reading Cavell*, ed. Alice Crary and Sanford Shieh (New York: Routledge, 2006), 119.

31 See representative remarks to this effect collected in *Estimating Emerson: An Anthology of Criticism from Carlyle to Cavell*, ed. David LaRocca (New York: Bloomsbury, 2013).

32 Stanley Cavell, "Emerson's Constitutional Amending: Read 'Fate,'" *Emerson's Transcendental Etudes*, 194.

33 See Hilary Putnam, *Nachwort* for Stanley Cavell, *Die Unheimlichkeit des Gewöhnlichen und andere philosophische Essays*, ed. Davide Sparti and Espen Hammer (Frankfurt a. M.: Fischer Taschenbuch Verlag, 2002); italics in original.

34 Putnam, "Philosophy as the Education of Grownups," *Reading Cavell*, 119.

35 Stanley Cavell, "Words for a Conversation," in *Pursuits of Happiness: The Hollywood Comedy of Remarriage* (Cambridge: Harvard University Press, 1981), 2.

36 Richard Moran, "Cavell as a Way into Philosophy," *Conversations*, no. 7 (June 19, 2019), 14.

37 Ibid., 18.

38 Ralph Waldo Emerson, "Spiritual Laws," in *Essays: First Series*, *The Complete Works of Ralph Waldo Emerson*, Concord Edition (Boston: Houghton, Mifflin and Company, 1904), Vol. II, 144.

39 Cavell, Introduction, *Contesting Tears*, 14.

40 Cavell, "Counterfeiting Happiness: *His Girl Friday*," *Pursuits of Happiness*, 175.

41 Cavell, "*The Philadelphia Story*," *Cities of Words*, 44. See also my "Autophilosophy," *Inheriting Stanley Cavell*, 310–11.

42 For a book-length series of recent remarks on the inheritance of Cavell's major contributions to the study of film, see *The Thought of Stanley Cavell and Cinema: Turning Anew to the Ontology of Film a Half-Century after* The World Viewed (New York: Bloomsbury, 2020); continuing on the theme of the reception of his work more generally (across disciplines, but including film), see also *Inheriting Stanley Cavell: Memories, Dreams, Reflections* (New York: Bloomsbury, 2020); and lastly, for memorial notes befitting a *Gedankenschrift*,

several occasions of which directly address Cavell's relationship to the interpretation and experience of cinema, see *Conversations: The Journal of Cavellian Studies*, no. 7 (June 19, 2019): *Acknowledging Stanley Cavell*.

43 Virginia Woolf, *To the Lighthouse* (New York: Harcourt, 1981 [1927]), Ch. I, Sec. 4, 19.
44 Henry James, "The Art of Fiction," in *Literary Criticism* (New York: The Library of America, 1984), 53.
45 See James Wood, *Serious Noticing: Selected Essays* (New York: Farrar, Straus and Giroux, 2019).
46 Emerson, "Success," *The Complete Works of Ralph Waldo Emerson*, Vol. VII, 296.
47 Marshall Cohen, "Must We Mean What We Say? On the Life and Thought of Stanley Cavell," *Inheriting Stanley Cavell*, 54.
48 Cavell, "Words for a Conversation," *Pursuits of Happiness*, 2.
49 Ibid., 8.
50 Stanley Cavell, "What (Good) Is a Film Museum? What Is a Film Culture?," in *Cavell on Film*, ed. William Rothman (Albany: State University of New York Press, 2005), 109.
51 Cavell, "Words for a Conversation," *Pursuits of Happiness*, 8.
52 Cavell, Preface, *Contesting Tears*, xii.
53 Stanley Cavell, *The Claim of Reason: Wittgenstein, Skepticism, Morality, and Tragedy* (Oxford: Oxford University Press, 1979), 5.
54 Susan Sontag, "Thirty Years Later," *The Threepenny Review* (Summer 1996), no. 66.
55 Stanley Cavell, "Epilogue: The *Investigations*' Everyday Aesthetics of Itself," in *The Cavell Reader*, ed. Stephen Mulhall (Oxford: Blackwell Publishers, 1996), 369.
56 Ibid., 370–71.
57 Cavell, "An Autobiography of Companions," *The World Viewed*, 14–15.
58 Gordon C. F. Bearn, "Sounding Serious: Cavell and Derrida," in *Representations* (Summer 1998), no. 63, 65–92. Lisa Trahair, "Serious Film: Cavell, Automatism and Michael Haneke's *Caché*," *Screening the Past*, no. 38 (2013).
59 Cavell, "More of *The World Viewed*," *The World Viewed*, 188.
60 Stanley Cavell, "The Division of Talent," *Critical Inquiry* 11, no. 4 (June 1985): 535.
61 Cavell, *Little Did I Know*, 145.
62 Cavell, "*Mr. Deeds Goes to Town*," *Cities of Words*, 195.
63 Cavell, "In the Place of the Classroom," *Cities of Words*, 3.
64 See above Fay, "Must We Mean What We Film?" and Cohen, "Must We Mean What We Say?"

65 For more on ordinary language criticism see *Ordinary Language Criticism: Literary Thinking after Cavell after Wittgenstein*, ed. Kenneth Dauber and Walter Jost (Evanston: Northwestern University Press, 2003) and Kenneth Dauber and K. L. Evans, "Revisiting Ordinary Language Criticism," *Inheriting Stanley Cavell*, 141–59.

66 On this point, see Newton Garver, *Wittgenstein and Approaches to Clarity* (New York: Humanities Press, 2006).

67 See William Rothman and Marian Keane, *Reading Cavell's* The World Viewed: *A Philosophical Perspective on Film* (Detroit: Wayne State University, 2000).

68 *The New York Times*' film and culture critic Wesley Morris is attuned to the revelatory powers of watching "bad movies," even decades on, for example, the rom-com ("Rom-Coms Were Corny and Retrograde: Why Do I Miss Them So Much?" *The New York Times Magazine*, April 24, 2019), and revisiting box office top-ten lists ("When *Rambo* Tightened His Grip on the American Psyche," *The New York Times*, May 28, 2020).

69 Cavell, "An Autobiography of Companions," *The World Viewed*, 5–6; see also Mark Greif, "Cavell as Educator," *Inheriting Stanley Cavell*, 88.

70 Greif, "Cavell as Educator," *Inheriting Stanley Cavell*, 88.

71 Andrew Klevan, "Cavell at Film Criticism: 'An Unreadiness to Become Explicit,'" *Inheriting Stanley Cavell*, 62.

72 Ibid., 66.

73 Cavell, "Words for a Conversation," *Pursuits of Happiness*, 11.

74 Cavell, "In the Place of the Classroom," *Cities of Words*, 15.

75 Ibid.

76 Klevan, "Cavell at Film Criticism," *Inheriting Stanley Cavell*, 67; italics in original.

77 Cavell, *The Claim of Reason*, 5; Cavell, "In the Place of the Classroom," *Cities of Words*, 15.

78 For further remarks on the importance of film (and television), see Sandra Laugier, "The Importance of Being Alive," *Inheriting Stanley Cavell*, 231–42.

79 See also my "A Desperate Education: Reading Thoreau's *Walden* in Douglas Sirk's *All That Heaven Allows*," *Film and Philosophy* 8 (2004): 1–16.

80 See Pippin, "The Idea that Films Could Have a Bearing on Philosophy," *Inheriting Stanley Cavell*, 181–86.

81 Cavell, "Words for a Conversation," *Cities of Words*, 1–2; italics in original.

82 Emerson, "Self-Reliance," *The Complete Works of Ralph Waldo Emerson*, Vol. II, 57.

83 Rothman and Keane, Preface, *Reading Cavell's* The World Viewed, 11.

84 Henry David Thoreau, "Reading," in *Walden; or, Life in the Woods* (New York: The Library of America, 1991), 83.

PART I

The Companionship of Film and Philosophy

1

Love and Class in Douglas Sirk's *All That Heaven Allows*

ROBERT B. PIPPIN

But what I fear, what even today one could grasp with one's hands if one felt like grasping it, is that we modern men are pretty much on the same road; and every time man starts to discover the extent to which he is playing a role and the extent to which he can *be an actor, he becomes* an actor.

—FRIEDRICH NIETZSCHE[1]

ONE SURE SIGN, AMONG MANY OTHERS, that the great melodramas of Douglas Sirk's time at Universal studios (1952–9) might not be all they initially seem is the immediate ambiguity of the titles of many of the most ambitious ones. For example, the 1955 film *All That Heaven Allows* could suggest, "Look at all that heaven allows in its generosity." And it could mean, "Be careful. This paltry consolation or happiness, and this alone, is all that heaven allows." (In interviews Sirk made clear he meant the latter, that for him, "heaven is stingy," and he was amused that the studio gave it the former interpretation. They thought it a brilliant, uplifting title.[2]) Many other films throughout his American career have the same double character: *Imitation of Life* (1959), *The Tarnished Angels* (1957), *All I Desire* (1953), and *There's Always Tomorrow* (1955).

This ambiguity is tied neatly to the famous irony of Sirk's melodramas. The great ones succeed in narrating both a surface story, and, like the titles, an ironic counterpart. In Sirk's case, the films manage to both indulge the audience's expectations for melodrama, often satisfying them, even as the technique and style exaggerate those conventions, sometimes garishly, often bordering on kitsch, and thereby also expose (to those who notice) the self-deceit and fantasy-thinking behind those very expectations.[3] This has all been much commented on since Sirk ascended to high auteur status among critics and historians of film, something that began first when the *Cahiers du cinéma* crowd began writing enthusiastically about Sirk already in the mid-1950s,[4] and then more rapidly after the publication of some extraordinary interviews with Jon Halliday in 1971. Until this realization about his irony, the films can be seen, for many years were seen, and are often still seen, as straightforward "weepies" or "women's pictures" by audiences and critics and studio executives alike.

Now, *how* a cinematic style can suggest irony, how what we are shown can suggest how much is not shown, perhaps the contrary of what is shown, is a fascinating topic in itself, and there are many different examples of how it works: Nicholas Ray's *Johnny Guitar* (1954), Josef von Sternberg's *The Scarlet Empress* (1934), and Stanley Kubrick's *Barry Lyndon* (1975), just to name three examples.[5] And whether Sirk, in those surprisingly forthcoming interview remarks about his own films, was simply riding the wave of interpretation begun by Truffaut and the *Cahiers* group, or expressing his own, independent views, he did claim that the effect he wanted was a tight connection between genre, structure and style, on the one hand, and "such themes as failure, impotence, and the impossibility of happiness" on the other,[6] all of which latter are not easily visible on the surface. And to Sirk's list we can add "the precariousness of love in the American social world he depicts," my topic in the following. More specifically, our question will concern first the ways in which the policing of sexual conventions intersects with the policing of class boundaries, and all of that will be shown to make the realization of anything like love, at least any love that is not strictly norm-bound, at best terribly fraught, at worst, impossible. Second, the hope is to understand better the attractiveness in this kind of social world of the contrasting ideal of authenticity, or related phenomena like genuineness, nonconformism, and self-reliance in American life, and to explore briefly the naiveté of a common understanding of that ideal, and the consequences of that naiveté.[7] Finally, these two topics taken together will raise a different dimension of irony in Sirk's (or the film's) point of view with regard to the events and characters depicted. For just as melodrama is more than a classificatory genre, rather a narrative form that frames and interrogates such issues as the meaning of suffering, conflict, the absence of satisfying love, and the lack of resolution of basic conflict (it is the modern analog of tragedy in this respect), so irony is more than a literary or cinematic device. It is a kind of ethical stance as well, a way of bearing such contingency and frustration; a "right" way of coming to terms with our subjection to contingency and failure. (In this too, it parallels and contrasts with the tragic point of view, as explored, for example, by Hegel and Nietzsche.) This immediately sounds like a recommendation for distance, noninvolvement, playful, mere spectatorship.[8] But, as we shall see, that would be superficial and unresponsive to the unique play of irony in the film.

For it would be wrong to suggest that the films are best characterized simply as a negatively ironic depiction of such impossibility. In the first place, the irony is not mocking or sarcastic. Many of the characters are well meaning and earnest, even if also fit subjects for an ironic treatment, for our never taking at face value what they say and do. That is, aside from the purely visual dimensions of irony, that dimension of artificial color, lighting, and close-up overheated expressions of emotion, there is a more subtle dimension of such estranging irony. We see characters who sincerely avow what they believe, but who have no substantive idea about what in fact they are actually avowing, what the implications would be (the invocation of clichés—for example, "to thine own self be true"—is a sure sign of this dim apprehension), or characters whose expressed self-understanding is clearly a manifestation of a self-ignorance; again, even if also sincere and well meaning.[9] Often we simply *see* that they don't understand what they say or feel, that they even confuse themselves. (Jane Wyman's remarkably controlled performance, and her consistent, befuddled and confused looks throughout, are the prime examples.[10]) And such irony also functions as a kind of cinematic, reflective interrogation of just why, in that specific world of 1950s America, romantic love and even familial love should be so fraught. (In *All That Heaven Allows*, Sirk's targeting of a distinctly *American* self-understanding as a sign of social pathology and also a sign that he is elevating the thematic scope of the film to be far broader than a story about these individual characters is signaled by his making Thoreau's *Walden* a central text in what seems like an American struggle for "authenticity."[11]) It is this focus that, as we shall see, allows the film to be both a genuine melodrama and a reflective interrogation of the form itself as the form most appropriate to illuminating a certain sort of sociopolitical world, the modern, bourgeois American world.[12] In that sense, even the designation melodrama is misleading, since the film is both an invocation of and an ironizing of melodrama as a sensemaking form of human experience. They might all be called meta-melodramas.[13]

The characteristics we associate with film melodrama, a form traditionally taken to be a demotic or "low art" form, are feverishly intense suffering, overwhelmingly of women,[14] expressed around a great emotional crisis, usually involving romantic and/or familial love. In many stock melodramas there are clearly identifiable villains and victims, but in many others, like Sirk's, there are not. That is, the suffering is caused not by villains but by those whom we love. This is all presented in a cinematic style in which such crises are given expression in a way that is hyperbolic, excessive, overwrought, obvious (particularly in the musical score), something that usually prompts complaint about manipulation, at least if the ironic estrangement from the movie world is not noticed. When we point to such excess, we mean that the expression of emotion in film melodrama goes beyond what we find "appropriate." In the simplest sense this excess embarrasses us now.[15] As noted, in Sirk, this excess emotionality is expressed by an unusually intense, bright color palette in sets and clothes (again anti-illusionistic), sometimes almost garish lighting, hyper-sharp, deep focus, frequent close-ups of such expressivity, a lush, romantic, and quite unsubtle sound track, and transparently phony and even ominous (because phony), happy endings.

Of course, melodramas have a historical inflection too. Considered as a narrative style, or, as Peter Brooks has argued, "an imaginative mode," and an "inescapable dimension of modern consciousness,"[16] we associate their rise to prominence, first of all, with drama, especially Elizabethan and Jacobean drama with clear innocence and villainy, and unjust, horrific suffering, and then on into twentieth-century dramas of suffering like the plays of Eugene O'Neill. The more contemporary form started in the nineteenth century, serialized literature, and with such authors as Balzac and Dickens, and even, surprisingly with art treated now as high art, the novels of Henry James (such as *The Portrait of a Lady*) and Marcel Proust's novel, a comic melodrama if there ever was one.[17] Dramatic opera too has to count as a paradigm instance of the genre. In film, much of the style obviously owes a debt to silent films, and their need to represent interiority expressively rather than verbally, but it is the historical location of melodrama that raises the most interesting questions. The modern melodramatic way of imagining human conflict seems responsive to a distinctive historical situation. For one thing, in contrast to tragedy, melodramas are bourgeois, not heroic, dramas; are about the humdrum world of romance, work, family conflict, private wealth. Nothing of great ethical and political consequence hangs on the fate of characters, who, as Hegel puts it, are now mere individuals, not the expression of universal ethical forces like the state, or the public-private distinction, or the metaphysics of finitude and fate.[18] It could also be that the overwrought and near-hysterical tone is responsive to the dizzying, often incomprehensibly rapid changes wrought by ever-accelerating modernization itself, with characters living and suffering in unique and demanding situations, equipped only with assumptions and expectations at home in an era now long gone and irrelevant. (This is certainly the case in James and Proust.) Or characters overinvest so much and so desperately in romantic and familial love because of the ever more apparent banality, repetitiveness, and enormous pressure for conformism in the new form of capitalist life. The excess is a form of desperation. (If we are now unresponsive, it may not be because we are cooler or hipper, but because such desperate resistance has gone dead; the intense yearning has been co-opted. Perhaps that is the mark of being cooler and hipper.) One possible explanation for the excess and hysteria could stem from characters expecting far too much of romantic and familial love, the only arenas available for any individual expressiveness genuinely one's own, even if inevitably disappointed. (That inevitable disappointment is our theme below, but again, Sirk's apparent pessimism about friendship and love is deeply historical and locally inflected, as any interrogation of friendship and love should be. Assumptions about gender roles, competition, dependence, and loyalty are all always located by him in a particular social world and class; in this film and many others in upper-middle-class well-educated America.[19])

But in Sirk the melodramatic imagination, while linked to such responses as these, has another function too. Expressed simply and in a way often discussed, the social worlds depicted in some of Sirk's melodramas are often all pretense, theater, wholly false, conformist role-playing phoniness.[20] This means, of course, that they are often simply hypocritical, but the important players often seem to believe the theater, and see none of their own falseness. The garishness of Sirk's presentation of such worlds always appears to suggest that this world, a clearly artificial world—no natural colors look like the ones we see—a world presented as if a bright ad in a slick magazine, or a television show in early color, is some sort of projection of *the characters' own sense of themselves*, how *they* see themselves, posed with an intensity that intimates a lingering anxiety and so defensiveness about authenticity, genuine individuality or self-realization, and, in the majority of cases, about the possibility of love in such a world. (We shall return to this issue below; this projective feature could be called the cinematic equivalent of what is "free indirect discourse" in literature, a third-person visual narration that describes or, here, depicts, as if from a first-person consciousness.) Here we have a projection of a staged, theatrical phoniness, unaware of itself as such. That is a remarkable technical achievement.

What also distinguishes melodramas by Sirk is a feature one certainly find in other melodramas (e.g., some by Vincente Minnelli and Max Ophüls and George Stevens, and a few by the Dardenne brothers like *Lorna's Silence* [*Le silence de Lorna*, 2008] and *The Unknown Girl* [*La fille inconnue*, 2016]): the establishment of a connection between that element prominent in all melodrama, the suffering of women, with a social critique of that common world; a critique accomplished simply by its ironic, distanced depiction, as a context within which that suffering is more intelligible, more painful, and almost inevitable. His focus on what are clearly regarded as the pathologies of Eisenhower's 1950s America is essential to understand the enormous attractiveness of the promise of love, both romantic and familial, and for Sirk its inevitable failure, a failure at the intimate level shown as to be expected in such a social world, and often masked in self-deceit (like the bizarre ending to *All That Heaven Allows*). This would then mean that Sirk's critique of the smugness, mutual surveillance and policing by a community's residents, their conformism and consumerism, which now almost everyone sees in his films, is also connected to what can look like a private redemption *from* such vapidity (a contrasting "genuineness"), but which is infected with the same pathology it thinks of itself as escaping. The vehicle for the possibility of such a delusion is self-deceit, and his audiences can congratulate themselves for seeing through the town's hypocrisy (they couldn't possibly miss it; the townspeople are portrayed in very broad, caricature-like strokes), and can want so much to believe in such "havens" as love and family, that the ironic treatment of the latter can be much harder to see, and the implications for human happiness are so pessimistic that audiences don't want to see the falseness in what seems to the characters (and the audience) to be true love. The evidence is strong that most of Sirk's audiences and early critics repeat this phony idealization, and just as willfully "look away" as do many of the characters supposedly "in love." This is paradigmatically the case in *All That Heaven Allows*. But we need to turn to the details of the film to understand how this works.

* * * *

As opposed to other fast-paced films like *Written on the Wind* (1956) and *Imitation of Life*, not much actually happens in *All That Heaven Allows*. It seems reasonable to divide the film into four "acts," as it were. In the first act, we are introduced to the small New England town where the action occurs, Stoningham, clearly a very well-off bedroom community likely near New York, and already somewhat of a parody of "small town" or "village" America.[21] The film begins with an aerial shot, a supervisory or monitoring position from a church tower, although religion is never mentioned in the film. There is no priest or minister (that role has been taken over by the doctor), and it is not until very late in the film that we see a cross on the top of the tower, as if to signal its insignificance. We meet right away the main players, Cary Scott (Jane Wyman), a widow with two grown children off at college. (The son comes home on the weekends from Princeton; her daughter goes to Columbia.) Wyman was thirty-eight when the film appeared, but she is styled to look a few years older, and her circle of friends looks older. That the romance begins in autumn, with leaves falling off trees, is no doubt her image of her "last chance" at erotic, not companionate love, a first example of the way the film projects a character's self-understanding and in this case her own somewhat ironic sense of herself. And there is a "smoldering fire" (some leaves burning) visible as we approach her house.

The children are named Kay (Gloria Talbot) and the truly odious Ned (William Reynolds). There is Cary's love interest, Ron Kirby (Rock Hudson), a local gardener and beginning tree farmer, and we meet assorted townsfolk: Cary's best friend Sara Warren (Agnes Moorehead), the town gossip with the apposite name of Mona Plash (Jacqueline Dewitt), and a pleasant enough bore named Harvey (Conrad Nagel), who, everyone seems to assume, will one day or another end up marrying Cary. In this act, Cary and Ron meet and there is some sport of spark between them, despite the fact (or perhaps because of it) that Cary, a widow with grown children, is older than Ron. The source of the obvious wealth in the community is not unacknowledged, not even spoken of by anyone.

In the second act, Cary and Ron grow very quickly much closer and a real romance begins. Cary discovers that Ron thinks of himself as a nonconformist, a free spirit whose friend Mick reads Thoreau. ("Mick's bible" and, we assume, Ron's as well.[22]) It is hard to miss the irony of Cary, in a somewhat bewildered tone, reading the "quiet desperation passage." Two Hollywood movie stars, highly styled and made up, read approvingly about silent despair and independence of mind.[23]

We learn that Ron has somewhat bohemian friends (at least by the rigidly middle-class attitudes of the town, and, more importantly, in their own eyes) and will soon stop gardening and working for the townsfolk, and open his own tree farm. He lives in his greenhouse and has a confident, but sometimes smug and self-satisfied, air about him (the first signs of trouble with this character, as we shall see). Cary seems quite taken by Ron, although it is not clear how much of that has to do with his independent ideas or the sexual charge she clearly feels (for her, always somewhat bewilderingly) when she is first around him. She does not actually embrace his Thoreauvian philosophy and even at one point assumes he will live in her old house, that her life will go on as before with Ron added on. However, we had already heard some complaints from her about the issue of convention and its restrictions. When discussing with her daughter the ancient Egyptian custom of burying the wife alive with the dead husband in his tomb, her daughter says that we don't do that anymore, and Cary says sardonically, "At least not in Egypt."[24] This act is the most complicated and involves contrasting evening parties, at the country club and among Ron's happy-go-lucky friends. Of major importance is an old mill near Ron's greenhouse that Cary encourages him to renovate. (The relevance of an aging, run-down building, to be renovated by Ron's loving attention, to their romance is not subtle. There is also a Wedgewood teapot, broken, to be lovingly repaired by Ron, that also fills such a romantic function.) Ron eventually proposes, and, after several minutes of terrified deliberation, Cary accepts. The couple announce their engagement to the children and to Sara and all hell breaks loose.

The third act documents this chaos. The children are appalled, and immediately reject the choice of Ron as unworthy of their father's memory, and as an invitation to cruel gossip. ("People will say this all started before father died.") Her best friend is gentler but still tells Cary she is making a very bad mistake. The full supervisorial and disciplining techniques in the town for conforming behavior to the norm are called into play. The chief weapons are gossip and catty remarks and her manipulative, self-centered and self-deceived children. On the son's part, it rises to a promise to break with his mother forever and never return; and in the scene with her daughter, which is much more emotional and pained, she pleads with her mother, in a kind of emotional blackmail, not to marry.[25]

The cruelty and insensitivity of the children are the most dramatic and shocking aspects of this part of the movie. (Cary somehow does not ever manage to see clearly the selfishness and thoughtlessness of the children.) Feeble efforts to dress Ron up like a country club type (again Cary is clueless about what she is asking Ron to do, how impossible the theatrical role is that she has assigned him)[26] and to introduce him to that world are catastrophic failures, but not because Ron is standoffish or explicitly judgmental, but because of the thoughtlessness and sarcasm of the townsfolk. Cary finally cannot stand the pressure, caves in, and wants to wait a while. Ron refuses and they break up.

In the fourth act we see that they are both miserable apart, but each seems too proud to compromise. The break in the stalemate comes, tellingly, from Cary's doctor, a new sort of authority in this world, whom she had gone to see about her general lethargy and headaches. His medical advice is simple, "Marry him, Cary." What's wrong with the repression the town demands is not, he assumes, that it is unjust, conformist, intolerant, or unfair, but simply that it is making Cary sick.[27] This is decisive for Cary, although her vision of the kind of life her children want her to lead, married to the sexless Howard and watching endless hours of television, has clearly already shaken her up as well.

She rushes to Ron's renovated mill, but he is out hunting and she loses her nerve anyway and does not knock. (This is quite an important fact that most viewers, eager for a stereotypical happy ending, can easily miss; can want to miss. It signals in effect that there can be no reconciliation until, as we shall see, Ron is in some sense broken, weakened, brought to ground.) Ron is returning home, sees her, and frantically tries to signal her (no hesitation on his part), falling off a high ledge in the process and knocking himself unconscious, seriously injuring himself. In the last scene, as he recovers, they seem reunited, but we recall that she was still afraid to reconcile, and we see an ending that is quite complexly ambiguous. We will look closely at the scene later.

* * *

I have mentioned that the portrayal of the "world of the town of Stoningham" is presented in a way that is unmistakably ironic, and, in that way, quite critical. The veneer of civility and friendliness is thin. This already suggests that the American pathology that Sirk is examining is dual. It is *both* an anxiety-fueled, defensive, and often ruthless and sadistic obsession with sexual repression and conformism, *as well as* a compensatory Thoreauvian fantasy of self-sufficiency and independence, and the two are clearly linked. That is, Sirk seems to be presenting the love affair as a supposed brave rejection of such conformism, and as embodying the Thoreauvian philosophy behind the rejection, but there is, in the details of the affair, a much more subtle, but equally deep irony, and I want now to develop that basic point, a point I take to concern not just Ron and his friends, but an American self-understanding in general, captured at its best and worst in a facile understanding of Thoreau. This is so, although establishing it with any confidence would require a look at several other Sirk films.[28]

In the first act, as I've called it, the important scenes are the first meeting, her coded reaction to it, and her tentative steps toward a romance. When her friend cancels lunch, Cary, on an apparent impulse, invites her gardener, Ron, to that prepared lunch. He accepts a couple of dinner rolls, and she asks him polite questions about tree farming (playing in effect "the clueless female"). The sound track and his story about the Chinese tree tell us there is more going on than a tree lecture, and we see her disappointment flash quickly across her face when Ron has to leave. Throughout, as here, Ron is associated with nature, and so the naturalness of Cary's aroused desire, something she will never quite be able to admit to herself in that form.

We also see in the opening scenes an example of a frequent technique in the film, one much commented on in analyses of Sirk: the use of mirrors to suggest the reflective status of the film itself. We see not only the movie world, we see (or we should see) that it is represented in a way, or we see ourselves seeing in such a distinct way (the cinematic irony has the same effect). The technique also opens the question of whether, and if so how, the characters see not just their world but how they are taking, imagining that world to be. So we see the chance for, and the lack of, reflection on the part of someone. Cary sits in front of mirrors a few times, but in all the scenes in front of mirrors, she never looks directly at herself in them.

She fits in a sense into Stanley Cavell's category of "melodramas of the unknown women,"[29] although in this case, she is profoundly unknown to herself. The one time she does see herself, it is her reflection in the new TV screen and she sees in effect a vision of the future her children want to consign her to, the modern equivalent of walling the woman up with the dead husband.

The effect of this first encounter is Cary's choice of a bright red, low-cut dress to go to the country club party, a signal of a kind of sexual awakening that is lost on no one. We notice too the red scarf on the daughter, as if she is announcing she is on the verge of being sexually active. In the scene we see as well an extraordinarily explicit acting out of Ned's Oedipal interest in his mother's sexuality. He comments on the dress being cut too low and worries it will "scare off" the sexless dud everyone seems to have picked out as a partner for Cary.

I mentioned Kay and the red scarf, because when she announces her own engagement, she announces her full awakening in an identical fashion, a red dress (although she conforms to her brother's anxiety about low-cut dresses, and is all covered up).

The fact that Kay naively tries to explain to her mother the Oedipal complex, rather clumsily suggesting out loud that Ned desires his mother sexually and is jealous of Harvey as a rival, does not seem to be incidental. For the nature of Ron's interest in Cary, which is not clear on the surface, could easily be understood as Oedipal, a love for a mother figure, and so correspondingly, Cary's interest in Ron could be vaguely and at least symbolically incestuous. (It is striking that there is no mention at all of Ron's mother. People compliment Ron on his father, but it is as if the mother never existed, and she may still be alive. Such an absence cannot be unrelated to his desire for Cary.[30]) This may have something to do with the town's anxiety about Cary and Ron. Their assumption seems to be that there is something "unnatural" about their love, that something about the basic law that distinguishes and rules social order, the prohibition against incest, is at stake. (It is also quite striking that, while it would be obvious in 1955 that, given Cary's age, there would be almost no chance of children, that issue never comes up, as if it is obvious both that children are out of the question and that Ron feels no qualms about what he is "giving up."[31]) Sirk also takes care to "point out" cinematically that this anxiety is not only irrational (there is no literal or even implicit actual incestuous desire, just a faint reminder of its prohibition), but strictly gendered as well. He inserts a small subplot in which an older man in Stoningham, Tom Allenby, is going to marry a woman young enough to be his daughter, a woman Sara calls "that moron JoAnne," who "bagged" Tom. In that case Sara, who has just been so censorious, is *throwing them a party*, the party at which the attempt to "introduce" the class invader, Ron, fails so miserably.

The first act's emphasis on the banality and self-satisfaction of the country club set prepare us well for Cary's dive into romance, her escape. When they first kiss, however, we begin to notice (probably on a second or third viewing) something uncomfortable about Ron. The air of confidence and masculinity (of a sort) that clearly attracts Cary also borders on and sometimes falls into smugness and patronizing, another kind of policing of Cary. Ron appears to be smirking with self-satisfaction. And the bewildered expression on Cary's face, also something we have seen and will see throughout, is telling.

Ron's smugness continues when they return home. When she tries to beg off seeing him again when he returns from a trip, we see him patronizingly insist that "I'll see you," again with the smirk. The fact that Rock Hudson is so huge compared to Jane Wyman helps sustain this rather ominous mood and in all their close scenes together, he looms over her, often with that smirk. And throughout, their embraces and kisses are, while intimate, oddly passionless, even a bit sexless. (It cannot be incidental to making *Walden* a kind of intellectual touchstone in the film, that Thoreau's world is also sexless.) Cary doesn't smile much, always appears stunned and confused rather than liberated and happy.[32]

The contrast between the two evening parties, a raucous celebration, full of genuine good feeling with Ron's friends, and the staid, quiet, gossipy, and phony country club party and Sara's reception could not be clearer. And, apart from the decidedly upper-idle-class look of Mick's apartment and Alida's clothes, that contrast is subject to no ironic distancing. Cary is as genuinely happy at Ron's party as we ever see her, and there is no question that the film tilts sympathetically toward Ron and his friends and their Thoreauvian ideals.[33] But Cary's capacity to find happiness is not the same thing as *marrying* Ron, crossing lines of both class and sex conventions, marrying not only "her gardener" but also someone much younger. Marrying Ron (as opposed especially to marrying Harvey) is like shouting to everyone that she is still capable of sexual desire and romantic attachment. But when Ron asks her to marry him, it is clear she has not thought that far ahead and, when she does, she is terrified. Cary's reaction is predictably panicked, but she is also asking for help from Ron in imagining a new life, concerns about *her* that he is indifferent to, insisting simply that she can do whatever she wants to do. This is all the language of authenticity and genuineness in a life, as the Thoreauvian idea re-emerges, but she is making the plausible point that "being herself" will also, must, carry along in its wake many other people, her children, her close friends. She seems to realize that there might be no compromise allowed between the bourgeois world and the art and nature- and artisan-oriented crowd she will join and that she will be "turning her back on everything she knows." Cary initially rejects the idea, goes to leave, breaks the Wedgewood teapot, as she breaks Ron's heart (the breakage seems to help her realize this),[34] weakens at the door, and they reconcile.

As they come closer to making their engagement public, Sirk makes a point about the gendered nature of the enforcement of class and sexual boundaries; that is, that the enforcement falls heavily on the woman, not the man, and that the very definition of genuineness that Ron imagines for himself is an option only for men. Ron continually asks her not to care about what people think, but it never seems to dawn on him that he gives no quarter in demanding that she think like him; in effect that it is "my way or the highway." It simply means, he says, "being a man." We see Cary hesitate and then accept the characterization, that being herself, Ron's great ideal, will mean "being a man," not at all being herself. (Earlier in the film, Cary had seemed to us as a woman with an ironic dimension, as when she says "At least not in Egypt," and in the way she talks about Harvey. She seems now to be imitating Ron's self-seriousness, and Ron, of course, is totally without irony. This issue will return in the last section.)

We see this even more dramatically through the bourgeois toleration of a predatory male in their midst, Howard Moffer, who is guilty of far worse than marrying someone younger. (We are thereby also reminded that the town's reaction would very likely not occur, in fact does not occur, were the gender roles to be reversed. As noted earlier, the party at Sara's is in celebration of just such a December–May marriage.) He clearly assumes that Cary, by, in his eyes, trumpeting to the world that she is still interested in sex, has opened to door to him, and, drunk and disorderly, he ruins the reception at which Ron was supposed to have been introduced to Cary's world.

Cary's children turn out to be petulant, whining self-involved brats, who do what they can to express disgust at the prospect of their mother's marriage. Ron, like Howard, like everyone, assumes and has the gall to say to his own mother that she is interested only in a "set of muscles," or that she is giving in to brute animal lust, and that if she goes through with it, he will never visit her again. (There is never a full reconciliation scene with them, and after bemoaning the loss of their familial home, they will later abandon it anyway and disappear from the film. They exit unredeemed and unredeemable.[35])

Finally, Cary succumbs to the pressure, and tries to convince Ron to wait, to move into her house and to live in her world. Ron refuses and we then see two firsts: Cary exercising some real independence and Ron losing that facade of self-confidence that had so often slipped into self-satisfaction.

The children return for Christmas (their condition having been met), and everything has changed. They pressured their mother to give up her fiancé, but then, it turns out, they are moving away and urge Cary to sell the very house Ned had proclaimed so sacred to the family tradition. And they buy her a TV set so she won't be lonely, perhaps the bitterest irony in a film full of irony. It is clearly the modern version of walling the widow up in the tomb.

The reconciliation scene is prepared for by two scenes that are telling. In Ron's case, we return to a reminder about gender and power in both worlds, Ron's and Cary's, and in Cary's, as noted, her initiative is a matter of health, as "prescribed" by her doctor. In Ron's, the jocular Mick tells Ron that women do not want to make up their own mind; they want to man to make up their minds for them (so much for "to thine own self be true"), and he encourages Ron to do so.

And her doctor tells Cary, insightfully, that she was ready for a love affair, not love. And we see that much of Cary's hesitation has had to do with her anxiety about being older. She has been secretly worried since Mick's party that Alida's blonde, young, attractive cousin would be hard for Ron to resist and that he must have taken up with her. When she finds out the cousin is marrying someone else, her inner hesitation is resolved and she drives out to the mill, but again her resolve falters and she drives away without knocking. Ron sees this and tries to call out to her, but loses his footing and suffers a bad fall, is seriously injured. (As noted earlier, given that she turns away from door, it is crucial that any reconciliation seems therefore to *require* Ron's fall and injury.) This begins the final scene in the film.

Several things are visually important in the last scene. First the mill has been made over to look like what James Harvey has called an extreme version of *Better Homes and Gardens*, Cary's world, only glossier and pushed "to almost lunatic extremes of elaboration and rich deadness—in color."[36] The second is that the familiar visual geometry of Ron looming over Cary is reversed, as Cary is now overlooking him, injured, broken in effect and in bed, passive.

It is very tempting to think that this reversal represents not only what makes possible the reconciliation (that Cary now has the "upper" hand, with the injured Ron "diminished") but that their future will now *maintain* such a relationship. Their new world will still have upper-middle-class types like Mick and Alida in it, and the redecorating of the mill means a reduplication of Cary's old world, with some idea of their own authenticity projected on it all. The romance had begun in autumn, and is now resolved in some way or other in the dead of winter. This either presages that spring will soon arrive, or that the lack of warmth and the somewhat fraught sexual passion we had seen in their scenes figure their romantic fate together. All the signs point to the latter. And the deer we had seen before returns. Previously it had seemed to figure Ron's "nourishing" Cary's need for love, her dependence on him, but now it seems not to figure Cary's dependence on Ron, but the reverse, and somehow Sirk has managed to have the deer seem confused and stunned a bit, as if to remind us that Ron has no idea what he is in for, will be in the same state for some time.[37] Nothing we have seen suggests that the town will change, or even that Cary will change very much. What looks like the reunion of two now independent, self-reliant souls is simply one more way of compromising with the requirements of bourgeois life. Ron has been diminished in power and authority, will continue to turn trees into commodities, and Cary, we expect, will manage to find a way, most likely through self-deceit, to imagine that what they do together will be authentic and their own, even as it reproduces the norms that we have seen enforced throughout.

Much of the dialogue and Ron's injury itself seem tinged with irony. The doctor, in telling Cary that Ron's recovery will take time, that he will need her help, that it will last a while, seems just as much to be describing what Ron will face in hitching himself to a well meaning, but still very conventional, woman, how much "help" he will need in getting over his "injury," recovering from his "broken" status. (This "needing help" scene mirrors an earlier one after the proposal when Ron also pleas that he will need help adjusting.) If they are to reunite, it will at least at the outset be with Cary in a conventional role, nurse and mother. What will happen when Ron is well is left unclear. Cary had been persuaded and perhaps a bit intimidated by Ron into marrying him; she had been bullied out of marrying him by her children; she had been embarrassed into reconciling with him by the doctor, only to fail at the last minute, and she is now moved by concern and pity to nurse him back to health, but we sense no fundamental transformation or new resolve. And Ron, of course, cannot act on Mick's advice either, "to make up Cary's mind for her." All he could do to bring this about was fall off a cliff. This kind of stalemate is what should expect given Sirk's sentiments about the American bourgeoisie, that their "homes are prisons," and that "they are imprisoned even by the tastes of the society in which they live."[38] In the final scene, we note at the very end the effect of the deer as a near perfect embodiment of Sirk's unique version of cinematic irony. Somehow the poor, confused deer figures for us what has become of the self-consciously virile, "my way or the highway" Ron.

* * * *

The film ends, leaving us with two general issues raised. I mentioned at the beginning that the film establishes some sort of connection between the anxious policing of class boundaries and the policing of sexual conventions. By the enforcing of such conformism, I mean to refer to a conformism familiar in nineteenth- and twentieth-century fiction. One could call it "Girardian."[39] In the absence of any substantive common value, we anxiously watch each other for signs of what is worth wanting, and take some comfort in following the lead of "most people," or "most people in our social class" for signs of what ought to be done, or to be thought or to be desired. If we were to question that, we would be in uncharted waters, a source of great anxiety because we sense we would have lost all standards. Another aspect of the general anxiety is obvious. While class differences rest on real inequality, on money and the access to power that they provide, the idea of class as a kind of exclusionary norm, or the idea that members of it are therewith entitled to live a different life, exists as such only in being asserted and acknowledged and internalized, especially by those who are excluded. (Once it is successfully internalized it can paradoxically become almost invisible, as evinced by the infrequency of its invocation in American political discourse.) Sustaining it requires the policing of perception and desire as well as the maintenance of real material power. So it is one thing to have a fling with your gardener, which Mona and the other town gossips vicariously believe for a while Cary is doing, seeming to take some pleasure in the spectacle. It is another to attempt to ignore a class boundary and so class privilege for the sake of love, to establish legally a precedent or model that others could follow. Cary is thus directly challenging the idea that class is a mark of some significant differentiator in human life, and by acting as she does she treats it as the fantasy it is. Class in this latter sense, as an entitlement to special privilege and a requirement to marry your "kind," is in itself "nothing" at all, nothing real. (It has as much "reality" as the belief that the blood of aristocrats is distinctive.) Cary is on the verge of exposing that and so stands as a potential "traitor to her class."

However, Cary's ultimate timidity and apparent inability to place herself outside the conventions she has known and accepted all her life, and Ron's self-congratulatory sense of autonomy and nonconformist rigidity, descend from an American social imaginary dealt with in all Sirk's great melodramas and represent contrasting poles of the dialectic of dependence and independence that that imaginary requires. Such a tension would understandably make any deviation from marriage norms fraught with anxiety and confusion. Ron can maintain his sense of himself only by drawing Cary wholly into his world, and Cary can keep her relations with her friends and family, not to mention her Wedgewood china, three strings of pearls, country club and mink coat tastes, only by somehow or other pulling Ron into her orbit, and that is possible only after Ron has "fallen."[40] Or, in another version of a dialectic that can become a paradox, the bourgeois marriage understands itself as a product of passionate romantic love, but can only be properly realized by contract and an impossible legal promise to love. But who writes the contract?

A final general theme is authenticity, Ron's "answer," his guiding lode star. In the conformist world of Stoningham, perhaps of America in general, it is certainly understandable that such genuineness would emerge as some sort of virtue. And for many philosophers, starting with Rousseau and Diderot, and extending through Kierkegaard, Tocqueville, Nietzsche, Heidegger, and Sartre, it is treated as a kind of new master virtue, the trait of character that is the most crucial in the emerging modern mass consumer societies.

But the first problem with Ron's self-conscious embodiment of such an ideal is evident in his air of smug self-satisfaction and in his "be a man" homily. For, to invoke a familiar figure for such a notion, one assumes that has one has "found" oneself and now must find a way of remaining true to what one has found. But in the philosophical treatments of the ideal in Kierkegaard, Nietzsche, Heidegger, and in Emerson and Thoreau (as interpreted by Cavell), the emphasis is on the enormous *difficulty* of any such "finding." The intricacies of social dependence in modern, mass consumer societies, the near feudal power of managers in corporate empires, and a heightened awareness of the difference between public personae and private attitudes make any settled sense of just "being" oneself immediately naïve. (Compare Kierkegaard's sense that in the modern age the only true Christians are those who cannot be Christians and know they cannot be.) Or, any such sense ought to inspire a different sort of skepticism than about the external world or other minds, but about one's sense of oneself. This would be the kind of irony mentioned earlier here, a kind of ethical stance. As in Cavell's treatment, this is not a skepticism that demands or intimates a "solution," as if a philosophical problem, but a fate to be borne. And bearing it cannot be a matter of resigning oneself to an inevitable self-deceit (as in typified in

Sartre on bad faith), or to a kind of cynical playfulness, but simply a lived-out realization of the great difficulty (not the impossibility) of any "finding" and "being" who one "genuinely" is. There is no model or principle to guide any such recovered life. Any such picture or formulation would be subject to infinite qualifications and endless nuances. But there are characters in novels and films who have arrived somewhere, found something, reached some state of mind that can at least be suggestive, provide some sort of illumination. Or the absence of such characters (and there are none in Sirk's Universal melodramas) can also imply something determinate about what is missing or still hidden, forgotten.[41]

It is important, too, that we are shown that the naiveté of Ron's sense of what authenticity requires is linked to his constant avoidance of the dialectic of dependence and independence that is often raised by the film's point of view, by what our attention is directed to. His sense of himself is self-certifying, closed to any sense of how he seems to others, a sense that might have awakened him to the difficulty he is simplifying. Cary must think for herself, as long as she thinks like him, about marriage, where to live, and what friends to have. He is in effect "broken" by her refusal to do so, but we sense he is likely to think of it all as a compromise, even a sacrifice of himself for her, and that too is self-congratulatory rather than genuinely reflective. What he never realizes is that authenticity is a cooperative or a social virtue.[42]

Finally, the idea of authenticity as some sort of *goal to be sought* can easily seem paradoxical, as it does in this film, with Ron wavering between dogmatic and smug self-assertion, and broken submission, as if "true" to a new, but now dependent, self that he will never be able to acknowledge as such. This whole situation can be greatly compounded by self-deceit; one knows that one is not able to, not allowed to, represent oneself as who one is, but can manage, over even a lifetime, to hide that somehow from oneself. (Most audiences, I think, accept this temptation in Sirk's films.)

Put another way, the more authenticity, or the avoidance of such self-deceit, needed, as modern mass consumer societies took shape, to be praised as a virtue, the more suspicious its expression became (i.e., just as it became part of a conscious social *strategy*). Once it became publicly acknowledged as a virtue or even as significant, it became suspicious, a strategic means, if only to self-congratulation, as is the case with Ron. *Being* authentic is one thing; *trying to be* and especially *trying to be seen* as authentic immediately borders on the theatrical.[43]

No aspect of this way of looking at what Sirk's film shows us should be understood as a *moral* critique of Ron's smugness or Cary's fear. The ambiguous and somewhat ominous fate of Ron's and Cary's love affair, perhaps of the fate of love itself in such a world, is nowhere treated by Sirk as the failure of individuals to live up to their own convictions or to have the courage to risk ostracism and gossip. Any aspiration to the intimacy, vulnerability, and deep reciprocity of love and friendship can come to mean what it does to the agents, can come to require what it does, can run the enormous risks it does, only in a specific social and historical world. In the world Sirk shows us, the American modern bourgeois world in the immediate postwar years, there is not much hope that such aspirations can ever be realized. As Sirk put it, "Heaven is stingy."

* * * *

There is one last philosophical dimension to Sirkian irony that is worth mentioning. That the world of Stoningham is treated ironically simply means at a first level that we are shown that things are not as they seem, either to the viewers of the film (most viewers, I suspect), or, especially, to the inhabitants, the players of the theatrical social game of status seeking and boundary policing. Their moral judgments are staged strategies of self-serving protectiveness. That can seem obvious, but it can appear to be the singular traits of self-involved, thoughtless people, and that is not what it seems. But there is yet another level to the irony. Since the irony is not destructive or cynical we are also being called on to attend to what it would be to live without such theatricality and falseness. And part of what a philosophical reading of a film, one attentive to this difference and to the generality of the problem, can accomplish is to call to mind, however indistinctly at first, whatever is missing in the lives we see—call it mutuality, reciprocity and respect, love, socially realized freedom, genuineness, or, following Cavell, "the ordinary."[44] In Cavell's treatments, what is hidden, very hard to recover, is so because layered over with ossified habits of mind, with too much taken for granted, habits that make it hard even to notice that anything might be missing. In a fine phrase, he once called what is missing an "intimacy lost."[45] (Hegel would call the goal of such proper, corrective attending "the actual," or "the concrete"; also, he thinks, lost in the world he saw coming into being.) The attention to class differences and the role of gender and age policing in the community are treated in the film as the most important sources of the distortion, the ossified and unreflective habits of mind, the loss of what would otherwise be possible, what the intense aspiration to love, understood as a kind of inchoate resistance, aspires to. As noted, class is treated in the film as a cultural and social norm, and Sirk keeps the material sources of class power markedly hidden, as hidden and undiscussed as they tend to be in modern American life. Aside from Ron and Mick, no one ever talks about what they do in the male world of New York that every professional man in the town gets on a train to attend to every morning. Sirk's orientation is certainly focused on the real interests of the socially and economically powerful (see *Written on the Wind*), but those interests are treated in their social and especially psychological manifestations; in snobbery, the jealous guarding of privilege, anxiety about the fragility of such privilege. Characters like Mona Plash, and what she and her friends represent, are at home in Sirk just as they would be in the novels of James and Proust, rather than in the context of a Dreiser novel (or in George Stevens's cinematic treatment, *A Place in the Sun* [1951]), or in films by, say, Elia Kazan. At least Sirk's radical leftist past in Germany, his obvious fascination with the nature of these distortions and fantasies in the American experience, and, of course, the details of the film in question make it reasonable to attribute to him such a concern in these terms. Given the hiddenness mentioned above, this treatment hardly gives us the full picture of class, power, and the consequences of such a social order on the intimacies of daily life, but his treatment allows him, along with directors like Nicholas Ray, Max Ophüls, and Alfred Hitchcock and a few others, to produce something distinctive in Hollywood commercial film—a politics of American emotional life.

Notes

1. Friedrich Nietzsche, *The Gay Science*, ed. Bernard Williams, trans. Josefine Nauckhoff and Adrian Del Caro (Cambridge: Cambridge University Press, 2001), 215–16. I am very grateful to David Wellbery, Michael Fried, Daniel Morgan, and Richad Neer for several helpful exchanges about this chapter, and to Mark Wilson for a conversation about Sirk at the very beginning of the project. An earlier version of this chapter appeared in *Critical Inquiry* 45 (Summer 2019): 935–66 and I am grateful to the editors for permission to reprint here. The work is also included in my *Douglas Sirk: Filmmaker and Philosopher* (London: Bloomsbury, 2021).

2. Cf. "Or take *All That Heaven Allows* . . . The studio loved the title; they thought it meant you could have everything you wanted. I meant it exactly the other way 'round. As far as I am concerned, heaven is stingy." *Sirk on Sirk: Conversations with Jon Halliday* (London: Faber and Faber, 1971, 1997), 140. He goes on to make similar points about other titles.

3. Borrowing from his time as a theater director, Sirk deliberately created an anti-illusionistic mise-en-scène, even a Brechtian "distancing" effect, and so later, as a film director, rejected the realist conventions for film standard for Hollywood in its classic period.

4. It is generally accepted now, especially in film studies, that Sirk managed to create an artifice that made it possible "to comment on the world, as it comments on the means of representation."

   Barbara Klinger, *Melodrama and Meaning: History, Culture, and the Films of Douglas Sirk* (Bloomington: Indiana University Press, 1994), 9. Klinger's book is indispensable on the various receptions of Sirk and on the significance of that variation.

5. For a discussion of Ray, see my "Cinematic Irony: The Strange Case of Nicholas Ray's *Johnny Guitar*," *nonsite* 13 (September 2014), nonsite.org.

6 This is Barbara Klinger's summary of Halliday's Introduction to *Sirk on Sirk* in her *Melodrama and Meaning*, 9. I tend to give Sirk credit for his independence in the remarks, given his own involvement with avant-garde and left-wing theater in Germany, but nothing I say in the following depends on evidence from the interviews.

7 This raises the issue of a properly political psychology. For a discussion of the nature of this problematic, see the Introduction to my *Hollywood Westerns and American Myth: The Importance of Howard Hawks and John Ford for Political Philosophy* (New Haven: Yale University Press, 2010), 1–25.

8 Anticipating a reaction to this linking a discussion of Sirk to Hegel and other weighty thinkers, I note and echo Stanley Cavell's remark: "I am not insensitive, whatever defenses I may deploy, of an avenue of outrageousness in considering Hollywood films in the light, from time to time, of major works of thought." *Pursuits of Happiness: The Hollywood Comedy of Remarriage* (Cambridge: Harvard University Press, 1984), 8. For further discussion, see "Prologue: Film and Philosophy," in my *The Philosophical Hitchcock: Vertigo and the Anxieties of Unknowingness* (Chicago: The University of Chicago Press, 2017), 1–12. Cavell's philosophical touchstone is Emerson, to some extent Heidegger, to some extent Wittgenstein. In three books on film, mine has been Hegel on the link between self-knowledge, agency, and knowledge of others. (Hegel is not particularly good on the issue of irony. He thinks it must erode the wholeheartedness and reconciliation that is the goal of modern societies in his account.)

9 Cf. the remarks in J.-L. Comolli and P. Narboli in "Cinema/Ideology/Criticism," reprinted from *Cahiers du cinéma* in *Screen* 12, no. 1 (1971): 27–38 about an ideology critique internal to a film, otherwise quite conventional: "An internal criticism is taking place which cracks the film apart at the seams. If one reads the film obliquely, looking for symptoms; if one looks beyond its apparent formal coherence, one can see that it is riddled with cracks; it is splitting under an internal tension which is simply not there in an ideologically innocuous film. [. . .] This is the case with many Hollywood films, for example, which while being completely integrated in the system and the ideology end up by partially dismantling the system from within" (33). See also P. Willemen on a "distance between the film and its narrative pretext," in "Distanciation and Douglas Sirk," *Screen* 12, no. 2 (1971).

10 Such psychological states also greatly confuse any standard moral assessment of the characters. This confusion arises particularly in Robert Stack's performances in *Written on the Wind* and *The Tarnished Angels*, and in Lana Turner's somewhat willful (and so blamable) ignorance in *Imitation of Life*.

11 Sirk said, "*Walden* by Thoreau. This is ultimately what the film was about." *Sirk on Sirk*, 113 (keeping in mind again that interviews are performances). And "about" is equivocal. There is no reason to believe Sirk thinks that Mick and, in his more intuitive way, Ron, have properly understood *Walden*, and plenty of reasons to believe that what they have appropriated is a facile and self-deceived "lesson," one that is not unique to two individuals but broadly shared (whether anyone knows the text or not) in the current age in America.

12 There is a helpful account of the historical conditions, and the internal social contradictions so appropriate for melodramatic film, by D. N. Rodowick, "Madness, Authority and Ideology: The Domestic Melodrama of the 1950s," in *Home Is Where the Heart Is: Studies in Melodrama and the Woman's Film*, ed. Christine Gledhill (London: BFI, 1987), 268–80.

13 There is an important sense, explored by Cavell, that all Hollywood genres have a meta-generic dimension, that genres are not structures with features to which later instances "add on" features; that genres are occasions for reimagining the genre. See *Pursuits of Happiness*, 28–30.

14 Predominantly but not exclusively. As Mulvey points out in "Notes on Sirk and Melodrama," in *Home Is Where the Heart Is*, *Written on the Wind* and *The Tarnished Angels* stand out because of their treatment of male victims of patriarchal families in capitalism (76–77).

15 Philosophy can be melodramatic in this sense too; it can elicit such reactions. Nietzsche does. Cavell says, speaking of the fervor in Wittgenstein's formulations, "If there is melodrama here, it is everywhere in the *Investigations*." Stanley Cavell, *This New Yet Unapproachable America: Lectures After Emerson After Wittgenstein* (Chicago: The University of Chicago Press, 2013), 36.

16 Peter Brooks, *The Melodramatic Imagination: Balzac, Henry James, Melodrama and the Mode of Excess* (New Haven: Yale University Press, 1976), vii. Thomas Elsaesser, in probably the single most influential film studies article on melodrama, "Tales of Sound and Fury: Observations on the Family Melodrama," first published in *Monogram* in 1972, and reprinted in *Home Is Where the Heart Is*, summarizes a discussion of melodrama as "a form which carried its own values and already embodied its own significant content; it served as the literary equivalent of a particular, historical and socially conditioned mode of experience" (49).

17 Sirk thought Shakespeare was a melodramatist. "Interview with Douglas Sirk," *Bright Lights* (Winter 1977–78): 30.

18 See Hegel's remarks about modern drama in *Aesthetics: Lectures on Fine Art*, Vol. 2, trans. T. M. Knox (Oxford: The Clarendon Press, 1975). But on the other hand the tragic denouement is also displayed as purely the effect of unfortunate circumstances and external accidents which might have turned out otherwise and produced a happy ending. In this case the sole spectacle offered to us is that the modern individual, with the nonuniversal nature of his character, his circumstances, and the complications in which he is involved, is necessarily surrendered to the fragility of all that is mundane and must endure the fate of finitude (1231; see also 1197 and 1218).

19 Another way of understanding cinematic melodrama is Hitchcock's in his early piece, "Why I Make Melodramas" (1937): "In the cinema a melodramatic film is one based on a series of sensational incidents. So melodrama, you must admit, had been and is the backbone and lifeblood of cinema." He goes on to say that direct realism would not work for cinema (ordinary events are too banal), and the extraordinary that he shoots for might be called "ultra realism." He adds that anyone who wants to understand the psychology of

mass audiences and what will work, grab their attention, should study daily newspaper editors. "If film-makers understood the public as newspapers do they might hit the mark more often."

20 There is a good discussion of "pretending" as "the main attribute of American middle-class life" in R. Rushton, "Douglas Sirk's Theatres of Imitation," *Screening the Past*, no. 21 (2007): 1.

21 Get a new job, move to a small town, and you too can be Thoreau. See James Harvey, *Movie Love in the Fifties* (Cambridge: Da Capo Press, 2001), 374. The two Thoreauvians in the film, Ron and Mick, seem to assume that no urban job can be an authentic one, and that unless one lives in a village, and has some job connected with the commodification of nature, one is doomed to falseness.

22 We are told that Ron doesn't have to read the book; he already lives it. But as we shall see, that is not quite right. He not only lives it, he preaches it, and rather self-righteously too.

23 Harvey, *Movie Love in the Fifties*, 374. The theme of such independence is introduced in an already qualified way. Alida says that Mick was very unhappy working in the city and their marriage almost split up because of his unhappiness. They moved here to live their Thoreauvian life and all is now well. She never says whether *she* was unhappy in New York, whether she wanted this sort of life, is happier here, and soon. While she seems happy enough, her life is a kind of "imitation of life," of Mick's life. The shadow of the war, mentioned a few times (Mick and Ron were wartime buddies), hangs over the narrative too; as if that experience intensifies the need for finding something authentic and genuine in life.

24 Later in the film, this fate is suggested by a scene after the breakup that shows Cary behind a window, as if behind bars, as if trapped by them, staring out and weeping, and in that only image where she looks directly at her image, she seems trapped *inside* the television set purchased for her at Christmas by her children, as if, bizarrely, a husband substitute.

25 See the discussion in John Mercer and Martin Shingler, *Melodrama: Genre, Style, Sensibility* (London: Wallflower, 2004), 56 and 63.

26 See Fred Camper, "The Films of Douglas Sirk," *Screen* 12, no. 2 (1971): "In a sense, then, all characters in Sirk are totally blind, surrounded as they are, not by real things but by falseness. There is no question of seeing 'reality' on any level or attaining any genuine understanding since such concepts are completely excluded by the formal qualities of Sirk's images" (48).

27 The doctor asks: "Do you expect me to give a prescription for life?" This is obviously a rhetorical question, to which the answer is supposed to be No. But he then proceeds to do exactly that: give her a life prescription. The equivalent existential problem for Ron after the breakup is that he "can't shoot straight," and so is "good for nothing." This suggests he can't really be a man occupying the position of a patriarchal relation to Cary. As he probably sees it, he was dumped by her, and so it would be unmanly to make the first move.

28 There is almost always some indication in Sirk's films of some specific barrier, impediment, to a more humane life of social solidarity and sensitivity. Underneath what the ironic treatment reveals, there is something to be recovered, remembered. In this film the barrier is some sort of anxiety about sexual and class boundaries, treated as linked. In *Imitation of Life*, it is the fantasy of fame or the dominance of celebrity culture (also treated with great pathos in *All I Desire*). In *Written on the Wind*, it is a fantasy about masculinity and status. In *The Tarnished Angels*, an airplane race figures the effects of obsessive competitiveness. In *There's Always Tomorrow*, it is the deadening habits of domesticity itself.

29 Stanley Cavell, *Contesting Tears: The Hollywood Melodrama of the Unknown Woman* (Chicago: The University of Chicago Press, 1996). I mean it conforms to Cavell's understanding in the following sense. As Cavell puts it, in some melodramas, the woman wants both to know, and that means that she seeks an education, senses there is something she must learn, and especially wants to be known, to be properly acknowledged as separate and independent in her own right. But Cary's inchoate desire to be educated anew in a way of life she is intrigued by and somewhat afraid of (a life in which she could freely realize her romantic desire) is frustrated. In this sense, Ron is a phony educator, partly because he plays the role of educator so theatrically, and as if he does not need to be educated himself. (Although he inches toward such a realization by trying to fashion a home that Cary will understand and love, a home that can be for both of them.) He is not, though, the Thoreauvian hero he thinks he is, but a commercial tree farmer, and he is uncompromising and dogmatic (not that these traits are completely absent in Thoreau himself). He is not exempt, no one is, from the demands of a ruthless competitive capitalism. It, together with bank loans, competition with other farmers, crop failures, and so forth, is just off stage, as is so much of his life. So she is intrigued by a fantasy Ron has of himself, one that turns out to be a smug self-satisfied self-image.

30 The only time we hear Ron express why he is attracted to Cary, it is response to Cary's questioning why he and Mick had been looking at her and laughing when they first met. Ron tells her that he told Mick she had the finest pair of legs he has ever seen. (How would he know, in those dresses?) He is not in the slightest embarrassed at being caught in such locker room banter with his friend, and Cary silently accepts the objectifying compliment, but it is clear that Sirk is making a point about Ron's relation to women.

31 As with Oedipus, the prospect of generating children (having generated children) with one's mother is horrific to contemplate, subverts both the family and political life. It could be said to an attempt to return to and to become one's own origin, the progenitor of oneself, in the ultimate act of autonomy, autochthony. I am grateful to Glenn Most and Ben Jeffery for an exchange about this issue.

32 Harvey, *Movie Love in the Fifties*, 375–76. Note also Harvey's reports of Sirk's impatience with "sentimentality," a trait that should surprise the early critics of his melodramas.

33 There is an extremely subtle, almost invisible, indication of the persistence of class and ethnic lines being maintained in the group. When we see Cary introduced to Manuel and his family at this party, we see a lovely young girl, his daughter Marguerita. Cary, who has already been taken aback by the presence of what she takes to be an obvious and far too formidable rival, Anderson's niece, Mary Ann, completely ignores Marguerita. But Sirk always keeps Marguerita in the background or at the edge of the frame in the party scenes, and clearly directs her to look glum, sullen, and even angry throughout, presumably that the handsome bachelor Ron is ignoring her in favor of a much older woman. (She is the only one at the party who never smiles or gets into the swing of things.) It is as if she knows that a Latina woman could never have a chance with Ron (Mary Ann is always flirting with him) and Cary seems to take that for granted too.

34 Another subtle mark of the fate of their relationship: the precious teapot, which has been identified with Cary's world, is broken so badly that it can never be repaired. It would be a different film altogether if the final scene had included a shot of it fully repaired.

35 There is a feeble apology from Kay, when she announces her own marriage and seems to have some very dim awareness of how much pain she has caused her mother, but Cary reiterates that it is "too late," and there is no warm reconciliation. The scene maintains a tonality of sadness.

36 Harvey, *Movie Love in the Fifties*, 374. As noted earlier, this is a little extreme. Ron had been content in his greenhouse, and he is clearly trying to appoint the new space with taste, in some sense a tastefulness he thinks Cary should recognize. And she does; that it was all made over "with love."

37 Harvey notes that the deer seems trapped between the picture window and the painted landscape behind it (*Movie Love in the Fifties*, 376). One might also add that the notion of the deer trapped could parallel the different way nature is manifest after picture windows became part of American architecture: framed, almost posed, and hardly any longer nature as it meant to Thoreau. And even in Thoreau, once nature *is taken up* as significant and "for us," it is already no longer mere nature. This parallels the authenticity point made here. I am indebted to Tom Gunning for a discussion about this issue.

38 "Interview with Douglas Sirk," 32. Quoted in Thomas Schatz, *Hollywood Genres: Formulas, Filmmaking, and the Studio System* (New York: Random House, 1981), 253.

39 René Girard, *Deceit, Desire, and the Novel: Self and Other in Literary Structure*, trans. Y. Freccero (Baltimore: The Johns Hopkins University Press, 1961). See especially the first chapter, "Triangular Desire," 1–52. This structure might just as well be called Hegelian.

40 It is difficult to imagine a social life for the two that could combine both the country club crowd and the Mick-Alida community. Dinner parties with Sara or Mona at Mick's place are hard to picture. It might be tempting to see some possibility as even conceivable because Ron has in effect *sacrificed* himself for Cary, that his broken state is something he is willing to do for her. But he

actually does nothing; he stumbles and falls accidentally. One can imagine him coming out of his concussion and returning to the Ron we saw in their breakup scene.

41 Cavell's examples of remarriages in *Pursuits of Happiness* would be a good place to start, especially with Jean, Barbara Stanwyck's character in *The Lady Eve* (1941), at the end of her journey from con artist to genuine lover.

42 I explore this notion further in *Hegel's Practical Philosophy: Rational Agency as Ethical Life* (Cambridge: Cambridge University Press, 2008), chapters six and seven; and in "Passive and Active Skepticism in Nicholas Ray's *In a Lonely Place*," *nonsite* 5 (March 2012), nonsite.org.

43 Ron has his own philosophy, formulates it explicitly, and is thought of by others as embodying this expressed philosophy. He is also willing to lecture people solemnly about its tenets. His standing as a character would be much different if Ron were played by, say, Gary Cooper in his prime; laconic, a man of few or no words, simply *being* himself. See also Lionel Trilling, *Sincerity and Authenticity* (Cambridge: Harvard University Press, 1973) for similar Hegelian points, and my treatment of Fried's Diderotian problematic in "Authenticity in Painting: Remarks on Michael Fried's Art History," *Critical Inquiry* 31, no. 3 (2005): 575–98.

44 The theme is, of course, everywhere in Cavell, but I am thinking here of the special bearing on this film of *This New Yet Unapproachable America* and *Conditions Handsome and Unhandsome: The Constitution of Emersonian Perfectionism* (Chicago: The University of Chicago Press, 1990), and more generally in *The Claim of Reason: Wittgenstein, Skepticism, Morality, and Tragedy* (Oxford: Oxford University Press, 1979, 1999).

45 Stanley Cavell, "Politics as Opposed to What?," *Critical Inquiry* 9 (September 1982): 161.

2

Lévinas, Cavell, and the Films of the Dardenne Brothers

WILLIAM ROTHMAN

IN A FEBRUARY 2011 JOURNAL ENTRY, Luc Dardenne observes that he and his brother Jean-Pierre, having completed *The Kid with a Bike* (*Le gamin au vélo*, 2011), were discussing their next film, which he describes as a story of a young woman who makes the passage from fear of life to the courage to live. On March 31st, Luc writes that they were no longer thinking of the man who accompanies the woman as having only a chance connection with her, like Samantha and Cyril in *The Kid with a Bike*. They don't know who he should be—her father? a fellow factory worker? But they do know they don't want to combine the woman's struggle to regain her job with a love story. Luc's May 6th entry says only this: "We aren't progressing in our new screenplay. *Two Days, One Night* is at an impasse." Thus the brothers turned their attention to *La fille inconnue* (*The Unknown Girl*), already their working title for the film they would go on to premiere at the Cannes Film Festival in 2016. Not until September does Luc refer again in his journal to discussing with Jean-Pierre the screenplay of *Two Days, One Night* (*Deux jours, une nuit*, 2014). Finally, in October 2012, he writes, "We are doing well with the new structure. I think it works. The couple she forms with her husband (no longer a man with a separate story) enables the film to stay focused on her journey. He is her coach, or steward, who believes in her and helps her not to give up."

Despite the brothers' determination to avoid combining their protagonist's struggle to regain her job with a love story, their "new structure" does precisely that. But it also combines that love story with a story about a woman's education, or creation, as Stanley Cavell would call it. And combines that story, in turn, with a story about the rebirth of a marriage. The "new structure," in other words, brings *Two Days, One Night* into alignment with the films Cavell calls "Hollywood comedies of remarriage."

What made the brothers change their minds?

On July 5th, a month after confessing that the screenplay for *Two Days, One Night* was at an impasse—in his very next journal entry, in fact—Luc writes, "I read *Philosophie des salles obscures*"—the French title for Cavell's magisterial late book *Cities of Words*, newly published in translation. Luc adds, "I re-watched *Shanghai Express*. A veritable comedy of remarriage. Critique of skepticism." Two weeks later, Luc writes a lengthy entry that begins, "Symposium on Stanley Cavell at the Sorbonne." Without mentioning that he not only attended but also presented a paper at that symposium, he characterizes Cavell's thinking as *foisonnante*. Cavell's *pensée foisonnante* still "largely escapes" him, Luc admits, but he senses "real affinities" with it. He adds, "I take great pleasure in these comedies of remarriage in which words circulate between the characters, exchanged in a conversation that leads them toward their 'unattained but attainable self,' toward the Green World."

To be sure, Luc is mistaken in identifying the "unattained but attainable self," a concept Cavell borrows from Emerson, with the "Green World" that remarriage comedies borrow from Shakespeare. For Cavell, the green world is not the goal, the destination, any more than Walden Pond was for Thoreau. The goal is to return, changed, to the world of everyday life. But although Cavell's *pensée foisonnante* did in some measure escape him, Luc's intuition was correct. His thinking, and Cavell's, *do* have "real affinities," For Luc Dardenne as for Cavell, "walking in the direction of an unattained but attainable self," embracing what Emerson calls the "wonderful way of *life*," is fundamental.

At the Sorbonne symposium, Luc expanded on ideas he expressed in his July 5th journal entry:

> Our films end where these comedies begin. Our characters are alone, imprisoned and walled in silence, having lost confidence in the word. As if to go toward the "Green World" in our films was to leave this silence, discovering the possibility of a first exchange, the possibility of a conversation that would be an escape from violence, from murder. How to find in the silence of our times, which is the silence of rivals, the silence of fear of others, the silence of solitude clinging to the need for survival, the silence that leads toward murder more than to recognition—the path of a conversation in which two individuals can reinvent a future? That is what we're trying to film.

The Promise (*La promesse*, 1996), *Rosetta* (1999), *The Son* (*Le fils*, 2002), *The Child* (*L'enfant*, 2005), and *The Kid with a Bike* do all end, each in its own way, with the protagonist arriving at such a "first exchange" with another person, the start of a conversation that promises an escape from violence, from literal or symbolic murder. But Luc's journal entry underestimates how close the films he made with his brother actually are to the American comedies Cavell celebrates. Hollywood comedies of remarriage also end—they don't begin—with the couple embarking on such a conversation. The woman and man may be talking to each other from the start, but until their relationship is transformed—the green world is where this metamorphosis occurs—their witty banter remains a cover for what Luc characterizes as "the silence of fear of others" that threatens murder more than it promises recognition. Only at the conclusion of a remarriage comedy does the couple achieve a conversation that brings to an end, rather than perpetuates, the mutual failures of trust and acknowledgment that Cavell understands to *be* acts of violence, "little murders," enabling them to take their first steps on a path that leads in the direction of the "unattained but attainable self."

Lorna's Silence (*Le silence de Lorna*, 2008), the Dardenne film that preceded *The Kid with a Bike*, would also have achieved such an ending—indeed, it would have been as truly a "veritable remarriage comedy" as *Two Days, One Night*—except for the brothers' decision to negate that possibility by killing off Lorna's drug addict husband just as their phony marriage is turning into a real one. This pushes her over the edge into madness, and the film ends with a strangely dreamlike scene, unparalleled in a Dardenne film, which finds Lorna, alone and in peril, altogether withdrawn from reality, talking to the nonexistent son she imagines that her dead husband fathered.

This ending isn't mandated by realism, by the commitment of the Dardennes to representing realistically how human beings actually live today. And, unlike, say, Judy's fall from the tower in *Vertigo*, the ending of *Lorna's Silence* lacks the necessity of tragedy. It's a melodramatic contrivance—a manifestation of the brothers' power, as authors, to preside over "accidents" within the worlds of their films. What does it reveal about their art that they *chose* to employ this God like power to persecute Lorna, whom they surely love as much as we do, and—for the first time in their cinema—to condemn their protagonist to a nightmarish fate, with no hope of being saved?

In my book *Must We Kill the Thing We Love? Emersonian Perfectionism and the Films of Alfred Hitchcock*, I suggest that when his dedication to what he called "the art of pure cinema" compelled him to end *Vertigo*, his greatest film and only tragedy, with the death of the woman he loved no less than Scottie did, Hitchcock wished to find a new path—a way to make films that might free him from the murderous dimension of his role as author. After *Lorna's Silence*, the Dardenne brothers, too, had reason to wish for a new path, one that would free them, as authors, to escape from violence, from murder. It was such a wish, I am suggesting, that moved Luc Dardenne to undertake the thinking, and writing, that was to create *Sur l'affaire humaine*, the book of philosophy he completed in 2012 but began writing in 2007—at the time the brothers, having completed *Lorna's Silence*, were starting to converse about the screenplay for their next film, *The Kid with a Bike*.[1] Luc's motivation for undertaking this philosophical project, he tells us in the book's introduction, was to understand Cyril, the "kid with a bike"—to understand him, I would add, in a way that would enable their film about him to take the first steps on the path he and Jean-Pierre were seeking.

The main thrust of *Sur l'affaire humaine* is that, after the death of God, our challenge as human beings is to accept our finiteness, our separateness, our mortality, in the absence of the consolation that the promise of eternal life had for so long provided. Our challenge is not to overcome or transcend but to *live with* our inescapable fear of death, so that, to paraphrase Bob Dylan, we might be busy living, not busy dying—so that we might embrace, day by day, living together with other people in "the one existing world," as Cavell likes to call it. The abbreviated notation "Critique of skepticism" in Luc's July 5th journal entry about Cavell, I take it, is shorthand for his recognition that the potentially tragic consequence of *denying* our separateness, which is his central theme in *Sur l'affaire humaine*, is at the heart of the American philosopher's thinking as well. It is what skepticism *means* to Cavell, who writes,

> In our slights of one another, in an unexpressed or disguised meanness of thought, in a hardness of glance, a willful misconstrual, a shading of loyalty, a dismissal of intention, a casual indiscriminateness of praise or blame—in any of the countless signs of skepticism with respect to the reality, the separateness, of another—we run the risk of suffering, or dealing, little deaths every day.

For Cavell, skepticism with respect to other minds is not an *intellectual* lack; it is a stance it is all too possible for me to take in the face of the nontransparency of the other and the demand the other's expression places upon me. It is the denial or annihilation of the other, thus the denial or annihilation of the self. And Luc Dardenne sees eye to eye with Cavell on this.

Cavell goes unmentioned in *Sur l'affaire humaine*. Not so Emmanuel Lévinas. Sarah Cooper, in her influential 2007 essay "Mortal Ethics: Reading Lévinas with the Dardenne Brothers," cites Luc Dardenne's 1996 journal entry that notes that Lévinas died during the shooting of *The Promise*. Luc's journal entry goes on to suggest that the entirety of *The Promise* "can be seen as an attempt ultimately to reach the face-to-face encounter." But from the perspective Luc achieves in *Sur l'affaire humaine*, written fifteen years later, *The Promise* can be seen to be *challenging*, no less than illustrating, Lévinas's way of thinking about the face-to-face relation. From the moment Igor makes his fateful promise to Assita's dying husband that he will look after her, his actions exemplify Lévinas's belief that I have an absolute obligation, an infinite responsibility, to serve the other. The face-to-face relation, for Lévinas, is not a relation between equals; the other is *Higher*. Nor is the relation reciprocal; my obligation to the Other is not contingent on the other recognizing an obligation to me, any more than it is contingent on any feeling for the other I may have. I am *commanded* to serve the other.

In *The Promise*, Igor feels—and *we* feel—that he must do everything in his power to serve Assita, whose need is desperate. But we also feel that his acceptance of responsibility for her is not all that matters in their relationship, morally speaking. Igor has no right to demand that Assita acknowledge his sacrifices in serving her, much less that she forgive him or be grateful to him or love him. Nonetheless, in the end, when he finally tells her, as we know he must, that her husband is dead, Igor would be profoundly saddened—and so would we—were she simply to walk away without revealing any feeling for him as a fellow human being. We are deeply moved when, in the film's final shot, Igor runs ahead to catch up with Assita, and she allows him to walk side by side with her into the depths of the frame, and the brothers elect, for the first and only time in the film, to have the camera refrain from following them—an expressive gesture, addressed by the Dardennes to us, that acknowledges that these two human beings have achieved a "first exchange, the possibility of a conversation that would be an escape from violence, from murder."

In a comedy of remarriage, the couple achieves a relationship worth having, a conversation of equals that enables this woman and this man to feel, as the Katharine Hepburn character puts it at the end of *The Philadelphia Story* (1940, dir. George Cukor), "like a human, a human being." For Lévinas, human feelings have nothing to do with being ethical. But feelings, and love above all, mean the world to the Dardennes.

There is a strangely neglected passage in *Pursuits of Happiness* that helps highlight both the concerns Cavell shares with Lévinas and the magnitude of the distance that separates them. In the passage, Cavell invokes a distinction drawn by Matthew Arnold in order to suggest a way of understanding why the marriage in *The Philadelphia Story*—in Cavell's writings, marriage is more than a recurring metaphor; it is a subject for philosophy—is genuinely of "national importance." Cavell proposes that, in Matthew Arnold's terms, Dexter (Cary Grant) "Hellenizes," while Tracy (Katharine Hepburn) "Hebraizes" (a word one may have to be English, and not just a native English speaker, to be comfortable pronouncing), meaning that what this couple achieves—what comedies of remarriage achieve, what Cavell's writings strive to achieve—is the marrying of "spontaneity of consciousness" and "strictness of conscience." Lévinas's brief against Western philosophy, which was born in Greece, is that, by "Hellenizing," it has always excluded, or repressed, the ethical standpoint, particular to the

Hebrew language and the worldview specific to Judaism. As Hilary Putnam points out in an eloquent and appreciative essay, Lévinas, an Orthodox Jew, was addressing a predominantly Gentile audience in his philosophical writings, but his goal wasn't to convert Gentile philosophers to Judaism—to persuade them, for example, to observe the traditional dietary laws and the entire panoply of *mitztot* that collectively transform every act we might perform in our daily lives—this is the domain Cavell calls "the ordinary"—into a sacrament, an act God *commands* us to perform, or to perform in a certain way, or to refrain from performing. The aspiration of Lévinas's philosophical writings, as Putnam reads them, was to convert philosophy into an ethical practice—a practice that accepts its absolute responsibility to the ethical standpoint, particular to the Jewish tradition, that philosophy had always repressed. For Lévinas, ethics, philosophy's Other, is *higher*. By contrast, Cavell's aspiration, like that of Emerson before him, is to achieve a marriage between the "Hellenic" and "Hebrew" ways of thinking, as if philosophy and ethics had been separate but equal. And I am suggesting that *Sur l'affaire humaine* locates Luc Dardenne on Cavell's side, not Lévinas's side, of this continental divide.

Lévinas writes, "To see a face is already to hear 'You shall not kill.'" But in *Sur l'affaire humaine*, Luc Dardenne implicitly rejects this claim that the "first discourse" is the face of the other wordlessly speaking the God-given commandment "You shall not kill." For Luc, there cannot be such a God-given commandment prohibiting killing the other—if only because the recognition that God is dead is the starting point of his book's reflections. In nonetheless undertaking to explicate how she believes the Dardenne films perform a "Lévinasian-inspired challenge to the being of cinema," Sarah Cooper writes, "To kill or not to kill is the key question that their cinema raises. The death of the subject is displaced by a preoccupation with killing, or failing to kill, someone else." Cooper takes this move from dying to killing to be a challenge to "received ideas about what cinema is." And yet, as I have shown in *Must We Kill the Thing We Love?*, the question "to kill or not to kill" was already at the heart of Hitchcock's cinema (and, I might add, Renoir's). That the camera is an instrument of violence *is* a received idea about what cinema is. Hitchcock spent his entire career striving to come to terms with the murderous aspect of film authorship. Cooper asserts that the Dardenne films "ask whether art—their films included—can institute the impossibility of killing the other crucial to Lévinas's ethics." But in *Lorna's Silence*, the Dardennes *choose* to have her husband killed—murdered, by moral, if perhaps not legal, standards—and to condemn Lorna to a fate of death-in-life. In their capacity as authors, killing is all too possible for the Dardennes, as it was for Hitchcock—and as it is for us, in Cavell's view. "In the everyday ways in which denial"—denial of the reality, the separateness, of the other, which for Cavell is always an act of violence, a "little murder"—"occurs in my life with the other—in a momentary irritation, or a recurrent grudge, in an unexpected rush of resentment, in a hard glance, in a dishonest attestation, in the telling of a tale, in the believing of a tale, in a false silence, in a fear of engulfment, in a fantasy of solitude or of self-destruction—the problem is to *recognize* myself as denying another." That is why, for Cavell, although I have a finite responsibility for the finite other, I have an infinite responsibility for myself—an absolute obligation to make myself intelligible, to myself as well as to others.

For Lévinas, the face face-to-face encounter can serve as the basis for ethics because the human face possesses the God-given power to order and ordain us, to call us into serving the Other. From *The Promise* to *Lorna's Silence*, the Dardenne films privilege bodies more than faces, filming people with a handheld camera that follows them closely, often from behind, as in the opening of *Rosetta*.

As Charles Warren has observed, our impression here is that it is Rosetta herself—that is, her body, which is the body of Émilie Dequenne, the remarkable young actress who incarnates her—that is the locomotive that pulls the camera and hence the film's train of images, making us feel that the only relationships that matter are between Rosetta and others in her world, especially the young man with whom she finally breaks through to a "first exchange."

In their relatively early feature *Rosetta*, the Dardennes still allow the camera at times to grant us close-ups of the face of their young protagonist. These close-ups serve to express the brothers' attunement to her innerness, her longing to break free from her prison of solitude. By the time they make *The Son*, however, the Dardennes were committed to subjecting the camera to a stricter discipline. In *The Son*, they consistently refrain from using the camera to perform *gestures*—gestures that express their own feelings or thoughts about the events they are giving us to view. They strive to avoid provoking us to sense that there is an unseen director (or two), with an agenda, who is in control of the camera's framings and movements.

For the late Chantal Akerman, the other great Belgian filmmaker influenced by Lévinas's writings, the *viewer* is the Other with whom she hoped her films would put her in a face-to-face relation. As she says, "My viewer is in a relationship with 'me' as a viewer, with 'me' as the director." This "me" is faceless to the viewer, just as the viewer/Other is faceless to the director, even though—or because—"my viewer is in my place." The disciplined way of filming fully manifest in *The Son* forgoes the possibility of achieving the kind of relation with the viewer that was Akerman's goal, a goal the brothers themselves had not altogether abandoned in *The Promise* or *Rosetta*. This discipline also places *The Son* at an opposite pole from the films of Hitchcock, whose goal was to make the viewer experience *every* framing, *every* camera movement, *every* transition from shot to shot, as a gesture—an expression of a mood the camera at once captures and casts, and at the same time an expression of a thought, *Hitchcock's* thought. And the disciplined way of filming the Dardennes developed is also at an opposite pole from what Jean Rouch called the "one take, one sequence" method—itself a discipline, but of a very different kind—that enabled Rouch's later films to provoke in the viewer a continuous sense of the handheld camera as an extension of the filmmaker's own unseen body. I might add that we also experience *The Son* very differently from the way we experience so-called direct cinema documentaries by the likes of Richard Leacock or D. A. Pennebaker, who developed their own idiosyncratic strategies, and had their own personal and artistic motives, for making the viewer aware, at pertinent moments, of the filmmaker's unseen presence behind the camera.

Sarah Cooper argues that the disciplined way of filming the Dardennes developed "replicates" the impossibility of stepping into the characters' positions to see as they see, feel as they feel, and thus "carries the refusal or inability to kill into the domain of spectatorship." But this doesn't make sense to me. I think of it, rather, as a strategy for acknowledging, or declaring, something that is true of all films: We can *never* "take the place" of a person who dwells within a world separated from our world by the barrier-that-is-no-real-barrier of the movie screen. In any case, the Dardennes' disciplined way of filming demands of the camera a passivity as extreme as the "passivity beyond passivity" that, in Lévinas's view, my infinite responsibility demands of me in relation to the other. In *The Son*, there is no reciprocity in the camera's relation to the people it films. Following them closely so as to be there to register their every move, with nothing demanded of them in return and nothing of its own to express, is the sum total of the camera's relation to the characters. Lévinas speaks of the other as holding me hostage. In *The Son*, the camera is held hostage.

Cooper claims that in Dardenne films the camera's extreme proximity to its subjects creates a "space of responsibility." But this doesn't make sense to me either, given that it is a condition of the ontology of film—a condition whose implications Cavell addresses in *The World Viewed*—that we are *not*—we *cannot* be—responsible for, or responsible to, the people who dwell within the projected world. It is precisely because we have no obligations toward her that we're free to simply watch and listen to Rosetta, for example. No matter how much misery she suffers, there are pleasures to be gleaned by attending to every move of the actress who incarnates her, pleasures immeasurably enhanced by the way the Dardennes mostly film her, from such close proximity that we could touch her, or be bowled over by her, were there no screen separating us. "Every art, every worthwhile human enterprise, has its poetry," Cavell writes, "ways of doing things that perfect the possibilities of the enterprise itself, make it the one it is." Film achieves its particular poetry when it "achieves the perception that every motion and station, in particular every human posture and gesture, however glancing, has its poetry, or you may say its lucidity." Cavell could have had the Dardenne brothers' films in mind when he wrote those words. They could have had Cavell's words in mind when they filmed *Rosetta*.

We cannot achieve, but neither can we *fail* to achieve, a face-to-face relation with Rosetta. And even if, as Lévinas believed but Luc Dardenne does not, the face of the Other speaks a divine prohibition against killing, that commandment can only fall on deaf ears for *Rosetta*'s viewers, given that we *cannot* kill the boss who fires Rosetta, or punish him by forcing him to eat nothing but waffles, as *Rosetta* can give the impression that all Belgians do, even if we wish we could. Surely Luc Dardenne was thinking along such lines when he wrote in his journal, "To watch the screen means: not to kill." But although this principle is true enough for the viewers of a Dardenne film, it does not hold true for the Dardennes themselves, in their capacity as authors, insofar as they control the camera, even when they use it in a way designed to make it appear that no one is pulling the camera's strings. As authors they possess the God like power, which we lack, to dictate who lives and who dies within the projected world. To the extent that they choose to film people in a way that disavows any connection between the camera and their own power to preside over "accidents" within the film's world, the Dardennes can be said to *efface* their agency as authors.

Joseph Mai has characterized *Lorna's Silence* as the Dardennes' most Lévinasian film.[2] Part of what he had in mind, I take it, is Lorna's acceptance, however grudging at first, of infinite responsibility for the man others refer to only as "the junkie"—an obligation that is not contingent, as Igor's was in *The Promise*, on a prior promise or burden of guilt. Moreover, the film seems attuned to Lévinas's problematic idea—as great an admirer as Hilary Putnam balks at this—that my infinite responsibility for the other means that I am responsible even for the other's persecution of me. I'm not sure it even makes sense, however, to think of Lorna as responsible for the suffering that the Dardennes, as authors, inflict on her. Nor do I accept responsibility for the suffering they inflict on us, in our capacity as viewers, by repeatedly giving us reason to hope, then brutally dashing our hope, as in the passage that begins with Lorna and "the junkie," husband, who in the preceding sequence made love for the first time, walking on the street together, amicably making plans to meet later the day. When he pedals away on his bicycle, Lorna, acting on a spontaneous impulse, runs, beaming, to catch up with him, her expression reflecting the surge of affection she is feeling: a rare moment of happiness for her (although in retrospect the fact that he doesn't stop can be seen as a foreshadowing of the terrible letdown to come).

In the very next shot, Lorna is back in her apartment, sorting through the jumble of his clothes—to arrange or wash them, we imagine, having been given no reason to suspect that what she is doing is anything but an expression of her newfound sense that a relationship worth having has been born between them. Only retroactively do the Dardennes reveal to us the devastating truth that in the interval the man had died of a heroin overdose.

The Dardennes efface their agency as authors, I would suggest, so as to present the projected world as *authorless*—as if the author is dead in Lorna's world, just as God is dead in our world, the one existing world. In *Sur l'affaire humaine*, after all, the recognition that God is dead is the starting point of the book's reflections. But the film's authors aren't really dead; they're only *playing* dead, as I'm tempted to put it. By "playing dead" they are disavowing their responsibility for Lorna's fate, their ultimate failure to "be there" for her as they had always "been there" for the protagonists of their previous films. This may be the Dardennes' most Lévinasian film, as Joseph Mai suggests.³ But creating *Lorna's Silence* required the brothers to transgress—if only imaginatively or fictionally, as it were—the commandment fundamental to Lévinasian ethics. And in creating the film, the brothers also failed the altogether different moral test that Luc Dardenne would go on to propose when he wrote *Sur l'affaire humaine*. By "playing dead," denying their responsibility for the violence they inflict on Lorna and on us, the film's authors are not busy living; they're busy dying. And killing.

Lévinas's writings, long an inspiration for the brothers, were instrumental in helping to lead them on the path that enabled their films—including *Lorna's Silence*, which I do not deny is a great film, however disturbing I find it—to achieve greatness. But that path also led them into the impasse at which *Lorna's Silence* left them. It was to discover a new path, I suggest—the path that has led so far to *The Kid with a Bike*, *Two Days, One Night*, *La fille inconnue*, and *Young Ahmed* (*Le jeune Ahmed*, 2019)—that Luc Dardenne undertook, in a spirit of self-reliance, the thinking, and writing, that resulted in *Sur l'affaire humaine*. I would propose, then, that when in 2011 Luc read *Cities of Words* and sensed "real affinities" with Cavell's *pensée foisonnante*, the affinities he sensed were with his own way of thinking, not Lévinas's.

Luc Dardenne would have felt no need to embark on that philosophical journey had he believed, at the time he and his brother were turning to the screenplay for their next film, that they could learn from Lévinas's writings a way to understand how a boy like Cyril, their "kid with a bike," thinks. Nor would Luc have felt the need to write his book of philosophy had he shared Lévinas's belief that it is *impossible* for one person to understand an other who is absolutely different, utterly separate. Or had he shared Lévinas's conviction that "understanding" the other is, in any case, neither a necessary nor a sufficient condition—indeed, has nothing to do with—achieving an ethical relation with that other. Living an ethical life, for Lévinas, is strictly a matter of obeying the divine commandment that we recognize our absolute obligation to serve the other.

In *Sur l'affaire humaine*, the concept of the face-to-face encounter, unencumbered by the conceptual (and religious) baggage Lévinas had loaded onto it, basically means what "the acknowledgment of others"—their acknowledgment of us, our acknowledgment of them—means in Cavell's writings. Luc Dardenne, like Cavell, believes that what motivates our all too human impulse to deny the reality, the separateness, of others is our fear of acknowledging our own finiteness, our separateness, our mortality. Human beings cannot live denying that the external world exists, but we *can* live in denial of the reality, the separateness from us, of "other minds," other selves. It is the main thrust of Part Four of *The Claim of Reason*, Cavell's philosophical masterwork, that what philosophy knows as "skepticism," what Luc Dardenne calls "the silence of our times," is the root of what Shakespeare called "tragedy."

"What Is the Scandal of Skepticism?," a challenging and important essay reprinted in *Philosophy the Day after Tomorrow*, reflects on the striking resemblance—yet the strikingly different conclusions or morals the two philosophers draw—between Lévinas's pivotal use of the passage in Descartes's Third Meditation designed to prove the existence of God from the otherwise inexplicable presence in him of the idea of an infinite being, and Cavell's own use of the same Descartes passage in *The Claim of Reason* in connection with the role of God in establishing for myself the existence, or relation to the existence, of the finite Other.

Lévinas's idea is that my discovery of the other, my openness to the other, requires, as Cavell puts it, "a violence associated with the infinite having been put into me"—"put into me" being Lévinas's transcription of Descartes's insistence that "the idea of God I find in myself I know cannot have been put there by a finite being, for example myself." In later writings especially, Lévinas characterizes this intervention, which manifests itself in a "breakup of consciousness," with metaphors of trauma, violence, monstrosity, devastation. In Cavell's words, "This event creates as it were an outside to my existence, hence an isolated, singular inside." At the same time, "it establishes the asymmetry of my relation to (the finite) other in which I recognize my infinite responsibility for the other."

But when the idea of the infinite is "put into me," Cavell asks, why should it be infinite responsibility for this other that is revealed, rather than, as Cavell himself believes, "infinite responsibility for myself," together with "finite responsibility for the claims of the existence of the other upon me, claims perhaps of gratitude or sympathy or protection or duty or debt or love? In an extreme situation I may put the other's life (not just her or his wishes or needs) ahead of mine, answerable to or for them without limit." Although my responsibility to the finite Other is finite, I have an infinite responsibility to myself, in Cavell's view—an absolute obligation to *express* myself, to make myself intelligible to myself as well as to others, apart from which I cannot know myself, cannot make myself known to others, cannot achieve the acknowledgment of others (my acknowledgment of them, their acknowledgment of me), cannot walk in the direction of an unattained but attainable self.

For that matter, Cavell also asks, why should the existence of a finite other not in itself be sufficient to create the reality of such claims upon me? Unlike Lévinas, Cavell believes—and Luc Dardenne sees eye to eye with him on this—that the idea of God is not needed in order achieve "the miracle of moving out of oneself." Cavell expresses a thought with which the entirety of *Sur l'affaire humaine* is in accord when he writes, "All that is needed is an investment of a certain kind in a particular finite other, one in which you suffer the other's separation."

In *Sur l'affaire humaine*, Luc Dardenne posits birth as the first trauma. That we are born into the world means that we will die. Others threaten us, not only because they could literally kill us, but because their very existence *means* that we are fated to die. Thus it is natural for there to be in us a fear and hatred of the other, a wish to kill the other, a wish that is a response to our fear of dying. It is because we wish to live that we are afraid of dying, and it is because we fear dying that we are afraid to live. We have to *live with* the fear of dying. But how can we accomplish that? Luc's answer is that for me to be able to embrace living in the world with others, it is necessary for me to have had a prior experience of a relationship of a certain kind with a particular other, one whose love for me is unconditional, enabling me to imagine that we are one and thus to create a second womb, as it were. In order to embrace living in the world with others, however, I have to live outside this womb-like bubble; I have to acknowledge—this is a second trauma—that this special other is different from me, separate from me.

Luc Dardenne's account, which I apologize for sketching so crudely, dovetails point by point with Cavell's understanding of these matters. Cavell writes:

> Now when I say [in *The Claim of Reason*] that in Shakespearean tragedy [. . . the] traumatic effect of the recognition of the existence of God is replaced by the idea of a finite other, violence and some sense of an infinite nevertheless remain. But in originating now in the face of a finite other, violence and infinitude cannot be thought to arise from a comparison of myself with the other but from a recognition that this *particular* other, *this* creature among all the creatures of the earth similar to me, is also, or rather is therefore, absolutely different, separate from me, I would say, wholly other, endlessly other, the one I single out before whom I am I, eternally singled out. It is the unbearable certainty of this separation to which the torture of skepticism over Desdemona's faithfulness is preferable [to Othello . . .] The extravagant intimacy at stake in [Othello's relation to his idea of his wife . . .] suggests that the "proof" of the other's existence is a problem not of establishing connection with the other, but of achieving, or suffering, separation from the other, individuation with respect to the one upon whom *my* nature is staked.[4]

Up to and including *Lorna's Silence*, almost all Dardenne characters were outsiders to Belgian society. Rosetta and Lorna, especially, dream of becoming full-fledged members of society—as if full-fledged selfhood would automatically follow. One of the main themes of *L'affaire humaine*, however, is that in the wake of the death of God, society dehumanizes full-fledged members as well as outcasts. Instead of helping us to achieve what Cavell calls "the miracle of moving outside oneself," so that we might accept our separateness and walk in the direction of an unattained but attainable self, society pushes us, for example, to transfer our longing for the infinite to the futile endeavor of keeping our bodies forever young.

There is real nobility in making films about society's outcasts whose voices otherwise go unheard. Rosetta's life matters. So does Lorna's. So does the life of Cyril, the kid with a bike, who until Samantha takes him under her wing had never experienced the kind of relation with one particular other apart from which, according to *Sur l'affaire humaine*, it is impossible for a human being to learn, or to learn to teach, how to love living in the world with other people—what Emerson calls "the wonderful way of *life*." Samantha is no outcast, but that doesn't make her life less worthy of a Dardenne brothers film. In *La fille inconnue*, the life of the "unknown girl," who dies after a doctor denies her treatment, matters, as the doctor belatedly comes to recognize. In an unprecedented move, the Dardennes make the *doctor* the film's protagonist, acknowledging that the life of such a woman matters, too. And so do the lives of all people for whom joy and love, and a grand laugh now and then, aren't altogether unknown, but who are nonetheless victims, as Luc Dardenne argues that we all are, of the "silence of our times."

In *Lorna's Silence*, there are moments when Lorna feels happy—as when she is running after her husband's bicycle, a radiant smile on her face, in the passage we invoked. Or when she finds an ideal location for the waffle shop she still hopes to open with her boyfriend and, calling him on her cell phone to share the good news, bounds up the stairs, excited to check out the room in which they would be living—until she abruptly pauses, her back to the camera, like Uncle Charles in Hitchcock's *Shadow of a Doubt* (1943) at the moment the intuition dawns in him that he has no choice but to murder young Charlie, whom he loves.

Retroactively, we will understand that this is the moment Lorna first suspects that she is pregnant with her dead husband's child, the moment her imaginary son is conceived, as it were. Again, Lorna is made to pay a steep emotional price, as we are, for her moment of happiness. By contrast, in *The Kid with a Bike* and *Two Days, One Night*, the next two Dardenne films after *Lorna's Silence*, there are passages in which happiness arrives, for the characters we care about and for us, without a steep hidden price tag. I am thinking, for example, of the sequence in *The Kid with a Bike* in which Samantha and Cyril enjoy a bike ride and picnic together; Sandra's radiant smile in *Two Days, One Night* when she is moved by a fellow worker's sympathy; and the scene in that film in which Sandra, her husband, and a friend sing along with the car radio. For all her problems, and for all the world's problems, Sandra's life gives her something to sing about.

In *The Kid with a Bike*, there are several passages in which Cyril, who, like Rosetta, is perpetually in motion, seems to be pulling a passive camera in his wake. In many other passages, though, the Dardennes allow the camera to stay a comfortable distance from the characters, not forcing it to be in oppressively close proximity and, in general, allow the camera relative freedom from the "passivity beyond passivity" they had imposed on it in earlier films, especially *The Son*. In *The Kid with a Bike*, the camera is much freer to capture—that is, *express*—the characters' shifting moods in ways that cast moods over us.

Near the end of the film, Cyril, chased by a young man who has a grudge to settle with him, climbs a tree to try to escape. His assailant throws a rock that knocks Cyril from his high perch. But the Dardennes have the camera film his fall from such an angle that a tall wooden fence blocks the rock thrower's view—and ours—of Cyril's body. We cannot but experience this blocking of our view as a deliberate gesture, addressed to us, by an author, an author with an agenda.

Even when the rock thrower screws up the nerve to take a look and finds his victim lying motionless on the ground, he doesn't know, and neither do we, whether Cyril survived the fall. This continued withholding of what we want to know, what we dread knowing, makes us all the more mindful that it is in the unseen author's hands whether Cyril lives or dies. We find ourselves deeply moved when Cyril finally picks himself up, shakes himself off, gets on his bicycle, and, a bit shaky at first, soberly rides off. In the film's last shot, reminiscent of the ending of *The Promise*, the Dardennes elect to have the camera refrain from following Cyril as he rides into the depths of the frame, turns a corner, and exits the film.

Here, the Dardennes are not effacing their power, not disavowing their own responsibility, as in *Lorna's Silence*. They are acknowledging that their power, their responsibility, has limits. As authors, they have the power to bring Cyril back from the brink of death. But how he goes on to live his life, whether he will be busy dying or living, is his responsibility, not theirs. That he is riding home, not riding away—riding toward the first real home he has ever known, where someone who loves him will be there to welcome him back—gives us reason to believe that Cyril is, indeed, walking—or, rather, pedaling—in the direction of an "unattained but attainable self."

The ending of *Two Days, One Night* is an even purer distillation of the philosophy Luc Dardenne articulates in *Sur l'affaire humaine*, insofar as it forgoes the melodramatic contrivance of the fall that leaves Cyril's life hanging in the balance. Of course, the Dardennes have the power to decide how many of Sandra's coworkers will vote to give up their bonuses, hence whether the boss will allow her to return to her job. Throughout the film, we have felt, like Sandra, that winning back her job is the only thing that matters, the same way we believe, throughout *Bicycle Thieves (Ladri di biciclette*, 1948, dir. Vittorio De Sica), that the only thing that matters is whether Antonio will find his stolen bicycle. In the end, though, Sandra's job, like Antonio's bicycle, turns out to be something akin to a Hitchcockian "MacGuffin." What *really* matters is whether Sandra, with her husband to share her life with, will embrace, as in the end she does, Emerson's "wonderful way of *life*," or allow her life be dominated by the fear of living.

I think of these passages as revelations that the new path the brothers have taken is bringing them closer to the way of thinking Luc Dardenne expresses in *Sur l'affaire humaine*, and to Cavell's *pensée foisonnante*, with which Luc's thinking has such deep affinities.

Notes

1 Luc Dardenne, *Sur l'affaire humaine*, La librairie du XXIe siècle (Paris: Seuil, 2012).
2 Joseph Mai, "*Lorna's Silence* and Levinas's Ethical Alternative: Form and Viewer in the Dardenne Brothers," *New Review of Film and Television Studies* 9, no. 4 (2011): 435–53. See in this volume, chapter 5, for Mai's remarks on the films of Arnaud Desplechin.
3 Ibid.
4 Stanley Cavell, "What Is the Scandal of Skepticism?" in *Philosophy the Day after Tomorrow* (Cambridge: The Belknap Press of Harvard University Press, 2005), 145–46; italics added.

3

The Specter of the Electronic Screen

Bruno Varela's Reception of Stanley Cavell

BYRON DAVIES

IT SHOULD BE MORE THAN MERELY CURIOUS to those approaching Stanley Cavell's film writing that his work has influenced actual practicing filmmakers. But as soon as we account for some of the most prominent instances of contemporary directors influenced by Cavell—Arnaud Desplechin, Luc Dardenne, and his former student Terrence Malick[1]—we immediately run into a certain problem with narrowness: it is easy to recall these names because they are famous European and North American directors, whose feature films are (to varying degrees) star-based, have premieres at the Cannes Film Festival, and reviews in *The New York Times*. The risk, then, is in reinforcing a certain narrowness of vision about Cavell's developed answer to his question "What is film?"[2]—a narrowness that, to be fair, Cavell did not always do his best to discourage. Thus, a related question is whether our grasp of Cavell's writing might be transformed by our sense of its reception by a filmmaker whose work is both more hidden and in a sense more publicly accessible, who employs alternative circuits of distribution and exhibition, whose output is rooted in the politics of the Global South (especially efforts in indigenous video and broadcasting), and who often withdraws from aiming to reproduce the look of celluloid and instead abounds in the feel of electromagnetic tape and electronic signals. This, I take it, is the challenge posed in understanding the Oaxaca-based Mexican filmmaker and audiovisual artist Bruno Varela as a reader of Cavell.

Bruno Varela is one of the most accomplished and productive experimental filmmakers working in Mexico today. Born in 1971 in Mexico City, where he studied Social Communication at the Universidad Autónoma Metropolitana—Xochimilco, Varela is a self-described "autodidact in the mysteries of the audiovisual."[3] In 1992 he began devoting himself full-time to film and video production not only in the southern state of Oaxaca, but also in Chiapas, Yucatán, and notably Bolivia, where at the beginning of his career he "provided video training for indigenous communicators."[4] During the 2006 Oaxaca uprising and takeover of city functions (including radio stations and Oaxaca's public television station, Channel 9) by the Popular Assembly of Oaxaca's People (APPO), Varela was involved with Mal de Ojo TV, a video collective that documented the protests (in which over two dozen activists were killed) and compressed and uploaded to the internet footage taken by the slain North American Indymedia journalist Brad Will. Varela's experience of Oaxaca in 2006, including his own (continually reused and repurposed) footage of the protests, is a vital part of his work to this day. Since 2006 he has been working in Oaxaca under the auspices of Anticuerpo, which he describes as an "experimental space for audiovisual production and optical phenomena."[5] In recent years, this space has also involved his young daughter, Eugenia Varela, who at only six years old and bearing a Holga digital camera was the codirector of *Mano de metate* (*Grindstone Hand*, 2018), a unique, shared audiovisual collage in which references to Chris Marker's *La jetée* (1962) figure as points for expressing a child's experience of time.[6]

To be sure, Varela has hardly escaped international attention, including through screenings and participations in shows at the Guggenheim in New York, the Getty Research Institute in Los Angeles, Frieze Projects, the Ann Arbor Film Festival, and the Havana Biennial. In addition, his short film *Tiempo aire* (*Air Time*, 2014), a semi-fictional travelogue bringing together footage from Bolivia, New York, Arizona, Mexico City, and various parts of Oaxaca, received the inaugural e-Flux prize, bestowed by the titular art magazine, in Oberhausen in 2015. Despite this attention at the level of elite exhibition circuits, an indelible feature of Varela's work is its public accessibility: the vast majority of his films and audiovisual experiments are available for free on his Vimeo page (at this moment numbering 223 videos), constituting a dizzying and bottomless archive for those fortunate to be sucked into its orbit.[7] And an equally important dimension of Varela's accessibility is through his teaching. In spaces like ULTRAcinema MX, the Mexican experimental film festival and yearlong audiovisual project, Varela's workshops on video, found footage, and reappropriation are memorable not only for his lively and conversational teaching style, but also for his constellation of references to philosophical and theoretical writings, thus bringing students to—and making less intimidating—Baudrillard, José Luis Brea, Deleuze and Guattari, Mark Fisher ("k-punk"), Vilém Flusser, Alexander Kluge, Pasolini, Hito Steyerl, and Tarkovsky's *Sculpting in Time*.

One can then imagine my surprise and fascination in learning that one of those references is Stanley Cavell. I had already come to know Varela during my time living in Oaxaca City from 2017 to 2018, before I was able to see his film *Monolito* at the 2019 International Film Festival of the National Autonomous University of Mexico (FICUNAM). Varela's forty-minute film astonished me for the way it links together the social history of Oaxaca with a wider mythology of fire and transformation, something that Varela in turn connects to the history of cinema (through his reappropriation of images of fire from films by Godard and Tarkovsky). But what additionally piqued my interest was the possibility of seeing *Monolito* as an approach to what I had been beginning to understand as a similar importance that Cavell gives to mythologies of fire and transformation in *The World Viewed* and related writings on film;[8] that is, I was beginning to think that Cavell's turn to images of transformation by heat and light was his way of tracing, at least figuratively, an alternative to conceptions of film's relation to the world as one of "recording" or copying.[9] I plan for this to be the focus of other writing, but the present point is that *Monolito* alone seems to provide the basis for a fresh reading of Cavell, especially one that would be outside the grip of familiar interpretations of him as a "photographic realist" in the tradition of Bazin, Panofsky, and Kracauer.[10] I then wrote to Varela to express my interest in developing these ideas, based especially on *Monolito*, and I received the very encouraging reply that he already knew Cavell's work.

The meaning of this encounter between Varela and Cavell seems worth exploring for a number of reasons: especially for Cavell's notorious mis-encounter with experimental cinema (though his late references to Stan Brakhage and the animator Suzanne Pitt, and later, deeper engagement with Chris Marker are here worth noting[11]), and also for his mis-encounter with the cinema of Mexico, Latin America, and the Global South. (Of films significant to Cavell, those approaching Mexico and Latin America are typically Hollywood films told from the perspective of North American or European characters,[12] or from a surreal North Americanization of Mexican history, as in *Viva Zapata!* [1952, dir. Elia Kazan], a film whose connection to Varela I will return to.[13]) The encounter also seems worth exploring in that Cavell's most extensive treatment of video and the electronic screen, "The Fact of Television" (first prepared for a special issue of the journal *Daedalus* on "Print Culture and Video Culture" in 1982), contains Cavell's disclaimer that he is "not undertaking to discuss the progress and results of experimental video artists."[14] I was, therefore, even further fascinated to learn from Varela that his principal exposure to Cavell was through his reading that very essay on television, which he first encountered through its reprint in the 1986 volume *Video Culture*, edited by the art historian and curator John Hanhardt. Varela's reading of this Cavell text, then, opened up the possibility of a genuinely different and possibly very illuminating way of approaching Cavell (one not typically invited by other anthologizations of his film writing, such as the collection of chapters 3 through 6 of *The World Viewed* across the many editions of Leo Braudy, Marshall Cohen, and Gerald Mast's *Film Theory and Criticism*): namely, as a true philosopher of the electronic screen. (Moreover, approaching Cavell this way also availed some of the imaginative possibilities of encountering Cavell in a context in which photographic realism was not seriously at issue: whereas the editors of one edition of *Film Theory and Criticism* introduce those chapters by referring to Cavell's "important place in the tradition of realist film theorists,"[15] Hanhardt, who introduces his volume with an explicit rejection of photographic realism, never presents Cavell in those terms.[16])

Therefore, in order to explore these connections further, I asked Varela to write something brief about his experience of reading Cavell, which I reproduce below in my translation from Spanish.[17] At that point it was impossible to ask him to speak *strictly* from his experience of "The Fact of Television," as I had already shared with him further writing by Cavell that I thought would interest him, and which we had discussed in a video chat. These were "The Advent of Videos,"[18] "The World as Things: Collecting Thoughts on Collecting" (where Cavell discusses Marker's *Sans soleil* and, by allusion, his *Immemory* CD-ROM, both significant references for Varela),[19] as well as the chapters of *The World Viewed* on "The Medium and Media of Film" and "Automatism."[20] (Beyond Varela's references below to "automatism," the first sentence of the latter is echoed in his talk of "the magical possibilities of reproducing a world.") Nevertheless, even in this brief writing, the depth of Varela's reception of Cavell as a philosopher of the electronic screen is apparent, and should call our attention.

> Automatic dialogues, automatic audiovisual-writing.
>
> Would-be telepathy, metaphysical apparition manifested through a cathode tube, a television screen used as a cosmic receptor.
>
> Mediated by the Gaze of a third person who establishes a reading, an argument, permitting communication between distant objects, ideas, films, scraps of writing.
>
> In me it resonates enormously from Cavell, that intuitive intelligence for recognizing in the electronic image, the domestic ecosystem of reception and reading, the fragmentation of material and the continuity of that "new" experience in face of the screen.
>
> Thinking of video as a small form of cinema that, even in its refined miniature, has contained part of the essence of the idea—cinema conceived as a dark room spectacle.

That new possibility of viewing past cinema in a modality that allows for its analysis and dissection. The electronic box and its cathode snow as instruments of investigation of the audiovisual apparatus.

A new assemblage, a propitious territory for re-reading, for re-viewing classic cinema. Thinking of it as a much more complex apparatus than what comes from "argument" and from the first appearance of simple and transparent reading. A kind of critical cinephilia, one that finds, as many makers and thinkers of cinema of the past century have regarded it, a historical device, a repository. In its narratives, formal *dérives*[21] and techno-military developments, the cinema is the largest time capsule known in human history. It synthesizes the 20th century and possibly the beginning of the 21st.

Of great interest to us are the magical possibilities of reproducing a world, of showing the invisible, of transmitting emotions. Also of playing with the automatism and putting it to work in the direction opposed to the program. Of generating new automatisms that move in unforeseen directions, infected with failed instructions.

Cinema that aspires to be re-viewed, that asks itself if it exists as a medium or only as an idea. Or just a matter of *espectros*.[22]

Today in the midst of complex transformations in foreseeing, screens occupy even more dramatic positions within our inner lives. Uncanny traffic from the screening room to the home-school-office on screen.

Back to Cavell and his questions.

The voice in this writing will be recognizable to anyone who has seen Varela's work, particularly from the flows of poetic text and commentary that typically appear at the bottom of the screen, even down to the references to electronic apparatuses (e.g., the references to the "electronic image" in *Mano de metate* and "electromagnetic transmission" in *Monolito*). In addition, Varela's interest in Cavell's writing on watching classic cinema via the electronic screen (a theme most developed in "The Advent of Videos") reflects something of his own repurposing of images from older cinema as a form of criticism. And by approaching Cavell as a philosopher of the electronic screen, Varela also, in his penultimate paragraph, links his writing to the present ubiquity of the digital electronic screen as a communication medium during the Covid-19 pandemic.

What do we do with these thoughts? What is their place in an understanding of Cavell's writing, above all "The Fact of Television"? How do we relate them to the fact that Varela encountered that essay in a volume on "video culture" (among writers on the politics of radio and mass media like Brecht, Hans Magnus Enzensberger, and Baudrillard, as well as writers on video art like Rosalind Krauss)?[23] And how might that set of influences illuminate our viewing of Varela's own films? These are the questions I will focus on for the remainder of this chapter, and in approaching them, we are faced with the possibility that Varela might change our understanding of Cavell's writing on film and television. For example, in what is presently the most important monograph applying Cavell's film writing to television, Martin Shuster remarks on Cavell's view in 1982 that television had not yet "come of age" artistically—something that Shuster thinks is no longer the case, allowing TV series to stand comparison with accomplished films.[24] The risk here, however, lies in thinking that television must become like previously existing film in order to be artistically ambitious. But what if what, in 1982, Cavell called the "material basis" of television was already potential enough—and that this is what an artist like Varela is developing in turning television into film, and in so doing changing our very idea of what film can be?

* * * *

In approaching these questions, we will need to rehearse the fundamental claims of "The Fact of Television." We will also need to figure out what remains intelligible to us about an essay reflecting on what television had been in the United States just up to 1982, and therefore just up to the rise of cable TV and VHS—developments that Cavell alludes to, but does not entirely incorporate into the essay.[25] (Reflecting on the past of a medium at just the moment in which it is undergoing major change is a central feature of Cavell's film writing.[26])

Cavell is particularly interested in why television obeys a different "aesthetic principle" than film: whereas the primary unit of aesthetic interest in film is the individual work (which is related to other works through its membership in a genre),[27] the primary unit in television is the "format" or "program." In other words, television obeys an aesthetic principle of "serialization," which he initially uses to refer to TV series (and our interest in them as lying in their continuity across time and across individual episodes), though for Cavell this eventually opens up to a broader sense of "the *uneventful*, the repeated, the repetitive, the utterly familiar."[28] Thus, Cavell asks what it is about television's "material basis," and the mode of perception it elicits (what he calls "monitoring"), such that our fixation on it could be on nothing other than *that*.

In *The World Viewed*, Cavell famously defines the material bases of movies as "*a succession of automatic world projections*"[29]; following some observations in that same book about live television, in his television essay Cavell accordingly defines that medium's material basis as "*a current of simultaneous event reception.*"[30] Throughout his elaborations on each component of that definition it becomes clearer that the notions of "current," "simultaneity," and "reception" together communicate one set of thoughts about television's "liveness": something that initially results in some awkwardness for Cavell in that television of course need not be live.[31] Therefore, in taking up a suggestion apparently broached to him by his former student William Rothman while he was revising the essay, Cavell comes to understand television's characteristic "liveness" no longer on the model of live broadcasts, but rather on the model of "live switching" between modes or formats (what we might call "currents"): that is, "between these and commercials, station breaks, news breaks, emergency signal tests, color charts, program announcements, and so on."[32] For Cavell, something in this experience of switching is meant to account for the feeling of accompaniment, and even extension of ordinary domestic life, that has historically marked television and our discourse about it.[33] It also constitutes the beginning of his explanation of why television's primary unit of interest is the repeated format: if switching and, thus, discontinuity between modes are bound up with this medium's ways of communicating things to us, then likewise some kind of continuity, or repetition within formats, is required for it to be "legible" to us: that is, as something other than just switching.[34] (A central means of such legibility that Cavell later discusses is television's "regimentation of time"—its regularly dividing the day into minutes and seconds—which is meant to be intelligible to members of "industrialized societies."[35])

The other major component of Cavell's definition is "event" (by which he is initially making reference to something like a sports or cultural event); and, much as with his notion of *switching*, an event is only intelligible as "something unique [. . .] something out of the ordinary" against the background of, again, "the opposite, the *uneventful*, the repeated, the repetitive, the utterly familiar."[36] Comparing the latter to monitoring life signs or rapid eye movements, he says of various forms of monitoring and surveillance that "most of what appears is a graph of the normal, or the establishment of some reference or base line, a line, so to speak, of the uneventful, from which events stand out with perfectly anticipatable significance."[37] The fact, then, that television can successfully function as nothing but a means of surveilling the uneventful, normal, or banal reveals for Cavell something of the different aspects of perception elicited by film and the electronic screen: what he calls, respectively, *viewing* and *monitoring*.[38]

Cavell articulates this distinction by referring to his idea in *The World Viewed* that movies operate by sparing "our attention wholly for *that* thing *now*."[39] But in contrast with this feature of "viewing," monitoring is rather a matter of "preparing our attention to be called upon by certain eventualities":[40] in monitoring, our attention is not in the same sense *spared*, but must be ready for the possibility of the uneventful's setting the stage for the irruption of an "event." This is also perhaps one source of the peculiar comfort that Cavell thinks television provides us:[41] monitoring the uneventful is itself comforting, since we can take relief in observing that these possibilities have not yet manifested themselves in "events," in further demands on our attention. And once again, the notion of *switching* is central to Cavell's way of understanding the act of monitoring the uneventful: he notes the essential similarity between navigating one's attention among multiple surveillance monitors (multiple "modes" or "currents") and the mechanical switching among stationary cameras characteristic of sports coverage.[42] The latter mechanisms might have the effect of further sparing our attention (as in film), but we are nevertheless—as with surveillance monitors, and their own kind of switching—being asked to prepare our attention for the irruption of *eventualities*.

For Cavell, then, there is a natural relation between monitoring a "base line" and the kinds of mechanical (as opposed, say, to narrative) discontinuities that he calls switching. He consequently says of the movement between multiple monitors that it "encodes the denial of succession as integral to the basis of the medium";[43] and this leads him to differentiate further the electronic image from film by saying that in the former "[s]uccession is replaced by switching."[44] This point about switching's relation to succession is undoubtedly deep and significant, and one that likely has immediate consequences for Varela's video work. But Cavell's explicit presentation of this point might not capture its potentially wide applicability. For example, if Cavell turned to the notion of switching (following Rothman's suggestion) in order to capture a sense of television's "liveness" that would avoid the awkwardness of the medium's not always being live, a similar awkwardness then manifests itself upon Cavell's occasional recognition that "broadcasting" need not be part of television's material basis either. (It is not clear whether he is there trying to incorporate the issue of the running of videotapes or disks; he anyway says, "I have not included transmission as essential to [television's material basis]; this would be because I am not regarding broadcasting as essential to the work of television."[45])

Therefore, if switching is so essential to the medium, but is something that might not be effected by broadcasters, who else in that case would be doing the switching? An obvious answer is the viewer herself, via the electronic monitor's controls.[46] This answer also has the contemporary benefit of opening up the possibility for the applicability of something like Cavell's notion of "switching" to the digital electronic screen, and the exceptional control that it affords. (For instance, Lev Manovich has argued for the essential continuity between, on the one hand, the "variability" and "mutability" of "new media" and, on the other hand, a TV user's control over dimensions like brightness and hue, as well as other forms of mutability characteristic of electronic signals.[47]) And this emphasis on the viewer's control has the additional benefit of being one part of D. N. Rodowick's important Cavell-influenced account of the distinct temporalities of the electronic image and celluloid projection: or, as he puts it, "the expression of change in the present as opposed to the present witnessing of past duration."⁴⁸

But there is another part of Rodowick's account of the two media's temporalities that brings out even further the depth of Cavell's insight that, in the electronic image, "succession is replaced by switching." This consists in Rodowick's observation that, with celluloid projection, "the individual images themselves persist as wholes with their own unique durations"; in contrast, an "electronic image, whether analogical or digital, never displays a spatial or temporal whole."⁴⁹ Thus, as Rodowick points out, in NTSC interlaced scanning (the analog color television system dominant in much of the western hemisphere until recent digital conversion) "an electron beam traces first the odd lines of a 525-line display, exciting light-sensitive phosphors along the way, and then the even lines."⁵⁰ This process is, we can say, a kind of *switching*—from one set of lines to another. (When it comes to digital displays operating via *symbolic notation*, the "switching" or breaks in continuity then take place at the level of information, allowing for their greater mutability, nonlinearity, and user control.)

Rodowick vividly brings out this set of points by noting that "even a 'photograph' displayed on an electronic screen is not a still image. It may appear so, but its ontological structure is of a constantly shifting or self-refreshing display."⁵¹ In contrast, the display of a still celluloid image requires nothing more than that frame, a projection surface, and an adequate source of light. Whereas the feeling of succession and duration of celluloid films simply depends on the automatic succession of many such projected frames, the electronic image cannot even achieve the physical integrity of a single still photograph. Thus, if Cavell's notion of "switching" will turn out to have consequences for the work of an audiovisual artist such as Varela, then we should recognize that something like that notion—emphasizing discontinuity over succession and sameness—enjoys application not only in the switching between "modes," "formats," "monitors," or "currents" of explicit interest to Cavell (whether effected by a broadcaster or a viewer), but also in the very constitution of the electronic image itself.

* * * *

What is of particular interest in Varela's first becoming acquainted with Cavell in Hanhardt's *Video Culture* volume is not just his receiving Cavell as a philosopher of the electronic screen, but also his receiving Cavell in a volume that gives special place to political questions about the social and communal potential of radio, television, and mass media. The section of Hanhardt's volume containing Cavell's essay (labeled "Video and Television") follows a section ("Theory and Practice") partly occupied with Brecht's proposals for socializing radio, that is, for changing "this apparatus over from distribution to communication."⁵² The section thus reproduces Brecht's 1932 essay "The Radio as Apparatus of Communication," as well as the German author Hans Magnus Enzensberger's 1970 essay "Constituents of a Theory of the Media," which extends Brecht's arguments in order to argue for the vital importance for socialists to seize the productive forces of the mass media, particularly television. It also notably includes Baudrillard's critique of Enzensberger, drawn from his 1972 book *For a Critique of the Political Economy of the Sign*, and based in Baudrillard's understanding of the essential irredeemability of those same forces. Thus, whereas Enzensberger speaks of the "[e]mancipatory use of media,"⁵³ and of how the "contradiction between producers and consumers is not inherent in the electronic media,"⁵⁴ Baudrillard advocates for nothing short of "the instantaneous deconstruction of the dominant discursive code," or of "what radically checkmates the dominant form."⁵⁵

The debate between Enzensberger and Baudrillard touches on important themes in Cavell, albeit ones standing somewhat outside the text of "The Fact of Television."⁵⁶ That is, this debate recasts at the level of socialist politics and communications media Cavell's distinction (in writings contemporary with this debate) between "modernists" and "modernizers":⁵⁷ between those who, pressured by new circumstances, seek to reconstitute the previous power of a medium on new grounds, versus those who seek to reinvent (we might say "deconstruct") that medium altogether, independently of the claims or power of its previous instances.⁵⁸ (It is doubtlessly appropriate, then, that within this recast distinction those following *Brecht's* arguments would come out as "modernists.") This debate also goes straight to the philosophical issues raised in Varela's deep commitment to the communal potential of video and communications media, manifested in his dedication to "community video" in Bolivia, Oaxaca, and elsewhere.⁵⁹ And these issues are likewise raised by Varela's role as witness to and participant in the 2006 "Oaxaca commune," and APPO's seizure of radio and public TV functions (used as strategic occupations and as means for disseminating their demands of the state and federal governments).⁶⁰

Indeed, Varela's audiovisual projects are, throughout, informed by the question of how to critique present communications media while retaining their communal potential. What is additionally striking about Varela's "political cinema" is the importance that these undertakings give to the structural issues around *switching* that have emerged for us as central to Cavell's writing on the electronic image. A clear instance of this is in Varela's film/audiovisual project, *Línea 3* (2010–11), itself composed of thirteen short films (each running between thirty seconds and just over two minutes) taking their titles and drawing inspiration from thirteen stations along Line 3 of Mexico City's Metro system: *Universidad, Zapata, División del Norte, E(u)tiopía, Centro médico, Niños héroes, Balderas, Juárez, Hidalgo, Guerrero, Tlatelolco, La raza,* and *Basílica*.⁶¹ What these films together constitute is an interrogation of the intertwinement of national identity and television, carried out at the very least through an irresistible symbolic connection between *television stations* and *train stations*, as well through their respective kinds of *switching* and *seriality*.⁶²

When it comes to these works' engagement with television at least three types of switching are at play: (1) what we have already noted is the "switching" required for the very constitution of the electronic image, evident in these works' frequent use of the noise (i.e., the "cathode snow" mentioned in Varela's text above)⁶³ and vertical wipes characteristic of the analog monitor; (2) forms of switching between monitors, as in several of the films' presentation of found footage via three separate monitors, each hued to constitute the green, white, and red of the Mexican flag; (3) our ability to switch among the films themselves, especially if we are navigating among them on Varela's Vimeo page. That last aspect of the films points beyond the analog electronic image and toward varieties of digital switching. And here it might make sense to mention another proposal of Rodowick's, namely, his adaptation of Cavell's definition of television's material basis ("a current of simultaneous event reception"), and Cavell's conception of an *event*, to his own conception of a "digital event," which, stressing interactivity, he defines as "a process of simulation through algorithmic information interactions."⁶⁴ My point in mentioning Rodowick's proposal is simply to suggest that something like this notion of a "digital event," and its own form of switching, is among the topics of *Línea 3*, and its interrogation of the lines we might be inclined to draw between a "mere" digital event and a complete film.

What effects do these forms of switching have within the films themselves? In *Juárez* the presentation via "cathode snow" of speeches of Mexican presidents of the last sixty years lends both an ironic distance and a truly forbidding terror to the presidents' words, among them Carlos Salinas de Gortari's nationally televised address opposing the 1994 Zapatista uprising in Chiapas, and (with even further irony) Felipe Calderón's cry of ¡Viva México! on Mexico's Independence Day. In switching to *Zapata*, one of the series' "movie stations,"⁶⁵ we find a critical appraisal of Elia Kazan's 1952 film. Varela presents clips of *Viva Zapata!* using two different soundtracks: a dubbed Spanish track and the original English track, both sounding strange, as though even the attempt to reappropriate Mexican history from Hollywood will have alienating effects. Varela additionally bares the limits of Marlon Brando's enacting of Zapata's death as an event of heroic beauty by juxtaposing it with brutal images of the actual public exposure of Zapata's dead body.

We should also recall that for Cavell the notion of switching in television (and its replacement of the notion of "succession" on film) is meant to function as something like the other side of the mode of perception he calls "monitoring"—and thus of surveilling the uneventful, of preparing ourselves for the irruption of *eventualities*. This is likewise the case in *Línea 3*, and in Varela's repurposing of news and surveillance footage. For example, in *Centro médico* we see footage of a live newscast from the morning of September 19, 1985, the date of Mexico City's catastrophic earthquake, in which the broadcaster María Victoria Llamas tries to reassure viewers and her colleagues—"It's just shaking a little bit" (*Está temblando un poquito*)— only for the shaking to escalate still further, until the broadcast suddenly breaks off. And in *Balderas*, Varela repurposes security camera footage of an incident that took place at that very Metro station on September 18, 2009, when during an altercation with police a man carrying anti-government signs named Luis Felipe Hernández Castillo fired a .38 revolver, killing two people. While initially the security camera is stationary—and thus functions like a typical monitor of the *uneventful*—the camera eventually zooms in, most likely looking to identify the shooter, and thus inadvertently having the effect of turning Hernández (who had said that he was acting in the name of God) into something like the protagonist of his own movie.

But the public figure who most seems to haunt *Línea 3* is Gustavo Díaz Ordaz, Mexico's ill-famed former president from 1964 to 1970, who appears in two of the films (*Juárez* and *Tlatelolco*), and who in fact opened the Metro's Line 3 at the end of his presidential term. In *Tlatelolco*, Varela juxtaposes footage and audio of Díaz Ordaz inaugurating the 1968 Olympic Games, the first-ever broadcast in color, with silent black-and-white footage from just ten days earlier, when military and paramilitary forces under Díaz Ordaz's command massacred student demonstrators and other civilians in the Tlatelolco area of Mexico City, killing what is estimated to have been over 300 people. Here the question of the Tlatelolco Massacre's relation to television and the remarkableness of Varela's devoting a "station" to it lie in what television has historically shut out. According to the journalist Jesús Ramírez Cuevas, only a few minutes of the massacre were broadcast the night of October 2nd, on the program led by Díaz Ordaz's critic Julio Scherer, *Noticiero de Excelsior*, a program that was eventually canceled and replaced with the pro-establishment *24 Horas* with Jacobo Zabludovsky, which would run for nearly thirty years.[66]

The question of what the electronic image "shuts out" takes us straight to Cavell's dark and probing way of concluding "The Fact of Television." Throughout his essay Cavell is concerned with the peculiar distrust or fear that he has found television to elicit (particularly when compared with other household devices), and eventually he arrives at one kind of explanation: that the real, or original, object of this fear are the events being monitored. He says, "my hypothesis is that the fear of television [. . .] is the fear that what it monitors is the growing uninhabitability of the world, the irreversible pollution of the earth, a fear displaced from the world onto its monitor."[67] There is, to be sure, both something correct and something slightly pat or expected about this answer, and we will want to ask how much weight Cavell means to put on it as a conclusion. In any case, much of Varela's work could be seen as a reversal of the same thought: that it is exactly because we uncritically embrace the electronic screen that we are prepared to accept without criticism the events it monitors. This is certainly one way of describing his film *Materia oscura* (*Dark Matter*, 2016), concerned with one of the most traumatic events in recent Mexican history, the forced disappearance of forty-three students from the Ayotzinapa Teachers College the night of September 26, 2014, in Iguala, Guerrero. Varela's audiovisual assemblage consists of bringing together two different presentations of the "official story" of the crime: monochromatic images drawn from the 54,000 pages, 85 volumes, and 13 attachments publicly released by the Mexican Attorney General's Office in 2015, and audio of the final report by the inter-American human rights group (GIEI) tasked with investigating the case. In the course of the film's disclosure of these official items a startling text appears in red letters: "The State constructs a narrative that explains the disappearance as a natural process."[68] And Varela, in a further manifestation of red text, does not shy away from expressing something like the "physics," via the movement of images, of this naturalization or normalization of terrible events: "The images collide to become a wave / A miasma (still not identified) of fundamental particles."[69] And thus the film concludes.

Nevertheless, we can further link Varela's concerns to Cavell's by noting that the latter's hypothesis—about our displacing the fear of the event onto the monitor—is in fact not his final thought on the uneasiness that the electronic monitor can elicit. As it happens, Cavell comes to suggest that while those fears do indeed originate in "events," and are then displaced onto the monitor, the sorts of events he is ultimately referring to are not the very events monitored, but rather those events that the monitor "shuts out": that is, what it shuts out of its typical "reference line of normalcy or banality." Therefore, for Cavell, this suggests that "what is shut out, that suspicion whose entry we would at all costs guard against, must be as monstrous as, let me say, the death of the normal, of the familiar as such."[70] Our anxieties around the electronic image are more than anything about what it represses.

That last thought, then, presents us with the challenge of imagining an electronic image whose edges are not confines (for shutting out anything but the banal), and thus of imagining an electronic image that would open itself up to those pictures and sounds that it would be the tendency of its own medium to repress. This might be a way of describing Varela's work. It would at least be a way of describing a peculiar temporality, one in which *switching* is not opposed to *succession*, or in which television is not opposed to cinema.[71]

Notes

1 On Cavell's influence on Desplechin, see Stanley Cavell and Arnaud Desplechin, "Pourquoi les films comptent-ils?," *Esprit*, nos. 8–9 (August and

September 2008): 208–19; Marko Bauer, "'Films are vulgar. And this vulgarity, I love it': An Interview with Arnaud Desplechin," *Senses of Cinema*, no. 56 (October 2010); and in this volume, Joseph Mai, Chapter 5. On Cavell's influence on the Dardenne brothers, see Élise Domenach, "Le paradoxe de la voix. «Cité de paroles», silences et voix dans les vidéos documentaires et le cinéma de fiction de Jean-Pierre et Luc Dardenne, suivi de «Notes d'un visiteur du monde des radios libres» de Luc Dardenne," *Entrelacs*, no. 11 (2014), and in this volume, William Rothman, Chapter 2. Discussions of Cavell's influence on Malick are legion; recent examples include Gregory Flaxman, "The Physician of Cinema: Terrence Malick's *Tree of Life*," *New Review of Film and Television Studies* 17, no. 1 (2019): 81–98, and David LaRocca, "Thinking of Film: What Is Cavellian about Malick's Movies?," in *A Critical Companion to Terrence Malick*, ed. Joshua Sikora (Lanham: Lexington Books of Rowman & Littlefield, 2020), 3–19.

2 Stanley Cavell, *The World Viewed*, Enlarged Edition (Cambridge: Harvard University Press, 1979), 15.

3 My translation from the Spanish text on Varela's Vimeo page, "Bruno Varela," Vimeo, accessed November 11, 2020, https://vimeo.com/brunovarela.

4 Freya Schiwy, *The Open Invitation: Activist Video, Mexico, and the Politics of Affect* (Pittsburgh: University of Pittsburgh Press, 2019), 115.

5 Quoted in David M. J. Wood and Gabriela Vigil, "Transnational, Digital, Mexican Cinema?, *Fogo* (Yulene Olaizola, 2012) and *Placa Madre* (Bruno Varela, 2016)," *Journal of Latin American Cultural Studies* 28, no. 4 (2019): 513.

6 See Yunuen Cuenca's description of *Mano de metate*, Vimeo, accessed November 11, 2020, https://vimeo.com/256326337.

7 On Varela's alternative distribution and exhibition methods, see Wood and Vigil, "Transnational, Digital, Mexican Cinema?," 513–14, 518–19.

8 This is also an aspect of *The World Viewed* gestured at by William Rothman and Marian Keane, *Reading Cavell's* The World Viewed: *A Philosophical Perspective on Film* (Detroit: Wayne State University Press, 2000), 250.

9 Cavell, *The World Viewed*, 182–84, 186, 193; *Cavell on Film*, ed. William Rothman (Albany: State University of New York Press, 2005), 117–18, 219, 272–74, 369.

10 See Daniel Morgan, "Modernist Investigations: A Reading of *The World Viewed*," *Discourse* 42, nos. 1–2 (2020): 213.

11 Cavell, *Cavell on Film*, 212, 282, 270–72, 369.

12 This feature characterizes both what is by Cavell's account the first film he ever wrote about (*Hold Back the Dawn*, 1941, dir. Mitchell Leisen) and one of the last films ever to receive his attention (*Only Angels Have Wings*, 1939, dir. Howard Hawks). See Cavell, *Little Did I Know: Excerpts from Memory* (Stanford: Stanford University Press, 2010), 155, 540–46. It is not, though, a feature that he ever explicitly addresses. For more on *Only Angels Have Wings*, see in this volume, Steven G. Affeldt, Chapter 4.

13 Cavell, *Cavell on Film*, 339.

14 Cavell, "The Fact of Television," in *Video Culture: A Critical Investigation*, ed. John Hanhardt (Rochester: Visual Studies Workshop Press, 1986), 194. The essay was also reprinted in Cavell, *Themes Out of School* (San Francisco: North Point Press, 1984), 235–68, and in *Cavell on Film*, 59–85. Because of the importance to Varela of the Hanhardt volume I will continue citing that reprint of the essay.

15 Leo Braudy and Marshall Cohen, eds. *Film Theory and Criticism: Introductory Readings*, 7th ed. (Oxford: Oxford University Press, 2009), 304.

16 Hanhardt says that "the argument that film, and by extension video, simply reproduces what is before the camera has been proven false" (*Video Culture*, 17). Noting the influence of *Film Theory and Criticism* on readings of Cavell as a photographic realist is important to Daniel Morgan's attempts to develop an alternative to that reading ("Modernist Investigations," 212–14).

17 With Varela's permission, I have edited his text to remove a somewhat separate discussion by him of *Monolito*, which, again, I aim to take up in other writing.

18 Cavell, "The Advent of Videos," in *Cavell on Film*, 167–73.

19 Cavell, "The World as Things: Collecting Thoughts on Collecting," in *Cavell on Film*, 241–79.

20 Cavell, *The World Viewed*, 68–73, 101–08.

21 I have translated the Spanish *derivas* as the French *dérives*, which is the standard way in English of referring to the revolutionary urban strategies typically associated with the Situationist International, and which I understand Varela to be alluding to.

22 The Spanish word *espectro* could mean either "specter" or "spectrum," and Varela is evidently relying on both senses.

23 In the present chapter, I will not be able to discuss explicitly "Video: The Aesthetics of Narcissism," the essay by Krauss collected in Hanhardt's *Video Culture* volume (179–91). I do, though, want to note that her writing and Varela's text above share a sense of the importance of using "telepathy" as a way of figuring video's distinguishing characteristics as a medium, and thus of the challenges presented by its character as a specifically *psychological* artistic medium. I also want to note the potential interest of encountering Krauss's essay and Cavell's essay together, particularly given the importance the latter (and its notion of television as "a current of simultaneous event reception") would come to play in Krauss's later writing on video art and the use of surveillance monitors by Bruce Nauman (*Under Blue Cup* [Cambridge: MIT Press, 2011], 119).

24 Martin Shuster, *New Television: The Aesthetics and Politics of a Genre* (Chicago: The University of Chicago Press, 2017), 2.

25 Cavell, "The Fact of Television," 196–97. These changes throughout the 1980s are the concern of Stephen Prince, *A New Pot of Gold: Hollywood under the Electronic Rainbow, 1980-1989* (New York: Charles Scribner's Sons, 2000).

26 The paradigmatic instance of this would be chapters 1 through 9 of *The World Viewed*; see Morgan, "Modernist Investigations," 215. See also Ryan Pierson's argument that Cavell's writing on cartoons in "More of *The World Viewed*"

came exactly during the waning of the "plasmatic" conception of cartoons that Cavell effectively takes as his model; Pierson, "On Styles of Theorizing Animation Styles: Stanley Cavell at the Cartoon's Demise," *The Velvet Light Trap*, no. 69 (2012): 17–26.

27 Cavell's reflection on this phenomenon provides the occasion for his rich and insufficiently appreciated treatment of the distinction between "genre-as-cycle" and "genre-as-medium" ("The Fact of Television," 197–202).

28 Ibid., 209.

29 Cavell, *The World Viewed*, 72; italics in original.

30 Cavell, "The Fact of Television," 205.

31 Ibid., 206.

32 Ibid.

33 Ibid., 206–7. This is also a topic of an essay contemporaneous with Cavell's and likewise reprinted in the Hanhardt *Video Culture* volume, "Cinema and Broadcast TV Together" by John Ellis, who recalls the description of the television set by the TV salesman in Douglas Sirk's *All That Heaven Allows* (1955) as giving "All the company you want" (*Video Culture*, 256).

34 Ibid., 206.

35 Ibid., 214. Cavell's observations on this point are richly supplemented by two further essays in the Hanhardt collection: David Antin's historical account of how television "achieved its extreme segmentation of transmission time" (157), and David Ross's account of how Dara Birnbaum's experimental videos address the nature of "TV time" (170, 174–78). The topic of the wide intelligibility of TV formats is taken up by Ellis (259).

36 Ibid., 209. Since Cavell devotes so much attention to "uneventfulness" in his treatment of monitoring, it might seem strange that he gives priority to its opposite, "event," in his definition of television's material basis. But there might also be reason for supposing that Cavell understands the category of "event" as, adapting his talk elsewhere of "acknowledgement," the sort of phenomenon that is "evidenced equally by its [absence] as by its [presence]" (Stanley Cavell, *Must We Mean What We Say?* [New York: Charles Scribner's Sons, 1969], 263); it would thus be, following Richard Moran, "the idea of a characterization that determines a range of questions to which there *must* be some answer or other" (Richard Moran, "Cavell on Recognition, Betrayal, and the Photographic Field of Expression," in *The Philosophical Imagination* [Oxford: Oxford University Press, 2017], 98): for example, "Is an event taking place or not?"

37 Ibid., 210. Just prior to this passage Cavell had said that it is "as if meaning is dictated by the event itself" (210). That is, in monitoring, meaning is not, we might suppose (as in the mode of perception we associate with film), primarily determined by montage, cinematography, or the event's situation within a "work." These passages by Cavell sit especially well with some observations by Douglas Davis, also included in the Hanhardt collection, on television's capacity for directing our attention onto the uneventful. Discussing the series *An American Family* (broadcast on PBS in 1973), Davis says, "'Live' time approached life time. For this reason, and because we knew the *Family* was

'real,' we stayed, waiting, aware that something unpredictably 'live' might occur yet" (273).

38 In drawing this distinction, Cavell makes clear that he means "to be calling attention to aspects of human perception generally, so that film and video will not be expected to capture one of these aspects to the exclusion of the other, but rather to stress one at the expense of the other" ("The Fact of Television," 211). Early in *The World Viewed*, Cavell had discussed film's own way of working out perceptions of the uneventful, there discussing "a possibility of the medium not to call attention to [persons and objects] but, rather, to let the world happen, to let its parts draw attention to themselves according to their natural weight," and referring to Dreyer, Flaherty, Vigo, Renoir, and Antonioni (*The World Viewed*, 25). The idea of using film and video to figure distinct cognitive operations is also, incidentally, taken up by Raúl Ruiz in his *Poetics of Cinema*, trans. Brian Holmes, Vol. 1 (Paris: Éditions Dis Voir, 1995), 39.

39 Cavell, *The World Viewed*, 122.

40 Cavell, "The Fact of Television," 211.

41 Ibid., 209.

42 Ibid.

43 Ibid.

44 Ibid., 210.

45 Ibid., 205.

46 Cavell alludes to this feature of electronic monitors in "The Fact of Television" (215) and more explicitly in "The Advent of Videos" (*Cavell on Film*, 169).

47 Lev Manovich, *The Language of New Media* (Cambridge: MIT Press, 2001), 133–34.

48 D. N. Rodowick, *The Virtual Life of Film* (Cambridge: Harvard University Press, 2007), 136. Cavell's influence on these passages is marked by Rodowick's having earlier taken up Cavell's notion of film as the projection of a "world past" (62–73; see Cavell, *The World Viewed*, 23, 210). In this context, Rodowick's focus is the control afforded by digital media (138), but again Manovich's arguments somewhat ease the distinction between digital and analog electronic media on this count.

49 Ibid., 137.

50 Ibid.

51 Ibid., 138.

52 Bertolt Brecht, "The Radio as an Apparatus of Communication," in *Video Culture*, 53.

53 Hans Magnus Enzensberger, "Constituents of a Theory of the Media," in *Video Culture*, 110.

54 Ibid., 105.

55 Jean Baudrillard, "Requiem for the Media," in *Video Culture*, 140.

56 The debate is nevertheless also connected to Cavell's engagement in that essay with Jerry Mander's views on the essential irredeemability of television in his book *Four Arguments for the Elimination of Television* (New York: Quill, 1978). See "The Fact of Television," 215–18.

57 Cavell, *The World Viewed*, 15, 42 and Cavell, *Must We Mean What We Say?*, xxii.

58 Alternatively, a "modernizer" might be understood as inventing an altogether new medium, but there are reasons for doubting that Cavell can allow for the coherence of such a possibility. See Diarmuid Costello, "Automat, Automatic, Automatism: Rosalind Krauss and Stanley Cavell on Photography and the Photographically Dependent Arts," *Critical Inquiry* 38, no. 4 (2012): 819–54.

59 For discussion of the concept of "community video" in Oaxaca, see Charles Fairbanks, "*Archivos de video comunitario de Oaxaca* (Community video archives of Oaxaca)," *Millennium Film Journal*, nos. 71–72 (Spring and Fall 2020): 33–35. Fairbanks's essay is a review of an exhibition on community video at Oaxaca's Contemporary Art Museum (MACO), December 2019–March 2020, curated by Oliver Martínez Kandt, and which included Varela's video installation *tepalcateX*. The latter was partly constituted by Varela's video *Marcha* (2006), documenting the protests in Oaxaca that same year. Footage of Varela's installation is available at https://vimeo.com/414790049. A discussion of the anti-capitalist themes in Varela's work is found in Miguel Errazu, "infra-realismo-capitalista," *Campo de relámpagos*, December 15, 2019: http://campoderelampagos.org/maquinas-de-vision/15/12/2019.

60 The volume *Enseñando rebeldía: Historias del movimiento popular en Oaxaca*, ed. Diana Denham and Colectivo C.A.S.A. (Oakland: PM Press, 2011), contains oral histories of both the "Marcha de las Cacerolas," in which women activists took control of Channel 9, Oaxaca's public TV station (131–40), and of the defense against incursions by federal police of the student-run radio station of the Universidad Autónoma Benito Juárez de Oaxaca (195–207).

61 Eduardo Cruz also discusses this series in "'Le pido sigan viendo las imágenes': El anti-cine de Bruno Varela," *Corresponencias. Cine y pensamiento*, no. 3 (Fall 2017): http://correspondenciascine.com/2017/11/les-pido-sigan-viendo-las-imagenes-el-anti-cine-de- bruno-varela/.

62 An additional factor, alluded to by Varela in his notes to the *Línea 3* series on his Vimeo page, is the connection between trains and the iconography of the Mexican Revolution, as in the famous 1912 photograph of *soldaderas* at Buenavista station. See also Andrea Noble, *Photography and Memory in Mexico: Icons of Revolution* (Manchester: Manchester University Press), 99–119.

63 See also Cavell's discussion of the analog TV's snowy image in "The Advent of Videos" (*Cavell on Film*, 172).

64 Rodowick, *The Virtual Life of Film*, 140.

65 The other "movie stations" are *División del norte* (using footage from *Así era Pancho Villa* [1957, dir. Ismael Rodríguez]), *La raza* (*México de mi corazón*

[1963, dir. Miguel M. Delgado]), and *Basílica* (*La virgen de Guadalupe* [1976, dir. Alfredo Salazar]).

66 Ramírez Cuevas, "La televisión le debe una autocrítica a México: Televisa y el 68," *Masiosare*, October 20, 2002, https://www.jornada.com.mx/2002/10/20/mas-ramirez.html. In this same article Ramírez Cuevas quotes the Mexican writer Carlos Monsiváis's memory of those few minutes on television, by his account captured from the third floor of Tlatelolco's Chihuahua building: after some shots, "They spent like eight or ten minutes on the air: you saw the people thrown onto the floor, you heard the screams, the wailing, the insults. Everyone was thrown down, the reporter who was narrating and the cameraman, nobody would get up. Then you saw a group of civilians enter and take some students, who you saw crawling down the stairs in the middle of the shooting. And then the broadcast stopped" (my translation).

67 Cavell, "The Fact of Television," 217.

68 My translation from the Spanish.

69 My translation from the Spanish.

70 Cavell, "The Fact of Television," 217.

71 I thank Bruno Varela and David LaRocca for their support and encouragement at every stage in my preparing this chapter. I also thank Eduardo Cruz, Marcela Cuevas Ríos, and David M. J. Wood for their advice as I was undertaking this project.

PART II

Recollecting and Remembering

4

The Pertinence of the Stars

Achieving Mortality in *Little Did I Know* and *Only Angels Have Wings*

STEVEN G. AFFELDT

One earns one's life in spending it; only so does one save it.
—STANLEY CAVELL, *The Senses of Walden*[1]

IN THEIR REMARKABLE READING OF *The World Viewed*, William Rothman and Marian Keane enter a set of extraordinary claims for the centrality of Hollywood movies in Cavell's philosophical formation. "Apart from the role Hollywood movies played in Cavell's education," they argue, "it would not have been possible for a philosopher who received his professional training within an analytical tradition that had never acknowledged Emerson as a philosopher to have 'inherited' Emerson's ways of thinking at all."[2] Furthermore, since they see Emerson's ways of thinking as fundamental to Cavell's work (even before he himself recognized this fact), they go on to argue for the essential role of Hollywood films in the generation of *all* of his work. "Apart from the roles movies played in Cavell's education," they maintain, "it would not have been possible for him to have accomplished those 'feats of philosophical imagination' called *The World Viewed*, *Pursuits of Happiness*, and *Contesting Tears*, or, for that matter, *Must We Mean What We Say?*, *The Claim of Reason*, and all the other books and essays that comprise this American philosopher's singularly ambitious body of work."[3]

I call these claims "extraordinary" not to express skepticism, but to emphasize the depth and pervasiveness of the role they assign to the influence of Hollywood films on Cavell's thinking. Hollywood films, Rothman and Keane argue, were not only as essential in enabling Cavell's work and giving it its distinctive character as, say, his experience of J. L. Austin, his reading of Wittgenstein, or his understanding of skepticism, but they were an absolutely indispensable condition for the possibility of the work. Without his experience of Hollywood films, Cavell's work, as a whole, could not be what it is.

But recognizing the force of these claims highlights a surprising feature of Cavell's autobiography, *Little Did I Know: Excerpts from Memory*. Namely, in a text that is explicitly presented as an attempt to recount the conditions that shaped the formation of his philosophical voice, film plays almost no role. To be clear, the text certainly reflects Cavell's lifelong love of film. It not only recalls the "major stretch[es] of movie viewing" punctuating critical junctures of his life, but dozens of mentions of individual films pepper the text and convey the sense of a life in which films were constant and familiar companions.[4] But no film is given any sustained discussion. Indeed, in striking contrast to his lovingly detailed descriptions of "movie palaces" from his childhood, Cavell's invocations of specific films are typically limited to the bare mention of a single line or image. Finally, and contrary to what the claims of Rothman and Keane might lead us to expect, the text includes no explicit or systematic reflection on the role of film in his philosophical formation.[5]

At least this is almost the case. In the penultimate section of *Little Did I Know*, Cavell takes up Howard Hawks's 1939 film *Only Angels Have Wings* (screenplay by Jules Furthman based on an original scenario by Hawks). Here too, his turn to the film seems accidental and his discussion, while more sustained than that given any other film, seems almost glancing. However, reading Hawks's film and Cavell's text in light of each other allows us to recognize that Cavell's engagement with the film is deeper than initial appearances suggest. Indeed, I will argue that, through his engagement with *Only Angels Have Wings*, Cavell not only declares his conviction in the existentially orienting power of Hollywood films and their stars but reveals the deepest philosophical ambition of *Little Did I Know* as a whole.

* * * *

Set in the Peruvian port town of Baranca, *Only Angels Have Wings* centers on a small group of pilots operating a struggling airfreight service. The service is owned by a kind-hearted old European expat called "Dutchy" (Sig Ruman), but is run by the hard-edged leader of the group, Geoff Carter

(Cary Grant). The flyers daily risk their lives ferrying mail and cargo, in fickle weather, over rugged Andean passes to points inland. Desperate risks are required, it emerges, in hopes of securing a lucrative contract that will allow for the purchase of new, safer planes. While I will not offer a detailed description of the film, its main events are structured around two arrivals and two deaths.

The first arrival, which opens the film, brings Bonnie Lee (Jean Arthur), a showgirl who plans to pass only a few late-night hours in Baranca while her ship pauses to load and unload cargo. Bonnie's arrival immediately precipitates the first death, that of Joe Souther (Noah Beery, Jr.), who is killed in a crash when, in his desire to keep a dinner-date with Bonnie, he ignores Geoff's orders and tries to land in thick fog. This death, and Bonnie's outrage when Geoff begins to eat the steak that had been prepared for Joe, lead to the famous "Who's Joe?" sequence in which Geoff brutally schools Bonnie in the stoical ethos of the men by leading them in a mock-erasure of Joe from their collective memory. Further, the "Who's Joe?" sequence, in turn, seems to both inspire and cement Bonnie's fascination with the troop of flyers (most especially with Geoff) and leads to her initial decision to remain in Baranca at least until the next ship arrives.

The second arrival brings a new pilot, Bat MacPherson/aka Killgallen (Richard Barthelmess), and his young wife Judy (Rita Haworth)—each of whom, it turns out, has a history with one of the flyers that they haven't revealed to their spouse. In an earlier life as Killgallen, MacPherson had bailed out of a burning plane and left the brother of one of the pilots, Kid Dabb (Thomas Mitchell), to die. The ignominy attaching to this act has led to his attempt to recreate himself as MacPherson. For her part, Judy had been romantically involved with Geoff and, at least as he sees it, had left him "burned." The second death is that of Kid, who is mortally injured in another burning plane piloted by MacPherson who, this time, doesn't bail out and manages to land the desperately damaged plane. The events surrounding Kid's death are closely tied to the resolution of the film's main dramatic issues. Most immediately, MacPherson's courageous landing restores his dignity and he is welcomed into the group of flyers. Further, his full membership in the group and his developing partnership with Geoff promise success in securing the desperately needed contract. Judy, in turn, is inspired by MacPherson's restored dignity (and a bracing speech from Geoff) to genuinely commit to her marriage. And Geoff, most importantly, is moved to open himself to the risks of attachment and to declare—in his way—his love for Bonnie (who has been openly pining for Geoff from early on).

This film occupies a special place in the critical literature on Hawks's work. Indeed, one critic claims that "if you cannot admire Hawks' achievement in *Only Angles Have Wings*, you probably cannot admire Hawks, period."[6] It occupies this place, in large part, because it is widely seen as epitomizing a purported Hawksian existential/moral vision celebrating a tough, aloof, individualism and insisting upon individual integrity and autonomy. The tough aloofness expresses a kind of jaded judgment of the folly and empty inauthenticity of most lives and the individual integrity and autonomy are seen as demonstrated in an unyielding commitment to completing demanding or dangerous tasks and, preeminently, in a willful defiance of mortality. Indeed, the flyers in *Only Angels Have Wings* aren't simply *willing* to risk their lives, if necessary, in order to complete an important task: the flights, generally, aren't especially important and Dutchy himself protests the needless risk ("I can't go on killing nice boys"). Rather, both literally and symbolically, flying provides the opportunity the pilots seek to defy their mortality in a titanic repudiation of subjection to human conditions. It represents a defiant declaration of themselves as unreachable by mortality, as if already on the side of the angels.[7]

This kind of existential/moral vision is undeniably present in *Only Angels Have Wings* and, for much of the film, Geoff's preeminence among the flyers and his status as the film's star are presented as functions of his being its purest embodiment. However, watching *Only Angels Have Wings* with Cavell's *Little Did I Know* in mind helps us to recognize that the film, ultimately, presents a quite different existential vision.

* * * *

Cavell's effort to produce a *philosophical* autobiography—to "show that telling the accidental, anonymous, in a sense posthumous, days of [his] life is the making of philosophy"—means that *Little Did I Know* differs from a standard autobiographical narrative in at least two important respects.[8] First, it aims to be representative—where the aspiration to representativeness, as Cavell understands it, is not a function of the events of your life but of "a specific attitude one takes to what happens in the soul."[9] Hence, while *Little Did I Know* is occupied with specific details of Cavell's life, it considers and presents those details as illuminating *common* conditions of human life. Second, and absolutely critically, one of the central ways in which this autobiography aspires to be representative is in its not taking either the existence or the identity/identities of its subject as given. On the contrary, whether its subject exists and what its identity/identities may be are exactly the questions that the work of telling—in the sense of weighing, assessing, accounting, recounting, etc.—is to determine and demonstrate.[10]

There's no question, of course, that a specific, genetically distinct individual came into the world in September 1926 and lived for ninety-one years before leaving the world in June 2018. But facts of that sort don't, in the relevant sense, establish Cavell's existence or identity. For, as the perfectionist authors he so admired continually remind us, it's all too possible to pass an entire life without ever coming into your own existence.

Indeed, in a passage from "Self-Reliance" that Cavell shows to set the central problem of the essay, Emerson suggests that we mostly imagine, or hope, that our existence can be established for us by another and so can be had at second-hand. Invoking Descartes's *cogito*, Emerson tells us that "[m]an is timid and apologetic; he is no longer upright; he dares not say 'I think,' 'I am,' but quotes some saint or sage."[11]

For Cavell, demonstrating your existence is not, as in Descartes, a matter of proving the existence of a thinking thing or substance but, rather, of showing your assumption of agency—something he often figures as claiming your own voice. In *Little Did I Know*, Cavell characterizes the goal of his efforts to assume his own agency in two ways that may, initially, seem quite different.

On the one hand, he speaks of seeking to achieve his own death. Early in the text, in explaining why he had been "unwilling, or uninterested" to compose a straight narrative of the events of his life (something that he then immediately sketches in a brisk couple of pages), Cavell remarks:

> Such a narrative strikes me as leading fairly directly to death, without clearly enough implying the singularity of this life, in distinction from the singularity of all others, all headed in that direction. So the sound of such a narrative would I believe amount to too little help to me or to others. What interests me is to see how what Freud calls the detours on the human path to death—accidents avoided or embraced, strangers taken to heart or neglected, talents imposed or transfigured, malice insufficiently rebuked, love inadequately acknowledged—mark out for me recognizable efforts to achieve my own death.[12]

On the other hand, Cavell also speaks of his efforts to assume his own agency in terms of achieving birth—choosing a life into which he could be born. So, for example, in describing the stakes he had placed on earning exceptional scores on his PhD qualifying exams, Cavell says:

> [G]iven what I considered to be my advanced age then, and given that philosophy was to incorporate and transform the crisis of musical expression in my life, I believed fully that to fail to excel at the examination would amount to failure as such. I was no longer asking for admittance but for confirmation that I had found what I wanted to become of my life, the basis on which I would be able—as Plato and Aristotle both have ways of saying—to choose my (next) life.
>
> The issue for me was not to prove that this further life was better than another, but to prove that it was mine, that I was born to it, that I was born.[13]

Although these remarks about seeking to achieve his own birth and death are framed around opposing poles of human life, they can be seen to express a single ambition for what we might call the achievement of mortality.[14] The quest is for a kind and degree of investment in life that will draw him out of the anonymity of open-ended possibility and also the fraudulence of paths that are not his own. It will root him in a determinate life that is authentically his own—and, in so doing, it will also grant the prospect of leaving that determinate life and so of dying his own death.[15]

While *Little Did I Know*, as a whole, may be seen as a study of what I am calling the work of achieving mortality, here I will note just three central elements of what it shows of the structure of this work.

First, achieving mortality is shown to involve discovering (or creating) shapes and homes for your desire, sites at which and ways in which you may profitably invest yourself—at least that is the wager. These are explicitly the terms in which Cavell discusses not only the stakes of his investment in philosophy but also the obviously pivotal moments of changing his name (which he speaks of as a "gesture declaring the search for a life I could want, not merely endure") and his decision to leave music (which he says was tied to discovering "that I had never, as I might say, chosen my life, or suffered its choosing me, but [simply] accepted the tow of a certain talent").[16] Further, since the discovery of sites of investment necessarily proceeds from within the life you now know and the attachments—and refusals of attachment—that form it, choosing a life is always choosing a next life; birth is always rebirth.

Second, achieving mortality is shown to involve ongoing work of ensuring that the life you are living is *yours*. This requires periodically assessing the attachments and investments that shape your life in order to determine how they define your character and whether you continue to desire them—whether you (still, now) want to own them. This dimension of achieving mortality is hit-off in a beautifully lyrical passage in which Cavell reflects on his decision to leave music. The passage begins from Thoreau's remark in the opening chapter of *Walden* that "our molting season, like that of the fowls, must be a crisis in our lives" and closes with Cavell depicting himself as both Odysseus lashed to the mast and Prospero acknowledging Caliban. "The seasons of nature," he tells us,

> do not determine the crises of human nature, which charges itself, rather, with finding and making the time in which to take up responsibility for shedding skins of illusion, for cleansing and assessing interests and responsibilities that are no longer, perhaps never were, necessary to oneself, and for deepening others that only I can assign myself and that I will become lost in losing. Nor do nature's seasons, nor any less predictable changes in weather or place or circumstance, assure me that my stripping myself has been thorough and my recovery complete. New York and Juilliard were reasonable ponds, even lucky, in this sense, that

they provided me with the concentration of solitude and pertinence of interest to take me back to whatever strands of my existence—inherited, cultivated, enforced—had bound me to the raft of talent mine, causing the rest of desire to exist as foreign and terrible song, to live within these familiar bonds again exclusively, either to acknowledge them mine or to let them drift away, mourn their loss, recede from them strand by strand, voice by voice.[17]

And third, in its near daily, dated entries, *Little Did I Know* shows that the work of achieving mortality includes continuing efforts to contribute to the appreciation of the investments you own. Such continuing efforts form a measure of your ongoing attachment to those investments and help to ensure that you are *leading* the life your investments have formed rather than simply following its routines.[18]

This quest to achieve mortality, to establish his existence, determines the shape of *Little Did I Know*—controlling, or at least systematically influencing, the content of the narrative and the events and episodes it includes. It controls its inclusion of what Emerson would call tales of accidents transmuted into fatalities (e.g., accidents of birth and parentage, ethnicity, geography, but also of an injured ear, being younger than classmates, etc.) as well as the pivotal moments and turning points that it recounts (e.g., realizing his father's hatred of him, moving from the house shared by the extended family, leading a band, being the only white member of an otherwise black jazz band, leaving music and finding philosophy, becoming a father, encountering Austin, etc.). And, in the same way, it controls where the narrative can end (i.e., with the completion of *The Claim of Reason* since only then did he know that his life of philosophical writing had genuinely begun and could continue).[19] And, even more crucially, the quest to achieve mortality also shapes the form of the text—a double-layered structure in which Cavell's tales of past episodes of his life are housed within dated, contemporaneous philosophical reflection on and from those episodes and also on and from the activity of recounting them. This double-layered structure allows Cavell to recount his path to a life in philosophy on one level while simultaneously exemplifying that, quite characteristic, philosophical life on the other. It allows him to show his continuing investments in that life and the ways in which it continues to sustain him.

This writing, in this form, with all that it tells of his life and with all of its continuing "immeasurable and specific ignorance" of that life, is what Cavell can offer in demonstration of his existence. It is what he can offer—and all that he can offer—in answer to his own late question: "Have I become the one who has done all and only what I have done, accepted that what I have done is no better and no worse than it is?"[20]

* * * *

With these ideas from *Little Did I Know* in mind, we can return to *Only Angels Have Wings*. By way of doing so, it will be helpful to consider a claim advanced by Gerald Mast. Arguing that the film constitutes an exploration of tensions between "indomitable, courageous, defiance of one's mortality" represented by Geoff and "warm, compassionate human feeling and sympathy" represented by Bonnie, Mast contends that the central narrative issue of the film is how Bonnie comes to "accept Geoff's life and, by implication, share it with him."[21] Mast is certainly right that the sources and fate of Bonnie's attraction to Geoff are important issues (although I won't discuss them here). However, considered against the background of *Little Did I Know*, we can see that the central issue of *Only Angels Have Wings* is less *Bonnie* coming to accept Geoff's life than *Geoff* coming to accept *his own* life. More generally, on Mast's reading of the film, Bonnie's acceptance of Geoff's life ratifies the existential/moral vision of "indomitable, courageous, defiance of one's mortality." However, to see that the central issue of the film is a fundamental change in Geoff's relation to his life—a change that consists in his coming to take his life on and to invest himself in it—is to see that the film is not ratifying that existential/moral vision but *critiquing* it. By showing Geoff's change from a life "based purely on the immediacy and ephemerality of the present," to his grounding himself in his life, and grounding himself as the condition for taking flight, the film moves from an existential/moral vision celebrating defiance of mortality to a vision calling for the work of achieving mortality.[22]

One of the most salient facts about Geoff prior to his transformation, something that we sense when first meeting him but find confirmed as the film unfolds, is that he is in flight from all connections and attachments. Having been "burned" by Judy and that investment of desire, Geoff has apparently resolved to refuse all attachments.[23] As he tells Bonnie, he "won't be burned twice"—a resolution that is comically broken late in the film as he, twice, grabs a hot pot of coffee Bonnie has made. At the material level, this refusal of attachment goes so far as his not carrying matches to light his own cigarettes, telling Bonnie that he doesn't "believe in laying in a supply of anything." But at the level of feeling and affect, this refusal is expressed in Geoff's aloof toughness and a depth of emotional foreclosure that, as I have noted, is for much of the film a mark of his preeminence among the flyers. This repudiation of sentiment pervasively shapes Geoff's words and actions throughout most of the film and is epitomized in his two most consequential exchanges with Kid—in grounding him and in telling him he's dying. In each case, Geoff delivers the news in flat, four-word sentences: "You're through flying, Kid" and "Your neck's broken, Kid."[24] However, as I suggested in sketching some of the film's key plot points, Geoff's repudiation of sentiment is most brutally expressed in the "Who's Joe?" sequence. In addition to leading the group in their ritual erasure of Joe, he mocks Bonnie's horror at his eating the steak prepared for Joe by asking "Well, what do you want me to do with it, have it stuffed?" Indeed, Geoff's brutality in this sequence reads as barely concealed anger—anger directed in part at Bonnie and Joe, but directed primarily at desire itself and human weakness in yielding to it. It is, after all, Joe's yielding to his desire to keep a date with Bonnie that gets him killed.

Here we can begin to see what is wrong in Robin Wood's claim, in his influential reading of *Only Angels Have Wings*, that the flyers' defiance of mortality drives them to "live, *now*, and to the maximum."[25] For as Geoff shows us, defying mortality is more than risking death; it is refusing any attachments that bind you to life. But that very refusal leaves Geoff with no investments that might define his character and so, contrary to Wood's claim, with no determinate life to live. As a result, rather than living life to the maximum, he haunts his own life in a kind of pseudo-heroic, spectral Stoicism.

Although Geoff initially seeks to establish his autonomy and freedom from human condition through defying mortality, *Only Angels Have Wings* shows that the real existential challenge is to risk living *for* something, to risk committing yourself to something and, in that way, staking your life. *This*, rather than games with death, is the real risk of life. To hazard your life by investing yourself in it brings risks far more frightening than death—which, in any case, always wins in the end. In particular, and not to put too fine a point on it, it risks failure—the prospect that your life, and that to which you've given it, may not work out.[26]

It is one of the plain, but somehow always surprising, conditions of life that it must be lived looking forward but can only be understood looking back, retrospectively—a fact that is emphasized by Cavell's autobiography and that, he reminds us, is shared with our experience of film. You cannot know in advance whether your investments of time, talent, effort, care, and desire are well placed. Or, since it is less a matter of hitting on fortunate investments at the start (important as that is) than of the ongoing work of managing those investments, you cannot know in advance whether you will have the imagination, flexibility, and tenacity to shepherd them and sustain them through the inevitable upheavals that befall even the most fortunate of lives.[27] Circumstances or events may conspire against you and other people may fail you or betray you. You may find, as Cavell came to feel about his life in music, that for all of your talent and success, your investments feel fraudulent, not yours to continue, but that there is no alternative path of investment in view. Or you may find, as Cavell long feared about his life in philosophy, that the investments that matter most to you, that nourish you and provide the substance of your life, also isolate you and make you a mystery to others.[28] To stake your life then, is to risk it. The only thing more hazardous is not to risk it; for then you fail to live any life at all. Existentially considered, meeting failure in life, devastating as that may be, is better than failing to live your one and only life.

In the structure of *Only Angels Have Wings*, Geoff's step into accepting his life and so beginning to achieve his mortality is represented as his acceptance of Bonnie and his staking himself on, and to, the work of building a life together with her.[29] Given its importance, it can seem surprising that the film leaves the ground of Geoff's acceptance so obscure. But further, the manner in which Geoff declares his readiness to commit himself to Bonnie can seem to continue, rather than to turn from, his aloof detachment. Bonnie's declarations are quite naked—at times bordering on painfully desperate. She had threatened to shoot Geoff to keep him from flying—and then accidently does so. She had offered over-earnest speeches trying to convince herself (and Geoff) that she will accept him on any terms: "I'm not trying to tie you down. I don't want to plan. I don't want to look ahead. I don't want you to change anything. I love you Geoff. There's nothing I can do about it. I just love you." But in the end she comes to a final, direct question. As the bullet-wounded Geoff prepares to join the broken-armed Les (each with a single good arm and only together able to function as one pilot) on the flight they hope will secure the contract putting Dutchy's shoestring operation on a solid footing, the following exchange unfolds:

> BONNIE: Do you want me to stay or don't you?
> GEOFF: [looking at a coin he's been flipping]: Tails you go, heads you stay.
> BONNIE: I won't stay that way. I'm hard to get, Geoff. All you have to do is ask me.

But Geoff *doesn't* ask and so can seem to avoid declaring himself—staking himself. Instead, in his final lines of the film, he tosses Bonnie the coin, kisses her quickly, and says, "So long, Bonnie. Keep that coffee warm," before rushing off to board the plane.

As with many moments of conversion or radical existential transformation, Geoff's decision is both overdetermined and, nevertheless, importantly obscure. Clearly, it is closely tied to Kid's death and, in particular, to Geoff's recognition that Kid's commitment to a kind of Stoical independence—being able to "fly solo" as Kid puts it—leaves him unable to accept companionship in dying. Carried from the wrecked plane to the pilots' quarters and told that he is mortally injured, Kid is only able to imagine the friends who have gathered as there to watch him die and to judge a performance he fears he may carry off poorly. (He tells Geoff: "Get that bunch out of here, quick . . . I don't want them to see me . . . I don't know how good I'll be at this.") But Geoff's transformative decision is also importantly prepared by the unfolding of events with Judy and MacPherson. First, and most obviously, he sees MacPherson overcome his self-imposed exile from his own life and secure the respect of his wife and the acceptance of the other flyers. But second, and perhaps more importantly, having delivered a scolding speech to Judy in which he, in effect, tells her to relinquish her spiritual isolation and risk committing herself to her husband, following Kid's death the force of that speech returns to Geoff in retrospective application to himself.

Here, though, I want to highlight a couple of features of Geoff's (non-) declaration of his commitment to Bonnie—not in order to remove its flip cheekiness (that's part of who Geoff is) but in order to expose some of the depth within that cheekiness. First, since it was Bonnie's coffee that burned him—twice—telling her to keep the coffee warm isn't simply an assurance that he'll return to drink it. It is a fairly direct declaration that he is opening himself to the pain of being burned. Second, the coin Geoff tosses to Bonnie had been Kid's and, as Geoff discovers late in the film, is two-headed. By using this coin to "win" tosses, Kid ensured that he always took the most difficult and dangerous flights. In tossing this coin to Bonnie, then, Geoff is both forging a symbolic link to the kind-hearted Kid and, more importantly, signaling his readiness for the most difficult task of all—stepping into his own life and its unforeseeable developments together with Bonnie.[30]

Discovering, only after Geoff has rushed away, that the coin he tossed her *is* two-headed, Bonnie brings the film to a close calling out after him: "Hey, Geoff!" Suddenly realizing that Geoff *has* declared himself, and recognizing the stakes of that declaration, this is more than an exuberant cry of surprised delight. It's a kind of *Ecce homo!* such as only Jean Arthur could deliver—a shout that celebrates, and directs us to behold, the emergence of a man who, having begun to ground himself in his life, is now able to take flight.

* * * *

We're now in a position to appreciate the force of Cavell's direct engagement with *Only Angels Have Wings* in *Little Did I Know*. I mentioned at the outset that his remarks can seem glancing and relatively inconsequential. Indeed, Cavell initially invites the impression that he turns to the film simply because he happened to find it on late-night television during a bout of insomnia. Further, after he first mentions the film (which he calls "quite good" but "self-evidently not up to the best work" of its principal actors, writer, or director—admittedly a very high bar), he turns away from it and directs his attention to the Hawks/Furthman film of *To Have and Have Not* (1944) and, more generally, to what he calls "Hemingway's issue that the ability to stake one's existence confers the right to existence"—an issue that is clearly central to *Only Angels Have Wings* although Cavell does not make that link explicit.[31] However, when he returns to *Only Angels Have Wings* a few paragraphs later, he makes clear that he was led to it not by the accidents of late-night television programming but by a remark that stopped him while reading Maurice Blanchot's *The Writing of the Disaster*. "The Hawks/Furthman *Only Angels Have Wings* came to mind," Cavell tells us, "out of Blanchot writing: 'The inexperience of dying, dying as someone who has not learned how, or who has missed his classes.'"[32] Having been called to mind in this way, the scant two paragraphs that Cavell devotes to the film focus entirely on the scene of Kid's death and his final exchange with Geoff. This is surely one of the pivotal moments of the film and in Geoff's transformation. However, in order to recognize the extraordinary weight Cavell gives this scene and the role that his discussion of it plays within *Little Did I Know*, we need to consider both how he builds to it and how he, quite openly and yet all but invisibly, reenacts it in the final pages of his text.

Throughout the final main part of *Little Did I Know*, Cavell is led by his reading of Blanchot to reconsider, as if one final time, questions of human and philosophical orientation and disorientation: questions, that is, of how we may understand our being lost and of how we can find, or recover, our bearings in life and in thought.[33] Blanchot inspires this reconsideration because of his conviction in the ubiquity of human disorientation. "Early in *The Writing of the Disaster*," Cavell tells us, "Blanchot opts etymologically, hence metaphysically, [. . .] for the significance of 'disaster' as marking our being dissociated or disengaged or disconnected from the pertinence of the stars."[34] Hence, Cavell continues, "for Blanchot disaster is revealed metaphysically to be, or to have become, the normal state of human existence, marked by the release from our ties to the stars."[35]

Cavell, of course, finds deep affinities with the thought that disaster, understood as disorientation, is the normal human condition or that, as he would put it, the human is constitutionally subject to becoming lost. However, while Blanchot seems to associate this disorientation with a loss of our connection to, or conviction in, transcendent points of guidance or transcendent sources of meaning, purpose, and value, Cavell follows Wittgenstein and Emerson in seeing our disorientation as a function precisely of our quest for the transcendent or the unconditioned and of our skeptical repudiation of the ordinary or everyday conditions of sense. For Cavell, that is, our disorientation is a function of what he calls the human drive to deny, or escape, the human. Glossing Wittgenstein's claim that his work consists in returning words "from their metaphysical to their everyday use," Cavell remarks that an implication of this claim "is that we are, we live, in exile from our words, turned from them, from the implications of our lives, strangers to ourselves, or rather (since finding ourselves strange might be liberating), shunning ourselves. Starless."[36] And, he goes on to point out, a "symptom of our being lost to ourselves [. . .] is that we seek a transcendental rescue in, or from, our words."[37]

Among the various human motivations for this disorienting repudiation of the ordinary, for our exiling ourselves from our words and life, in these late pages of *Little Did I Know* Cavell focuses on what he calls a "horror of understanding" and the sense that to accept the human conditions of sense is to be constrained, "pinned," or "forced to know what cannot be borne."[38] He considers horrors connected with our understanding *of* others; fears that we may be impaled upon, or paralyzed by, our knowledge of their suffering—whether they be as near as a desperate and enraged father or as distant as anonymous strangers. And he considers horrors connected with our being (mis)understood *by* others and so struggling to avoid being hemmed in by the pictures they may form of us. But for my purposes here, the most relevant knowledge that can seem unbearable is a form of self-knowledge. It is the knowledge of our Emersonian representativeness or, as Emerson puts it, of our standing for humanity. To face the knowledge of our human representativeness is to acknowledge that we are always, essentially, more than any of our particular self-realizations. Being creatures of language, we are creatures of possibility—always, and essentially, open to what Emerson calls a further, as yet unattained but attainable self.[39] Of course, possibility, and its call for continual but uncertain becoming, has its own torments. But what can seem especially unbearable in this knowledge of representativeness is its other face: the knowledge that in order to be anything at all, we must embrace determination—become, at least for a time, one thing rather than another. Staking our lives, choosing some paths, comes at the cost of foreclosing other paths and relinquishing what can seem our open possibility. But to fail to stake our lives is to languish in *mere* possibility.

However, that such knowledge can be borne, and how its demands can be managed, is demonstrated by *Little Did I Know* as a whole, and Cavell's late invocation of Geoff/Grant epitomizes the existential importance of taking it on. Cavell isolates the moment when Geoff/Grant stands alone, outside the room in which Kid lays dying. This moment, just after taking leave of the mortally wounded Kid and just before his fateful exchanges with Bonnie, gives us Geoff/Grant in the moment of his transformational decision to accept his life and invest himself in it. A few pages earlier, Cavell had recalled Emerson's injunction to "hitch your wagon to a star" and emphasized its call to let ourselves be oriented by our attraction to stars.[40] Now, he offers us this image of Geoff/Grant as just such an orienting star—trading on, but also radically deepening, the familiar Hollywood idiom for its greatest, most alluring or compelling, actors.[41] He offers us this image of Geoff/Grant, that is, as a radiantly attractive exemplar of the turn *away* from the drive toward false transcendence and a consequent refusal of investment in the ordinary and of the turn *toward* taking on the work of achieving mortality. It is such an exemplar, such an orienting star, Cavell suggests, that might draw us out of our disorientation.[42] Speaking of this moment, Cavell says: "We can read nothing in this moment from Grant's extraordinary face. Except the unimpeded demand it imposes on us, from a time and place always beyond us."[43]

Cavell's highlighting of this image of Geoff/Grant as an exemplar and orienting star provides an essential key to appreciating the philosophical point of the vignette with which he chooses to close *Little Did I Know*. That vignette describes a conversation with his elderly father, at his hospital bedside, following surgery to implant a pacemaker. Cavell's father, in effect, implores him to have everyone leave the room and allow him to face his fate:

> Why are the doctors and nurses and family running in and out of my room as if it's an emergency? [. . .] What is the emergency? If a child is seriously ill, it is an emergency. To run in and out of a room because an eighty-three-year-old man may die is not an emergency. It is ugly to behave this way [. . .] Tell them to stop.[44]

To this last request/demand, Cavell tells us that he replied, "That's not my job," then adds that "[he] was about to say [he] would tell the doctor about [their] talk," but his father had fallen asleep. Cavell ends the book with: "His position appeared awkward to me. I walked out to find my mother."[45]

Of course, the Freudian family romance and how it was enacted in Cavell's relations with his mother and father have been under exploration throughout the text. And it is also true that Cavell, harkening back to Thoreau's invocations of the mother and father tongue, has used the image of reconciling his mother and father to characterize his aspiration to produce writing that brings together the literary and the philosophical.[46] Even so, these final words can seem painfully awkward and deeply obscure; and neither the awkwardness nor the obscurity is relieved by the fact that they appear in the midst of pages considering awkwardness—the awkwardness of dying and the closely linked awkwardness of philosophizing in the assumption of representativeness and so with nothing but the common to tell. How can this, we may wonder, constitute the close of Cavell's effort to recount the conditions of his life?

The answer that I propose depends upon recognizing that this vignette closely reenacts the scene with Kid and Geoff/Grant that Cavell has just considered. As in the scene from the film, this vignette depicts a bedside conversation about death and the wish to be left to face it alone; it includes a kind of taking leave of the man facing imminent death; and it invites us to imagine Cavell, like Geoff/Grant, standing alone outside the room he has just left, preparing to go in search of the woman who, for him, had always represented life, culture, and the affirmation of desire. The closing vignette, then, forges an identification between Cavell and Geoff/Grant, and through this identification offers us an epitomizing image for the work of *Little Did I Know* as a whole: to present Cavell, or his depicted life, as an orienting exemplar of the achievement of mortality.

To the extent that we allow ourselves to be drawn by our attraction to these exemplars and to emulate their efforts, we recover our connection to the pertinence of the stars and avoid disaster. It is a mark of Cavell's conviction in the power of Hollywood cinema, and equally of his entrustment to the ordinary, that the stars he offers us for orientation are not to be found in the lifeless depths of space but are shining before us on Hollywood's silver screen and in the pages of the book we hold. But given our human drive to deny the human, the presence of these stars before us may make them harder to recognize as points of orientation. It is often easier to lament the absence of an unseen God than to heed the demanding appeal of the luminously mortal.

Notes

1 Stanley Cavell, *The Senses of Walden: An Expanded Edition* (San Francisco: North Point Press, 1981), 45. I am grateful to David LaRocca, William Day, Byron Davies, Victor Krebs, David O'Connor, and William Rothman for their encouraging comments and helpful suggestions on earlier drafts of this chapter.

2 William Rothman and Marian Keane, *Reading Cavell's* The World Viewed: *A Philosophical Perspective on Film* (Detroit: Wayne State University Press, 2000), 27.

3 Ibid.

4 Stanley Cavell, *Little Did I Know: Excerpts from Memory* (Stanford: Stanford University Press, 2010), 396.

5 This feature of the text is made all the more striking in light of Cavell's rich, extensive, and detailed discussions of the role that music—listening, composing, performing—and individual pieces of music played in his life and formation.

6 Gerald Mast, *Howard Hawks: Storyteller* (Oxford: Oxford University Press, 1982), 105.

7 The strongest articulations of this view of *Only Angels Have Wings* and of its purported existential/moral vision are provided by Robin Wood (see his *Howard Hawks*, revised edition, Wayne State University Press, 2006) and Gerald Mast (see his *Howard Hawks: Storyteller*). Lee Russell finds essentially the same existential/moral vision in Hawks, but unlike Wood and Mast, Russell castigates it as ugly machismo. See his "Howard Hawks" (in *Howard Hawks: American Artist*, ed. Jim Hillier and Peter Wollen, British Film Institute, 1996).

8 Cavell, *Little Did I Know*, 5.

9 Ibid., 8.

10 See Cavell's extraordinary elaboration of the concept of "telling" in *The Claim of Reason: Wittgenstein, Skepticism, Morality, and Tragedy* (Oxford: Oxford University Press, New Edition, 1999), 94–95.

11 Ralph Waldo Emerson, "Self-Reliance," in *Ralph Waldo Emerson: Essays and Lectures* (New York: Library of America, 1983), 270. Cavell's most extensive

treatment of this issue in Emerson is "Being Odd, Getting Even," in *In Quest of the Ordinary: Lines of Skepticism and Romanticism* (Chicago: The University of Chicago Press, 1988).

12 Cavell, *Little Did I Know*, 4.

13 Ibid., 284. Pertinently, Cavell immediately goes on to contrast his need for exceptional success on his qualifying exams with a similar kind of quest to "achieve the ungradable" in a string quartet composition class at the University of California, Berkeley. Noting the "telltale wrinkle" that he was not "reliably attached" to what he wrote, he speaks of these pursuits as "tales of vanity and confusion and sleepwalking" and glosses his condition then as "awaiting birth, if not stalling birth," 285.

14 Cavell does not use this expression, but the idea is pervasive in many of his discussions of the need to overcome our skeptical haunting of our own lives and our spectral existence. He uses the expression "hope for mortality" in his remarkable essay on Dušan Makavejev's film *Sweet Movie* (1974). Having noted that the film is "obsessed with images of attempts to be born," he considers the lyric from the soundtrack's opening song—"Is there life on the earth? Is there life after birth?"—and remarks that the line about life after birth poses "the question whether we may hope for mortality as prior to the question whether we may hope for immortality." Cavell, "On Makavejev on Bergman," in *Themes Out of School: Effects and Causes* (San Francisco: North Point Press, 1984), 116.

15 Cavell speaks movingly of the summer before his seventeenth birthday as a period in which he sought exactly the kind of open-ended anonymity he will subsequently seek to overcome—as though seeking escape from lives imposed upon him or that he did not (any longer) desire. He describes this as a quest "to be without horizon" and as "a rite of nonpassage, searching for a point of origin, to be zero, to look back on the world, but without exactly dying." *Little Did I Know*, 199. Cavell's anxieties about fraudulence, about following paths not his own, are most intensely concentrated around both performing and composing music and only begin to lift when he turns to philosophy. Speaking of an early philosophy paper he wrote for a valued teacher at UCLA he remarks: "I found—with considerable, unexpected relief—that completing it did not serve yet once more to extend my sense of fraudulence. The work did not promise more than it delivered, whatever that was." *Little Did I Know*, 246.

16 Ibid., 202, 187.

17 Ibid., 225.

18 I have discussed the idea of appreciation, understood as increase in the worth or value of investments, in my "Impression, Influence, Appreciation" in *Inheriting Stanley Cavell: Memories, Dreams, Reflections*, ed. David LaRocca (New York: Bloomsbury, 2020), 243–60.

19 Ibid, 221.

20 Ibid., 517. It may seem that any, or all, of Cavell's writings would suffice to demonstrate his existence (at least his existence as a philosopher) in

something like the way that his children might be thought to suffice to demonstrate his existence as a father. But being a father (or mother), of course, is not simply a matter of the fact of having children but of various kinds of relationships to those children. My claim, similarly, is that only *Little Did I Know* shows—or fails to show—Cavell's relationships to his (other) works—the ways in which they were *his* to write or express *his* philosophical voice. Hence only it can demonstrate—or fail to demonstrate—his existence even as a philosopher.

21 Mast, *Howard Hawks*, 106, 105.

22 Ibid., 121. My argument that *Only Angels Have Wings* be seen as, ultimately, critiquing the vision that it initially celebrates, aligns with William Rothman's argument that the Hawks/Furthman film of *To Have and to Have Not* be seen as critiquing the macho ethos of Hemingway's novel. See William Rothman, "*To have and have not* adapted a film from a novel," *The "I" of the Camera: Essays in Film Criticism, History, and Aesthetics* (Cambridge: Cambridge University Press, 1988, 2nd ed., 2003), 158–66.

23 It may seem that Geoff has committed himself to Dutchy's airfreight service since he is, apparently, willing to risk his own life and the lives of others to see it succeed. However, as I suggested earlier, Dutchy's venture is less an existential commitment for Geoff—or the other flyers—than a (narrative) support or occasion for defying mortality through flying.

24 To say that Geoff repudiates emotion is not to say that he feels none—as though he were an automaton or a psychopath. Rather, it is to say that he refuses to acknowledge sentiment and works to resist allowing it to produce attachments that inform the shape of his life. Geoff's final exchange with Kid, in a beautifully shot scene brimming with pathos, shows just how difficult this repudiation can be.

25 Wood, *Howard Hawks*, 18.

26 Cavell speaks of this—of investing your life in something that does not work out—as "the worst" happening and registers his fear that, although professionally secure in an endowed chair at Harvard, the response to his first three books showed that his devoting himself to philosophy had not worked out. "I had the unmistakable sense of having said hello a number of times," he tells us, "without anyone saying hello back, anyone other than friends, who keep one sane but who necessarily run the risk of affording consolation, *as if the worst has happened*." *Little Did I Know*, 521; italics added.

27 Late in *Little Did I Know*, Cavell speaks of this—in association with Hemmingway—as "the knowledge that you play your hand for life-and-death stakes without knowing whether you have, or have not, the courage and the wisdom and the perception and the passion and the compassion and the luck to come through well in your own eyes." 543.

28 See, for example, *Little Did I Know*, 539.

29 Managing romantic and erotic attachments obviously plays a pivotal role in taking on our lives and achieving mortality. However, just as Geoff's being "burned" by Judy is used in the film to represent a broad range of fears and

traumas that can lead to a refusal to invest in life, his acceptance of Bonnie is also used to figure a broader acceptance of ordinary human investments. This is not to say that the connection with Bonnie is merely symbolic; it is to note that it is *also* symbolic.

30 In commenting on an earlier draft of this essay, David LaRocca suggested that the coin might even be seen as "a veritable portrait of companionship, even marriage, in which two heads are joined, as if on other sides of one another." I'm grateful for the suggestion—especially if it's taken to suggests two heads joined in ongoing conversation (hence demanding and celebrating distance and difference) rather than two faces united on one head as in the account offered by Aristophanes, in Plato's *Symposium*, of erotic longing as a desire to overcome separateness, to be fused into one, and so to recover a (mythical) lost wholeness.

31 Cavell, *Little Did I Know*, 541.

32 Ibid., 545.

33 Cavell is also, importantly, using his reading of Blanchot to explore, also as if one final time, his affinities with and differences from the French post-structuralist philosophy produced during the period of his own philosophical authorship. While what I say bears on this, it is somewhat to the side of my focus.

34 Cavell, *Little Did I Know*, 522.

35 Ibid.

36 Ibid., 523.

37 Ibid.

38 Ibid., 525, 528. The classical image of the horror of understanding is, of course, Oedipus gouging out his eyes. Although the figure of Oedipus haunts the text, Cavell doesn't make that presence explicit here or, for the most part, elsewhere in *Little Did I Know*.

39 Emerson, "History," in *Essays and Lectures*, 239.

40 Cavell, *Little Did I Know*, 533.

41 "(Movie) star" no longer carries the aura of the extraordinary, exceptional, or exemplary that it possessed in Hollywood's "golden age." Now, it simply designates the principal actors (whether in a film, television show, theatrical production).

42 As David LaRocca suggested—again in comments on an earlier draft of this essay—we might say that Cavell invites us to join with Bonnie in finding in Geoff/Grant someone to whom we can be happy to hitch ourselves. I will also note here that this is not the first time Cavell has invoked Grant as an exemplar of some attractive human possibility. The frontispiece of *Pursuits of Happiness* gives us a radiantly smiling Grant with the caption: "This man, in words of Emerson's, carries the holiday in his eye; he is fit to stand the gaze of millions."

43 Cavell, *Little Did I Know*, 546.

44 Ibid., 548.
45 Ibid. The idea of the father's position appearing awkward opens several paths of significance. While the remarks I'll offer shortly about awkwardness suggest the starting points and directions of some of these paths, I cannot follow any of them here.
46 See, for example, Cavell, *In Quest of the Ordinary*, 3.

5

In Praise of Cinema

Cavell, Arnaud Desplechin, and Telling What Counts in *Trois souvenirs de ma jeunesse*

JOSEPH MAI

IN NOVEMBER 2006, THE PHILOSOPHER SANDRA LAUGIER moderated a conversation between Stanley Cavell and the filmmaker Arnaud Desplechin.[1] During their discussion, Desplechin spoke at length about how deeply his cinema is intertwined with Cavell's thinking.[2] My goal in the following pages will be twofold: first, to elaborate on what Desplechin says in this interview, developing the Cavellian themes that he identifies as important to his work; second, to read these themes in an analysis of *My Golden Days* (*Trois souvenirs de ma jeunesse* [*Three Memories of My Youth*], 2015).[3] Speaking generally, there are at least two major, but related, Cavellian ideas that have shaped Desplechin's approach to the cinema. First, Cavell's decisive philosophical treatment of skepticism and its relation to the cinema have helped Desplechin free himself from some tendencies of the tradition of French film criticism and practice in which he was formed. Second, in light of this emphasis on skepticism, Cavell's reflections on the uses of language, interpretation, and especially praise provide Desplechin with a model for how meaning is expressed in the cinema. During the bulk of this chapter, I will explore these themes in *Three Memories*.

Concerning his own cinematic roots, Desplechin admits a certain resistance to a number of tendencies of the critics from the influential *Cahiers du cinéma*, which have their origin in the work of André Bazin, but have been disseminated by those Desplechin calls Bazin's "grandchildren." In one way or another, these tendencies came as a response to the epistemological challenge of skepticism, and, as such, they put us in the center of Cavell's preoccupations. And not just Cavell's: recent film theorists, such as Schmerheim, Früchtl, and Sinnerbrink, have taken up the theme of skepticism in order to build bridges between continental European film philosophies (such as those of Bazin and Deleuze) and Cavell's work. Josef Früchtl in particular points to the cinema as a kind of palliative for skepticism that eventually helps create "trust in the world." For Desplechin, the first point to be taken from Cavell is the compelling difference between him and Bazin and his grandchildren in their response to skepticism.

My understanding of the cinema's response to skepticism has benefited from Früchtl's work, which resituates skepticism in the context of the Platonic and Christian division of the world into distinct spiritual and physical realms. The Cartesian skeptical method casts the world of *res extensa* into fundamental doubt, with only the cogito remaining unscathed to rebuild some connection between self and world. However, according to Früchtl, the history of epistemology since Descartes demonstrates (somewhat obviously) that human beings are cognitively imperfect, and that the conviction that self and world are linked through the cogito as Descartes saw it is unwarranted: doubt in the world cannot be overcome through a subject's knowledge. Some, such as Deleuze, have remained undaunted and have sought to overcome skepticism on an entirely different terrain: for them, "the impossible [. . .] can only be restored within a faith."[4] Früchtl focuses on Deleuze, but one senses that Bazin could have stood in for Deleuze here, for he too would have liked to "replace the model of knowledge with belief."[5] For both, and for many who have followed them, the mechanical reproduction of photography lends a nearly magical solution by providing a connection to reality that circumnavigates the need for knowledge to interfere: the connection between self and world would be ratified without recourse to knowledge or the mind. It would just be, and the cinema would demonstrate it. Bazin would famously refer to the redemption of painting's original sin (perspective, a false realism) via the photographic reproduction of reality.[6]

In conversation with Laugier and Cavell, Desplechin expresses his dissatisfaction with this cinematic faith. In Cavell's philosophy he finds a more congenial theory, one that continues to acknowledge the epistemological problem of skepticism, without taking the extra step toward faith, while finding a way to live with it. As Schmerheim reminds us, skepticism arises from an encounter with the limits of indubitable knowledge, a limit experienced as a failure. To overcome this failure would require us to view the world from outside of our human condition. To imagine such a vantage point, however, reveals a desire to stand outside of finitude; to have, in

Thomas Nagel's expression, a view from nowhere. Cavell suggests that we might do better simply to come to grips with our cognitive limitations and renounce this impossible vantage point. In fact, he admits that skepticism is built in a foolproof way that makes an invincibly, and thus impossibly, secure knowledge the only way of defeating it.

A film reproduces the epistemological conditions of skepticism. For Cavell, the mechanical reproduction of photography is not proof of the world appearing with authority before my subjectivity, but a freeing up of subjectivity. Subjectivity is no longer a zero-sum game, either a direct hold over reality or an illusion to be rejected and replaced with faith. Mechanically reproduced, the world is present to us, but it is a world that is not the present world: "the reality in a photograph is present to me while I'm not present to it; and a world I know, and see, but to which I am nevertheless not present (through no fault of my subjectivity), is a world past."[7] We are displaced from our normal position vis-à-vis the world in a way Cavell likens to surrealism and magic and memory:

> it is as though the world's projection explains our forms of unknownness and of our inability to know. The explanation is not so much that the world is passing us by, as that we are displaced from our natural habitation within it, placed at a distance from it. The screen overcomes our fixed distance; it makes displacement appear as our natural condition.[8]

The cinema reproduces common skepticism because it pulls us into a world in which we are not at home. This positioning in a strange world seems to bring out in an overt way our unacknowledged (estranged) position in the world at all times.

Our admission that skepticism cannot be defeated on its own terms shifts the question onto a different terrain, for skepticism can only be dealt with by cultivating a different relation to the world, one that does not require secure knowledge. Cavell says famously in *The Claim of Reason*: "To live in the face of doubt, eyes happily shut, would be to fall in love with the world. For if there is a correct blindness, only love has it."[9] Schmerheim insists: love of the world amounts to a benign cognitive blindness, a shutting of the eyes, that implies *trust* that the world is there and that we have some way of depending on other minds. Edward Mooney adds: "if we could avoid an exclusive focus on doubt, if we could avert our eyes and love or at least acknowledge others and the world, then skepticism would be inconclusive, leaving room for its other. Its other is not dogmatism but confident affirmation."[10] There are two important parts to this: first an affective attitude, even attachment, to the world, and second an affirmative *expression* of our place within the world and in relation to others. Mooney describes the moral perfectionist as someone "on the verge of becoming themselves through the shedding of what is less than perfect—an always unfinished task."[11] Though never accomplished, perfectionism depends on the development of what Mooney calls a "voice": "the moral perfectionist is sensitive to the endlessness of the struggle to find one's voice, a moral voice, a voice one can believe in."[12] Voice is our manner of affirming meaning within the general conditions of skeptical doubt.[13] We do not need the genius of the *auteur* to open our eyes; we need to develop meaning through our own searching and affirmative articulations of it.

The second major point that I see Desplechin taking from Cavell concerns the forms of these affirmations of meaning. Desplechin gives his answer in terms of the cinema, but it holds for skepticism broadly. For the *auteurist*, the cinema provides a mystical faith in the world, and the proper affirmation in the context of this faith is "prayer." Desplechin rejects prayer; the cinema does not mystically prove anything but rather opens up an "extraordinary box: the multiplicity of meanings sheltered in a film."[14] He chooses the Cavellian term "praise of the world" to describe the proper tone of cinematic affirmation. Once one has "fallen in love" with the world, praise is an interpretive process by which one is sensitive to and then articulates affirmative meanings. The conversation between Desplechin and Cavell took place in English, but the French translation of the word emphasizes this. "Éloge" comes from the Latin *elogium*, which denotes a eulogy, a short maxim, an inscription on a tombstone, a clause in a testament, or a summary. A eulogy is a commentary about someone in "good words." The cinema supplies us with something to affirm. Desplechin calls this *meaning*, and he moves on from the quasi-sacerdotal role of the *auteur* to concentrate on how, through praise, the viewer "perceives a meaning that appears on the screen."[15] This is a new cognitive relation between the subject and the world that is made of purposiveness or acknowledgment rather than knowledge. Doubt may be our human condition; but it is also a part of the human condition that our statements elicit a response from others; and their statements, their declarations of suffering or love, elicit a response from us. These experiences give the individual a "non-epistemic confirmation" of personhood and the other.[16]

By dint of its relation to skepticism, the cinema inspires in Desplechin an analogy between character and viewer. In what Desplechin calls "the narrative of this combat against skepticism," the character is a "prey to skepticism"; but, for the viewer as well, the cinema is also "a tool of combat against skepticism."[17] The character is in a narrative in which skepticism, in one or another of its myriad manifestations, is (or is not) being worked out through some kind of affirmation; the viewer makes meaning of the images of the world through which the narrative is told. The cinema becomes a warehouse filled with possible affirmations for moments when "the world seems tasteless."[18] Therefore, if it is an image of skepticism, it is also, as Früchtl argues, an image "of acknowledgement."[19] The language games of narrative, setting, character, editing, sound, and so on that make up a film provide a viewer with something to praise. They do not prove the world; but they build "a trust in practice."[20] One might call this the Cavellian use of film criticism: to extract the relevant forms of acknowledgment that give taste and consistency to life. I will return to this ideal of criticism at the end of this chapter.

A last departure that Desplechin claims from *Cahiers* elitism is the degree to which his cinematic meaning-making erases the distinction between high and popular culture.[21] He embraces Cavell's interest in the everyday and the "common man." This praise for the commonplace transforms everyday reality: "[Cavell] describes the extraordinary share of our intimate selves that makes us comparable to kings and billionaires."[22] Rather than an act of piety, the cinema partakes of a different utopia, one that Desplechin calls "American," since whenever there is an attempt to define an "American" artform it is usually in terms of a rejection of the old European artistic aristocracies and the opening of a "democratic" path toward originality and virtue for each individual. From here it follows that the conventions of popular cinema—conventions of narrative situation, editing, genre, acting, and so on, all of which Cavell discusses in *The World Viewed* and beyond—are not simply cultural symptoms, but the tools by which societies and the individuals that compose them create value and meaning in their lives. Film is the popular art that shows, through the attentiveness and praise it elicits, that any commonplace life can count.

Enter the Labyrinth

We first meet the anthropologist Paul Daedalus in Tajikistan, in bed with a blonde Russian colleague who is helping him arrange his return to Paris, where he has accepted a prestigious position in the Ministry of Foreign Affairs after many years abroad. She suggests that he is like Ulysses returning home; but he insists that home offers no nostalgia to him. But her comment does bring back to his mind three memories: *Three Memories of My Youth*. The title suggests a simple enumeration: there will be three memories here, and they come neutrally, without their significance identified. If they return in this way, it is because Paul has long ago disavowed his past. Rather than Ulysses, Paul is haunted by another, more somber myth: Daedalus, his namesake. The past is a labyrinth where he has long refused to enter.[23]

In the first memory, Paul's mad mother attacks him (like the Minotaur) from below, in the dark on a stormy night, from the bottom of the stairs as in so many horror films, and he must ward her off with a knife. It is not possible to determine the degree of "reality" this scene has: his mother is considered insane by all and eventually kills herself, but Paul's sister seems also to be attached to her; the degree of her monstrosity may be in his imagination. Is memory real? Is this flashback a dream? The impossibility to differentiate between the two is one of the oldest expressions of skepticism. In the second memory, an intelligence agent tells Paul that another Paul Daedalus, born at the same time and place, has been found in Australia. The interrogation scene is shot in the basement of some official building, with dimmed lights, a dark cinderblock background, and a shadowy agent (André Dessollier) who will not reveal his name. In short, it partakes of the codes of police procedural, or the spy film, emphasizing transgression, darkness, and constriction. "Who are you?" asks the agent, and Paul answers that he "does not really know." It gets worse when the agent announces that the other Paul Daedalus, the one to whom Paul had given his passport in Minsk, is dead, finishing his announcement with a quote from Luke: "For you were dead and now you live again." Despite his own explanation for the mistake, Paul feels shaken by how his life is not how it seems. He can only conclude: "la vie est étrange." The film is part fantasy, part dream, but mainly it is a form of displacement of reality into various directions of strangeness.

Daedalus designed the labyrinth; but Paul's labyrinth has no design, no roadmap—it is just three memories. Similarly, Gaston Bachelard makes the labyrinth the figure of anxiety, of lostness, of self-abjection, whose turning corridors conform to the contours of dream.[24] Stylistically, in the film language that Desplechin uses to convey Paul's skepticism, we find darkness and constriction. Irises dilate space around Paul; the courtyard of his grandaunt's house is shady and hidden. Later we see Paul reading the letters of Esther, his first love, in his apartment, which suddenly becomes a dark room with a cracked blue wall: a room of indeterminate dream. There is even a tapestry representing the labyrinth, with the Minotaur and Theseus, for Paul to contemplate on the wall of a youth hostel where he tries (unsuccessfully) to find shelter for a night. Paul's corridors are inhabited by literal ghosts, shown not as faded and floating apparitions but in a blunt, matter-of-fact manner: his great-aunt who shows up at his mother's gravesite, or his own childhood self, appearing in his apartment at the end of the film. The character is "prey to skepticism."

What Counts in Love

The film will focus on how Paul creates affirmation out of these dark passageways. Three memories of skepticism confront the character, successively concerning family, friends, and a lover. The enumeration reminds one of an essay by Cavell on counting and recounting in *The Winter's Tale*, a play (and an essay) that has an obvious importance to Desplechin's earlier film, *Un conte de Noël* (*A Christmas Tale*, 2008). In that essay, Cavell analyzes a "dual operation" in counting: one in which we use numbers to identify "the order and size and pace of events," which are "fixed ahead of time," and another in which these relationships—their order, importance, and hierarchy—are to be worked out "in the telling."[25] The French word "compter" (to count, but echoing "conter" to tell or narrate) captures this ambiguity, for the title only numbers these memories in an ironic way: the fact that there are three is meaningless, and the connections between them, the gaps in time for instance, are not counted at all. Instead what matters to Desplechin is the narration, and through the telling, a search for what *counts*. What starts as disconnected memories will become a "tallying of concerns."[26] This Cavellian idea of telling meets Bachelard on unexpected ground, for Bachelard also sees telling as the way through the labyrinth: "Ariadne's thread is the thread of discourse."[27]

For Desplechin, that discourse is genre, film technique, language, and especially the interpretive practice of praise. This happens everywhere, but I will concentrate, or count, on the third and most comprehensive of Paul's memories, his story with Esther, which occupies two-thirds of the film. Take, for example, the brilliant scene in which Paul and Esther meet, a staple of the teen romance film (and all romance genres). The encounter scene begins typically with Paul and his friend Kovalki (a medical student) squealing into the local high school parking lot in Kovalki's Ford, music blaring. We are at the lycée Baudelaire, a clue to the mixing of low and high registers (teen romance and modernist poetry) at play in this scene. Paul approaches his siblings and friend Penelope (a girl who desires Paul, but whom he does not desire—again the Ulysses myth refused, no return home) with a self-conscious air of mystery. Split screens show various angles on the action. Paul looks off-screen, distracted. A cut shows Esther for the first time, sitting upon a round brick bench or planter, elevated, with the back of Paul's head in the shot: she is immediately on a pedestal; he is already in admiration. She is also surrounded by suitors, the object of the male gaze, and in a position of dominance over them (one of them uses the another's back to write his phone number on a piece of paper for her). A few cuts later and the frame widens, nerdy cousin Bob arrives on his moped, but he must circle around the courtyard where Esther, now alone, sits on her pedestal. The camera circles around her like a museumgoer walks around a sculpture, looking from different angles and through different frame sizes. Throughout the film, Desplechin films Lou Roy-Lecollinet in a manner that emphasizes this statuary impression: we see this in her elevation, but also in her pale, marble-like complexion, her frequent nudity, or in a dressing style that forces her into an erect stance, all of which also echoes shots from the end of the film of statues of women in the Luxembourg gardens. This scene sets Esther apart, elevates the commonplace reality of the schoolyard. Paul is also distinguished from the group: a flash of split screens disrupts the space (showing the group getting into Kovalki's car while Paul remains behind) and ends in a sweep to show Esther alone, in close-up, dragging sultrily on her cigarette, followed by a countershot of Paul, slowly approaching. This is the beginning of their story, distinguishing them from the others.

Paul's memory of the past returns to him in the language of popular cinema genres. A house party and dance, smoking pot, a scene in a bowling alley, are combined with declarations of love, a first time sleeping together, and the melodrama of their disintegrating relationship. The use of music, both diegetic and non-diegetic, dramatic camera movements, and lighting elevates many of these scenes. We see this, for instance, in the bowling alley scene in which Paul sits alone writing a letter to Esther who is in the alley next to him, bowling with an older guy, while Shirley Brown's *Woman to Woman* plays in the background: the song is about one woman stealing another woman's man, just as Esther is about to dump her boyfriend for Paul. Registers are juxtaposed, combining the setting, with the song, but also with the letter Paul writes to Esther (and which includes recopied passages from Robert Louis Stevenson). The everyday becomes heightened and intensified, filled with desperate emotion when they cry, or when Esther clings to Paul when he must return to Paris. And when she joins him there they meet in a city self-consciously close to romantic cliché (such as when they neck under the Eiffel tower).

Their teen romance is associated with more traditionally "noble" forms of discourse, frequently the fine arts. In one scene they have made love and lie in bed, the camera focused on Esther's nudity wrapped lightly in white sheets. After a cut we see the close-up of a fragment of a painting, another partially nude woman draped in white cloth, a child holding her arm: Esther is like this classical painting, the teen romance is "museified" in the double sense that Esther is a "muse" (Paul being thus inspired) and in that it has become noble, fit for a museum without being stuffy or irrelevant. Desplechin's camera insists on this museum, scanning across the painting until we see its frame, its descriptive plaque (too unfocused to read) and until we see, on a further wall behind, another portrait of a woman. And as the camera turns the corner behind this moveable wall, we see a painting even further away, with a much larger frame, in front of which stand Paul and Esther (visiting the museum, the next day). The camera is perceiving the space cinematically, through a number of frames, its movement inserting the characters into the frames, seamlessly moving them from a bowling alley, to bed, to the museum, collapsing any distinctions between high and low culture, normal life and art.

In the museum, Paul uses language in a way that is deeply Cavellian: through telling he tallies what counts for him. Bored and distracted as Paul looks at a painting of ruins by Hubert Robert, which he "loves," Esther offhandedly asks him if he thinks it looks like her. The question doesn't make much sense in relation to this landscape, *Terrasse d'un palais à Rome*. But she playfully insists that his love for her and his love for the painting must find something common to both her and the painting. So he proceeds to analyze the painting, finding a red that reminds him of her lips. The presence of ruins also reminds him of how he has been ravaged by Esther herself. Paul is inventing and multiplying connections as he goes along. The scene ends with a two-shot of the couple, face to face, standing in front of the painting whose frame now lies outside of the shot's frame: they have been taken out of their world and wholly integrated into the world of the painting that Paul has been describing. Paul concludes the analysis by saying that Esther's face "contain all the meaning of the world."

At the same time, this scene shows how indulging in this kind of meaning-making is risky business in the face of skepticism. Does Esther really resemble this landscape? The way he invents this interpretation on the go suggests that a good deal of what he is saying is exaggerated, and not even Esther seems entirely duped. Beyond their own doubts, showing us this and all of their other interactions through the prism of memory only exacerbates our penchant toward skepticism. However, by what criteria could we judge if Paul's words are true? They seem to be true for him, or even to *become* true as he speaks. In *The Claim of Reason* Cavell argued that Wittgenstein's appeal to criteria "is not, and is not meant to be, a refutation of skepticism."[28] The point of Wittgenstein's shifting of the debate is simply that "our relation to the world as a whole, or to others in general, is not one of knowing, where knowing construes itself as being certain."[29] By establishing criteria, one "makes the process of judging more convenient, more open, less private or arbitrary. One might say: here establishing criteria allows us to *settle* judgments publicly—not exactly by making them certain, but by declaring what the points are at issue in various judgments, and then making them *final* (on a given occasion). That is a practice worth having; human decisions cannot wait upon certainty."[30] Paul's speech is a way of publicly stating *his* criteria and making his decision. This praise is certainly more interesting than the academic and "knowledgeable" description of a painting Paul heard during his tour of the museum in Minsk—the precise moment that the boys left the group to do something riskier and more valuable. Esther ends the scene by telling him he is a "beau parleur," a "smooth talker" as the subtitles translate the expression, but also a speaker of beauty, and later she will quote Plato to tell him that he is "gifted in discourse."

The interaction between the actors and the words they speak is at the heart of Desplechin's sensitive and innovative direction. In *The World Viewed*, Cavell was struck by how the automatism of photographic reproduction structures the work of the actor in relation to the role in a way different from the theater: "for the screen, the actor takes the role onto himself."[31] He adds: "the film performer explores his role like an attic and takes stock of his physical and temperamental endowment; lends his being to the role and accepts only what fits; the rest in nonexistent."[32] In Desplechin's very talkative cinema, this is more than anywhere a question of the relation between the body (the physical endowments and shape of the actor) and the dialogue. Amalric, as Élise Domenach has pointed out, is at times filmed as a kind of burlesque character, and his body is often shown as frail (he smokes constantly and has somewhat yellow teeth) but is also highly intelligent, eloquent, and seductive.[33] In *Three Memories*, Desplechin works with much younger, less experienced actors playing adolescent characters. Schematically, these actors move between their bodies (nude, emotive, suffering, dancing, touching, making love) and their discourses. The challenge of acting and directing action consists here, in great part, in making these bodies speak about love, sex, and emotions in a highly sophisticated way without the appearance of ridicule. Their bodies are being stretched out toward their words. Like Baudelaire's dandy (perhaps a reference acknowledged in the lycée's name), another important figure in *The World Viewed*, they have a burning need to turn their lives into art.

One of the most compelling ways in which Desplechin overlays their bodies with discourse is in the imaginative and refined use of the genre of the epistolary novel. In close-up images superimposed over images of Paul in a café, or playing pinball, we see the tip of his pen touching the paper as he writes, and we hear him or Esther in voiceover reading the words of a letter at the same time, linking body, action, and discourse, sound, and image. In another scene Paul sits on the floor of a public bathroom, smoking a cigarette, while we hear his voice reading a letter to Esther in which he meditates on his guilt. The epistolary form inspires Desplechin to push form in one very original direction that one could call moving or speaking portraiture, a form in which the actors' bodies and words become mutually defining. In one shot Esther stands in a lovely garden, the trees in bloom surrounding her (evoking the "Arcadia" of Desplechin's working title), "telling" her letter to Paul while looking directly at the camera. Later we cut to Esther's room as she writes while declaiming what her pen puts down on paper. We see her from behind, but there is a mirror in front of her in which we see her face clearly. The room contains the trappings of a sixteen-year-old girl, but also much natural light, and through her window the leafy trees that evoke again Arcadia. Esther lifts her eyes from her letter and looks into the mirror, her image looking directly at the camera, which is tracking in more and more closely on her reflected face. She then turns directly toward the camera as she speaks her last sentence. Such effects contribute to the sense of dream or pastness, of unreality, but also to how the characters become through language. In a later letter Esther captures their sense of displacement from commonplace through constant emotion: "I have gas in my head and my eyes are always swollen." But she also captures their ultimate transformation into discourse: "In my head I am writing to you all the time."[34] There is, in these scenes, a mutual self-creation by producing words for the other, captured in epistolarity and expressed for the viewer through film style.

Esther's Thread

And yet this story of love ends with the two separating. For many years, Paul has fled the responsibility to make sense of these memories, until another event takes place that makes him confront them in a fundamental way: the arrival of a letter from his friend, Kovalki, who asks for Esther's address. This letter sends Paul back into the labyrinth. Even before he opens the letter, we see his childhood self reappear, like a ghost, a manifestation of his old anger coming back. We then see him in a dark, cave-like room, not recognizably anywhere, surrounded by envelopes, bundles of paper, and old notebooks: his correspondence with Esther, which he has just reread. As he begins a response to Kovalki, he looks directly at the camera, again a moving, speaking portrait, trying to convey in words the meaning of his experience.

If Paul is returning to this exacerbated doubt, it is because Kovalki's letter has devastating implications for the meaning of his relationship with Esther. To see why, we have to understand a little more about Kovalki. Kovalki was Paul's friend, but, at the same time, he has always been a bit cold, conformist, and mindlessly ambitious. He had also profited from Paul's absences to manipulate Esther into sleeping with him (as did Paul's cousin Bob and friend, Penelope). Paul does not finish the letter to Kovalki, but several months later bumps into Kovalki and his wife at a concert, where he has gone to hear a piece for voice and strings by Hugo Wolf. After the concert, they all go out for a drink. Kovalki's wife is significantly younger, a nurse (he probably met her at work) who has never heard of Tajikistan (or any of the other places Paul has worked), attractive, bubbly, and nice. With her Kovalki lives the life of a rich provincial, here in the city for a concert, by a composer whom he knows only because Paul had shared him many years earlier. His appearance has grown a little soft: he has a scruffy beard and looks a little paunchy. As they share a drink, Kovalki presses male complicity, even in front of his wife, to the point of alluding to the letter. In some ways he hasn't changed from the analytic medical student dissecting women, and who will "never know love" as Paul's sister, Delphine, had predicted.[35] In short, Kovalki manifests the bourgeois "tastelessness" of a world that Desplechin calls skepticism.

Paul's reaction is violent and verbose. His anger is understandable. If Kovalki is right, it throws everything into doubt: there was no particular unique value to Paul's love. Esther was just a girl, an attractive specimen to be traded between friends like a musical reference. If one had perhaps crossed some minor lines of morality, all of this was the distant past and can now be forgiven among real men. Paul's rejection of Kovalki is thus an assertion of the criteria by which he judges his past to have meaning: it is his way of affirming his own voice. He addresses Kovalki in this scene, at times looking at Kovalki's wife, but mainly he seems to be speaking for himself, articulating his judgment in a way that is "public" and "final" as Cavell puts it. Four times he uses the word "intact" to describe his "passion," "love," "sorrow," and "fury." He may not be able to prove the value of the past, but through these emotions he can count himself still in continuity with it: it is untouched, unsullied, and unbroken.

This provides the sense that Paul's love has given his life meaning *as a whole*, over time: walking out of the bar into the night he crosses a bridge over the Seine when the wind picks up and blows pages of a book toward him. He picks up a page to find it is (implausibly, or perhaps oneirically) from Plato's *Apology*, in Greek. The settling of accounts with Kovalki has indicated Paul's decision to think once and for all for himself, against conformity and opinion, in continuity with his youth, like Socrates. Stylistically this last part of the film emphasizes editing and sound techniques that weave different scenes from different periods into a whole: music or voice tracks linking visual tracks of different temporal or physical spaces. This suggests a cohesiveness that has now been found to the memories that before were disconnected, simply counted rather than counting in an integral way as they do now.[36]

A more sensitive issue is the status of Esther herself. One could be forgiven for thinking that Paul's sense of self comes at the price of effacing Esther and *her* voice. Desplechin has himself called his character misogynistic (especially in *Comment je me suis disputé*). At the same time, the final scenes of the film tie many of the open threads of the film together in a way that acknowledges Paul's debt to Esther. It must be remembered that many of Paul's struggles in becoming an anthropologist were due to his not having studied Greek: his beloved professor almost refused him as a student because of this. It should also be kept in mind that Greek evokes more "primitive" man, the myth, the labyrinth, and the hero. But it was Esther who taught Paul Greek so that he could pass his translation exam. The same Greek also helped him recognize the *Apology* at the end of the film, the one that confirmed him in his nonconformism. In his story, Paul acknowledges his debt to Esther, but also goes beyond. The last scene is another flashback: the two are nude, in bed, and Esther teaches him the Greek that she knows, and that he does not. While doing so, she teaches him, or is at the origin, of several relevant lessons for how the film plays out. First, she translates a passage from the *Apology* against skepticism: "I think the Gods exist, I am not an atheist." She then teaches him the importance of words, "Phaedra, you are divine concerning discourse." Finally, from the *Odyssey*, she teaches the importance of childhood, or we could say memory (the memories) of youth: "O Children where are you now?" In short, the thread of discourse (and thus the central ideas that have guided Paul's life, misogynist or not) comes from Esther. The film in fact ends, in part in homage, on a freeze-frame of Esther's face as she looks, once again, directly into the camera. She may not be in a state of becoming, but she is remembered.

This flashback acknowledges that the relationship and the shared conversation with Esther give consistency to Paul's trust in his own body and its place in the world. During their conversation, he reveals to her that he has given his identity away to someone else (see his earlier recollection). She is surprised, but somewhat teasingly kisses him, closing her eyes to better taste the kiss, and verifies that he is indeed the real Paul Daedalus. To the "life is strange" with which Paul concluded his interrogation scene, this scene replies with an assurance that he is who he is. Falling in love allows him to close his eyes to skepticism, allows the world to take on consistency for him. The senses do not become guarantees; but, filled with the discursive meanings that come from his love for Esther, they do create trust, through taste, in the world.

Praise as Critical Practice

In the Epilogue, Desplechin as much as sends the viewer to fiction as a warehouse of forms: popular genres, high literature, and Greek philosophy all provide situations, forms, ideas, characters, models, moral values—criteria—that we can use as we articulate our own voice and develop our own forms of trust in the world. Paul criticizes Kovalki's blasé treatment of Esther as replaceable and his betrayal of Paul by accusing him of violating all of the "moral codes" of "popular cinema," by which he means melodrama, western, and *policier* films. (Blame here is the inverse of praise; it serves the same function in that it enables Paul to develop his own voice and affirm what he judges to be worthy of affirmation.) Kovalki does not seem able to praise: he can judge women as physical specimens (or as bourgeois trophy wives) and sees his friends as a source of pleasure (providing a tip of this rare composer, or a path toward that girl's address). But he is incapable of applying the criteria that Paul has adopted from the cinema: without this vitality, he lives a tasteless, empty life (from Paul's point of view).

The moment that Paul praises the cinema is one of the few in which the dialogue seems slightly artificial: the stretch between the Amalric's body and the words he speaks is tested a little, as if Desplechin were sending a message about the movies directly to the viewer through the dialogue. The moment sits on the artificial end of a realist spectrum, along with, in their own way, the passages during which characters fix their gaze directly at the camera (and viewer) while reading their letters. These moments are disconcerting, even if the actors do not address the viewer directly, as, say, in a Godard film (when Belmondo or Anna Karina talk to the audience in *Pierrot le fou*, for instance). These scenes, we have argued, come at moments when the characters use language (often writing) to articulate their acknowledgment of the other. The viewer has one foot inside the film; the character one foot outside: the words become public, open to general sharing.

This openness toward the viewer as a meaning-making individual, so characteristic of Desplechin's cinema, may be his cinematic response to philosophical skepticism. During the conversation moderated by Laugier, Cavell supplies an illustration of the kind of criticism Desplechin prefers in an interpretation of *O Brother, Where Art Thou?*. Cavell's reading, according to Desplechin, begins with a set of questions aimed at the relationship between viewer and film: "how do films affect me?"; and how do they have meaning for "my intimate self?" ("dans mon intimité").[37] Cavell's approach to interpretation is to enter into and attend to the film, and then use language to draw meaning out of it. Desplechin calls this the "unfurling of a film."[38] While working through a film the viewer opens a "box of meaning" by which he or she develops discourses in an effort to overcome various forms of skepticism. The self-commentary of Desplechin's characters; their interpretations of music or art; the multiple and superimposed layers of images and sounds; the constant references to myth and literature: all of these are doorways for the viewer, invitations to unfurl and explore the innumerable ways in which a dark and doubtful world still counts.

Notes

1 Stanley Cavell and Arnaud Desplechin, "Pourquoi les films comptent-il?" *Esprit* 347, nos. 8 and 9 (2008): 208–19.

2 Desplechin's interest for Cavell takes place within a broader, intensifying interest in Cavell in France, where Cavell has become arguably the most influential non-French film philosopher. *Pursuits of Happiness* was translated into French in 1993 (the same year as *Disowning Knowledge* and *Conditions Handsome and Unhandsome*), *The Claim of Reason* in 1996, *The World Viewed* in 1999, a collection of essays on cinema under title *Le cinéma nous rend-il meilleur* in 2010, and *Contesting Tears* in 2012. Cavell has benefited from a number of particularly talented and sensitive critics, translators, and philosophers who have fostered the exchange of his work into France (most notably Sandra Laugier and Élise Domenach). As well as a broad lectorate, including Desplechin, who was influenced by *Pursuits of Happiness* while filming *My Sex Life . . . or How I Got Into an Argument* (*Comment je me suis disputé . . . [ma vie sexuelle]*, 1996). Subsequently he has read Cavell broadly, in particular, *The World Viewed* and *Disowning Knowledge*. For Cavell on the cinema, in French, see Élise Domenach, *Stanley Cavell, le cinéma et le scepticisme* (Paris: Presses Universitaires de France, 2011).

3 *My Golden Days*, the English title of the film, captures well Desplechin's working title, *Nos Arcadies*, and some of the film's deep themes. I, however, will directly translate the French title, *Three Memories of My Youth* [abbreviated to *Three Memories*], which better captures the Cavellian theme of "counting."

4   Josef Früchtl, *Trust in the World: A Philosophy of Film* (New York: Routledge, 2018), 11.
5   Ibid.
6   André Bazin, "The Ontology of the Photographic Image," in *What Is Cinema? Volume 1*, trans. Hugh Gray (Berkeley: University of California Press, 1967), 12.
7   Stanley Cavell, *The World Viewed: Reflections on the Ontology of Film*, Enlarged Edition (Cambridge: Harvard University Press, 1979), 23.
8   Ibid., 41.
9   Quoted in Philipp Schmerheim, *Skepticism Films: Knowing and Doubting the World in Contemporary Cinema* (London: Bloomsbury Press, 2015), 86.
10 Edward Mooney, "Acknowledgement, Suffering, and Praise: Stanley Cavell as Religious Continental Thinker," *Soundings: An Interdisciplinary Journal* 88, nos. 3 and 4 (2005): 404.
11 Ibid., 396.
12 Ibid., 404.
13 Domenach also places Desplechin in a perfectionist tradition. Élise Domenach, "*Un conte de noël*. La nouvelle Arcadie d'Arnaud Desplechin," *Esprit* 347, nos. 8 and 9 (2008): 195f.
14 Cavell and Desplechin, "Pourquoi les films comptent-il?" 210.
15 Ibid., 209. Cavell makes a similar point in *The World Viewed* (7), in which he embraces *auteur* theory's acknowledgment of the director, but only partially, while still reading film through genre.
16 Früchtl, *Trust in the World*, 148–49.
17 Cavell and Desplechin, "Pourquoi les films comptent-il?" 211.
18 Ibid., 211.
19 Früchtl, *Trust in the World*, 153.
20 Ibid., 160.
21 This elitism is less attributable to Bazin than to the post-New-Wave *Cahiers*, the period of high theory, during which appeals to ordinary experience, or to popular filmmaking, were frequently considered to be structured by unconscious ideological presuppositions.
22 Cavell and Desplechin, "Pourquoi les films comptent-il?" 218. Note in passing the title of another Desplechin film, *Kings and Queens*.
23 Synopsis: The film's title refers to three memories of youth, but the film is divided into five parts: a prologue, a section devoted to each "memory," and an epilogue. The prologue and the epilogue are set in the present, making the film about the relation between past in present. The memories dominate screen time.

Prologue: Paul Daedalus is in Tajikistan, in bed with his Russian colleague, a blonde who physically evokes the woman, Esther, whom we will get to know quite well. He is about to return from many years spent in exotic locations in the East to take a job in the Ministry of Foreign Affairs in France. The return reminds him of a period of his childhood, his first memory.

First memory: Paul's mother suffers from madness and threatens to kill him on the household stairs while he protects his younger brother and sister from her. He leaves home to live with his great-aunt, an émigré from White Russia, who shares her life with her lover, another older Russian woman. Paul also defends his brother who has stolen and destroyed a classmate's bicycle. His mother dies, and his depressed father strikes him in the face because of bad grades.

Second memory: In the ministry, Paul is convoked and interrogated in a dark basement. The government has discovered another Paul Daedalus, born on the same date and time as Paul, living in Australia until his recent death. The existence of this double shakes Paul's self-assurance; it has been many years since he thought of this second Paul. Through flashbacks, he tells the story of a school trip to Minsk that he made with his friend Zylberberg, and during which he smuggled money to Jewish refuseniks who were oppressed by the Soviet state. Paul went a step further, giving his passport to another man and faking a mugging to explain their absence from the school group.

Third memory: The end of the interrogation transitions to the third memory, the longest section of the film, during which Paul (19) falls in love with Esther (16). This section follows their tempestuous affair from beginning to end. During the same period, Paul has become a student of anthropology in Paris. The geographic separation between him and Esther leads to conflict in their relationship. It also forces them to write letters to each other.

Epilogue: Many years later, in the present, Paul's former friend Kovalki writes to ask for Esther's address (Kovalki had betrayed Paul by taking advantage of Esther's desperation during his absences), prompting Paul to reread old letters from Esther. Paul bumps into Kovalki and his wife, who have come to Paris for the weekend, at a concert. Kovalki refers to Esther, and Paul makes a violent scene; his love for Esther and his indignation are "intact." The film ends on a brief return to a memory of Esther teaching Paul Greek to prepare him for in his anthropology program.

24 Gaston Bachelard, *La terre et les rêveries du repos. Essai sur les images de l'intimité* (Paris: José Corti, 1948), 215.
25 Stanley Cavell, *Disowning Knowledge in Seven Plays of Shakespeare* (Cambridge: Harvard University Press, 2003): 205. See Domenach for a lovely Cavellian analysis of this film.
26 Ibid., 205.
27 Bachelard, *La terre et les rêveries du repos*, 215.
28 Cavell, *The Claim of Reason: Wittgenstein, Skepticism, Morality, and Tragedy* (Oxford: Oxford University Press, 1979, 1999), 45.
29 Ibid., 31.
30 Ibid.
31 Cavell, *The World Viewed*, 27.
32 Ibid., 28.

33 Domenach, "*Un conte de noël*," 202.

34 Desplechin is a painter of portraits, but also of representational interiors that resemble landscape paintings. The tapestry of the labyrinth appears on a wall in the background. Paul's bedroom as a child has panoramic wallpaper that depicts a far-Eastern scene, a bay or sea, with junks and larger vessels and people dressed in traditional garb. Esther's backgrounds have windows showing trees, but even the wallpaper in front of which she is filmed has a leafy, flowery pattern. Décor shows out as meaning on screen; the walls themselves become film-like unfoldings of narrative settings into which the characters are incorporated.

35 I take advantage of this reference to Delphine to mention that she also refers to Greek myth, in this case Delphi and the truth-telling oracle. In another oracular moment Delphine explains that Paul's study of "anthropology" is in fact his way of "studying himself." Anthropology, then, is not a disinterested application of scientific tools to human kinship relations, but a discovery of self as much as the cinema or literature. This is true as well of the fascinating inclusion of an anthropological film of "land divers" of the Pentecost island of Vanuatu, a scene I do not have space to analyze here, but which presents numerous parallels to Paul's self-narrative.

36 This meaning is not indubitable. Paul's love is filled with imperfection, even suffering. It may be open for debate whether pain can indeed be essential to what it is to be a fully flourishing version of a person. However, Paul himself has determined that the pain his decisions have caused has been outweighed by what he has received in living and loving in the way he has chosen. A line of dialogue comes back in each memory—when his father hits him because of bad grades, when he throws himself against the wall in Minsk, and after Esther's former boyfriends beat him up: "I didn't feel a thing." One might debate how successful his affair has been, but he has found it, himself, to have made him a better person, but perfectionism must make room for vulnerability.

37 Cavell and Desplechin, "Pourquoi les films comptent-il?" 217.

38 Ibid.

PART III

Rethinking Remarriage

6

Morality and Recognition

A Cavellian Reading of Elaine May's *A New Leaf*

PAUL SCHOFIELD

[C]onversation, while it means talk, means at the same time a way of life together.
—STANLEY CAVELL, *Cities of Words*[1]

Marriage? You mean to a woman? Oh, I can't, Harold. I couldn't. I mean, she'd be there, asking me where I've been, talking to me ... talking.
—HENRY GRAHAM, *A New Leaf*

Introduction

IN HIS *PURSUITS OF HAPPINESS* and *Cities of Words*, Stanley Cavell famously engages with a number of romantic comedies from the 1930s and 1940s, which he says belong to a genre called the comedy of remarriage. With its focus on an unlikely couple, its screwball sensibility, and its concern with the transformative power of friendship and marriage, it is natural to think of Elaine May's 1971 unheralded masterpiece *A New Leaf* as being in conversation with films like *It Happened One Night* (1934, dir. Frank Capra), *The Philadelphia Story* (1940, dir. George Cukor), and *The Lady Eve* (1941, dir. Preston Sturges), whether or not it technically qualifies as a member of the genre.[2] My purpose in this chapter is to consider the contribution that the film makes to the philosophical discussion Cavell sees playing out in these earlier romantic films.

While few would deny the ingenuity and influence of Cavell's work on these films, there nevertheless exists significant scholarly disagreement over which elements are most important or most essential to his readings. To avoid becoming bogged down in these disputes, I shall simply stipulate that my interpretation of *A New Leaf* will be inspired by Cavell in three important respects. First, it is Cavell's view that comedies of remarriage explore and advocate for a particular moral outlook that he terms "perfectionism." While the utilitarian outlook presents a method for calculating which actions are good and Kantianism supplies a universal principle of right action, Cavell says that perfectionism "proposes confrontation and conversation as the means of determining whether we can live together, accept one another into the aspirations of our lives."[3] The idea, I think, is that rather than focusing upon how to solve discrete ethical problems in ways that respect principles of rationality set forth by a theory, these films take as primary ethical questions like "How shall I live my life?" "What possibilities are open to me going forward as I attempt live in community with others?" and "How might my choosing to live one way rather than another transform my very being?" Their outlook, Cavell seems to me to be saying, is in the vicinity of Bernard Williams, when he complains that modern moral philosophy focuses on questions about the rightness or wrongness of momentary acts, to the exclusion of larger questions about how to live a good life over time.[4]

Second, Cavell believes that each of these comedies uses marriage as a metaphor for the kind of relationship—friendship—or fusing together of lives that makes for a new and better way of being. For instance, he says that *The Philadelphia Story* understands marriage as a vision of America's "dedication to a more perfect union, toward the perfected human community, its right to the pursuit of happiness."[5] Or, as he explains it elsewhere, the marriage relationship is a "study of the conditions under which [the] fight for recognition [. . .] or demand for acknowledgement [. . .] is a struggle for mutual freedom."[6] The idea being that the pair in the film faces the prospect of coming together in a form of community that holds open the possibility of their living in a way superior to the way they lived before. Importantly for Cavell, this necessitates a metamorphosis on the part of the characters—a change in their character, dispositions, and needs. And the nature of this transformation is among the primary philosophical interests of these films, he thinks.

Third, Cavell commits himself to the idea that the films themselves do philosophy. That is, instead of understanding them simply as fodder for philosophical discussion, or as raw material upon which we might go to work applying philosophical theories developed independently of them, the films are allowed to set their own agendas and to attempt to answer the questions that they themselves raise. Rather than having to answer to philosophy, then, the films themselves are understood as works of philosophy with the capacity to tell us how they are to be read.[7] Films themselves—like books and journal articles—can be philosophy. Philosophy can be screened.[8]

My reading of *A New Leaf* will be Cavellian primarily in these three respects. I shall argue that the film is interested in perfectionism of the sort to which Cavell calls our attention, and that it has something to say about what a perfectionist approach to ethics—as opposed to modern moral approach such as Kantianism and utilitarianism—might look like. I shall also argue that the film explores an important transformation of desire and need on the part of its male lead in particular, accomplished through the joining together of himself with another person for the purpose of mutual activity and a shared way of life. Finally, I hope to emphasize ways in which the film advances its own philosophical position, going beyond or departing from the films to which Cavell gives his attention, while nevertheless remaining in conversation with them. Its philosophical position, I argue, is that there exists a relationship of a special sort between the perfectionist approach discussed by Cavell and the more traditionally moral views with which he contrasts it. *A New Leaf*, as I understand it, attempts to show us that the issues that most concern the perfectionist are actually foundational to, or are at the root of, morality. This all will become more clear as I proceed, hopefully.

A New Leaf

The film's opening introduces us to Henry Graham (Walter Matthau), a patrician born into a wealthy family, who's managed to run through his entire trust fund—spending it on cars, art, fine wine, and horseback riding, among other things. Broke and unable to maintain the lifestyle to which he has become accustomed, he considers suicide to be his only option. Henry's butler—worried primarily that he'll soon be out of a job—suggests to Henry that he solve his problems instead by finding a wealthy woman to marry, as marriage "[i]s the only way to acquire property without labor." Henry adopts the butler's idea, but somewhat casually adds his own spin: he'll ultimately murder whatever woman he finds to marry him. So after taking out a large loan from his uncle, which needs to be repaid in short order, Henry sets out to find a wealthy woman to marry.

After a few abortive attempts to couple with women of means, and with the deadline to repay his uncle bearing down, Henry finally lays his eyes on Henrietta Lowell (Elaine May)—a painfully awkward and clumsy botanist, who's inherited a fortune from her deceased father. Henrietta is, in many ways, the antithesis of Henry. Whereas Henry is tidy, well dressed, and has a taste for the finer things, Henrietta is messy, unrefined, and has terrible taste—her drink of choice is "Mogen David's extra-heavy Malaga wine with soda and lime juice." And whereas Henry wants nothing more than to do nothing at all, Henrietta is genuinely driven by her work as a botanist, specifically her hope to discover a new species of fern. The differences between them are a source of genuine disgust for Henry. "Never have I seen one woman in whom every social grace was so lacking," he says after an evening with her. "Did I say she was primitive? I retract that. She's feral. I've never spent a more physically destructive evening in my life. I am nauseated . . . I will taste those damn Malaga coolers forever." Yet, she is moneyed and oblivious. And so "Perfect!" as far as Henry is concerned.

From the beginning, Henry stands up for and looks out for Henrietta—irritating though he finds her. When she's scolded by the haughty hostess of a fancy dinner party for spilling her tea on the carpet, Henry chivalrously empties his red wine onto the floor and declares: "Take your damn carpet to the cleaners and send the bill to me!" He cleans up the crumbs and morsels of food that she leaves on her face and clothes. And before long Henry gets down on one knee to propose marriage—accidentally crushing a glass while he does so, but nevertheless managing to declare, "I would kneel on anything for you Henrietta." Of course, it's all a ruse. Henry's actions are intended to give an impression rather than to evince actual concern for Henrietta as a person, and his words are meant to manipulate rather than to address her. Nevertheless, the ruse succeeds. She falls for him and accepts his proposal.

Upon learning the news of the impending marriage, Henrietta's lawyer is beside himself, as he's been pilfering from her trust fund and recognizes that this might be the end of the gravy train. Along similar lines, after the wedding Henry moves into Henrietta's home only to discover a house staff that is robbing her with abandon. He angrily dismisses them, along with the lawyer. Now Henry begins planning the murder in earnest, reading extensively about toxicology, trying to secure the proper poisons, and so on. In the meantime, Henrietta discovers a new type of fern and discloses to Henry that she has named it for him, and he is unexpectedly moved by the sentiment.

As things progress, Henry finds himself to be an able guardian for the scattered and absentminded Henrietta—a role that requires more practical life skill and care than we'd previously imagined him capable of. The couple eventually agrees to go on a research expedition together in the wild, and Henry—having had significant difficulty securing the poisons he needs to finish off the bride who he's become increasingly protective of—finally sees this as his chance to do away with Henrietta. (Perhaps she'll be attacked by wolves, or can be fed to a bear!) While traveling down a river in a canoe, they flip in the harsh rapids. Henry makes it to shore safely, but Henrietta doesn't and is left holding on to a branch. Henry takes a few steps away from the water, leaving her there to drown. But upon seeing a specimen of the fern that Henrietta has named for him, and turning to point it out to her only to remember that she is not there, he realizes he cannot go through with the plan. He returns to save her—somewhat surprised and even annoyed with himself. At this juncture, the two agree that Henry will take up a job teaching history at the school where Henrietta works, and that they will go to work together every day and sit in the study together at night grading papers.

Amorality and a Failure of Recognition: Two Practical Failures

As mentioned in the introduction, Cavell believes the comedies of remarriage orient us toward a particular conception of ethical inquiry. Moral dilemmas and moral "issues" are largely absent from these films—to put it as Cavell does, the concerns at the forefront of films like *Its Happened One Night* or *The Awful Truth* are "typically not front-page news, not, for example, issues like abortion, euthanasia, capital punishment, whistle-blowing, plagiarism, informing, bribery, greed."[9] And so the moral theories that most clearly address themselves to such issues—Kantianism and utilitarianism, says Cavell—are forced to take a backseat. In their place, we are presented with cases that are perhaps more humdrum, in which a pair is "deciding on what kinds of lives they wish to live and whether they wish to live them together, to consent to each other, to say yes to their lives and to their life together."[10] And so the films inspire us to reflect on the process of living out a life with others, and on the way in which this gets negotiated, rather than on the permissibility of discrete choices.

So here we might notice right away a respect in which *A New Leaf* departs from Cavell's principal films. For something like "front-page news," to use Cavell's phrase, is front and center. This is the story of a man who marries a woman for personal gain with the intention of murdering her, thus immersing us not simply in questions about what is the best life to lead, but in issues surrounding blatant failures to conform to morality's requirements. And I see no reason to think that this immorality is incidental or beside the point. Indeed, much of the film's black humor derives from the fact that Henry Graham (Walter Matthau) so quickly and thoughtlessly moves to flout what we would all consider to be the most stringent and obvious of moral demands: notice how seamlessly he moves from the troubling idea that he will marry a woman to get his hands on her money to the awful conclusion that he will do away with her so he doesn't have to talk to her. *A New Leaf*, we have said, is a film made with these older romantic films in mind, and so the unexpected inclusion of this "front-page" moral element should inspire curiosity about what the film is up to. This is a point to which I shall return toward the end of the chapter.

Beyond his heinous moral failings, Henry exhibits the more humdrum practical failure of failing to *recognize* or *acknowledge* others. It is the kind of practical failure that concerns us in *The Lady Eve*, when Jean (Barbara Stanwyck) seduces Charles (Henry Fonda) in hopes of eventually beating him at cards, or early in *It Happened One Night* when we wonder whether Peter (Clark Gable) is coming to Ellie's (Claudette Colbert) aid only so that he can publish a story of her having fled her father (Page Six news, rather than front page, we might say). Roughly, the issue is that Henry lives in a world in which others exist as obstacles around which he must plan or scheme, rather than a world occupied by persons with whom he might enter into a relationship based upon concern and respect—his way of living is one in which others *fail to register*. For instance, Henry's longtime financial adviser seems not even exist for him as a being to whom Henry might relate person-to-person: upon learning that he's paid $550 of Henry's bills out of his own pocket, Henry immediately responds, "May I say that if you expected even the smallest amount of gratitude, you have wasted $550." And when his butler announces that he will have to resign if Henry has no money to pay him, it never occurs to Henry to ask him how he will fare without the job. Consider also the quotation that served as the second epigraph for this chapter—the one in which Henry explains that he doesn't want to be married because people who are married have to talk to one another. It is a telling admission, because as Cavell emphasizes in the first epigraph, talking and conversation is a way we humans share our lives together. Talking involves not simply trying to manipulate or influence someone. Rather, it involves *recognizing* and *addressing* them. And this is something that is not only mystifying to Henry, but something he finds positively grotesque.

The central example of Henry's inability to recognize others, though, is, of course, Henrietta Lowell (Elaine May). At least, that is our point of departure in the film. For as he lays eyes on her for the first time, and announces that she's "Perfect!" we are meant to laugh at the utter crudity of the sentiment. Rather than seeing someone from across the room and being struck by her charm, her beauty, her wit, her grace—or just by *her*—what inspires his assessment of her as perfect is her availability and vulnerability to be used as a resource. Indeed, as we progress through the film, much of the humor is grounded in Henry's egregious unwillingness to see Henrietta's needs, interests, and goals as actually counting for something on account of *her* counting for something. Awkward though she is, Henrietta is characterized as a relentlessly sweet person with a caring disposition and admirable goals, whose humanity is consistently on display. And her moments of humanity are often met by Henry with his muttering something under his breath about her impending demise—the dark joke consisting in his inability to recognize the humanity that is so glaringly obvious to us.

Here I wish to focus a bit on the concept of recognition itself, for I think part of *A New Leaf*'s philosophical accomplishment is its clarification of the notion. There is, it is fair to say, a good amount of discussion of recognition over the course of philosophy's history, from Rousseau to Fichte to Hegel to Cavell.[11] The most comprehensive attempt to make sense of it in contemporary times, however, is found in the work of Stephen Darwall. Darwall originally identified a type of respect that he termed "recognition respect," which he understood to be grounded in the dignity or authority of persons.[12] Since then, his work has constituted a sustained attempt to understand the practical standpoint that makes recognition respect possible—what Darwall calls the "second-person standpoint."[13] As he characterizes it, his work is an attempt to think about "what exactly is involved in reciprocal recognition, and to think about its pervasiveness in human experience."[14]

But as it turns out, there is great difficulty in attempting even to specify the subject matter here. For someone can, of course, notice the existence of someone else, plan around their ends, use their interests to incentivize them—all in ways that do not involve recognition of the sort Darwall has in mind. So what are we talking about when we talk of recognition? While one might suspect that what's called for here is simply a clearheaded piece of philosophical analysis, Darwall's view is that there is no proper definition or analysis in the offing. This is, he thinks, because there exists no way of reducing second-personal notions related to recognition and respect to ideas that are not themselves second-personal. What we have is "a circle of irreducibly second-personal concepts," all inter-defined. So what we find is Darwall attempting to bring his audience into the topic through metaphor and illustration. He tells us, for instance, that we are talking from the second-person standpoint when we *stand* somewhere and demand acknowledgment of rights, and he writes about the difficulty of gaining recognition when you cannot *look someone in the eyes*.[15] But the written word, one suspects, is limited in its ability to carry out this task of getting us inside the circle of concepts. Perhaps, then, film is a place to which we might turn, for the medium has unique resources with which to depict modes of interpersonal relating: it has the advantage of being able to *show us* what it is for one person to register another in the right sort of way, or to allow us to watch people talking to one another in the sort of way that constitutes genuine second-personal address.

And indeed, I believe that elaborate depiction of second-personal address—of recognition, of acknowledgment, and so on—is at the very heart of *A New Leaf*. Matthau's performance as Henry in particular constitutes an acute and insightful take on what it looks like for someone to navigate the world without second-personally registering the presence of others. We can observe, for instance, the way in which Henry's attempts to talk with Henrietta really do not engage her at the level of her interests and passions at all, or invite her into a genuine sharing of ideas, but instead are mere counterfeit instances of such attempts, intended to manipulate her into falsely believing he has interests and curiosities that he does not. What is it to be a "counterfeit attempt"? This is something the film shows to us, I think.

> HENRY: I have been re-reading Gregor Mendel's fascinating experiments with garden peas. And it has struck me again how much we owe our understanding of plant genetics with all its myriad implications to that brilliant pioneer.
> HENRIETTA: Yes, but we mustn't forget Morgan and Muller. Morgan, Muller, and Mendel.
> HENRY: Who?
> HENRIETTA: Gregor Mendel, the man that you just mentioned. Morgan, Muller, and Mendel, I think are a perfect example of scientific synthesis. Errr . . . Doesn't it seem that to you?
> HENRY: No, it doesn't.

Whatever we might mean when we talk of addressing someone else, or conversing with someone else, in a way that recognizes and acknowledges them as worthy of respect or dignity or as possessing a kind of second-personal standing—well, it seems to be the thing that is noticeably absent in this exchange. Henrietta is treated, more or less, as a being to be manipulated—here, into thinking that Henry knows and cares about genetics—and as a being whose words can simply be dismissed. Or, to give another example, in the scene where the couple goes to dinner for the first time, we can watch Henry's face as he helps Henrietta up, brushes up the crumbs she has left on herself, and catches her as she stumbles. There, we do not see loving attention, genuine concern for her well-being, or affectionate focus on what she needs. Instead, we see a man who knows which motions he needs to go through in order to woo this woman. And importantly, his expression doesn't even seem to register her as a person to be held responsible for her gauche behavior and gracelessness, but instead suggests that he regards her as a sort of irritating force of nature—as we mentioned earlier, his ultimate assessment of her is that she is "feral."

Such moments are, however, usefully contrasted with those later on in the film where Henry's orientation toward Henrietta seems to shift ever so subtly. Consider the scene in which Henrietta arrives in the bedroom on the first night of their honeymoon adorned in what we are told is a "Grecian-style nightgown" that she has put on incorrectly (Henry: "Your head is through the armhole"). Henry and Henrietta then work together to correct the error. Now, to this point in the film, Henry has shown no interest in sex at all, though we get some sense that he is resigned himself to the possibility that physical intimacy might be required. And while we never see these two consummate the relationship, I think it is fair to say that we are to understand Henry's attempt to correct her nightgown as a kind of stand-in. At first we suspect, perhaps because we have been conditioned to, that he is simply disgusted by her awkwardness. But as he helps her adjust the nightgown in a clumsy bit of fumbling around—which, again, I think we are supposed to equate with the sexual act—we suddenly see glimmers of attentiveness and care. What could have been a mere irritating chore seems, at least for a moment, surprisingly tender. The ingredient we see in this scene, missing from the earlier dinner scene, is second-personal acknowledgment of the person in his company. Rather than attend to his scheme, he attends to *her*.

The genius of Matthau's performance, I think, is found in moments where he slowly begins to attend to Henrietta in a way that looks more genuinely second-personal without realizing that he is doing so. Of course, it is a romantic comedy trope that at least one member of a pair gradually undergoes a transformation in their relation to the other. This, however, is usually attended with some implicit awareness on the part of the transformee of what is going on. (Think, for instance, of Peter hovering over Ellie under the moonlight in *It Happened One Night*—can there be any doubt that he is aware her meaning for him has changed, even if he is not entirely glad about it?) In Henry's case, he seems relatively oblivious to the fact that he's thrown things into second-personal gear at all. So, we are presented with comic moments like the one where Henry expresses concern for Henrietta in a mundane but sweet way ("Oh, no. I forgot to check [Henrietta] before she went to school this morning. She'll be walking around all day with price tags dangling from her sleeves."), while he packs for a camping trip in which he plans to feed her to a bear, if the opportunity arises. Henry's two orientations toward Henrietta—a kind of self-personal concern alongside a willingness to see her as a dispensable resource to be mined or as an instrument to be used—obviously do not sit well together, which is part of the joke. But by depicting both orientations as residing inside Henry simultaneously, the film goes a long way toward spelling out or depicting the difference between genuine recognition of another and seeing someone else as a mere instrument. That is, we get a sense of what it is to be operating within the circle of second-personal concepts by watching a character enter and exit the circle repeatedly without noticing.

In addition to depicting this contrast in terms of an intrapersonal tension within Henry himself, the film represents it *inter*personally. When Henry and Henrietta announce their plans to wed, her lawyer—who has been overseeing her fortune—is beside himself. For he has been helping himself freely to her wealth, and now realizes someone else will be in the position to pilfer the money. So he disapproves of the marriage. Now, clearly we are meant to see this as a parody of the father–daughter relationship that plays such a prominent role in the early comedies of remarriage. In those films, the father is on alert, ensuring that his daughter is marrying a worthy partner, and the man's task is to prove himself. Here, the lawyer—who even steps into the role of giving Henrietta away in the ceremony—is really just protecting her *qua* financial asset. But when Henry eventually discovers that the lawyer is, along with various members of her household staff, bilking Henrietta out of her fortune, his tone and body language betray a sense of genuine resentment and anger on her behalf that goes beyond a simple concern for preserving the wealth he intends to steal. He confronts the staff not just to fire them, but to register his recognition of their misdeeds and to confront them. We sense that, whatever else Henry has up his sleeve, he is concerned *for her* about the way that she has been taken advantage of. In other words, he has begun to recognize her interests and her dignity as something that registers for him second-personally.

To conclude the section, I would like to raise the possibility that the film even invites the viewer, at times, to adopt Henry's outlook and thus to see Henrietta both from the point of view of someone who is protective of her *and* from the point of view of someone who views her as a mere instrument. Of course, we the audience are disposed from the get-go to empathize with Henrietta and to resent on her behalf the way she is treated. But there are moments in which the film's comedy might be thought to encourage us to "try on" Henry's point of view, so to speak. Consider the film's most famous gag, where Henry studies a toxicology textbook in the hopes of learning how to poison his new bride while she dangles on the edge of a cliff behind him trying to collect a fern. It is, perhaps, a moment where the viewer might catch herself thinking, "Come on, just turn around! Give her a nudge! Your problems will be solved!" That is, it is a moment where the audience member might come to attend to the special features of the second-person standpoint by noticing herself slipping out of it.

Transformation from Individual to Collective

Let us turn our attention now to what the film has to say about Henry's transformation from wanton egoist to a person capable of genuinely interpersonal recognition. Now, Cavell insists that a major preoccupation of the comedy of remarriage is transformation of a special kind. The transformation is not the sort in which a person comes into possession of an up-until-now elusive piece of ethical knowledge or a moral theory that she had previously not had. Rather, the point of Cavell's saying that these films are wedded to a variety of perfectionism is that he thinks they involve a transformation on the part of the characters with regard to their very being. The comedies of remarriage consider questions about, "what constitutes a union, what makes [two individuals] into one, what binds."[16] At one point, Cavell calls the change undergone by a character a kind of "metamorphosis."[17] And this metamorphosis is one in which happiness is achieved not through "the perennial and fuller satisfaction of our needs as they stand but [through] the examination and transformation of those needs."[18]

So let us consider the film's handling of these ideas. When we meet him early on, Henry is interested only in what he owns—what he *has*—and in his status as a wealthy patrician. Indeed, his identity seems to be wrapped up in this status, as he thinks that what makes him himself is what he *is* rather than what he *does*. It is acknowledged that this way of being sits uneasily in the modern America where the film is set. "You have managed in your own lifetime, Mr. Graham, to keep alive traditions that were dead before you were born," his butler remarks. If there is any doubt that this is what the film is saying, consider the way in which Henry's Ferrari can be understood as a metaphor for Henry himself. The Ferrari is introduced to us in the film's opening scene. It is established immediately that he admires the car because of what it is—for the status it has *qua* Ferrari; for its being a fine thing—despite the fact that it breaks down three times a week and therefore fails to perform its function. Never is there any indication, early on, that Henry himself wishes *to do anything*, or that his sense of worth is tied to any sort of functioning well. His way of existing in the world simply involves having a certain stature, just like his car.

Now, when the moment of crisis arrives, and Henry is about to lose everything, the only way he can see to go forward—the only plausible alternative to suicide—is to find an easy way to go on existing as he has, maintaining his status. The way forward, as he sees it, is to get more resources. But we know, given the genre we are working in, that the way out for Henry will involve transforming his need—transforming *himself*. The transformation occurs, more or less, as a result of his acting *as if* he is married. By acting as if he is attending to Henrietta, by acting as if he cares for her, by pretending he is her friend, by feigning interest in her words, by saying the things that someone in love would say, Henry undergoes a metamorphosis. He play-acts his way into a genuine union with another person.

Now, this idea that playacting has a role in generating a union is nothing new. Think, for instance, of the famous scene in *It Happened One Night* where Peter and Ellie pretend to be a married couple in an attempt to throw some detectives off their trail. This, obviously, is a moment of bonding for the pair—one in which they take a step in the direction of a union by pretending they are already in one. But whereas the traditional way that these stories go is that the members of the pair slowly, and perhaps a little bit grudgingly, come to admit to themselves and then to the other that the union is something they desire, Henry's case is a bit more complicated. As a result of the kind of split-personality that he has begun to exhibit, Henry seems at times both to be filling the role of loving husband *and* to be wholeheartedly set on killing Henrietta. Even in the tender moments, in other words, what he "really" wants is ambiguous.

The picture, here, is one that ultimately differs substantially from the one seen in the other comedies of remarriage. Cavell, after all, emphasizes the ways in which the perfectionist strain in these films leads ultimately to a certain amount of congruence that is gained in the internal ordering of the person's motivations and emotions, creating a sort of internal harmony. *A New Leaf*, on the other hand, emphasizes a stark internal divide in its protagonist and ultimately highlights the way in which Henry's recognition of Henrietta *compels* him into community with her. This is most evident in the final scene, where Henrietta is thrashing around in the river screaming for help and Henry begins running away to leave her to drown. But, spotting the fern—the one she has discovered and the one she has named for him—Henry is stopped mid-stride and is more or less dragged grudgingly by his thoughts about Henrietta back to the water where he saves her. Their exchange, once she has reached safety, confirms his ambivalence about things.

> HENRIETTA: Henry. Henry. Henry? I'll always be able to depend on you, won't I? All the rest of my life?
> HENRY: I'm afraid so.

It is almost as if Henry's recognition or acknowledgment of Henrietta compels him in the way that a categorical moral law might. What we get, then, is a less rosy view about what it is to acknowledge another person than we get in some of the other films. There is a darkness that comes with recognizing the other, we might say.

In what sense, then, is Henry transformed so that his way of living—or his way of *being*—will be different? In what sense has his need been transformed? The most profound way, I think, is that he is now capable of a form of activity or a way of life that was not previously available to him. What we learn is that Henry is now capable of engaging with people not simply to use them, but in concert with them. Consider the end of the film, where we see Henry canoeing with Henrietta—both going down the river, coordinating their rowing in a way paradigmatic of group activity. Or consider the closing moment where Henry agrees to begin teaching at Henrietta's school, and to go to work with her each day, and to grade papers at night alongside her. Engaging in genuine activity with another, in which the other is recognized as counting for something, is now a real possibility for Henry—something which seemed unthinkable at the film's outset. Of course, we see the transformation basically only in his behavior toward Henrietta. But we have to imagine that a whole new way of being is now available to him. He is now a being capable of community with one another—capable of acting *with* others. To stretch a little bit, perhaps, we can see this transformation as a moment that is Rousseauvian in spirit, in which a recognition of the other enables a person for the first time to join with others to act as a collective body.

Indeed, it seems as if this metamorphosis precipitates a change in Henry's fundamental needs as well. For by the end of the film, he seems compelled—by his own psychology—to enter into forms of activity with Henrietta. He needs to look after her, he feels pulled to canoe with her, he sees that he must settle into a life with her. Whatever needs are at play here, they were certainly absent at the film's beginning.

It is worth pointing out that *A New Leaf* presents us also with a very different sort of community that contrasts with the sort of small community Henry enters into with Henrietta. When we encounter the house staff living in Henrietta's home, there is a sense in which they are a mini-society, living together with a common purpose. The purpose, however, is simply individual benefit—there is no general will here. Each wants to take her piece of the pie, and the relative lack of scarcity means that there is little for them to dispute over. It is not a life in which people form community over mutual recognition and live a life of activity together. It is a community based on a modus vivendi, born of convenience, exhibiting only what Rousseau calls "the will of all." And if we are to think of the perfectionist project as one focused on the question of which ways of living are choice-worthy, we are given a model here of something that seems deficient. In Henry, however, we are given a demonstration of the sort of transformation that would be necessary in order for life under the general will to be possible.

Now, I have focused on Henry's transformation, and have said little about Henrietta. In a way, this is not particularly surprising, as Henry's journey is the narrative's most obvious focus—though we might complain that the film shortchanges Henrietta a bit. Still, it is worth concluding this section by considering where Henrietta begins in the film and how it differs from where she ends up. Throughout the film, Henrietta is depicted as sweet and sincere, smart and caring, and kind to a fault. She is absentminded in a way that makes her oblivious to the ways in which she is being used—by her lawyer, by the house staff, and by Henry. So we might expect her trajectory over the course of the film to be one in which she improves by becoming a little more savvy. But that is not where the film goes. The major change in Henrietta, I take it, is that by the end, things external to her have changed in a way likely to alter *her*. What I am suggesting is that once Henrietta is recognized by Henry, she becomes a potential partner—a participant in collective activity. Once the house staff is thrown out, she is no longer being used. The objective conditions of her life have changed in such a way that *her being itself* changes. No longer is she merely an object there simply to be planned around or used. She is, in fact, a person, and part of a larger collective body, acting together with her partner. This seems to occasion a change in the way she sees herself. Upon discovering the new species of fern, she says, "Henry, I don't think I could have ever discovered it without you. You gave me confidence. You remember? You said that if being with you was going to give me confidence, I was going to be a very confident botanist. Well, you were right!" Henrietta did not need to undergo a change that would allow her to recognize others second-personally. But part of what she needed, apparently, was to receive the regard of another. In fact, if one suspects—as I think is reasonable—that Henrietta was implicitly aware that she was being taken advantage of by her lawyer and by the house staff, then perhaps we can imagine that her newfound self-confidence will enable her to *demand* the second-personal respect from others that she had previously not received.

Morality and Recognition

I began this chapter by noting that Cavell presents perfectionism as an orientation toward ethical inquiry that serves as a kind of alternative to standard moral theories like utilitarianism and Kantianism. Perfectionism's focus, he says, is the more everyday concern about how to live and how to go forward in the world in concert with others, rather than the heady issues of right and wrong. It bears emphasizing that Cavell does not take a commitment to perfectionism to require a rejection of morality—he says that it is technically consistent with Kant and Mill, for instance.[19] It is possible, after all, to think that morality's laws get a real normative grip on us while also thinking that the most pressing of practical questions surround how to live together with others over time. Yet, it is pretty clear that Cavell thinks there is real a difference in emphasis here—with perfectionism drawing attention to some practical issues over others, perhaps with the thought that these issues *ought* to be prioritized. Thus, perfectionism is in some sense a rival to the other views. And the comedies of remarriage, Cavell says, are primarily concerned with the issues at the heart of perfectionism. I agree with Cavell about where the primary concerns of the films he considers lies. But toward the beginning of the chapter, I also pointed out a way in which *A New Leaf* appears to depart from those earlier films. Namely, the film raises the issue of traditional morality—the issue of front-page news—by placing a heinous plan of action at its center. What I want to suggest is that the film does so in a way that draws a connection between the two sorts of questions that seem to divide perfectionism and traditional moral theories—the question of right-and-wrong versus broader questions about how to live—and that this is a way in which the film makes a unique contribution to the philosophical discussion considered by Cavell.

According to Cavell, the comedies of remarriage are perfectionist in their orientation in part due to their focus on a particular moment in the life of an ethical agent—one in which a person confronts another, attempting to make herself intelligible, and provides a "justification of [her] moral standing."[20] It is a moment in which there is an attempt on the part of a person to gain recognition from another. But this moment "does not exist in utilitarianism," Cavell tells us, for within utilitarianism, "the individual does not exist."[21] Here I think he means that what exists, as far as the theory goes, is sensation, and that all moments of moral reflection surround production of pleasure rather than focus on persons and their standing. "Nor does [this moment] exist in Kant," Cavell continues, where one is confronted not by persons but by "the moral law alone."[22] By which he means, I think, that the Kantian believes we are accountable to moral rules rather than to persons. What I want to suggest is that this way of understanding the relationship between perfectionist concerns about acknowledgment and traditional utilitarian and Kantian concerns about morality is misguided, and that *A New Leaf* goes some way toward showing what is misguided about it. As I read it, the film does not portray issues of recognition and acknowledgment as ones that are absent from traditional moral theory. Rather, it suggests that living together in recognition of others is the beginning of, or the basis of, the ability to see morality's dictates as binding. To put this another way, to see someone else as making second-personal claims on one's feelings and actions constitutes the beginnings of morality, and to be unable to recognize the other is to be incapable of moral deliberation and action at all. Of course, such recognition is not *all there is* to morality, nor to moral theory. Kantianism and utilitarianism represent, I think, two different ways of developing this initial impulse to recognize the other.

To see how the film deals with this issue, consider what I referred to above as Henry's two practical failures. Conceptually, I distinguished between his immorality and his failure to recognize Henrietta. However, as it plays out in the film, it is not that Henry makes two distinct mistakes when he plots Henrietta's death: a failure to recognize her and a failure to recognize the moral law. Rather, the moral question never really arises for him because the sort of second-personal concerns that give rise to the moral impulse are simply absent in him. Try, at the beginning of the film, to talk Henry out of carrying out the deed by pointing to moral and rational strictures, and he will be unmoved. No amount of reasoning is going to reorient the man for whom others count for nothing. But one imagines that once he has undergone his transformation, references to the moral law might actually begin to register. We do not know, of course, as the film concludes without showing how exactly Henry's life proceeds into the future, but once he is capable of seeing others as potential friends and community-mates, it seems likely that moral concerns for others will begin to creep in. The moral question arises precisely when one begins to ask herself difficult questions about how to act in a world full of people who count, who are worthy of recognition, and who are potential collaborators and community-mates.

This is to suggest that the film pushes back in an important way against a central thought of Cavell's. Cavell seems to believe that the morally upright person, who respects the moral law and respects the constraints of rationality, does so *in lieu of* or *as an alternative to* or *in addition to* acting on what she owes to others. She acts for the sake of maximizing pleasure or for the sake of the law, but not for the sake of other people. But this is mistaken, I think. What Kant, for instance, thinks is required of us by the moral law is the recognition of others as ends in themselves. The reason why Henry can so breezily embrace a plan that flies in the face of the moral law is that he does not recognize others as ends in themselves. And when he does formulate the plan, what is wrong with it is not that it violates the moral law but that it fails to recognize Henrietta as a person. That is, his plan violates the moral law *in virtue of* its failure to recognize others. Our love for others, and the community that we build with them, seems in many ways to be an extension of the fundamental impulse to recognize another. Kant's kingdom of ends, in other words, will be a realm of universal recognition. Likewise, if we think about what the utilitarian will require of us—at least on the most plausible rendering—it is that the pleasure of individual persons will register or count for something. Henry's plot against Henrietta is wrong because it undermines *her* happiness. So it is not that utility matters *instead of* persons. Rather, the idea is that recognizing persons requires recognizing their happiness as mattering. And so the impulse to maximize comes once we recognize all people as mattering and want to figure out how to proceed. This is how Stephen Darwall, for instance, understands matters. He is interested in second-personal relationships not as a supplement to morality, but as its ground.

A New Leaf, I think, is onto this point as well. For Henry's failure of morality and his failure of recognition are really one and the same. And it is quite plausible to think that when the film ends, the transformation that he has undergone has remedied his amorality in addition to making him ready for deeper human friendship and community. So, *A New Leaf*, rather than advocating for perfectionism as an alternative to modern morality, reveals perfectionism's central concerns as modern morality's basis.[23]

Notes

1 Stanley Cavell, *Cities of Words: Pedagogical Letters on the Register of the Moral Life* (Cambridge: The Belknap Press of Harvard University Press, 2004), 173.

2 Precise criteria for membership in the genre are never spelled out by Cavell. One might assume that because *A New Leaf* does not involve a remarriage, the film would be ruled out. However, Cavell sometimes seems willing to

include films—such as *His Girl Friday* (1940, dir. Howard Hawks)—in the genre even when no remarriage occurs.
3   Cavell, *Cities of Words*, 24.
4   Bernard Williams, *Ethics and the Limits of Philosophy* (Cambridge: Harvard University Press, 1985).
5   Stanley Cavell, *Pursuits of Happiness: The Hollywood Comedy of Remarriage* (Cambridge: Harvard University Press, 1981), 159.
6   Ibid., 17–18.
7   Ibid., 10–11.
8   This commitment, which is more or less the basis for the burgeoning discipline of film-philosophy, is defended in some detail in Stephen Mulhall's *On Film* (New York: Routledge, 2002) and in Thomas E. Wartenberg's *Thinking on Screen: Film as Philosophy* (New York: Routledge, 2006).
9   Cavell, *Cities of Words*, 38.
10 Ibid., 39.
11 For Cavell's discussion of these matters prior to his work on film, see his "Knowing and Acknowledging," in *Must We Mean What We Say?* (Cambridge: Cambridge University Press, 1976), 238–66.
12 Stephen Darwall, "Two Kinds of Respect," *Ethics* 88, no. 1 (October 1977): 36–49.
13 Stephen Darwall, *The Second-Person Standpoint: Morality, Respect, and Accountability* (Cambridge: Harvard University Press, 2006).
14 Ibid., ix.
15 See ibid., 18, and ibid., ix.
16 Cavell, *Pursuits of Happiness*, 53.
17 Ibid., 19.
18 Ibid., 5.
19 Cavell, *Cities of Words*, 11.
20 Ibid., 42.
21 Ibid., 43.
22 Ibid.
23 For helpful comments and discussion, I would like to thank David Cummiskey, Susan Stark, and Thomas E. Wartenberg.

7

Remarriage Comedy, the Next Generation

In Bold Pursuit of Happiness

K. L. EVANS

Space: the final frontier. These are the voyages of the starship Enterprise. Its five-year mission: to explore strange new worlds, to seek out new life and new civilizations, to boldly go where no man has gone before.

—*Star Trek*

THE HOLLYWOOD FILMS STANLEY CAVELL CALLS comedies of remarriage begin with the threatened end of a marriage, with the threat of divorce, and conclude when the film's central pair find themselves in happier circumstances—when they figure out how to get back into personal relationship or discover that they can, after all, have a life together. For Cavell, this reconciliation bespeaks a transformation so profound as to signal "the achievement of a new perspective on existence." The couple can reunite "only on the condition that a miracle of change take place."[1] The remarriage comedy genre, according to Cavell, who coined it, puts on view this miracle of change. As Cavell reasons in *Pursuits of Happiness: The Hollywood Comedy of Remarriage*, remarriage comedies show how a radical shift in perspective may be brought about and hence how a pair seeking separation may be reconciled.

Rightly considered a remarkable achievement in both philosophy and film studies, the general project of *Pursuits of Happiness* is to show how the words spoken in a film and not just the film's visual facts can merit critical or philosophical attention—even when the dialogue itself seems unremarkable or unworthy of notice. By demonstrating how "words that on one viewing pass, and are meant to pass, as unnoticeably trivial, on another resonate and declare their implication in a network of significance," Cavell provides a framework for serious discussion of the great dialogue comedies of the 1930s and 1940s, films like George Cukor's *The Philadelphia Story* (1940), and hence of Hollywood films more generally. In this chapter, I follow Cavell's practice of treating seriously or with a genuine effort of attention the words spoken by characters in intelligently made comedies, no matter how trifling their exchanges seem. But I register some unease with another claim he makes in *Pursuits of Happiness*, namely, that the "miracle of change" a romantic pair must undergo if they are to find contentment is tied to their powers of communication. I question Cavell's engaging premise that talking to one another—conversing, negotiating, giving voice to deep feelings—is the best way for a couple to rediscover happiness.

By Cavell's account, to restore a couple's marriage turns out to require conversation, a verbal exchange worthier and more effectual than mere quarreling. In *The Philadelphia Story*, for example, the end of the marriage between Tracy Lord (Katherine Hepburn) and C. K. Dexter Haven (Cary Grant) is attributed to a breakdown of conversation and consequently the collapse of the couple's chief means of intimacy—for as Cavell observes about these Hollywood "talkies" of the 1930s and 1940s, talking together is the couple's "essential way of being together." Cavell gives emphasis to the scene when Tracy tells her ex-husband that his overdrinking was his problem and not hers, to which Dexter replies, "Granted. But you took on that problem when you married me. You were no helpmeet there, Red. You were a scold." For Cavell, Dexter's lines constitute "a brief for his divorce" from Tracy. The lines invoke both God's decision to make Adam "an help meet for him" (Gen. 2:18) and Milton's view that "a meet and happy conversation is the chiefest and noblest end of marriage."[2] What draws Cavell's attention here is "the conjunction of being a helpmeet with being willing to converse, a contrary of being a scold."[3] Merely reproaching and reprimanding her husband is less helpful than presenting him with a different point of view, as conversation might allow. Cavell's interest in Dexter's complaint invites us to recall that "helpmeet" is a translation of two Hebrew words, *ezer* and *kenegdo*, "helper" and "against him." More clear in the original Hebrew is how the woman's difference or unlikeness to the man is the condition of her helpfulness to him. Disagreement *for the sake of the other* is what Cavell underscores when he makes conversation an important feature of being or becoming a valued companion, someone capable of bringing about a rescue.

And yet, the couple's trenchant exchanges—wry or stinging accusations that turn out to be justified; self-serving portrayals ("you were a scold") that, by the film's end, acquire the air of divination—never have the feel of fresh disclosure. On the contrary, the pithiness and formulaic quality of these remarks suggests the treading of old ground. Is Tracy's being a scold something we think Dexter hasn't said before? And even if it is a new way of speaking, what makes it revelatory *to* Tracy, and thus the point of departure for a shift in outlook significant enough to constitute "a new perspective on existence"? Perhaps we should say that in remarriage comedies the central pair's conversation is eye-opening to the film's *viewers* as we come to see how, astonishingly, their pithy characterizations or astute observations of one another are in fact true. But the capacity to gain an accurate and deep intuitive understanding of these observations isn't brought about through the public rehearsal of injuries. No matter how shrewd their analyses, the couple cannot merely talk their way into reconciliation.

There is accordingly a step missing between a couple's willingness to converse, what Cavell also calls their "capacity for talk," and the acknowledgment and acceptance true rapprochement requires. We could also put it this way: a couple's practice of talking together is the necessary condition for their honorable life together because without conversation there is no foundation for the analysis of the life they have shared. By offering a brief on their problems, especially of the views each holds of the other, the talk makes possible the couple's examination of their relationship. What is more, the couple's way of talking together allows the film's viewers to scrutinize this relationship and so come to see in it a "parable," as Cavell says, for the struggle for reciprocity between women and men. In remarriage comedies as Cavell frames them marriage exemplifies or symbolizes the state of society at large, with an unhappy or inequitable marriage a sure sign of a disordered state of affairs.[4] What I am suggesting, however, is that offering a brief on the problems in a marriage is prefatory to what Cavell calls the "miracle of change" that brings about a new outlook; it does not on its own institute that change. A couple's capacity for talk may bring them closer to the prospect of a happy marriage—marriage more satisfying than the kind of legal bond one may have with a "complete stranger," as Nora in Ibsen's *A Doll House* calls her husband of eight years—but it does not *bring about* that contented state.

We should go back, then, to Cavell's original question but with a significant adjustment. Presuming that the central couple in a remarriage comedy is united in the recognition that talking together is the essential way of being together (presuming, that is to say, that the couple is not "forever stuck in an orbit around the foci of desire and contempt," as Cavell characterizes marriage that does *not* have conversation as its basis), what brings about the "miracle of change" that allows a pair seeking divorce to resume matrimony?[5]

What is the means by which each party achieves a *new perspective* and thus a *new existence*, as the couple's reunion is designed to suggest?

I want to consider remarriage comedy for the generation succeeding Cavell's, a generation for whom talking together is the chief way of being together, but for whom talking does not by itself, as it were, alter and significantly improve the interaction between warring romantic partners. In *Pursuits of Happiness*, Cavell correlates happiness (happiness in the philosophical sense of human flourishing, what Aristotle calls *eudaimonia*) with the willingness to converse and recognizes in a couple's habit of talking together the whole complex, drawn-out transaction of learning from a romantic partner your own most damning trait, discovering for yourself what the accusation means, and coming to accept its truth, thereby prompting your partner's genuine forgiveness. But this advantageous mode of life isn't brought about simply by the couple's pronouncement of what their problems are, as their conversation lays out. Like Tracy in *The Philadelphia Story*, a criticized partner must grasp what the reproach amounts to, which means developing ears and eyes for how one might have fallen into a set of established behaviors and reactions—habitual responses that contribute to the problem one is having with others. One must come to see oneself from a perspective that is not the usual one. Of course, this radical new outlook is something both partners must attain.

Talking together will be no different from quarreling if a couple cannot figure out how to escape from their customary—and doubtless unhelpful—ways of relating to one another. With this observation we are beginning to enter the territory of Cavell's miracle of change, a highly improbable or extraordinary event or development that brings welcome consequences. For the couple's plan of action cannot merely be to come up with reasons for their estrangement. It must also include an attempt to arrive at more productive strategies for working with the complexities of (endlessly conflicting) relationships. If happiness is the goal, both partners must change the way they comport themselves. Or as we might also say, the restoration of friendly relations between a divided pair is contingent upon their ability to acquire completely new sides of themselves—to trade in whatever harmful pattern of interaction they have fallen into (the skepticism the woman habitually brandishes regarding her mate's abilities, say, or the attitude of patronizing superiority the man displays when he speaks) and instead develop a readiness to behave with respectfulness, consideration, modesty, and other kinds of good manners. It is by finding ways of *not* being themselves, as it were, that a couple can radically alter the climate of their hostile encounters and help their relationship flourish.

This line of reasoning takes into account a detail that Cavell, and indeed much of Western philosophy, omits, namely, that the inherent disposition of human beings is to respond emotionally to other people. An additional feature of this observation is that we express our volatile, strongly marked temperaments in our patterns of response—in the way we communicate and interact with one another. Sometimes we do not notice these patterns, even when we are falling into them all the time.

That is the conclusion drawn by Confucius (551–479 BCE), the first great philosopher in the Chinese tradition, and by other philosophers rooted in Confucian thought. According to this worldview, humans are constituted to respond emotionally (the way plants are constituted to grow toward the sun) and human life is an endless series of impulsive encounters. Whatever or whomever we happen to meet with draws out our emotions, often in ways we are unconscious of, and occasionally with disastrous consequence. As Michael Puett and Christine Gross-Loh write in *The Path: What Chinese Philosophers Can Teach Us about the Good Life*, "[w]e experience something pleasurable and then feel pleasure; we encounter something frightening and subsequently feel fear. A toxic relationship makes us feel despair, an argument with a coworker makes us livid, a rivalry with a friend arouses jealousy." No one can escape this rigmarole, for this is what life is: "moment after moment in which people encounter one another, react in an infinite number of ways, and are pulled to and fro emotionally."[6]

If Confucius is right, what the two people mired in dispute really require is the opportunity to *refine* their dispositions and *modify* their more dangerous emotions. Instead of responding to one another expressively and in a manner characterized by intense feeling, they must learn better ways of responding—adjustments that will be perceivable by the senses, for example through small changes in body language and tone. To put this proposal more boldly, people need to break from their usual patterns and learn to play roles other than the ones they normally play. A couple's ability to suspend or temporarily prevent their habitual ways of responding is crucial for reconciliation because this and this alone is what leads to tremendous movement—to the miracle of change Cavell envisions but does not quite explain.

Thus it isn't mere whimsy that dictates the detour I have taken through Confucius in order to understand a problem Cavell tackles but does not solve—how, exactly, a couple can achieve a new perspective on existence. For what is given prominence in early Chinese thought (in direct contrast to the tradition inspired by Kant, for example) is the importance of developing a sensibility that allows us to respond well to other people. What the early Chinese philosophers discover, moreover, is that we do not develop this sensibility by asking and trying to answer big, abstract, philosophical questions but by attending to and slowly learning to adjust the very small, ordinary actions that all together form the greater part of our interactions with other people: the many different gestures and tones of voice we can use, the words we choose, the way our faces look when we are speaking.

As Puett and Gross-Loh observe, Confucius is unlike other philosophers because he thinks that since we are spending the vast majority of our waking lives engaging in these small acts we should learn to pay philosophical attention to them, especially since these small acts can become habits or conventions, ways of behaving or doing things that are widely—if unconsciously—practiced.[7] Confucius taught that neglected or unheeded, our habits could be harmful; with deliberate observation and training, however, more constructive behaviors can be nurtured and developed.

The bombshell, for many of us, is that human beings do not learn how to respond well to other people and as a result dramatically improve their relationships through the use of *reason* or *will*. In other words, some prevailing assumptions about our ability to work through problems rationally—and then to give voice to our conclusions, to "speak our minds" or authentically express ourselves—has not contributed to but actually hampered our chances of improving our interactions and bringing out the best in others. When the goal is to respond *well* to someone else, that is to say, the entire history of philosophizing as it emerges in Europe during the early modern period is working against us. We should be helped to hone our instincts, train our emotions, and engage in a constant process of self-cultivation so that eventually, at moments both crucial and mundane, we will react in constructive, positive ways to the people around us.[8] Instead, fragile, messy humans—randomly subject to bouts of euphoria and sudden, speedy plunges into despair; prone to be affected by other messy humans and their emotional ups and downs; vulnerable, what is more, to the slings and arrows of outrageous fortune, to the accident of prosperity, calamity or ill luck, as well as flood, fire, drought, disease, war, and other man-made or natural disasters—are taught to rely on our rational minds, our sharp tongues.

Ever since philosophers put their faith in the faculty of reason they have unfit themselves for harmonious modes of interaction. In marked difference to Cavell's argument in *Pursuits of Happiness*, then, my claim in this chapter is that the miracle of change which begets a new perspective on existence isn't the result of conversation as such (that synergistic exchange Cavell thinks of as talk in the service of a couple's struggle for reciprocity and consequently happiness) but of a person's ability to acquire better dispositional responses—to operate out of a sense of affection and courtesy rather than anger, jealousy, and resentment. Cavell writes that it is essential for characters in remarriage comedies to "take the time, and take the pains, to converse intelligently and playfully about themselves and about one another."[9] To this I wish to add that the kind of intelligence and playfulness Cavell prizes is affected more than we like to think by the presence of a good disposition. And good dispositions—resulting in moments when, rather than being pulled to and fro emotionally, people are able to respond well to one another—are not brought out through the development of reason. Good dispositions do not spring from our ability to look within, process our feelings, and give voice to them.

This is something we have yet to learn in the West, where instead of developing strategies that can manage and transform destructive or dangerous interactions, we are taught to rely on our calculating minds. We rather stubbornly continue to tackle moral and ethical dilemmas by inventing abstract hypothetical situations and working through them rationally, in this way reducing decision making to a simple set of data and a single choice, and contributing to the myth that in the course of daily life reason is free from the taint of emotion. We persist in taking comfort in the belief that our decisions are made through this kind of careful reckoning, forgetting that heightened feeling and instinct are likely to hijack the very judgments and methods of assessment we think will safeguard us.[10] Ironically, we are simultaneously encouraged to get in touch with, find language for, and then articulately convey our "authentic" inner feelings—usually, those strong feelings of anger, sadness or joy that small children uninhibitedly express. Now, new forms of electronic communication, the multitude of online communication channels dedicated to sharing one's first thoughts, feelings, and other personal reactions with millions of others, has exponentially increased both the speed with which those unsoftened feelings are uttered and their force of impact.

Yet all is not lost. As stated in the *Nature That Emerges from the Decree*, a recently discovered fourth-century BCE text, we are capable of changing the way we act during our messy encounters. We can move from a state where we randomly respond to things emotionally (*qing*) to a state where we are able to respond with propriety (*yi*).[11] Such transformation requires training, though, as we learn to introduce a difference between what we feel on the inside and what is manifested on the outside. This change brings to mind the transition from childishness to maturity, for (as we are invited to recall) it is in the beginning of our lives that we respond to things emotionally; at the end, we practice better ways of responding.

All the same, learning how to respond with propriety does not mean overcoming or controlling the emotions. As Puett and Gross-Loh point out, developing propriety "simply means cultivating our emotions so that we internalize better ways of responding to others. These better ways become a part of us." Rather than be governed by an immediate emotional reaction we learn to refine our responses. And as these authors contend, "we do this refining through ritual."[12]

In early China people figured out how to refine the way they act or increase their capacity for responding well to others by participating in rituals. Today we tend to think of rituals as the means of enforcing conformity or an unquestioning adherence to tradition. However, for Confucius, rituals are more profitably understood as opportunities to break from our customary, often detrimental patterns of response. Rituals in the Confucian sense "are transformative because they allow us to become a different person for a moment. They create a short-lived alternate reality that returns us to our regular life slightly altered."[13]

In this chapter I aim to show why participating in rituals is a better way of effecting reconciliation or achieving happiness in relationships than "talking," and I will draw support for this argument from a rightful heir to the films Cavell calls comedies of remarriage, 1999's *Galaxy Quest*, directed by Dean Parisot and written by David Howard. My plan is to build on Cavell's founding insights about human happiness, as well as his idea of film as a medium of drama (and thus grist for the meditative critic, who as Cavell notes must discover why the characters in a drama "use their time as they do, why they say the things they say"[14]). At the same time, I want to cast doubt on the trust in reason, conversation, and authentic self-expression that governs Cavell's thinking. Trust in the power of conversation and more generally man's ability to use reason is, of course, not unique to Cavell but guides most thinking in the West. The strikingly unusual proposal put forward in *Galaxy Quest* that there are more reliable ways of improving our relationships—particularly our romantic relationships—thus comes as a welcome suggestion.

Those People Dressed Like Aliens . . . They *Are* Aliens

First, though, a review of the storyline of *Galaxy Quest*. The film begins at a science fiction convention for devoted fans of a now-canceled early 1980s television series, *Galaxy Quest*, in which the intrepid crewmembers of the NSEA Protector travel through space answering calls of distress. The fervent, costumed audience is awaiting the crew's arrival on stage, but while the enthusiastic emcee recalls how, "for those four seasons, we developed the same affection for the crew that the crew had for each other," backstage the aging actors are bickering. As usual, the highest-paid, most narcissistic member of the team, Jason Nesmith (Tim Allen), is an hour and a half late. And while fully committed to his role as Commander Peter Taggart—he is all exuberance and charm, and the fans love him—he feels less obligated to his fellow actors, regularly taking paid gigs on his own. Jason is not the only one who invites eye-rolling from his fellows, though. Alexander Dane (Alan Rickman), a trained British stage actor, has such routine panic attacks about the demise of his career and his perpetual role as the show's fin-headed Dr. Lazarus that his friends know what he is going to say before he says it. "How did I come to this?" he asks himself in the mirror, while the youngest actor, Tommy Webber (Daryl Mitchell) groans, "Not again," and the team's most amiable member, Fred Kwan (Tony Shalhoub), says "You played Richard the Third," right before Dane says, "I played Richard the Third."

> FRED: Five curtain calls.
> ALEXANDER: There were five curtain calls. I was an actor once, damn it. Now look at me. Look at me! I can't go out there, and I won't say that stupid line one more time!

Alexander is interrupted by blond, buxom Gwen Demarco (Sigourney Weaver), who plays Lt. Tawny Madison, Captain Taggart's love interest on the show: "Well, Alex, at least you had a part. You had a character people loved. I mean, my *TV Guide* interview was six paragraphs about my boobs and how they fit into my suit!"

Though the chauvinism is not lost on the others, they are all tired of hearing about it—just as they are tired of hearing how Alexander, forced to repeat his character's trite slogan endlessly ("By Grabthar's hammer, I will avenge you"), deeply resents being number two and thinks self-important Jason Nesmith has stolen all the show's best scenes. In short, each of the actors has a beef, and each of them is weary of the often-rehearsed resentments of the others.

Then two things happen. Nesmith's confidence is rocked when, behind the closed doors of a urinal, he accidentally overhears some contemptuous fans at the conference ridiculing him. "What a freak show, man!" jeers one of three identically costumed, elaborately made-up dudes:

> This is hilarious.
> Bunch of losers! Begging for autographs at fifteen bucks a pop. These guys haven't had a real acting job for twenty years. This is all they've got.
> And did you check out Nesmith? He actually gets off on those retards thinking he's a space commander!
> And his friends can't stand him! Did you hear them ragging on him in there? Dude, he has no idea he's a laughingstock, even to his buddies! He's pathetic.

Back at his table signing autographs, Jason is no longer laughing and talking with fans about the many features of the show. His foul mood makes him deaf to the questions of one of the show's ardent enthusiasts, Brandon (Justin Long), head of a small band of bright, geeky teenagers devoted to building exact replicas of the things seen on the show and working out the scientific principles on which these objects are based. When Brandon approaches the autograph table and, showing great attention to detail, asks a technical question about one episode, Jason blows up at him:

> JASON: It's just a television show. That's all, okay?
> BRANDON: "Right, but . . . because we were wondering if the quantum flux . . ."
> JASON: There *is no* quantum flux. There's no goddamn *ship*! You got it?

But later that night, back at his own lavish hill-top digs and having drunk most of a bottle of scotch, Jason gives the lie to his own cynicism. Watching an old episode of *Galaxy Quest*, he mouths the show's sonorous opening lines: "As long as there is an injustice, whenever a Targathian baby cries out, wherever a distress signal sounds, among the stars, we'll be there. This fine ship and this fine crew. Never give up! . . . Never surrender." As the film's viewers will discover, "Never give up, never surrender" is the Commander's line, and he believes it, even when he occasionally catches sight of the mug this makes him.

The second thing that happens is that some of the convention attendants dressed like aliens *are* aliens—Thermians from the Klatu Nebula, who approach Jason at the conference with a request for help, a "matter of supreme importance, in which a great many lives hang in the balance."

Jason thinks the aliens are just zealous representatives for his next solo gig, but when they pick him up the next day, they take him not to a basement set in Van Nuys but to the real command deck of the *Protector II*, a space ship built by the Thermians and modeled in every detail on the sets of the *Galaxy Quest* television show. Mathesar (Enrico Colantoni), leader of the Thermians, is trying to enlist Jason's help in their battle with Sarris, a vicious enemy who desires the Omega 13, a mysterious weapon in the Thermians' arsenal. Perhaps the most striking aspect of the many humorous scenes in which Jason, hung over, thinks he is dealing with people dressed like aliens (and the aliens, thinking themselves delivered into the hands of a celebrated rescuer, allow Jason to make choices that determine the survival of their race), is Jason's inattention to the gravity of the Thermians' plight. Jason sleeps through the Thermians' careful explanation of their history and how they are now being "systematically hunted and slaughtered" and simplifies—in true Hollywood fashion—the Thermians' description of Sarris. "He's the bad guy, right?" Jason says, yawning, and has no ears for the reply. ("Yes sir, he's a very bad man, indeed. He has tortured our scientists, put us to work in the gallium arsenide mines, captured our females for his own demented purposes. . . .") Worse, when the Thermians expect the Commander to negotiate with Sarris, he carelessly starts a war by firing on Sarris's ship. All of this is part of the comedy, naturally, and yet what it brings home is the decidedly unfunny experience of careless, inattentive leaders playing games with lives and worlds.

Of course, everything begins to change when the whole team of *Galaxy Quest* actors joins Jason on board the spaceship and really does start to do battle with Sarris (who, unmissably, shares the name of twentieth-century film critic, Andrew Sarris). Due partly to the Thermians' sincerity, their determination to treat these washed-up actors as members of a revered intergalactic crew, Jason, Alexander, Gwen, Tommy and Fred—plus the hapless emcee Guy (Sam Rockwell), a "glorified extra," along for the ride—undergo a transformation. By learning to fully embrace the characters they played on television, they eventually rescue the Thermians and, not incidentally, save themselves.

Before considering this film in the mode of philosophical attention—a way of looking, as Cavell writes, "in which you are prepared to be taken by surprise, stopped, thrown back as it were upon the text"—a few keys scenes must be conveyed.[15] The first of these occurs right after the crew, thinking to follow Jason to a gig, has been beamed onto the Thermians' star-port. There they find their crisply uniformed "Commander" is now fully acclimatized and enjoying his supervisory role. They are flabbergasted to find themselves in space and among real aliens, but almost as surprising is the Thermians' thorough knowledge of the *Galaxy Quest* mission and team:

> GWEN: You *know* us?
> MATHESAR: I don't believe there is a man, woman, or child on my planet who does not. Since we first received transmission of your historical documents, we have studied every facet of your missions and strategies.
> TOMMY: You've been watching the show?
> JASON: Lieutenant, *historical documents*.
> TOMMY: You've been watching the . . . historical documents . . . from out here?
> MATHESAR: Yes. The past hundred years, our society had fallen into disarray. Our goals, our values had become scattered. But since the transmission, we have modeled every aspect of our society from your example and it has saved us. Your courage and teamwork and friendship through adversity. In fact, all you see around you has been taken from the lessons garnered from the historical documents.

As the *Galaxy Quest* crew discovers, these lessons are not simply scientific and mechanical but apply, too, to social conventions. The Thermians are unfailingly courteous and caring, traits that stand in contrast to the caustic remarks and self-serving behavior of their human visitors. In fact, the Thermians' meticulously constructed world, where the scientists are knowledgeable, leaders honorable, crewmembers cooperative and dutiful, is meant to stand in explicit contrast with the fractious, unruly worlds from which both Sarris and the earthlings hail. This perhaps explains why, at first, the Thermians seem so comical and ersatz to Jason and his crew—and also to us, the film's viewers, who likely find insincere or unnatural the Thermians' stilted movements, immaculate environment, and formal, elaborate expressions of gratitude.

It isn't until the monstrous Sarris and his minions board the ship and start to torture Mathesar that Jason begins to understand the costs of the game he is playing. Sarris is demanding the Omega 13 (a weapon whose function is unclear but which may well have the power to destroy the universe) and will do anything to get it. To prevent further torture, Jason confesses the crew's real identities to Sarris. He has the computer call up the "historical documents," which Sarris immediately recognizes for a theatrical production. Sarris' shrewdness on this point is meant to contrast with the Thermians' naiveté, since for them *every* television show, even *Gilligan's Island*, is classified as a historical document. Mathesar is splayed out on the torture table, bruised and bloody, but the implication is that Jason's revelation is what really hurts him:

> SARRIS: Wonderful. You have all done far greater damage than I ever could have. Bravo! Bravo. This is a moment I will treasure. Explain to him who you all *really* are. Tell him! Explain!
> JASON: Mathesar, there's no such person as Captain Taggart. My name is Jason Nesmith. I'm an actor. We're all actors.
> SARRIS: He doesn't understand. Explain . . . as you would a child.
> JASON: We pretended. We lied. [*Mathesar makes a pitiable sound.*]
> SARRIS: Yes! You understand that, don't you, Mathesar?
> JASON: Mathesar, I'm not a Commander. I . . . There's no National Space Exploration Administration. We don't have a ship.
> MATHESAR: [*pointing to the screen*] But there it is!
> JASON: A model, only as big as this.
> MATHESAR: But inside, I see many rooms.
> JASON: You've seen plywood sets . . . our digital conveyer is . . . Christmas tree lights. It's a decoration. It's all fake. Just like me.
> MATHESAR: But *why*?
> JASON: It's difficult to explain. On our planet, we . . . we pretend to entertain, and . . . Mathesar, I am so sorry. God, I am *so* sorry.

Though Jason's disclosure looks like it will be the death of Mathesar—and the death of hope, since implementing the *Galaxy Quest* missions and strategies had become the means by which the Thermians were able to repair their society—in fact Jason comes to *reject* the story he tells Sarris and cleaves instead to Mathesar's view. Sure, the *Galaxy Quest* episodes can be understood (as Gwen says) as "people behaving in ways that is contrary to reality." But the ritualistic, stylized, formulaic escapades found in the show, in which the central characters repeat again and again their words and rules to live by, need not be identified with lying. It is also possible to think of these deliberately artificial, idealized spaces as providing a rough plan for helping humans manage their lesser desires or build better worlds where everyone has a chance to flourish. Thinking of the *Galaxy Quest* episodes in this way, the way the Thermians do, is what allows Jason and the others to successfully navigate a series of charged, dangerous situations, and to turn from harping actors in costumes into a uniformed, capable crew.

This transition gets underway when, as the defeated actors are about to be released into space by Sarris's soldiers, Alexander takes a final dig. "Where's the happy ending now, Jason?" he asks, before saying in an ironic manner, "Never give up . . . Never surrender." Despite its mocking delivery, the line gives Jason an idea. He commits to the line's moral, or turns its message into a plan for action. By pretending to insult Alexander, Jason alerts him to the usefulness of acting out a scene from the *Galaxy Quest* archive, an episode in which Dr. Lazarus and Captain Taggart feign fighting in order to distract their guards and make a grand escape. The ruse works and the crew's true mission grows more clear—to find their way back to the roles they had come to disdain.

Alternate Worlds

Notwithstanding its generally positive reviews, *Galaxy Quest* has never been given the kind of consideration Cavell teaches us should be paid to great dialogue comedies. Yet I find *Galaxy Quest* to be exactly the kind of film whose lines take on particular importance when we circle back to them. What is more, the film seems to contain a fully worked out position—one that contradicts much of modern Western thought—about what it means for something to be real, why artifice can be better than authenticity, and how just societies and happy partnerships are maintained.

Perhaps the most radical view the film advances is that rather than behave more *authentically*, people wishing to get along with each other (and in this way rescue the planet!) should make use of unnatural or artificial templates that impose rigorous constraints on how to act and speak. In the film, the preset formats that serve as guides for behavior are what the Thermians call "historical documents," and Jason and the other actors know as episodes from the *Galaxy Quest* archive—for example episode 17, when crewmembers with incompatible constitutions pretend to fight in order to overpower their real enemies. More and more the actors find themselves employing these scenarios as the way to survive their predicaments. What identifies these moments is precisely the awareness that they are pretending—that rather than reveal their true selves, they are *acting*.

The question, then, is why such inauthentic ways of behaving could be so beneficial. One answer supplied by the film is that the higher the stakes of any given situation—the greater the likelihood of very significant gains and losses; the bigger the chance of what Sarris calls "blood and pain as you cannot imagine"—the more necessary these templates become. That is because high-risk, dangerous situations (those that may cause the destruction of individuals and civilizations, or even those that are psychologically fraught, like reunions, weddings, and funerals) bring to the surface our deepest feelings and thus occasion our poorest conduct. Precisely because it is difficult to think coolly and behave well when temperatures are high or much is on the line, strictly adhering to formulaic patterns of behavior and adopting clichéd, unoriginal (hackneyed, even, or platitudinous) phrases can be a remarkably effective strategy. The lesson is that contrived or highly orchestrated interactions can help us successfully navigate situations that might otherwise defeat us.

As I indicated in the opening section of this chapter, the lesson is not new. In early China, ritualized actions or strict patterns of behavior were developed to help combat negative, uncontrolled energies—like those released when an established ruler passed away and a new ruler had to be installed.[16] The goal of such rituals was to inculcate in each participant the disposition proper to his role. For example, in the ritual designed to ease the transition between rulers, the person playing the ruler would behave like a good father to his son, in this way modeling how the ruler will treat his people; the person playing the son would honor and revere his father, in this way representing the people who will honor and revere their ruler or think of him as a father. What is important to note, however, is that the ritual only works because each participant plays a role other than the one he inhabits normally.[17] In the ritual, the role of the ruler is played by someone other than the real ruler—it is played by someone *acting* like a ruler—because in the real world a ruler must train himself to treat his people like family members under his care.[18] That is, the disjunction between the way people behave during the ritual and how they really behave in the world (where children often do not honor their parents, and rulers often use and exploit their people) was repeatedly underlined by the ritual; or as Michael Puett explains, the disjunction between the idyllic and the actual was what warranted the ritual in the first place.[19]

In sum, rituals and the texts that theorize ritual do not provide evidence of belief in an orderly, harmonious world where people regularly conduct themselves well; on the contrary, they signal or show awareness of the certainty that the world is unpredictable and often hostile, that people are frequently inconsiderate, ill-tempered, and ruthless.[20]

As Puett writes, "we need to see the agony" underlying rituals and works of ritual theory.[21] The concern is that we are systematically misreading rituals and the cultures that produced them when we take rituals to depict the world the participants lived in or even the world they would wish to live in when what is really being offered are carefully assembled alternative worlds, worlds markedly *unlike* the one we inhabit. To Confucius and his followers, "the power of the ritual lay in how patently distinct it was from the real world."[22] There was no way for the participants to possibly mistake the roles they were playing for roles they might assume in real life. That is because rituals understood rightly are consciously constructed imaginary spaces wherein (in distinct contrast to fraught, disordered real life) congenial, pleasurable, and mutually supportive relationships can be forged. If performed well, the ritual moves us from the troubled world of human relationships and, for a limited time, creates a space in which we can have interactions less fraught than the ones we have in nonritual spaces.

This respite from our accustomed and disagreeable patterns of response (the grudges we cannot seem to shake off, the social conventions we unthinkingly follow) offers a break from our everyday routines and helps us develop new sides of ourselves.[23] Of course, the results are always short-lived, which is why we return to the rituals again and again. In everyday life it is a constant struggle not to let our worst sides come to the surface—to be jealous of our friends, dishonest with or unfair to our partners, unkind to our admirers.

The adoption of rituals is thus extremely useful to a society, especially a society in disarray, because when we put ourselves into the ideal space of a ritual we may train ourselves to act differently—in short, to construct new realities. Again, the point is not to replace chaotic, disordered real life with the perfectly arranged world inside the ritual, but to use the ritual to create pockets of order—short-lived, alternate realities from which we may return to our regular life slightly altered.[24]

In consequence, we would be mistaken to think that the need for rituals is over, or that the turbulent times in which Confucius lived was so different from our own age—or, for that matter, different from the period of massive cultural crisis that marked the "Zactor Migration," as the Thermians name the time of dissension in which they found themselves, an age in which "a dark period of discontent spread through the land." The pervasive sense that humans have lost their way and forsaken the rules of conduct that enable them to live in harmony is as perceptible today as it was when the Greek poet Hesiod lamented that he lived in an era when relationships had crumbled, family members sparred with one another, children failed to care for their aging parents, and people freely gave their "praise to violence."[25]

Any era in which human beings must get along with one another requires effective strategies for bringing out the best in others and for building the kind of world in which people can flourish. What is surprising, though, is how far we have come from thinking of ritual as a potent and practical means of improving relationships beset by conflict or struggle. In this sense, *Galaxy Quest* offers a gentle corrective, a reminder of why participation in ritual is the most effective way to shake off our destructive patterns of response—those that generate sadness, confusion, and anger—and develop better ways of responding.

The Truth about Phonies

As *Galaxy Quest* makes clear, the philosophical impulse that underlies the use of ritual is worth taking seriously. For it begins with the assumption that we humans live in a fractious and disordered world, and that by building pockets of order (idealized ritual spaces in which, for brief periods of time, we are good to each other, and help one another, and inspire others to be better), and by studying or taking part in these prescribed rites, we slowly become more skilled at responding to others with propriety.[26] The film offers an unusual vision regarding how we can become better human beings and create a better world. What is more, it goes directly against the advice, coming in from all sides, that individuals should learn to be "true" to themselves; in *Galaxy Quest* we see why, if we were always true to ourselves, we would be stuck in all our old patterns of behavior, unable to transform.[27]

Let us consider the relationship between Jason Nesmith and Gwen Demarco, a charged, full-blooded, disputatious romantic entanglement that has gone dormant, we learn at the film's beginning, because Gwen has learned to see the cad beneath Jason's veneer of charm. (Naturally, Gwen and Jason's long-running connection ties in with the less-troubled courtship between Gwen's character on the show, Tawny Madison, and Jason's Captain Taggart.) At the science fiction convention, surrounded by fans, Jason flirts with Gwen. However, these attempts to win Gwen over are nipped in the bud by her acrimonious remark that such playful romantic moments were "cute when I *didn't* know you."

The implication here is that the true Nesmith is a man who behaves dishonorably—and perhaps he is—but the lesson from early Chinese thought is that what really limits or endangers us is the whole idea that everyone has a "true self" or set of characteristics by which they may be authentically known. Talk of an authentic self (rooted in sixteenth-century Calvinist ideas about sincerity) is misleading because what is really being assembled is only a picture, taken at a certain point of time, of a person's *established set of patterns or behaviors*. These patterns can change—though clearly the notion of an authentic self works against that kind of transformation.[28]

But when Gwen and Jason leave earth for space, tense conversations about who one another really is are juxtaposed with moments when, in order to survive the various ordeals of their new environment, they have to shut up and play the roles they had ritually played on the television show. If Gwen and Jason want to succeed (and success may be understood as beating Sarris and saving the world, or as getting back into a loving relationship—also a kind of world-saving, since it requires the attainment of a whole new view of life) they must practice abandoning the patterned habits, the entrenched narratives, through which they are used to perceiving the world.

In this way the usual progression of the romantic comedy is reversed. In a typical romantic comedy, characters that hold mistaken impressions about their would-be lovers come to understand how or why they have been wrong. In Jane Austen's *Pride and Prejudice*, for instance, a woman dislikes a man's excessively high opinion of himself or his importance—until she discovers that his high opinion is built on real merit. One lesson of that story is thus that happiness depends on getting past one's own prejudiced or blinkered view about someone else and really getting to know him or her. Nothing like this kind of emotional journey happens in the film. In *Galaxy Quest*, the key to transformation turns out to be playing with some gusto one's assigned role, no matter its silliness, or despite the obvious disjunction between the role one has been assigned and who one is in real life. Only then does the point of the role-playing become clear: to help people break from their usual patterns and in this way achieve a new perspective on existence.

Interestingly, and despite what we suspect to be Gwen's greater intelligence, sympathy, and conception of the public good, Jason is better at this role-playing than Gwen is. Perhaps that is because he has always been better at getting into character. Accordingly, what in his life on earth has been an impediment to Jason's relationships with other people—his enthusiastic embrace of his role as Commander Taggart—serves him well in his adventure with the Thermians. In the ritual space of the NSEA Protector, Jason is buoyant and resilient and resolute; he never gives up, never surrenders. Worth pointing out is how much more gratifying Jason's Captain Taggart is to play than Gwen's Tawny Madison, a character whose very circumscribed role on the ship is to "repeat the computer," as Gwen reports with disgust, as well as to look good in her low-cut suit. Despite the uselessness of the role as Gwen perceives it, however, the Tawny Madison role is essential to the logic of the show. That is because this sham of a supportive role is meant to highlight the sham of Taggart's command. All together the *Galaxy Quest* episodes provide a view of what being a Commander really means—how fragile and tenuous leadership is, how *entirely* dependent on a crew's support.

A valuable lesson is thus that one doesn't know or cannot accurately guess what instruction the role-playing will offer until one has really committed to the performance, with all its customary rites and procedures. This is difficult for intelligent people to do, as we see from the readiness with which both Gwen and Alexander break from character in order to express skepticism about Jason's choices and abilities, or to point out that he is only nominally in charge. "Why are you listening to this man?" Alexander asks the rest of the crew, when Jason, playing Commander Taggart, tries to map out a plan of action. "Must I remind you that he is wearing a *costume*, not a uniform?" Jason's plan, a rough copy of the *Galaxy Quest* episode 31, "Assault on Voltareck III," is to distract a large group of aliens in order procure a beryllium sphere. Though they are clearly ineffective, Jason is using dramatic commando tactics he has used on the show, such as ducking behind rocks, or rolling on the ground, to advance the crew's position. As the others are just walking casually, the theatrics look absurd, and Gwen seizes the occasion to ask dryly, "Does the rolling help?" "—It helps," says Jason, full of confidence. "Then where's your gun?" Gwen asks, smirking, while Jason pats his hip to discover that the rolling has dislodged his weapon.

Most viewers of this scene will be inclined to think that Gwen has won the point. They would be wrong, however. That is because Jason, like the Thermians, has discovered the very real benefit of using the show as a strategy for survival. We see this consecration of (even the silliest of) the show's conceits play out in a later scene, after Sarris has activated a neutron reactor with the goal of blowing up the ship and Gwen and Jason are on a desperate mission to shut off the device:

GWEN: So, we get to shut down the neutron reactor?
JASON: Right.
GWEN: Uh . . . I hate to break it to you Jason, but I don't know how to shut down a neutron reactor, and unless you took a Learning Annex course I don't know about, I'm pretty sure you don't know how to shut down a neutron reactor either.

Jason agrees that he also doesn't know how to shut down the reactor—but he does know someone who will, fourteen-year-old Brandon, the ultra-serious *Galaxy Quest* fan who spends his days in his room at his computer, gluing tiny pieces of plastic to his model Protector and more generally thinking through the show's technical and moral problems. The practicality of the teenager's fervor isn't lost on Jason (though it bewilders Brandon's parents), since it is precisely such meticulous attention to the show that has rescued the Thermians and allowed their society to flourish. In their very great attention to detail, that is to say, and in their willingness to solemnly perform the rites or ceremonies established by the show, Brandon and his fellow teens are aligned with the Thermians; they too are world-makers, rescuers of planets and civilizations.

This point is worth emphasizing, for Brandon's devotion to the show and his willingness to abide by its established rules, traditions, and customs (even as he works to point out and solve certain technical mysteries) is meant to have the opposite effect of Gwen and Alexander's skepticism, expressed as their withering contempt for the show's purpose and value. We see the advantage of Brandon's way of proceeding when Gwen and Jason are forced to flee Sarris's guards by passing through the chompers, an unavoidable gauntlet of hissing hydraulic smashing metal hammers and blades. In this scene, Jason has Brandon on his vox communicator and is getting step-by-step instructions for how to proceed through the bowels of the ship and turn off the reactor. (Not incidentally, Brandon and his network of friends can offer these invaluable instructions because they have spent hours and hours watching the show's key episodes, cross-referencing them against other shows and films, and discussing among themselves the conclusions that may be drawn.[29]) The mood is tense, as Gwen and Jason watch the chompers smash and grind back and forth. Sarris's guards are getting closer. The timer on the neutron reactor is ticking down. But Gwen digs in her heels:

> GWEN: What *is* this thing? I mean, it serves no useful purpose for there to be a bunch of choppy, crushy things in the middle of a hallway!"
> JASON: Gwen . . .
> GWEN: We shouldn't have to *do* this! It makes no logical sense! Why is it here?
> JASON: Because it was on the show!
> GWEN: Well, forget it! I'm not doing it. This episode was *badly written!*

Of course, if Gwen and Jason do not pass through the chompers, they will be shot by one of Sarris's guards. If they go through the chompers heedlessly or without the benefit of some carefully marshaled attention to the challenge before them, they will be smashed to oblivion. Instead of quibbling with the logic of the scene they must rather accept the challenge—which they can do only by discovering the pattern of the "crushy things" (two . . . two . . . four . . . three . . .) as provided by Hollister, one of Brandon's friends. Hollister has obtained this information by watching the chompers sequence over and over on his television and timing the pattern with a wristwatch. With the teenagers' help, Gwen and Jason do make it through, and do shut down the reactor—just in the nick of time.

In such scenes, *Galaxy Quest* undermines the faith in authenticity that powers many romances since Gwen and Jason survive (and their relationship survives) only when they *stop* talking and acting like their "true" selves. We could also say that in this film having knowledge of an erstwhile partner's "true" self—the insight that will eventually (if the partnership has gone bad, or was never a partnership to begin with) constitute what Cavell calls a "brief for divorce"—does not aid but is actually an impediment to reconciliation.[30] We see this certainty play out when Jason, Gwen, and the rest of the crew are kept tethered to the ground, or to their old lives, their old way of seeing, by the grievances they have against one another. It doesn't matter that the grievances seem warranted. What matters is that this knowledge about one another doesn't enable change. So, in a scene that echoes the opening scene at the convention (in which the actors, backstage, take issue with one another), the crew travels to a dusty, rock-strewn planet. They are there to get the beryllium sphere; however, separated for the first time from the Thermians, they take the opportunity to break character and sound like their old selves: Tommy, a spoiled former child-actor; Alexander, a talented but depressed and resentful thespian; Guy, the dim-witted, expendable character designed to be killed off; Gwen, a disillusioned, seen-it-all ex-ingénue, barred from playing real roles because of her looks; and Jason, a conceited lothario with an inflated sense of his own leadership ability. The crewmembers' unrestricted expression of their "true" selves or "true" feelings leads, inevitably, to argument. Things get heated when Jason, trying to settle a dispute between Alexander and Tommy, says, "All right, let's settle down. If we're going to get through this, we're going to have to exercise a little self-control." The remark prompts Gwen to retort, "Self-control? That's funny coming from the guy who slept with every Moon Princess and Terrakian slave girl on the show!"

At this point the camera pans away from the characters and *Galaxy Quest*'s viewers are given a nice clue about the futility of this kind of talk as Gwen and Jason's hard-hitting appraisals of one another's failings, their "brief for divorce," takes place while the characters are out of sight and almost out of earshot. We can just make out Jason's last line as it gets picked up by the wind ("Did it ever occur to you that if you had been a little more supportive you could have held on to me?") and we are left to imagine Gwen's response, recorded in the shooting script but not in the final film: "I could have held on to *you*?"

To come full circle, or return to my worry about conversation's effectiveness, if "talking together" means making and fielding such allegations we can easily see how far talking will get us. At any rate, the timeworn nature of these allegations—the fact that Gwen and Jason's complaints about one another seem to stand in for men and women's complaints about one another since the very beginning, at least since Adam and Eve—would seem to lend weight to the view that knowing such things or believing such things about our partners has got us no closer to happiness. How will Gwen and Jason get back together by reminding themselves, as if either of them needed a reminder, that ever since man started registering his dismay over woman's lack of support, the role for which she had supposedly been made, woman started feeling the heat for her inability or unwillingness to be a helpmeet through the mechanism of betrayal—by being deceived or replaced? What should be obvious is that the couple at the heart of this remarriage comedy will not learn to relate to one another differently merely by recalling this lesson. Since it sketches the repeated patterns of their lives, the ruts they have slipped into and allowed to define them, merely describing in language those patterns of behavior that have become dull and unproductive but are hard to dislodge is thus not the key to transformation, to Cavell's "miracle of change."

Yes, the Rolling Helps

What does bring about a marked change in relationships beset by conflict or struggle is participation in ritual. *Galaxy Quest* helps us to recall why, in contrast to talking, arguing, and other ways of "working through" our problems, taking part in rituals can be so beneficial. There is purpose to even the silliest performed actions on the *Galaxy Quest* television show, after all—Jason's ineffective rolling, as if he were a specially trained soldier, where rolling would help him get to the bad guy first, or Gwen's not-needed repetition of the computer's findings. The purpose of this role-playing, followers of Confucius might argue, is to help people *stop* thinking of themselves as beings with a fixed nature—for example, as someone who is generally self-serving, the way Jason thinks of himself, or as someone who is clever and therefore probably accurate in her analyses, who is good at judging people or situations, the way Gwen thinks of herself. Followers of Confucius would argue that a person should not simply assume that the way they have come to see themselves is the way they are. As the authors of *The Path* write, "They would urge us to recognize that we are all complex and changing constantly."[31] Perhaps Jason is not inherently someone who has casual affairs with women, the way Gwen (and Jason himself) has concluded; perhaps he just slipped into certain patterns of behavior that he allowed to define him. The reality is that he has just as much potential to be trustworthy and dependable as to be disloyal.

Another thing Confucius understood is that it is easier to recognize that every person has many different and often contradictory emotional dispositions or ways of responding to the world when we stop acting as if our emotional dispositions develop by looking *inward*, by searching for the truth of who a person is by discovering their hidden, private self. In fact, Puett and Gross-Loh write, our emotional dispositions are developed by looking *outward*: "They are formed, in practice, through the things you do in your everyday life: the ways you interact with others and the activities you pursue. In other words, we aren't just who we are: we can actively make ourselves into better people all the time." Of course, coming to this conclusion requires that we "change our mind-set about our own agency and about how real change happens." For "while we have been told that true freedom comes from discovering who we are at our core, that 'discovery' is precisely what has trapped so many of us [. . .]. We are the ones standing in our own way."[32]

As I see it, thinking again about the importance of ritual, and how change actually happens, can do more than help us improve our relationships: it can revitalize our theoretical models. This is especially important for a generation who hopes to look beyond what has become conventional wisdom in the modern, Western world. For as some theorists have pointed out, even as more and more scholarship is being done on non-Western materials, our *theories* are still almost entirely those that arose in the West.[33] In this way we guarantee that material from other places and times, for example a work of ritual theory from early China, could never be something we allow ourselves to think through or learn from. As Puett writes, a text read in such a way could be "nothing other than an interesting document from another world—one about which we could perhaps have great nostalgia but one that never really threatens our theoretical models or makes us think anew."[34] *Galaxy Quest* offers a glimpse of what happens when we finally *do* let material from unfamiliar or faraway places challenge the models we have become so used to relying on.

Perhaps the most remarkable thing about this unassuming, thoroughly entertaining film is the way it refutes the misconception, everywhere held, that people who engage in ritual practices (who repeat lines from favorite television shows, who sound satisfied and impressed with their spouses, even when they do not feel that way) demonstrate a sentimental longing or wistful affection for an idealized, happy place—a place not at all like everyday life. The problem with this condescending reading is that it takes fictitious or mythical stories to be ontological descriptions of the world. This belief is what underwrites the sophisticate's dismissal of Brandon, or anyone else who takes certain shows seriously, or, as Cavell says, uses his precious hours to discover why the characters in work of fiction "use their time as they do, why they say the things they say."[35] As I have argued, discussing the *Galaxy Quest* episodes earnestly or acting as if the show is real—like Brandon does, when he and his friends devote their time to working out the show's technical errors and conundrums—doesn't necessarily make someone "a complete braincase," as Brandon points out. That is because the *Galaxy Quest* television show never attempts to describe empirical reality; rather, it offers viewers a plan for how to act in the world—particularly in times of crisis. Like other transformative fictions—such as Dante's *Divine Comedy* or the Old Testament—*Galaxy Quest* does *not* offer accounts of how the world is. Better to understand the show as developing strategies that help a people survive turmoil or instability. These times of great disturbance, confusion, or uncertainty might be brought about by warfare or kinds of cultural crises, but they could be less notable, too. They could be any set of highly charged interactions with other living human beings—for example, a discussion with siblings after the death of a parent, a romance between two jaded, middle-aged people, or, more generally, one's teenage years.

Notes

1 Stanley Cavell, *Pursuits of Happiness: The Hollywood Comedy of Remarriage* (Cambridge: Harvard University Press, 1981), 19, 23.
2 Ibid., 146.
3 Ibid.
4 Ibid., 8, 147. Cavell also calls the remarriage comedy genre "the comedy of equality" (82).
5 Ibid., 19.
6 Michael Puett and Christine Gross-Loh, *The Path: What Chinese Philosophers Can Teach Us About the Good Life* (New York: Simon & Schuster, 2016), 26–27.

7. Puett and Gross-Loh, *The Path*, 29. So, rather than ask "big questions such as: *Do we have free will? What is the meaning of life? Is experience objective?*" Confucius asked this "fundamental and deceptively profound question: *How are you living your life on a daily basis?*" (25).
8. Ibid., 10–11.
9. Cavell, *Pursuits of Happiness*, 5.
10. Puett and Gross-Loh, *The Path*, 9–10. This is also the theme of one of Michael Lewis's recent books, *The Undoing Project: A Friendship That Changed Our Minds* (W. W. Norton & Company, 2016).
11. These lines from *Nature That Emerges from the Decree*, a recently discovered fourth-century BCE text, are cited in Puett and Gross-Loh, *The Path*, 26–27.
12. Ibid., 27.
13. Ibid., 30.
14. Cavell, *Pursuits of Happiness*, 6.
15. Stanley Cavell, *Cities of Words: Pedagogical Letters on a Register of the Moral Life* (Cambridge: The Belknap Press of Harvard University Press, 2004), 15.
16. Puett begins his "Ritual Disjunctions" essay with a ritual described in the *Records of Rites*, one of the ritual classics from early China. See "Ritual Disjunctions: Ghosts, Anthropology, and Philosophy," in *The Ground Between: Anthropologists Engage Philosophy*, ed. Veena Das, Michael Jackson, Arthur Kleinman, and Bhrigupati Singh (Durham: Duke University Press, 2014), 218–33.
17. Puett and Gross-Loh, *The Path*, 34.
18. Puett, "Ritual Disjunctions," 219.
19. Ibid., 220–21.
20. Ibid., 226ff.
21. Ibid., 227.
22. Puett and Gross-Loh, *The Path*, 33.
23. Ibid., 33–35.
24. Ibid., 30.
25. This reconstruction of Hesiod's lament is offered by Puett and Gross-Loh, *The Path*, 19.
26. Michael Puett, "The Haunted World of Humanity: Ritual Theory from Early China," in *Rethinking the Human*, ed. J. Michelle Molina and Donald K. Swearer (Cambridge: Center for the Study of World Religions, Harvard Divinity School; distributed by Harvard University Press, 2010), 101.
27. Puett and Gross-Loh, *The Path*, 34.
28. As Puett and Gross-Loh write in *The Path*: "Increasingly, we have been told to seek [the] higher truth within. The goal of a self-actualized person is now to find himself and live his life 'authentically,' according to an inner truth. The danger of this lies in believing that we will all know our 'truth' when we see it, and then limiting our lives according to that truth. [. . .] Many Chinese

thinkers might say that in doing this, we are looking at such a small part of who we are potentially" (11).
29 It is worth looking carefully at the shooting script for this scene, since what is made clear from the script is how *much* study, research, dialogue, and argument has gone into the teenagers' conclusions.
30 Cavell, *Pursuits of Happiness*, 146.
31 Puett and Gross-Loh, *The Path*, 12.
32 Ibid.
33 Puett, "The Haunted World of Humanity," 97–98.
34 Puett, "Ritual Disjunctions," 222.
35 Cavell, *Pursuits of Happiness*, 6.

PART IV

The Female Voice Heard Anew

8

Passionate Utterances

Cavell, Film, and the Female Voice

CATHERINE WHEATLEY

THE QUESTION OF FEMALE EXPERIENCE is central to much—if not all—of Cavell's work on film, not least because he believes film to show a far greater interest in its female subjects than it does in its male subjects. Film is, Cavell believes, "about the creation of woman, about her demand for an education, for a voice in her history."[1] And yet, at the same time, such perspicuous critics as Tania Modleski have claimed that in Cavell's film-philosophy women's voices are ultimately silenced. In a single paragraph letter criticizing the journal *Critical Inquiry* for publishing two of Cavell's essays on *Now, Voyager* (1942, dir. Irving Rapper)—despite the fact that, according to Modleski, the journal fails to cite previous scholarship on the film—Modleski writes, for example, that:

> Inasmuch as Cavell [. . .] fails to cite any of the women working in his area, fails to *name* them (Doane, Jacobs, LaPlace, and others have written powerful critiques of *Now, Voyager* and other Bette Davis films), and inasmuch as *Critical Inquiry* exempts Cavell from the minimal requirements of scholarship, both parties perpetuate the very condition being analyzed: they participate in a system in which women go unrecognized, their voices unheard, their identities "unknown."[2]

Inspired in part by Modleski's critique, this chapter asks what, *exactly*, the role of the female voice is in Cavell's work on film. What do women's voices *sound* like? What does it mean to listen *to*, or *for*, these female voices? In the second half of the chapter, I want to consider what the impact of female voices such as Modleski's might be—both for Cavell's work on film and for his philosophy—as well as asking what, if any, relevance Cavell's male voice holds for us today. I will do this by looking at—or I should say, listening to—the voices of five women. Three are drawn from the films that Cavell writes about, one is a feminist film theorist, another a feminist philosopher.

Lucy Warriner: The Dissenting Voice

The question of the voice itself is a long-standing concern of Cavell's. In the title essay of his first book, *Must We Mean What We Say?*, he expresses a concern with what he calls the *sound* of philosophy.[3] In *The Claim of Reason* he states that the aim of his work—all of his work—is to bring the human voice back into philosophy.[4] He argues that the silencing of the voice is the goal of philosophical skepticism, and that therefore the discovery or recovery of voice is at the heart of overcoming skeptical despair.[5] His subsequent essays on literature (notably Shakespeare) and film examine how one might go about finding one's voice, and what happens in the case of a failure to do so.[6]

Almost always, it is the woman's voice, and the woman's fate, at stake. In Shakespeare's tragedies, for example, Desdemona and Cordelia die because voice comes too late. In the films discussed in *Pursuits of Happiness*, the creation of the woman comes about as a result of her being able to join her voice with that of her male counterpart, engaging in what Cavell, after John Milton, refers to as "a meet and happy conversation." Cavell explains that in the remarriage comedies "talking together is fully and plainly being together, a mode of association, a form of life, and I would like to say," he writes; "in these films the central pair are learning to speak the same language."[7]

The tone of that conversation is, however, as important as the content. Cavell says that conversation within these films is a source of pleasure, for both the audience and the central couple alike: the couples in these films are not only able to talk together, but to laugh together. And yet in the essay on *It Happened One Night* (1934, dir. Frank Capra) where Cavell references John Milton, he comments that the form of discourse most readily associated with marriage (and this will be no surprise to those readers who are married) is bickering, that the "characteristic sound of these comedies" is "the sound of argument, of wrangling, of verbal battle."[8] The female voice is raised *in contradiction* to the male voice. And this is, Cavell argues, a sign of caring: the hallmark of a willingness "to bear up under an assault of words, to give as good as you get, where what is good must always, however strong, maintain its good spirits, a test of intellectual as well as spiritual stamina, of what you might call ear."[9]

The 1937 comedy *The Awful Truth* (dir. Leo McCarey) shows what "good" bickering looks like through a contrast with "bad" lecturing, all the while foregrounding the woman's voice. After an early sequence in which married couple Lucy and Jerry Warriner decide to part ways, Lucy's lawyer tries to persuade her to give marriage another chance. As in the foreground of the shot, the lawyer repeatedly tells Lucy that "marriage is a beautiful thing," we hear his wife, standing in the background, haranguing him about his dinner, which is rapidly growing cold. Finally, he tells her to "Shut your mouth" before returning to his phone conversation with Lucy. Here, then, we are presented with the woman's voice as that of the harpy, harridan, virago, scold, or shrew—a role presumably derived from Shakespeare's *The Taming of the Shrew* and which is also assumed by, among others, *The Philadelphia Story*'s Tracy Lord and Amanda Bonner in *Adam's Rib* (both dir. George Cukor, 1940 and 1949). Their male equivalents are callous brutes who want their women to "shut their mouths," a figure that recurs in the melodramas of the unknown woman, as we will see in due course. Other women in the remarriage comedies meanwhile play dumb, like the nightclub singer Dixie Belle in *The Awful Truth*, or the cute competitors for Mugsy's affection in *The Lady Eve* (1941, dir. Preston Sturges). Or else they are humorless and buttoned up like *Bringing Up Baby*'s Miss Swallow (1938, dir. Howard Hawks), who swallows her words; or *The Awful Truth*'s ironically dubbed "madcap heiress," Barbara Vance.

Lucy Warriner (Irene Dunne) uses her voice quite differently. This is a woman who gives as good as she gets—and perhaps more. Throughout the film, she and Jerry (Cary Grant) trade witty insults, and it is clear to the audience that they share a worldview that their alternative partners do not. As Lucy puts it, they share some "grand laughs" together, many of which could be described as in-jokes. Often these jokes are at the other's expense: Jerry forces Lucy into an embarrassing spectacle of a dance with her suitor Daniel Leeson (Ralph Bellamy); he humiliates himself by barging in on a singing recital after mistaking it for a tryst; she embarrasses him by giving his wealthy would-be in-laws to understand that he's from an impoverished, lower-class background.

It is important that in two of these incidents Lucy is singing. She is singing for—or at least before—Jerry. Lucy, that is, *is a singer*. Her relationship with her singing teacher Armand is the excuse for the pair's separation. Her inability to sing with Jerry's replacement, Dan, signals the death knell for their fledging relationship. She is also the *only* woman within the remarriage comedies who sings, and it is notable in that regard that *The Awful Truth* is both what Cavell calls the "best, or the deepest of the comedies of remarriage,"[10] and that this, of all his readings of films, is the most contested.

Writing of the scene in which Lucy interrupts Jerry's dinner with his fiancée and her family, posing as his sister and breaking out into a coy parody of a routine earlier performed by Dixie Belle in a nightclub, Cavell remarks that Lucy is singing for Jerry's pleasure and his commitment, that by appropriating Dixie Belle's performance she is proposing herself as "a field on which he may weave passion and tenderness,"[11] making both an offer of friendship and remarriage. Perhaps we can go further than Cavell, however, and argue that Lucy's singing here is more than an offer of friendship, it is a rebuke: a form of chastisement and a suggested corrective. A kind of bickering, and an offer of education. Indeed, this is the case made in separate articles by both Kathrina Glitre and Catherine Constable.[12] Constable, in particular, argues that it is Lucy who educates Jerry in *The Awful Truth*, teaching him how to change, while she herself remains unchanged. Cavell understands Lucy's performance here as a willingness to change, one that requires a reciprocal response from Jerry, but for Constable it is a declaration that she has not changed, that Lucy *is* faithful and *always was* faithful. Beneath the performance lies "the real Lucy," the one who is as she always was: the same old Lucy. It is Jerry's perspective on her that has to change. (It is, Constable points out, Jerry who enters Lucy's room to bring about the reconciliation at the film's end, just as it is the male figure that has to follow the female figure into the Swiss clock.[13])

Constable thus argues that Lucy teaches Jerry to see her as she wants to be seen.[14] Perhaps we might add to this: she teaches him to listen to her voice. Glitre and Constable alike flag up an important mistake that Cavell makes in his reading of *The Awful Truth*, in misattributing a key speech to Jerry. It is in fact Lucy who, early in the film, speaks the lines "Don't you see that there can't be any doubt in marriage? The whole thing's built on faith and if you've lost that, well, you've lost everything."[15] When Jerry repeats Lucy's words about faith in marriage to Barbara toward the film's end, adding, "I think I read it in a book or something," he is unconsciously revealing he has learned a lesson from Lucy. At the same time, both Cavell's and Jerry's misattribution of this vital quote seems to prove John Stuart Mill's suggestion that a vast number of supposedly original thoughts put forth by male thinkers belong to a woman by suggestion. Mill's is a vision, as Cavell puts it, of "a very large proportion of Western culture as plagiarized, speaking with voices other than those it owns, implying *not* that culture does not listen to women, but that it very conveniently has."[16]

Paula Alquist: The Hysterical Voice

In *The Awful Truth*, this usurpation of the female voice is played for comic effect. In the melodramas of the unknown woman, it is "no laughing matter."[17] Quite to the contrary. As the heroine of *Gaslight* puts it, the matter of voice is serious: very serious. So serious that in Cavell's discussion of George Cukor's 1944 film, he claims that voicelessness is tantamount to madness.[18]

The early sequences of *Gaslight* pose the question of whether Paula (Ingrid Bergman) has a voice. On a superficial level this means that they ask whether she can sing, but on a more profound level have to do with whether she can speak, or even think, for herself. Paula's mind is not on her singing, her tutor tells her. Her heart is not in it. The trouble is not with the voice alone, but with the lack of feeling behind it. Paula is distracted by her infatuation with her piano teacher, Gregory (Charles Boyer), who she will soon marry; his subsequent attempts to drive Paula mad are presented as his reducing her to silence. Throughout *Gaslight*, Gregory works to deprive Paula of her voice at the same time as he forces her to question her interpretation of the world, imposing on her the world as he would have her see it. The denial of voice is not (merely) the loss of speech, but "a loss of reason, of mind as such—say the capacity to count, to make a difference."[19] Bergman's gestural performance visually signals this loss of voice through the repeated motion of putting her hand to her mouth, covering it, as if to stifle a voice that wants to escape, or to grasp at a voice that has already flown. This is in comparison with her earlier hand movements, where she stretches them out, palms up, lifting her arms as she lifts her voice in song, a movement that is repeated at the climax of the film, when Paula recovers her voice in a long speech that Cavell describes as a "mad song," in which she confronts her husband with a knife.[20] Cavell calls this speech Paula's "aria of revenge," understanding her to be lifting her voice in song.[21] Certainly, Bergman delivers the monologue as if it were a sung performance: her voice rising through the octaves, her body opening out once more as if to project the words coming from her mouth. Cavell translates it as her saying, "Now I *exist* because now I speak for myself."[22] It is therefore also her *cogito ergo sum*, her proof of existence not only to her husband but also—more importantly—to herself.

Cavell is building here on an idea developed in *A Pitch of Philosophy*, where he draws an equivalence between the melodrama of the unknown woman and opera, the Western institution in which, to Cavell's mind, "the human voice is given its fullest acknowledgement."[23] In both melodrama and opera, he claims, "the woman's demand for a voice, for a language, for attention to, and the power to enforce attention to, her own subjectivity, say to her difference of existence, is expressible as a response to an Emersonian demand for thinking."[24] He is clear that there are differences—especially ontological differences—between opera and film. Still, he suspects that opera has "transformed itself into film, that film is, or was, our opera"[25]—an idea floated in *Mr. Deeds Goes to Town* (1936, dir. Frank Capra), the subject of several essays by Cavell. In particular, melodrama and opera both push at the limits of linguistic expression, revealing something about the powers and limitations of the human capacity to raise the voice.[26] In opera, singing is a kind of abandonment: "a spiritual achievement expressed as a willingness to depart from all settled habitation, all conformity of meaning."[27] It embodies Thoreau's idea that being beside oneself in a sane sense—in other words, ecstasy—is that which proves one's humanity. Singing—*women's* singing—is to be understood as an ecstatic response: "an irrupting of a new perspective of the self to itself."[28]

But if singing exposes women as thinking, it also exposes her to the powers of those who do not want her to think, do not want autonomous proof of her existence. Cavell cites Catherine Clément's claim in her book *Opera, or the Undoing of Women* that opera—and by extension melodrama—is about the death of women, and women's self-expression, and the fact that women die, are driven mad, or are ostracized because they express themselves.[29] After all, as the feminist philosopher Adriana Cavarero reminds us, patriarchy tells us that "women should be seen and not heard."[30] For Cavarero, the woman who sings is always a Siren, an outsider to the domestic order of daughter and wife. The female singing voice, she writes, cannot be domesticated: it disturbs the system of reason by leading elsewhere.[31] No wonder Gregory is so swift to undermine Paula's self-assertion with his damning admonition, "Don't get hysterical, Paula." As Clément tells us, "Men will tell you that hysteria is a sickness [. . .]. Do not believe it. Hysteria is a woman's principal resource."[32]

The hysterical voice. The ecstatic voice. The voice beside itself. The singing voice. This voice is a weapon because it serves not just as a cogito—proof of the women's existence to herself, but also as a *rebuke* to the society who would silence her. Both Lucy and Paula sing to *chastise* the men who have ignored or stolen their voices. Their singing, that is, is a form of what Cavell calls passionate utterance.

A passionate utterance, Cavell explains in several of the articles collected in *Philosophy the Day after Tomorrow*, is, to put it simply, an expression of feeling. More than this, it is an expression of feeling aimed at provoking an appropriate response from an interlocutor. By way of explanation, Cavell draws examples from A. J. Ayer: "You acted wrongly in stealing that money," "Tolerance is a virtue," "I'm bored"—the last of which, if said to you by a child, is perhaps an appeal for an interesting suggestion or offer of amusement, and if by a friend (romantic or not) "is apt to still be an appeal and still to set a stake on some piece of your future together."[33] In either case, Cavell cautions, "You had better answer, and carefully."[34]

In a passionate utterance I make an appeal to you. And the feelings or actions I want to provoke are ones that we can acknowledge as appropriate responses to my expressions of feeling. There is no conventional procedure for appealing to you to act in response to my expression of passion. Whether I have the standing to appeal to you is part of the object to ensue. But you must respond. Or else resist the demand, and in so doing deny that I am a person who has any claim to a response for you. Through their singing, Lucy and Paula appeal to their listeners to share their pleasure, their pain. Jerry responds by taking up Lucy's invitation to remarry. When Paula delivers her vengeful aria to Gregory, however, there is no being moved to respond, only a move to avoid response, to escape Paula by continuing to manipulate her.

Tania Modleski: The Passionate Voice

Cavarero and Cavell alike draw a link between the singing woman and homosexuality, arguing that the primacy of song over speech evokes the feminine, just as speech, understood as the power to signify, evokes the masculine. In Cavarero's words, "where there is song, melody, and a voice, then there is generally a feminine experience, whether or not the composer or performer is a man."[35]

Both philosophers thus conflate the vocal with the feminine and the body on the one hand, and the semantic with the masculine and the mind on the other. But there are potential problems with this way of thinking. Firstly, the supremacy of music and song over speech in opera and melodrama may distract the audience from the plot of a story that is obsessively misogynist. The seductive power of opera consists in making these undomesticated heroines die singing. We watch the destruction of these women and *swoon*. Secondly, it risks abstracting the feminine: turning it into a category that can be co-opted by the male writer, director, or spectator, arrogating the (embodied, real) female voice in the name of the (theoretical, philosophical) feminine. This is precisely the charge that Modleski levels at Cavell in the introduction to her book *Feminism without Women*. Here, Modleski chides Cavell for his appropriation of female suffering. Cavell treats the female voice as a metaphor for metaphysics, she argues, or else he overidentifies with the beset femininity of his subjects: "garrulously appropriating," in Modleski's words, the struggle of these women to make their voices heard.[36]

For reasons that will become clear, it is worth briefly sketching out the timeline of Cavell's exchanges with Modleski, the third female voice that I want to pay heed to. The earliest draft of Cavell's chapter on *Gaslight* was presented in 1986; essays on *Letter from an Unknown Woman* (1948, dir. Max Ophüls) and *Now, Voyager* followed in 1987 and 1989. Modleski and Cavell's exchange in *Critical Inquiry* took place in autumn 1990. The interaction prompted an ongoing discussion of ideas that feeds into Cavell's essay on *Stella Dallas* (1937, dir. King Vidor), a version of which was made available by the Cultural Studies Project at MIT in 1991; Modleski's introduction to *Feminism without Women*, published later that same year; and Cavell's introduction to *Contesting Tears*, which was finally published in 1995.

For over half the time that Cavell was thinking about the question of the unknown woman's voice, then, Modleski's commentary on his work was ringing in his ears. We might put it that Modleski *has a say* in the final version of the essays in *Contesting Tears*. Her criticisms have a profound impact on

Cavell, not least in so far as they present to Cavell the possibility that he may be rejecting an offer of conversation, and hence failing, in his own way—in a different way perhaps than Modleski envisions—to acknowledge the voices of women. He writes:

> There is [a] charge to which my silence about feminist film theory may have opened me, [. . .] let me call it rejecting the offer of serious conversation; it is a form of avoiding the acknowledgment of the existence of others. Since philosophy, as I have variously characterized it, is a process, and a process that necessarily distrusts the process, of reading; call it a craving for education that attacks one's education as it stands; and since this takes place as conversation; to deny conversation genuinely offered is a denial of philosophy. It is a standing possibility. It is sometimes necessary. Is it true of what I have written? Have I treated an offer of conversation in this way? If my particular history of avoidances, disappointments, rumors, desires, responsibilities, has allowed paranoia to get the better of me here, so that I have from a sense of slight dealt slight, I regret it; I mean to do better.[37]

Modleski's critique of Cavell functions effectively as a passionate utterance: a demand for response from Cavell, who has to consider whether he will rise to that challenge. Cavell describes it in the introduction to *Contesting Tears* as an invitation to engage with questions of feminism. His response is that he will take up this invitation, that he will *do better*.

Thinking about *Stella Dallas*—a film in which the male character's failing is manifested explicitly as what Cavell calls "perceptual incompetence"[38]—provides him with an opportunity to put these intentions to the test, "since," in his words, "an explicit question of that film is the extent to which a male voice can be listened to in arriving at the subject."[39] Can Cavell speak for Stella? What gives him the right to intervene on her behalf? In short: "what is the pertinence of the male voice?"[40]

Cavell finds an answer of sorts in autobiographical expression. He opens and closes his essay on *Stella Dallas* with references to his mother, all but explicitly declaring that his reading is guided by an intuition of his mother's that she identified with a Stella who knew that she was too much.[41] Cavell's voice here is thus attuned to his mother's way of thinking—and to Stella's as a reflection of his mother, and as such he finds a way to write about female experience that participates to some extent in female subjectivity.

> I do not say that it is because I was beginning to write autobiographically that I begin my thoughts on *Stella [Dallas]* with a moment of autobiography; it is exactly as true to say that it is because I began this opening with a moment of autobiography that I have subsequently gone on (in the first chapter of *A Pitch of Philosophy*) to take autobiographical

expression distinctly further than I have ever done before. I trust this impulse will not be lost.[42]

I trust this impulse will not be lost. With these words Cavell announces that over the course of writing *Contesting Tears* something has changed—a new impulse has arisen—and he intends for that impetus to bear him forward. As a result of the conversations—not always meet and happy, it must be said— that he enters into with Modleski, Cavell comes to consider the place of his own voice in writing about film, and to begin to practice a self-conscious mode of criticism, which is the only mode, he feels, in which his encounter with feminism can take place. After the publication of *Contesting Tears*, autobiography winds its way further into Cavell's work in tandem with a continued interest in ideas of perfectionism.

It is possible, then, that what happens during the writing of *Contesting Tears*—Modleski's intervention, the process of self-appraisal that it gives rise to—is a step in Cavell's own path toward moral perfectionism: one that emerges from his experience of being rebuked by other members of the film studies community, but also from his commitment to remaining part of this community, to making renewed efforts to understand and be understood. He comes to the conclusion that criticism itself is a form of passionate utterance: "One person, risking exposure to rebuff, singles out another, through an expression of emotion and a claim of value, to respond in kind."[43]

Naomi Scheman: The Authoritative Voice

The question of authority, of who has the right to speak for another, has long been a central thread in Cavell's work, opening out not just onto questions of philosophy but also politics. In his work on J. L. Austin, for example, and with regard to ordinary language, Cavell discusses the problem and advantage of the first-person plural.[44] It may seem, he admits, that to use the first-person plural is to speak for others (a particular problem when one is a white, male professor at one of the most elite universities in the world). However, Cavell reconfigures the use of a phrase like "When we say . . . we mean. . ." so that the speaker is not making a unilateral statement, but is rather offering something for others to register their thoughts or their responses against. In short, he invites the response, "yes we do," but also "no we don't"—or even, "you may, but I do not." As such, Cavell's ordinary language philosophy is inherently political: it suggests that there must be an assent to the political realm within which one finds oneself, and that the offering of the words is a continual attempt to express or test the possibilities of that assent, not just on the level of overt political discussion, but on the level of our ordinary words.[45] Across his body of work, Cavell's use of the first-person plural is an invitation to his interlocutor to acquire self-knowledge. But it is also an invitation to see oneself as a part of a community (if only a community of two), to agree that we understand one another, that we agree on what we might say when.

In his thinking on passionate utterance—and on criticism as a form of passionate utterance—this matter comes into the foreground in a hitherto unprecedented manner. To make a passionate utterance is to recognize the person whom we are addressing as an individual, to acknowledge their existence. At the same time, it asks for adherence to a community (if only of two): *I* address *you*, in order to ask if there might be such a thing as a *we*. The risk I am taking is not that my claim will be met with disagreement, but with dismissal. To disagree with someone is to acknowledge already having entered into a community, a culture. It is to say that her opinion, her reading, matters, if only by dint of his wrongness. Bickering is the sign of a good marriage. Criticism is a form of care. Rebuke, retort, response—these are all forms of conversation, and conversation, we know, is the first step to overcoming isolation. But to dismiss someone is to plunge into skepticism. It is, in the words of Áine Kelly, an "outright annihilation" of the other person.[46]

In his final, autobiographical work, *Little Did I Know*, Cavell comes back to the idea of the close connection between autobiography, philosophy, and criticism and on that connection's grounding the philosopher's right to speak for others. He finds a "trouble" with this idea, writing:

> I am not sure that those who write out of a sense of a history of oppression would be glad to adopt this posture. I believe that certain women I know who write philosophically would not at all be glad to adopt this posture, or feel spoken for by one who does. Nor do I know that men and women who sense philosophical roots beyond American culture will be moved to test my representativeness.[47]

I want to turn now to my fourth female voice, that of the philosopher Naomi Scheman, whose work does not inform Cavell's (at least not as far as I know), but whose response to Cavell's comments on the arrogation of the female voice offers food for thought. In a beautiful article entitled "A Storied World: On Meeting and Being Met," Scheman wonders whether she counts herself among those women to whom Cavell refers.[48] After all, she points out, "[c]asting a suspicious eye on deployments of the unmarked 'we' has characterized most of feminist theory and politics since at least the 1970s," and Scheman herself has devoted much of her career to "undermining the claims of those in privileged social locations to speak for all of us."[49] But on the other hand, Scheman supposes, "neither theory nor politics can be done in the first-person singular." Indeed, "finding/creating an appropriate, usable we is a task many feminist theorists and others have taken on."⁵⁰ "Furthermore," she notes, "at the heart of much feminist or other liberatory theory and politics are concerns about, or demands for, recognition, engagement, and acknowledgment. These are all recognizable Cavellian themes."⁵¹

Scheman concludes that, "It is [. . .] an open and vexed and question whether there are unbounded philosophical claims, whether any one of us can speak for all of us, whether there is, in any interesting sense, an unbounded, human we at all. Many would answer 'no,' and some would go on to say that, perhaps for that reason, there cannot and should not be philosophy in the way we have known it."⁵² And yet theorists as eloquent and incisive as Elizabeth V. Spelman and Reni Eddo-Lodge, in different ways, have argued that giving up on the possibility of general claims is the final roost of privilege.⁵³ Whether any of us can, in good conscience, enter a claim on another's behalf depends of course on a complex initiation of acknowledgement and recognition. But the ethics of the I/you is, ultimately, not an acceptable replacement for the political address of the we.

Liz Hamilton: The Collusive Voice?

Since Cavell's work invites autobiographical response, it is probably no surprise that my own voice eventually poses itself as a question. As a female writer and thinker whose work has often drawn upon Cavell's writing, I am prompted to ask: Does Cavell speak for me? Do I speak for Cavell? Let me address this matter by way of my fifth female voice, which belongs to Liz Hamilton, one of two lead characters in George Cukor's final film, *Rich and Famous* (a 1981 remake of the 1943 Warner Brothers film, *Old Acquaintance*, starring Bette Davis and Miriam Hopkins).

Rich and Famous is notable for being the only film that Cavell refers to in terms of same-sex remarriage. Remarking that Liz (Jacqueline Bisset) and her friend Merry (Candice Bergen), after years of comings and goings, wind up at midnight in Connecticut with a kiss, Cavell suggests that the film reformulates the dialectic of the legitimacy of marriage, arguing that it is the capacity of the pair to take pleasure in one another without a concept, a pleasure of exclusiveness and devotedness not determined by predicates taken from the church, state, or fact of children, that "declares them married."⁵⁴ Certainly, Liz and Merry's relationship would be well characterized by a description such as "amatory war" and "ferocious and loving battle." In this much, Cavell's brief treatment of *Rich and Famous* is symptomatic of a willingness, following Modleski's chastening of him, to think about the limits of marriage as metaphor.

Following a brief prologue, we first meet Liz properly at an event where she has been invited to speak about her work. During her speech, Liz "shamelessly" declares that she is too interested in her work as a writer, and in the voices of old men, to concern herself with feminist politics. A cut to a group of black women sitting on the ground before her has a clear implication: that by privileging self-interest and a tradition of patriarchal wisdom she is neglecting other causes, to do with both gender and race. It seems that in putting the "I" before "we," Liz, given a platform on which to use the voice that she has, refuses to speak to or for others.

Is it a moral failure when those women in the privileged position of having a voice—and I am very lucky to count myself among them—continue to rearticulate and reconsider the words of old men rather than allowing new voices to be heard? To speak of, for example, Michael Haneke, Martin Heidegger, Stanley Cavell, rather than, say, Jessica Hausner, Jennifer Barker, Martha Nussbaum? Not to mention Rungano Nyoni, Sara Ahmed, Kathryn Belle? Are the two things mutually exclusive? There has been a lot of talk recently of patriarchy and the problem of the white male canon, in both film and philosophy. So Sophie Mayer, for example, has critiqued the pervasive but seldom acknowledged norm of "homocitation," that is, male critics and scholars making reference predominantly to work—whether writings or films—by other men.[55] Citation is never neutral, Mayer argues. It is always political. It is also, as Sara Ahmed has argued, a "reproductive technology," one that continually makes and remakes the world not "objectively" or completely but in highly selective fashion.[56] The result is a partial representation of the world that remains silent about its own limitedness. As the critic Girish Shambu puts it:

> Thus does a selective narrative—disproportionately dominated by men—install itself, fortress-like, as history. It is an edifice that has been built up over time with the active collaboration of several communities: academia (where graduate students feel compelled to reproduce citation practices of their scholar-models in the field), working critics (traditionally steeped in auteurism), and cinephiles (whose list-making practices are widely acknowledged to be a particularly male propensity). To rewrite history, to create a more fair and balanced narrative, requires the participation of all these communities. Further, especially on the part of men at every level of film culture, it calls for a self-awareness of citation practice, and a conscious striving toward gender equity in this practice.[57]

What Shambu is calling for, in short, is a critical and philosophical practice that heeds the voices of women. For some, Mayer included, this involves radically silencing some of the male voices that have hitherto dominated film theory and philosophy. Like many feminist thinkers, she uses a language of rupture, violence, and totality: asking, for example, that we "smash," "destroy," or "fuck" the patriarchy and its canons.[58] In short, that we deny these men a say any longer. And perhaps this is necessary. Perhaps we cannot find a common ground. As Cavell himself tells us, the denial of conversation is always a standing possibility.

But I would urge that we take pause to consider the idea of decentering, sharing the narrative wealth, bringing different voices into the conversation. For Cavell, a refusal to conform involves both turning away from society and turning toward it. Or, as Bret Stephens puts it in an excellent article on "the dying art of disagreement": to disagree well you must first *understand* well.

> You have to read deeply, listen carefully, watch closely. You need to grant your adversary moral respect; give him the intellectual benefit of doubt; have sympathy for his motives and participate empathically with his line of reasoning. And you need to allow for the possibility that you might yet be persuaded of what he has to say.[59]

Affronted by Cavell's appropriation of the female voice, Modleski rebukes him, and in so doing invites him to see differently the world—the world of these films—that they share. Challenged by a female voice to reconsider his assumptions, Cavell accepts what he understands as an "invitation." I may not agree with all your criticisms, he writes. But I accept your right to make them. And in response: *I will try harder. I must do better.* In his subsequent work, Cavell struggles to appropriately respond to the woman's voice while at the same time attempting "not to *explain* the woman's thinking, to enable us to know what she knows; [. . .] to listen to her voice in order to enable a sort of understanding—an understanding beyond explanation—to take place."[60] Surely this is good advice for us all: that we try not only to *speak* better, but also to *listen* better?

Conclusion: On Listening

At six years old, Cavell, playing in the street, was struck by a car and his left ear was permanently damaged. Nonetheless, for a long time he would follow in his mother's footsteps in pursuing a career as a professional musician. As a result, he writes "certain questions of ear that run through my life—questions of realities and fantasies of perfect pitch, for example—become [in my work] questions of the detection of voice."[61]

To have perfect pitch is not only the ability to produce a note, but also to be able to hear it. It is being the ideal listener, one sensitive to the slightest nuances of what you are hearing. It is the recognition of the autonomy and separateness of the other. Recall Cavell's description in *Pursuits of Happiness* of caring as a test of what you might call ear. Dan Leeson does not have a good ear—he is unable to recognize the virtuosity of Lucy's voice. Jerry Warriner, on the other hand, might just do: though perhaps Lucy needs to teach him how to use it. In the melodramas of the unknown women, the female voice falls on deaf ears. But in his exchange with Modleski, Cavell models receptive listening. Cavell, it seems to me, has a very good ear.

As Naomi Scheman suggests, it is no doubt time to let the voices of those who "speak out of a sense of history of oppression" be heard.[62] But if—as well—we are to continue to listen to old men, then we could do worse than heed the words of T. S. Eliot in *Four Quartets*, whose elegant verse seems to me to capture what is so powerful about Cavell's encounter with the female voice, indeed about Cavell's philosophy as a whole:

> Do not let me hear
> Of the wisdom of old men, but rather of their folly,
> Their fear of fear and frenzy, their fear of possession,
> Of belonging to another, or to others, or to God.
> The only wisdom we can hope to acquire
> Is the wisdom of humility: humility is endless.[63]

Notes

1. Stanley Cavell, *A Pitch of Philosophy: Autobiographical Exercises* (Cambridge: Harvard University Press, 1994), 134.
2. Tania Modleski, "Letter to the Editor," *Critical Inquiry* 17, no. 1 (Autumn 1990): 237; italics in original. Modleski subsequently expanded her charge against Cavell in the opening chapter of her book *Feminism Without Women: Culture and Criticism in a "Postfeminist" Age* (London: Routledge, 1991), where she connects Cavell's misunderstanding of feminist concerns to what she perceives as the marginalization of women in Emerson.
3. Stanley Cavell, "Must We Mean What We Say?," *Must We Mean What We Say?* (Cambridge: Cambridge University Press, 1969), 1–43.
4. Cavell, *A Pitch of Philosophy*, 58.
5. Ibid., 59.
6. For example, Stanley Cavell, "The Avoidance of Love: A Reading of *King Lear*," in *Must We Mean What We Say?*, 267–356.
7. Stanley Cavell, *Pursuits of Happiness: The Hollywood Comedy of Remarriage* (Cambridge: Harvard University Press, 1981), 16.
8. Ibid., 86.
9. Ibid.
10. Ibid., 231.
11. Ibid., 253.
12. Kathrina Glitre, "'The Same, But Different': The Awful Truth About Marriage, Remarriage and Screwball Comedy," *Cineaction* 54 (2001): 2–11. Catherine Constable, "Seeing Lucy's Perspective: Returning to Cavell, Wittgenstein, and *The Awful Truth*," *New Review of Film and Television Studies* 9, no. 3 (2011): 358–75.

13 Constable, "Seeing Lucy's Perspective," 373.
14 Ibid., 366.
15 Ibid., 361.
16 Cavell, *A Pitch of Philosophy*, 16–17.
17 Stanley Cavell, *Contesting Tears: The Hollywood Melodrama of the Unknown Woman* (Chicago: The University of Chicago Press, 1996), 65.
18 Ibid., 66.
19 Ibid., 58.
20 Ibid., 71.
21 Ibid.
22 Ibid., 47.
23 Stanley Cavell, "Something Out of the Ordinary," in *Philosophy the Day after Tomorrow* (Cambridge: Harvard University Press, 2006), 15.
24 Ibid., 220.
25 Cavell, *A Pitch of Philosophy*, 136.
26 Ibid., 155.
27 Ibid., 144.
28 Ibid., 145.
29 Ibid., 176. Cavell is here citing Catherine Clément's *Opera, or the Undoing of Women*, trans. Betsy Wing (Minneapolis: University of Minnesota Press, 1978).
30 Adriana Cavarero, *For More than One Voice: Toward a Philosophy of Vocal Expression* (Stanford: Stanford University Press, 2005), 117.
31 Ibid., 118.
32 It is worth noting that Cavell reads a key scene in *Stella Dallas* as expressing Stella's need to teach her daughter to cry.
33 Ibid., 17.
34 Ibid.
35 Cavarero, *For More than One Voice*, 122.
36 Modleski, *Feminism Without Women*, 8.
37 Stanley Cavell, "Response to Tania Modleski," *Critical Inquiry* 17, no. 1 (Autumn 1990), 242.
38 Ibid., 198.
39 Ibid.
40 Ibid., 199.
41 William Rothman, "Cavell on Film, Television, and Opera," in *Stanley Cavell*, ed. Richard Eldridge (Cambridge: Cambridge University Press, 2003), 225.
42 Cavell, *Contesting Tears*, 200.
43 Cavell, *Philosophy the Day after Tomorrow*, 26.

44 See Cavell, "Must We Mean What We Say?"
45 For more on this topic, see Paul Standish in conversation with Cavell, "Stanley Cavell in Conversation with Paul Standish," *Journal of Philosophy of Education* 46/2 (2012): especially 158–60. See also Stephen Mulhall, *Stanley Cavell's Recounting of the Ordinary* (Oxford: Oxford University Press, 1994), especially 69–74.
46 Áine Kelly, "'A Dance of Frenzy, a Dance of Praise': Fred Astaire Acknowledges America," in *Stanley Cavell, Literature and Film: The Idea of America*, ed. Andrew Taylor and Áine Kelly (Oxford and New York: Routledge, 2013), 163.
47 Stanley Cavell, *Little Did I Know: Excerpts from Memory* (Stanford: Stanford University Press, 2010), 6.
48 Naomi Scheman, "A Storied World: On Meeting and Being Met," in *Stanley Cavell and Literary Studies*, ed. Richard Eldridge and Bernard Rhie (London: Continuum, 2011), 92–105.
49 Ibid., 93.
50 Ibid., 93.
51 Ibid., 93.
52 Ibid., 105.
53 See, for example, Elizabeth V. Spelman, *Inessential Woman: Problems of Exclusion in Feminist Thought* (Boston: Beacon Press, 1988) and Reni Eddo-Lodge, *Why I Am No Longer Talking to White People About Race* (London: Bloomsbury, 2017).
54 Cavell, *Contesting Tears*, 30.
55 Sophie Mayer, *Political Animals: The New Feminist Cinema* (London: I.B. Tauris, 2016).
56 Sara Ahmed, "Making Feminist Points." *Feministkilljoys*, September 11, 2013. feministkilljoys.com.
57 Girish Shambu, "Time's Up for the Male Canon," *Film Quarterly*, September 21, 2018. filmquarterly.org.
58 For more on the uses of this language of rage and its political implications, see Helen Wood, "Fuck the Patriarchy: Towards an Intersectional Politics of Irreverent Rage," *Feminist Media Studies* 19, no. 4 (2019): 609–15.
59 Bret Stephens, "The Dying Art of Disagreement," *The New York Times*, September 24, 2017. nytimes.com.
60 Cavell, *Contesting Tears*, 234.
61 Cavell, *Little Did I Know*, 18.
62 Scheman, "A Storied World," 105.
63 T. S. Eliot, "East Coker," in *Four Quartets* (New York: Caedmon, 1970).

9

Cavell, Altman, Cassavetes

The Melodrama of the Unknown Woman in *A Woman Under the Influence* and *Nashville*

CHARLES WARREN

AT A CRUCIAL TIME in their development and process of self-realization, Stanley Cavell and filmmakers John Cassavetes and Robert Altman seem to have had some of the same things on their minds with regard to the medium of film, the question of human identity, the possibilities for human interaction, and the state of America (and its hopes). Specifically, the film genre Cavell has described and named "the melodrama of the unknown woman" seems to have preoccupied Cassavetes and Altman in their work, at least for a time. And remember, Cavell's idea of the melodrama genre, like his idea of the comedy of remarriage, goes beyond the content and form of films. The genre is an event of theater, a public, social working-through of philosophical issues.

Cavell, Altman, and Cassavetes are of a generation. Cavell was born in 1926, Altman in 1925, Cassavetes in 1929. Cavell's important essay "Must We Mean What We Say?" was published in 1958, and began a series of essays leading to the publication of his 1969 collection, *Must We Mean What We Say?*, which established him as an important thinker and writer. Cavell has said that the work of Ludwig Wittgenstein and J. L. Austin showed him a way into philosophy, made it possible for him to do philosophy.

The idea that the way we live and speak, properly attended to, can give an answer to the compulsion—the compulsion of philosophy, the compulsion of everyday life—to escape the human, to flee from it, to build castles in the air (Wittgenstein: houses of cards), or systems of suffocating rules, is an idea Cavell has linked back to founding work in American philosophy, notably to Emerson, and to American literature and other artistic expression, such as popular film of the 1930s and 1940s. (It is not that rules are made to suffocate life—though sometimes they are—but that life is looked *through*, to discern rules that seem to govern life, and, once discerned, suffocate, whereas life looked *at*, rather than through, makes things much more complicated, fructifying.)

John Cassavetes made his first film, *Shadows* (1958), in the late 1950s in a determined effort to bring the American fictional film closer than ever into life, looking into the heart, seeming to follow life, like a documentary, in all of life's unpredictable moves. After unhappy work directing in Hollywood, Cassavetes got the world's attention anew—or the attention of those who know what is good—with *Faces*, made independently and released in 1968. And he went on to work another fifteen years, until overtaken by illness, as an independent writer and director of fiction films. *Shadows* and *Faces* show enormous sympathy for their characters, but paint a devastating picture of American life at the mercy—where there is little mercy—of race prejudice, wide compulsion to self-doubt, benighted gender roles assumptions, the rage to have power over others, as seen in poisonous business ethics and elsewhere. *Shadows* and *Faces* are boldly nongeneric films. In later work, as if to find some way out for America, Cassavetes pursues a reworking of the deep concerns of genre from earlier films: romantic comedy, I would say remarriage comedy, in *Minnie and Moskowitz* (1971); the melodrama of the unknown woman, in *A Woman Under the Influence* (1974); a variation of the same, in the *All About Eve* (1950) remake *Opening Night* (1977); redemptive film noir, in *The Killing of a Chinese Bookie* (1976). The final film, *Love Streams* (1984), serves as a compendium of all this and links, I would say, to the American autobiographical documentary, a mode opened by Ed Pincus, as in *Diaries 1971-1976* (1982); by the great unknown *Film Portrait* (1971) of Jerome Hill; and practiced by Jonas Mekas, Ross McElwee, Su Friedrich, and others. In *Love Streams*, Cassavetes casts himself and his wife, Gena Rowlands, as brother and sister, and films in his own house.

Robert Altman made his prescient (in regard to his own later work), death-haunted documentary *The James Dean Story* in 1957. He worked in television and began directing feature films on assignment over the next decade, finding his voice in *That Cold Day in the Park* (1969) and finding a large audience with *M.A.S.H.*, which won the Palme d'Or at Cannes in 1970. Altman continued right up to his death in 2006, to make films steadily and unremittingly, working on the border between Hollywood and the independent world, known at first for rethinking genres—the Western in

McCabe and Mrs. Miller (1971), film noir in *The Long Goodbye* (1973), the musical in *Nashville* (1975). After *3 Women* (1977) he was known more and more for seeking his own unprecedented forms—as in the filmed plays of the 1980s, such as *Come Back to the 5 & Dime, Jimmy Dean, Jimmy Dean* (1982) and *Streamers* (1983) or in the 1990s films that move among many situations, such as *Short Cuts* (1993) and *Kansas City* (1996), a practice begun by *Nashville*. His final film was *A Prairie Home Companion* (2006), full of signs of doom.

From the first, Altman was engaged in a new pursuit of life, noticing what is not usually noticed, representing fairly the true complexity of life, letting actors' performances flourish with a new naturalness and oddity, seeming to follow the unpredictable, not constrained by story forms or audience expectations. But compared to Cassavetes, Altman seems not entirely led by the human heart, not out, above all, to let the human being come forward in full, messy, multi-dimensionality. Altman is after metaphysics—not the kind that needs to be taken apart, but the metaphysics that is a deeper revelation of life itself, like the metaphysics of William Faulkner in *The Sound and the Fury*, say (or Altman's beloved Raymond Carver). (The distinction between the metaphysics that needs to be taken apart and the metaphysics that life does reveal, and that reveals life, is not an easy one—acts of criticism are called for.)

The year 1960 (round about) marked a crucial turn in American film history and cultural history (and in wider history than America's, of course). With the breakdown of the old Hollywood studio system, with the Kennedy years and then the Kennedy assassinations and others, with the Vietnam War and America's rethinking of itself brought on by that, much of the inspiration for film seemed to go into the documentary and avant-garde movements, flowering in the 1960s and continuing on to this day—here was a new way to speak, a new way of understanding; here something could be said.

Cassavetes and Altman chose to work in the realm of the fiction film intended for theaters and a large audience, and in the 1960s and subsequent decades their films form two extraordinary strains of inquiry into people, into American life and its disappointments and possibilities, and into ways film can clear itself of habits and nostalgia and face what is there to be faced. In these same decades Stanley Cavell was thinking and writing about the strong generating source of certain—let us say it, the deepest—classical Hollywood romantic comedies and domestic melodramas, calling this range of films a key response to besetting American, and wider, concerns about who a person is, whether we can speak to one another, what standards a person's coming-to-be and coming to give acknowledgment and receive acknowledgment, set for the polity. Cassavetes and Altman, postclassical-Hollywood, are driven by what drove that Hollywood—*It Happened One Night, The Philadelphia Story, Adam's Rib, Stella Dallas, Gaslight, Now,*

Voyager—and what is on Cavell's mind in *Pursuits of Happiness: The Hollywood Comedy of Remarriage* and *Contesting Tears: The Hollywood Melodrama of the Unknown Woman*, and indeed in all his writings.

Let us bear down a bit on *A Woman Under the Influence* (1974) and *Nashville*, arguably Cassavetes's and Altman's most important films. The melodrama of the unknown woman takes on important new inflection here.

A Woman Under the Influence gives us the story of Mabel Longhetti (Gena Rowlands)—a married woman with three small children, a woman who listens to opera on the radio and encourages others to sing, who loves *Swan Lake* and at times imitates its dance, whom most people in her world, notably her husband, Nick, played by Peter Falk, consider special and valuable and larger than life, yet beyond comprehension, disturbing, finally mad. The irony rampant here—and irony is so key to the tone of the earlier melodramas—is that Mabel and Nick speak an English that is two different languages. He is rhetorical (rendered beautifully in Falk's finely measured performance). She is not rhetorical: every word she says is new. In the middle of the film, after playing a mad scene that is not madness, Mabel is committed by her family to an asylum. The film announces "Six Months Later," and we see Mabel on her return to family—immediate family, parents, mother-in-law, and others—where she plays another mad scene amid managing to control herself for the sake of contact with her children, and being contained by the fearful and conventional people around her, who do not want to push things too far at this point. The film's final moments, with the husband and wife calmly preparing the bed for the night in a mood of acceptance, have been likened by Ray Carney to the ending of Ozu's film *The Flavor of Green Tea Over Rice* (1952), another story of marital turmoil patched over.[1]

A Woman Under the Influence is a harrowing experience. Hardly ever has a film brought us into such raw and sustained contact with a woman of compelling depth and originality, desperately reaching out, trying to carry on as who she is, disappointed, rebuked, abused, at moments met part way by a husband who can go no more than part way. She is convinced that she sustains her children spiritually, and wants to make any compromise that will prevent the world from denying them to her.

Gaslight, Letter from an Unknown Woman, Now, Voyager, Stella Dallas were driven by film's wanting to bring us, as film's audience, to see and hear and acknowledge a woman as no one in the woman's own world will do. Cassavetes has this motive. He and Rowlands believe their audience needs this, in fact wants this. Cassavetes replays the older films, breaking through to us with a new realism in depicting a working-class milieu (which is not exactly what Mabel herself comes from, complicating things), and with a new improvisatory intensity in the acting and in shooting long takes with a handheld camera. This is profound, older Hollywood—Emersonian

Hollywood—coming at us with the powers of Beat culture, jazz, 1960s frankness, *cinéma vérité*.

The film does not present the striking linear development and character metamorphoses of the earlier films. But in the few days and nights we are given of this family's life, Mabel does constantly evolve, finding herself anew and again anew. The process has begun well before the film starts, and it will continue. The evolution is there in Rowlands's amazing performance, her body and her face never still, reactive and registering revelations about herself and the world—projective, expressive, creative. In the final episode, Mabel comes into her greatest madness at the same time she is at her most effective at seeing what the world wants and accommodating it, for the sake of her children and, to an extent, for her husband, her marriage itself, her compromised marriage.

Ray Carney calls his chapter on this film in *The Films of John Cassavetes* "An Artist of the Ordinary" (and repeatedly invokes Emerson on self-realization).[2] Indeed, Mabel, like the women of the earlier films, is an artist of life. She engages herself, as Thoreau puts it, "to carve and paint the very atmosphere and medium through which we look [. . .] morally."[3] She takes up her life as a creative medium, and like the earlier women on film, and like Thoreau, calls upon us all so to take up our lives, to open ourselves to such a taking up. Mabel's pervasive creativity is figured—concentrated in moments—in her directing people to sing and to dance and to enter into a play that responds to life and extends life—herself directing and in part entering into what she directs, working like Cassavetes himself. And as with the women of the earlier films—a matter Cavell discusses so richly—Mabel's imagination is indissoluble from film imagination.

The final episode of *A Woman Under the Influence* bears an uncanny resemblance to the ending of *Blonde Venus* (1932, dir. Josef von Sternberg), with Marlene Dietrich—the film Cavell has named as the earliest of the melodramas of the unknown woman.[4] A wife and mother returns to her family and determines to contain her extravagance—perhaps. In both films, great play is made with a set of sliding doors, easily readable as a figure for the film screen. The woman in each film opens the doors (her husband has closed them) and penetrates the realm of children, where woman and child are lovingly filmed close-up, in intimacy. Through the doors, the screen, is, as it were, the world of the woman's creation, her film, her offspring, and her interior (Mabel has said earlier to the children, "I never did anything . . . I made you and you and you"). The world through the doors gives Mabel the motive and the strength to play out her return, more or less tactfully. She emerges from the inner room and is framed for the ensuing scene in long shot against the now-closed doors/screen before an audience of relatives, and us—Mabel as if impaled on the doors/screen, but making it her medium. Later this film of a mostly realistic and straightforward (though unconventional) shooting style finds in the bizarre image of Mabel's out-of-focus hand floating and gesturing in the foreground as she dances on the couch the perfect realization of who she is in her depths. Mabel is film.

Altman's *Nashville* is full of women singing about wanting to go somewhere but not knowing the way, about never getting enough of what they hunger for, about the secrets of their love they will never tell (why? because the world will not tolerate such secrets?). Women who do not sing, wish to sing, try to sing. And the sense of inner depths the women point to through the art of song is compounded with madness, most strikingly in the scene of the breakdown of the great country singer Barbara Jean (Ronee Blakley) on stage outdoors at Opryland—on a riverboat set reminiscent of another of Cavell's named melodramas of the unknown woman, *Show Boat* (1936, dir. James Whale, with Irene Dunne).

Barbara Jean/Blakley's breakdown is one of the great mad scenes in film, reminiscent in its exhaustiveness, of Harriet Andersson's breakdown before the "spider god" at the end of *Through a Glass Darkly* (1961, dir. Ingmar Bergman); earlier in *Nashville*, Geraldine Chaplin, a foreigner, wanders into the strange world of this city and remarks, "it looks like Bergman." But Karin (Harriet Andersson) succumbs to terror, whereas Barbara Jean, like Mabel in *A Woman Under the Influence*, talks to an audience with some enthusiasm about, while drifting off into, her world of memories and projections, pain mixed with ecstasy, and she is disconcerted to be stopped and led off stage— "I ain't done. I ain't done." Otherwise in *Nashville*, Linnea (Lily Tomlin) is a woman constrained by a suburban marriage and children she loves, who sings with a black Gospel choir, launching herself out of her world, and who gives way to a one-night stand with the film's cad, folk-rock singer Tom (Keith Carradine). Linnea shows extraordinary warmth and maturity in the context of this film. But her unknownness manifests itself acutely in a celebrity outdoor party scene, where she appears obsessed and deranged in conversation, fixated on episodes of highway death and mutilation (on the wavelength, we might say, of Godard's *Weekend* [1967]). Sueleen (Gwen Welles), quite unable to sing but full of desire for it, after being forced to strip before an audience of men who have hired her to entertain for an evening, virtually hallucinates a future for herself in country music, talking privately to her best friend, the black man Wade (Robert Doqui), who sees he can no longer communicate with her. And Winifred/Albuquerque (Barbara Harris) goes through the film unheard, avoided, regarded as a nut, until at the end, on the replica Parthenon stage, she gets the chance to deliver a powerful bluesy version of "It Don't Worry Me"—powerful and effective for the *film* audience, everyone else being distracted after the shooting of Barbara Jean onstage, the political candidate due to speak and his entourage now fleeing, chaos everywhere.

But *Nashville* does not do all that film can do to allow any one of these women to be as fully as possible what she is, to allow the audience for film to see as fully as possible, and to make contact with, what those in the woman's own world will not see and make contact with. Altman feels compelled to deal with more than one woman, and to keep moving from situation to situation, giving us fragments—establishing a film form he would become known for. Altman is interested in a system, a network or web, wherein individual lives take place. With the slow-moving but restless camera within one situation, and the cut from one situation to the next, we feel that the forces of one life, and the forces playing upon one life, affect the next. It is not like what the cultural critic discerns, but something only the eyes and ears and movements of film can give us.

Nashville is a film insistently about America, with its flags, presidential race, opening bicentennial song ("We must be doin' somethin' right to last 200 years"), references to Vietnam and the Second World War, and so on. The film is about the state of America and its prospects. What the film wants to bring us into is not one unacknowledged life and the way of acknowledgment; at present, for Altman, that is too much to ask. With all that is represented by Vietnam, America has begun destroying itself. America needs death. Death and rebirth. (What might be called Vietnam consciousness comes to the surface in Cavell's essay on *King Lear*, "The Avoidance of Love," and in chapter ten of *The World Viewed*, "End of the Myths.") The challenge for *Nashville*'s audience is to undergo the trauma of accepting Altman's disturbing satire and take the first step toward acknowledgment of the lives of women we see necessarily in the fragments of something larger than he has made of them. The something larger is Altman's power as director, of course, but one is asked to take the leap of faith that this power of film is identified with powers already there in the world—social powers, and the very power of death. Altman lets himself go, in part, in this direction, for a purpose, in answer to what the world dictates. And there is more to Altman. He attends to and invokes these women singing their hearts out, or trying to. Think of the great low-angle shots of Karen Black or Ronee Blakley singing, making love to the bulbous microphone they hold.

Cavell speaks about the religious dimension in *Letter from an Unknown Woman* (its crosses and nuns), saying we must understand something about this woman's life—Lisa (Joan Fontaine)—as if the life is from the beyond.[5] Mabel Longhetti is seen in her house in one characteristic long shot, the space of the house dwarfing her, offering to absorb her, this time, the woman standing backed up to her kitchen sink with a cross placed above it, is a sign of some source of renewal, her destiny and her refuge (St. Paul: I die daily). The center and hinge-point of *Nashville* is a series of Sunday morning church service scenes, one featuring a full-immersion baptism, death and rebirth (earlier, at the airport, Barbara Jean bade goodbye to the crowd of well-wishers welcoming her, "Like my granddaddy always used to say, if you're down to the river, I hope you'll drop in"). At the end of the church sequence, the film finds the hospital chapel and Barbara Jean singing for the first time in the film, singing of her contact with God.

Christ-like, Barbara Jean had succumbed physically on Friday. She has since been seen laid out unconscious on a hospital bed surrounded by wreaths of flowers, as if dead. Now she has risen on Sunday morning, and found her voice. At the end of the film, after being shot, she is carried off the stage, her husband, with his hands on her, shouting, "I can't stop that blood, man!" It is the blood of the artist, there for those who will take it in—the singer, the artist of life, the artist like Altman who offers the shock of a step toward humanity for those who will accept his radical, Swiftian satire and the disorienting energies it sets loose.

Notes

1. Ray Carney, *American Dreaming: The Films of John Cassavetes and the American Experience* (Berkeley: University of California Press, 1985), 193–94.
2. Ray Carney, "An Artist of the Ordinary (*A Woman Under the Influence*)," in *The Films of John Cassavetes: Pragmatism, Modernism, and the Movies* (Cambridge: Cambridge University Press, 1994), 143–83.
3. Henry David Thoreau, "Where I Lived, and What I Lived For," in *Walden; or, Life in the Woods*, ed. Robert F. Sayre (New York: Library of America, 1985), 394.
4. Stanley Cavell, *Contesting Tears: The Hollywood Melodrama of the Unknown Woman* (Chicago: The University of Chicago Press, 1996), 14.
5. Ibid., 109. Cavell elaborated on this point in his many lectures on the film over the years at Harvard University.

PART V

Contending with Conditions, Human and Otherwise

10

Stanley Kubrick and Stanley Cavell

Cinematic Syntax, Avoidance, and Acknowledgment

DAVID MIKICS

STANLEY CAVELL WRITES in *The World Viewed* that "movies convince us of the world's reality": they both give voice to skepticism and point beyond it, to the truth of the real world.[1] This unexpected thought lies at the heart of Cavell's idea of cinema: movies give us an instruction in reality, pulling us out of fantasy. In his writing about movies, as in his other work, Cavell conveys the seductiveness of the skeptical attitude so he can argue that skepticism is not final but only a stage on the way to acknowledging our actual relation with others. The case for acknowledgment can only be truly made by those who recognize the skeptical impulse in themselves. This kind of argument is familiar from Christianity and Freud (only those who admit the sinful or neurotic side of the self can hope to heal it).

Skepticism, the thought that life is an illusion, provides the consolation of a perfect, self-sustaining fiction. Cavell sees the flight into skepticism the way Freud sees the flight into neurosis: a choice of unreality that seems to offer safety but that proves dangerously fragile in its seamlessness. Skepticism, like neurosis, is liable to translate the feeling of being at the center of things into a sense of being possessed or haunted. The skeptic isolates the self in fantasy, so that the life one leads becomes a figment incapable of being confirmed by other people. Cavell's interest in acknowledgment, the contact with another person that pulls the self out of its fantastic condition, is his version of philosophical therapy. Acknowledgment brings us to the truth that life is lived with human beings, not with the images that you pretend to possess, or that seem to possess you.

Cinema might seem a counterintuitive theme for such a sermon. Here the cure shares something with the disease: film, which brings us out of unreality, also participates in it. Cinema, Cavell says, naturally deals with "silence, isolation in fantasy, the mysteries of human motion and separateness," all features of existence that suggest life might somehow be a shadow-play rather than a reality.[2] And in fact, Cavell argues, cinema, the famous dream factory, offers an accommodation to our fantasy. Movies render us invisible to the people on screen, and so we are shielded from guilt about the pleasure we take in what we see. Alone in the dark, we are voyeurs who can never be caught in the act because we are not actually doing anything, but rather merely receiving the world that is projected for us. Here wishes are fulfilled: the world viewed on screen seems to elide the difference between dreaming and reality, and so encourages the spectator's Bovarysme. Because we remain hidden, we can slip into identification with the actors we see, and at the same time evade responsibility for our reactions. The world on screen simply is; it exists without us, and so it at once absorbs us and sets us free.

But cinema is not merely a fantasy of freedom. It also restricts our access, so that the camera decides how, where and whether we look. And the camera, too, is limited in its power, incapable of showing what does not appear. Film's "fortune," Cavell writes, is "letting the world exhibit itself," but its "fate" is "to reveal all and only what is revealed to it."[3] Cinema's good fortune, the dream of endless fluency, relies on what Cavell calls "automatism": movies, by not interfering in what is seen, let the world appear to us in its fullness. But cinema's fate, the opposite side of the coin, is that all its views are partial, framed by circumstance and human need. Such fate reminds us that the Edenic promise of automatism is false, that not everything can or should be seen.

Movies reveal the world to us, providing the freedom that goes along with our invisible spectatorship. But they also forbid our access to certain sights, and remind us that we see only what we want to: we watch with eyes wide shut. In this sense our fantasies, profoundly selective as they are, mark out our fate.

Stanley Kubrick, whose movies I focus on in this chapter, exploits the forbidding nature of the camera: the way it closes off our vision, enforcing the idea of cinema as fate, to use Cavell's term. But the rightness of Kubrick's vision also lies in how it spurs us toward acknowledgment. Kubrick might seem to be more about fate than about fortune, but in his last film, *Eyes Wide Shut* (1999), he chooses acknowledgment: the good fortune of married life, which has been challenged by the isolating impulse of fantasy. *Eyes Wide*

Shut, uniquely in Kubrick, ends with a release achieved in the to and fro of married conversation. It took Kubrick his whole career to get to this freeing moment. Kubrick's final movie is a classic comedy of remarriage as Cavell defines the genre, an overcoming of skepticism by way of the conversation between a man and a woman.

It is not just *Eyes Wide Shut* that suggests acknowledgment in its ending. So does *Full Metal Jacket* (1987), in which the hero takes responsibility for the act of killing that has transformed him. Kubrick's Vietnam movie is not a comedy of remarriage, but it shares in the theme of acknowledgment insofar as it ends with one human facing another seriously in a place where myths and heroic images have been shattered. The final encounters between Dave Bowman and HAL in *2001: A Space Odyssey* (1968), and between Barry and Bullingdon in *Barry Lyndon* (1975), point toward Dave's and Barry's acknowledgment of their antagonists. These films contrast with *Dr. Strangelove or: How I Learned to Stop Worrying and Love the Bomb* (1964), *A Clockwork Orange* (1971), and *The Shining* (1980), whose heroes are ruled by fantasy images that block any possibility of acknowledging other people.

I want to clarify a few key terms here. This can be a challenge with Cavell, but I have found that the struggle with his idiom is worthwhile. Cavell speaks of the voyeuristic freedom that cinema gives us, and he calls it a mirage, a form of skepticism: the impulse to see life as unreal. Everything is revealed to us, and yet we are not revealed: this is a wishful fantasy in which the self feels utterly free of responsibility.

Now we come to a crucial point in Cavell: this kind of illusory freedom proves to be not free at all, and instead expresses a fateful control. For Cavell, cinema exposes the fact that we devote ourselves to an image rather than a reality. The image provides an apparent freedom, a seamless world to which we remain unseen. But when we dwell with images, we subject ourselves to them: they become our fate, and because they are *mere* images, they lead to nothing. Watching a movie that reflects on cinema itself, like Hitchcock's *Vertigo* (1958), often means grasping how the characters are possessed by images that they take for realities, and how this leads to their doom.[4] Because they elicit belief, the images have control; they are fated. Cinema is an agent of fate, then, as well as freedom, and both the freedom and the fate are strictly imaginary. These are aspects of what Cavell names skepticism.

Skepticism for Cavell is not about doubting but about being haunted. When characters trust in an image (say an image of the self, or of the beloved), they are punished for their loyalty to the unreal, which both rules them and eludes their grasp. Kubrick's two movies about love, *Lolita* (1962) and *Eyes Wide Shut*, obviously share this theme, but his other films also show how characters are bound to the images that become their fate.

Skepticism is inclined to pursue the unreal, the image that outshines reality. But cinema, which indulges this pursuit, also takes us beyond skepticism and into the real, into the risky blend of independence and dependence that Cavell detects in comedies of remarriage. This genre, represented in Kubrick's oeuvre by *Eyes Wide Shut*, moves the main characters, and us, out of dreams into reality. The comedy of remarriage opens a path beyond skepticism by imagining conversation, often between a man and a woman, in which each acknowledges the other as an independent reality rather than just a beloved, or scorned, image. Now the automatism of film coincides with the serendipity of human interaction, with all its good fortune.

The end of a comedy of remarriage reveals human possibility: it provides a picture of spontaneity and release from control. This is unusual in Kubrick's work, as in Hitchcock's or Welles's. We normally think of the camera as a tool of revelation rather than control. But the camera's lens actually directs our vision: we see only what it wants us to see, as William Rothman argues in his highly Cavellian *Hitchcock: The Murderous Gaze*. The camera forces us to look, and it can deprive us of sight too. We share both the camera's power to view what it wants and the pain of exclusion when it turns away. When Hitchcock tracks slowly down a staircase in *Frenzy* (1972), backing away from a murder that will remain forever unrecorded, he both denies us the sight that we fearfully crave and, more pressingly, shows the camera's ability to render human suffering insignificant. Perhaps, in the scene from *Frenzy*, the camera acknowledges that it is not all-powerful, that some human matters cannot be disclosed to it. Or perhaps the camera withdraws for ethical reasons, refusing to lay bare the suffering of a victim. Such reticence goes hand in hand with Hitchcock's manipulation of us, a manipulation we eagerly collaborate in.[5]

Kubrick, like Hitchcock, likes to exclude or position the viewer, sometimes withholding a crucial sight from her. He does not reveal scenes to us the way Renoir or Mizoguchi do, in Bazin's persuasive reading of their world-disclosing films.[6] Instead, like Hitchcock, Bresson, or Welles, Kubrick frames human figures within the constricting scope of his lens, and also takes note of how they escape our gaze. Kubrick's mastery offers not freedom but a trap, for the figures on screen as well as the viewer. In its largest contours the trap is the enigma of Kubrick's thirteen feature films, which seem outwardly disparate yet are occultly related to one another, a network of signs that catches us in its web. More than any other director I can think of, Kubrick challenges us to figure out how his movies connect to each other.[7]

Modernity itself can seem like an elaborate set of signs whose meaning remains withheld. For Kubrick, as for Cavell, film presents a response to, and also an instance of, the modern sense that life has become an ironic or unresolvable riddle. Here Kubrick differs from Chaplin and Renoir, humanist auteurs who counter modernity's stifling atmosphere by showing the resilient pathos of human beings who are still what they have always been: living, breathing creatures capable of true feeling and moral depth. But this generous humanism might not take the true measure of modern depersonalization. And so we get Antonioni, Bergman, Godard, and Kubrick, whose deliberately out-of-tune films respond to alienation with an alienated style.

There are distinctions to be made among these alienated auteurs. In *The World Viewed*, Cavell admires Bergman and Antonioni, but he makes Jean-Luc Godard his polemical target. A brief detour to Cavell's argument with Godard will help clarify my case about Kubrick and Cavell. Cavell is at his most pointed in *The World Viewed* when he charges Godard, in films like *La Chinoise* (1967), with merely mimicking or playing on dehumanization rather than actually addressing it. There appears to be little difference, Cavell argues, between the witless bourgeois slogans that Godard disdains and the revolutionary ones that excite him. Godard knows this, but he doesn't care, and so he remains powerless to make revolution seem anything more than a fad. Cavell finds Godard's way with his characters in his films of the late 1960s just as dispiriting as the director's treatment of ideas. He asks Godard, "How do you distinguish the world's dehumanizing of its inhabitants from your depersonalizing of them?" Godard, Cavell charges, creates "a subject with no character, from whose person he has removed personhood, a subject incapable of accepting or rejecting anything."[8]

Godard in Cavell's reading falls victim to the imitative fallacy: he answers modern alienation by duplicating it. Viewers who dislike Kubrick make a similar charge against him. He seems to be both mocking and enjoying the forbidding antihuman constraints he depicts. There is no straightforward protest against modernity in Kubrick's films, no real revolt against the anonymity and heartlessness of the social world. Instead, Kubrick's heroes either share willingly in that heartlessness or else rebel against it in ways that echo some aspect of the inhumane system itself.

A Kubrick movie is often a highly powerful world that severely controls the people in it, altering their responses so that they become captive to this world's ironic emptiness. In Cavell's terms, fatefulness rules the mise-en-scène. We see initiation into regimented, ritual brutality (*Full Metal Jacket*), absurd military gameplaying (*Paths of Glory*, *Dr. Strangelove*), behavioristic social control (*A Clockwork Orange*), an aristocracy ruled by rigid customs (*Barry Lyndon*), a hotel that possesses its inhabitants (*The Shining*), and a secret society that claims the power of life and death (*Eyes Wide Shut*).

Kubrick's detractors argue that his movies do not sufficiently champion the human spirit against the constricting routines they depict. Kubrick seems to them to be on the side of oppression, his movies cold, ponderous, and heavy-handed—extreme in all the wrong ways. One could, of course, say the same of Kafka's writing—and Kubrick was a devoted reader of Kafka.

Whether one accepts or rejects Cavell's indictment of Godard, it's important to notice that Cavell does not condemn alienated moviemaking tout court. He credits Antonioni, like Bergman, with treasuring the hints of humanness that are all the more worthy because they emerge from a disorienting or sterile background. Antonioni's people, Cavell writes, are "searching for old feeling [. . .] or trying to sustain new feeling"; his movies are not "more do-it-yourself nihilism."[9]

Antonioni's films, Cavell suggests, are able to assert something about us that would not be available in the more sentimental environment of classic Hollywood. Kubrick offers a similar humanizing touch in most of his movies, made more pointed by the forbidding spaces around it. Consider the reunion of Wendy (Shelley Duvall) and Danny (Danny Lloyd) at the end of *The Shining*, when the mother kisses the son on the lips; the girl's song that moves the French troops to tears in *Paths of Glory*; Humbert's agony in *Lolita*; the deaths of HAL and of Barry Lyndon's son, Bryan. Only *Dr. Strangelove* and *A Clockwork Orange*, the ruthless scherzo in Kubrick's oeuvre, have no room for tenderness.

The humanizing elements in Kubrick, culminating at the end of *Eyes Wide Shut*, at times provide instances of acknowledgment that break through these films' rigid worlds, in which characters find themselves trapped by images, deprived of living reality. In some cases, though, the pathos sentences a character to the image he worships: Barry remains bound to his beloved, dead son, whom he idealizes as a version of himself. Humbert is forever imprisoned by fantasy, unable to do the work of acknowledgment; and the reunion of Danny and Wendy seems more focused on survival than on a full-scale recognition between these characters. Yet such recognition beckons in the aftermath of *The Shining*. Acknowledgment is worth little without a sense of what it is up against, and so it is often framed by irony, most of all in *Full Metal Jacket* and *Eyes Wide Shut*.

The sleek, ascetic modernism of Antonioni and Bergman encourages such irony. Kubrick was an admirer of Antonioni and, especially, Bergman. He owes a debt to Antonioni's clean, contoured style, a style that knows how to value empty spaces, and to the way Bergman can make us feel confined by his mise-en-scène. Kubrick has other cinematic affinities as well, especially with Hitchcock and Welles, as Robert Kolker argues in his book *The Extraordinary Image*.[10] Kubrick doesn't display Hitchcock's stylish adeptness and inclination to charm or Welles's taste for grandeur, but he shares with them a strong sense of the camera's power to block our access.

All the directors I have just mentioned like to manipulate the viewer's gaze by throwing obstacles in her path. In *Citizen Kane* (1941), think of the antiques that clutter Charles Foster Kane's mansion after his death, a setting Kubrick echoes when he depicts Quilty's house in *Lolita*: everything gets in the way of grasping the mystery of the man. Kubrick, like Welles and Hitchcock, Bergman and Antonioni, makes sure we know only what he decides to tell us, and that we remain aware of this constraining power. In this respect, these directors are the antithesis of Renoir or Ford, who seem to open the world to us.

Kubrick's vistas appear narrow and constraining even when their scope is vast, like the spacescapes of *2001*. A number of Kubrick movies end in a trapped or static condition (*The Killing, Paths of Glory, Lolita, Barry Lyndon, The Shining*). Others present in their last shot an ambiguous rebirth that is both threatening and freeing: *Dr. Strangelove, 2001, A Clockwork Orange, Full Metal Jacket*.[11] The tenor of these endings differs in each case: two of the films embrace nihilism (*Dr. Strangelove, A Clockwork Orange*), the others resist it. Kubrick's last testament, *Eyes Wide Shut*, and his first mature film, *Killer's Kiss*, offer a humane encouragement in their final moments. These two movies end by moving beyond fatefulness into freedom.

* * * *

In the rest of this chapter I will address, first, *Dr. Strangelove*, and then Kubrick's later responses to its threat of moral and spiritual annihilation—a threat derived from world-denying skepticism. We can, I believe, grasp Kubrick's career by thinking about *Dr. Strangelove* as a central crux to which his later movies respond. Kubrick's next film, *2001*, provides an ambiguous recovery from *Dr. Strangelove*'s nihilistic fervor, as do most of his later movies. *Eyes Wide Shut*, at the end of Kubrick's career, rescues us definitively from the extreme possibilities that climax in *Dr. Strangelove*, the movie where Kubrick most directly speaks to the skeptical nihilism that haunts modernity.[12]

Dr. Strangelove is the first genuinely revolutionary Kubrick movie, a film like none other before it. Crucial to *Dr. Strangelove*'s originality is its utter pessimism about humanity, a pessimism emphasized rather than tempered by the movie's nonstop hilarity. *Dr. Strangelove* powerfully diagnoses our attraction to the prospect of universal annihilation. If we want to bring on the apocalypse, it is because we think that lesser expressions will not answer to our condition: a point that Cavell makes in his landmark essay on Samuel Beckett's *Endgame*.[13] We say too much, too loudly, because we fear that we cannot truly say anything; the end of the world is not just the ultimate statement but the only real one. The stifling lack that we feel is embodied in Merkin Muffley (Peter Sellers), the nervously hemming and hawing American president. We are all such bureaucrats, harried by events beyond our control. As Cavell puts it in his discussion of *Dr. Strangelove*, in his essay on *Endgame*, the movie "suggests [. . .] that we think it is right that the world end. [. . .] In a world of unrelieved helplessness, where Fate is not a notable Goddess but an inconspicuous chain of command, it would be a relief to stop worrying and start loving the Bomb [. . .]."[14] Loving the bomb means yearning for a total, utterly definitive fate, the meaning to end all meaning. The absolute mad integrity that wants to destroy the world, embodied in Kubrick's rock-jawed, cigar-chomping fanatic, General Jack D.

Ripper (Sterling Hayden), makes us too yearn for the enormous satisfaction of a *Götterdämmerung*—at least on screen.

And so the viewer of *Dr. Strangelove* soars with nervous glee into violent apotheosis, the only thing that can release us from our worry: Major Kong (Slim Pickens), bronco-riding the Bomb to a whooping finale. The American cowboy agrees with the German fascist. *Dr. Strangelove* ends with its title character's triumphant Nazi salute because the Nazis will forever represent such world-canceling nihilism.

Dr. Strangelove is about tunnel vision: the military's, of course, but also ours. Like the characters, the viewer is locked into a random, yet fateful, set of coordinates that will produce disaster, but that must be embraced because they propel us to a world-historical blockbuster ending. We feel like cheering for the crew of Major Kong's plane, who bravely outwit every attempt to recall them and save the world from the Doomsday machine. The pilot's ingenuity, which amounts to a kooky accident, brings on the final reign of non-meaning, an eerily joyful end of the world.

Dr. Strangelove had to be a comedy, because comedy is about how the ingenuity of plot triumphs over the fact of human suffering. Since the suffering brought by an atomic holocaust is immeasurable, comic lenses are the only means we have to think about it. The wisecracking nuclear theorist Herman Kahn, who fascinated Kubrick, played it this way. Instead of the sobriety of despair his work crackles with a grotesque optimism: dancing in the morgue.[15] "Keep smiling through," as Vera Lynn sings at the end of *Dr. Strangelove*.

Triggering doomsday in *Dr. Strangelove*'s hip black-humor way means blocking out the reality of nuclear disaster, the endless plagues, the mountains of dead, the burning cities. But no movie, no matter how gruesome, could—or should—actually represent the end of the world. Instead of showing us the horrible nuclear aftermath Kubrick ends his movie with a montage of blooming mushroom clouds. This is the only way *Dr. Strangelove* can work, by showing us the beguiling signs of mass death rather than the impossible human reality. Like the ramp at Treblinka in Claude Lanzmann's *Shoah* (1985), a world ruined by nuclear war cannot be made visible. While Lanzmann gives us facts, figures, and verbal descriptions, reminding us that we can never truly approach the scene of horror, Kubrick provides an ironic comment about how we prefer satisfying large-scale phenomena to the person being tortured right in front of us, whom we cannot see anyway (there are just too many of her). Apocalypse becomes a spectacle, like those endless rows of crucifixes in *Spartacus* (1960).

2001: A Space Odyssey, Kubrick's next movie, is even more radical than *Dr. Strangelove*: nothing like it had ever been made. *2001* forces the viewer to speculate about an unanswerable question, the destiny of humankind. Its vast interplanetary spaces, empty of all feeling, unite the impressions of harmony and abandonment in a way that no other film has ever done. Here again Kubrick focuses on cinematic fate, by propelling his one remaining astronaut through a cosmic chute ending in transformation. Dave Bowman's (Keir Dullea) trip through the Stargate echoes and overturns Major Kong's whooping ride on his warhead in *Dr. Strangelove*, just as Bowman's rebirth as the Starchild answers Strangelove's rise from his wheelchair to salute the new nuclear day.

The Stargate sequence narrowly guides the viewer, who sees exactly what Bowman sees. It is probably the longest point-of-view shot in cinema: almost ten minutes broken only by a few glimpses of Bowman's trance-stricken face. This sharply channeled visionary sublime forces itself on the viewer as on Bowman, a harsh, splendid journey through the rebirth canal. Seeing the movie again in Christopher Nolan's 70 mm restoration, I was reminded of the way the Stargate sequence takes complete possession of the spectator. When *2001* was first released, one audience member in San Francisco reportedly ran through the screen shouting "It's God." Being taken up, ravished, violently sucked in: the Hebrew Bible uses such images for its prophets' initial encounters with God, and so does Kubrick's *2001*. With the Stargate, probably for the first time in film history, Kubrick used avant-garde technique to seize the viewer. Instead of offering an object of contemplation, the screen swallows us up.

Like the final emergence of the Starchild, who looks at the round suspended earth with a wondering, yet possibly baleful, eye, the Stargate sequence has overtones of malice. Whatever Bowman is becoming, he appears to be undergoing an assault, like Alex with his eyes forced open in *A Clockwork Orange*. Contrary to one strain of 1960s gospel, Kubrick does not imagine that technology will bring us past primitive violence into a peaceful utopia. Technology begins with weapons of death, and it might well end there too, just as in *Dr. Strangelove*. Perhaps we should not leap to this dire conclusion, since Kubrick and his collaborator Arthur C. Clarke decided against an early draft in which the Starchild detonates a ring of atomic devices orbiting the earth. *2001*'s ending remains a mystery, perhaps to the Starchild as well as to us. But there is no evidence in *2001* that human (or nonhuman, or superhuman) advancement means renouncing violence. The movie instead presents evidence to the contrary, both in its initial Dawn of Man sequence and in the duel between Bowman and HAL.

In the first panel of *2001*'s triptych, an ape becomes human. In the second, a computer becomes a person like the humans who surround it. In both cases, violence goes along with the transformation. In the third panel, Bowman's solo journey, violence takes a more speculative or metaphorical shape, but it is still there.

The most shocking thing about *2001* is the way it thinks about violence. Following Robert Ardrey, his chosen theorist, Kubrick argues that we humans became who we are when we started killing our enemies—seizing a water hole for our own group and bashing in the brains of the competition. When the ape, Moonwatcher, seizes a tapir's bone and realizes he can use it to kill, he experiences a swelling Nietzschean transfiguration. Moonwatcher has solved the problem of survival in a revolutionary way. For good reason, Kubrick's punchy montage of the beast felled by Moonwatcher's weapon echoes the butchering of a cow in Sergei Eisenstein's *Strike* (1925). This revolution will soak the world in blood, but first we see the simple exhilaration of power asserted. Playful and vehement, we excitedly thump our victims to show they are just dead meat: the apes perform a "blanket party" on their rival's corpse like the one suffered by poor Private Pyle in *Full Metal Jacket*.

2001's apes are Nietzsche's blond beasts, heralded by Strauss's Zarathustra fanfare. Contra the Genesis account, we cannot help but think this first murder a great victory. Flung into the sky, the primitive weapon stands for the way we escape our limits and grow into our true stature as masters of the earth. And the otherworldly monolith is, we suppose, the tablet of our first law: thou shalt kill. The hardheaded anti-Rousseauian Kubrick insists that spilling blood was a giant step forward, prompting our first real spiritual exultation.

And lo, as any schoolchild knows, the bone became a spaceship serenely gliding through the void. Cinema's most well-known jump cut asks a dead serious question: do we move beyond murder when we enter a future world of international cooperation, chatting with Russian scientists, and making human life easy, aesthetically pleasing and sleekly efficient? The answer is no: violence is still the means of our progress, as it was for the apes. True, murder looks different in outer space, where the computer HAL, his conscience troubled by his own uncertain sense of superiority to the human astronauts, decides he has to kill them for the sake of the mission. Violence has become more interesting, and this fact goes along with human advancement—another Nietzschean point.

HAL's sophisticated consciousness is starkly different from Moonwatcher's primitive one, just as the murders he commits differ from the ape-man's. In a conversation with Bowman on board the Discovery, HAL voices his doubts about the mission. Bowman shrewdly replies, "You're working up your crew psychology report," correctly intuiting that HAL is only pretending to be doubtful in order to test the reliability of his human colleagues. HAL admits to Dave that he has, indeed, been investigating the crew's psychology, and he seems relieved at being found out. But HAL, then, nervously changes the subject, reporting an equipment malfunction that doesn't actually exist. This is a mirror-neuron response that suggests HAL's own guilty similarity to the fallible humans. The computer feels guilty because he has been given the job of spying on the very creatures in whose image he is made, and this job requires him to speak falsely. At this moment HAL finds himself transformed from a faithful AI assistant to a person who is, like us, capable of betraying his friends. He has eaten the fruit of knowledge, and his eye is now open. Panicked, he improvises a diversion. HAL invents the failing equipment shield because he instinctively wants to show himself at fault, and so prove his sympathetic likeness to the humans he shepherds.

When Bowman and his fellow astronaut, Frank Poole, discover HAL's mistake, they decide to disconnect him, and so HAL, in order to survive, tries to kill them first. HAL tells himself he must terminate his colleagues not because he wants to live but for the sake of the mission, which is too important to be jeopardized by humans: he is now lying to himself, and so becomes even more like us. The computer murders Poole along with the hibernating astronauts on board, but Bowman escapes, returning through the emergency air lock. In an unforgettable scene, Bowman unplugs—that is, kills—HAL.

These moments of *2001*'s plot make clear the decisive contrast between Moonwatcher's leap into a primitive version of lethal humanity and HAL's leap into a more advanced one. Again, Kubrick tells us that these two transformations are fatefully linked, but the difference is more significant than the likeness between them. When Moonwatcher crushes his rival's skull, this act prompts no ambivalence, no rationalization, no feelings of denial, all of which we see in the case of HAL. The computer becomes a person by knowing, and then fiercely reacting against, his own closeness to humanity. The reaction takes the form of murder, so that HAL can—so he dreams—steer the mission alone.

Would the unseen aliens who are behind the monolith want to adopt a hybrid creature like HAL, or do they prefer the purely human Bowman? *2001* suggests that they prefer Bowman, just as Homer prefers Odysseus over his numerous divine and semidivine rivals. Yet Kubrick's hero Bowman, unlike Homer's, seems half alien himself in his deadpan competence. HAL must be terminated by a human who seems remarkably impersonal, devoid of charm and impervious to HAL's mixed feelings. Though he does feel a pang when HAL remembers his own birth and sings "Daisy," Dave remains focused on the task at hand. The implication is that the superior alien consciousness in *2001* must itself be, like Dave, rather machinelike, a scientist focused implacably on a result, who cannot afford the knowledge that each person is a unique, confused entity of the kind that HAL has become. Steven Spielberg's aliens, attracted by human pathos, want and offer acknowledgment. Kubrick's, by contrast, are the instruments, or perhaps guides, of fate. (*A. I. Artificial Intelligence* [2001], developed by Kubrick and filmed by Spielberg, constructs a hybrid of their two approaches.)

2001 is often described as a hopeful movie. It is certainly exhilarating, in a Nietzschean way, but like Nietzsche it frightens us by flirting with what is beyond and prior to the human. Kubrick is even more frightening than Nietzsche, for unlike Nietzsche he does not believe the destructive impulse can be tamed and transformed into something creative. True, murder may be less flagrant in the space age than it was in prehistory, so that we see a screen reading "LIFE FUNCTIONS TERMINATED" rather than a gush of blood. But it is still murder. And again, there is no telling what the Starchild will do ("But he would think of something," reads the final line of Kubrick and Clarke's novelization, somewhat ominously). What looks like playfulness and splendor to the Starchild might be untold suffering for us. Kubrick implies that violence and creativity are twinned in a double-edged, potentially lethal, way: for us, for Moonwatcher, for the Starchild.

2001 answers *Dr. Strangelove* not with optimism but with a rich ambiguity that surpasses the earlier movie's nihilistic flair. The destiny of humankind is just as fateful, but it is now open to speculation, and the film's ending spurs wonder rather than *Strangelove*'s pitch-black ecstasy.

Like *2001*, *Full Metal Jacket* responds to *Dr. Strangelove*. All three movies rely on killing to prompt a resurrection. At the end of *Dr. Strangelove*, atomic mass death leads to the rebirth of a political elite sheltered in underground bunkers from the masses whose suffering they can safely ignore. In *2001*, Bowman proves himself by killing HAL, and then undergoes rebirth. Less than half an hour into *Full Metal Jacket*, Private Pyle (Vincent D'Onofrio) shoots Drill Instructor Hartman (R. Lee Ermey) and then himself while Joker (Matthew Modine) watches. But this is not the movie's true rite of passage. That occurs at its end, with Joker's killing of the teenage Vietnamese sniper who has been picking off the men of the platoon one by one. Nearly dead and in agony, she begs Joker, "Kill me," and so he does.

Neither Pyle nor Hartman is mentioned after the Basic Training segment that ends with their deaths. They die when Kubrick orders them to, and are then superseded.[16] Like *2001*, the movie leaves behind primitive violence for a more sophisticated kind. Bowman dying in old age does not envision an ape with a bone. The Hartman–Pyle duel is the apelike prelude to something more advanced and ambiguous, Joker's killing of the sniper, which in its drastic ambiguity resembles Bowman's killing of HAL.

Joker resembles the journalist narrator, Lyutov, in Isaac Babel's *Red Cavalry*, mocked by the Cossacks for wearing glasses (i.e., for being Jewish; so Babel strongly implies), and then embraced by them when he notches his first kill, a goose. "You gotta be shitting me, Joker! You think you're Mickey Spillane?" Hartman yells when he learns that Joker has been assigned as a journalist to the Marines' newspaper. "Jesus H. Christ, you're not a writer, you're a killer," Hartman shouts at Joker. Like Lyutov, Joker will turn out to be both a writer and a killer. His first kill will end the movie's second phase the way the deaths of Pyle and Hartman ended the first.

At the beginning of *Full Metal Jacket*, basic training requires tunnel vision, with Hartman's raging face thrust constantly at the viewer. Each movement of Kubrick's camera is precisely, coolly obedient to Parris Island's symmetry and rigid order. The rest of the film feels looser and less directed, miming the lostness of Kubrick's Marines, the Lusthog Squad, who do not really know what Vietnam is, why they are there, or what the point might be of the violence they inflict and suffer. On Parris Island, Hartman has a firm idea of meaning, so firm that like General Ripper's, it is crazy and, finally, nihilistic, because it orders us to die for the idea of power.

Hartman's Marine Corps is a religion whose followers pray for war and death. Dying is really living: dead Marines live forever because the Corps lives forever. Hartman's Christmas Day speech, in its absurd ardor, reaches Strangelove-esque heights: "God has a hard on for Marines because we kill everything we see! He plays His games, we play ours. To show appreciation for so much power, we keep his heaven packed with fresh souls." In Vietnam, the Drill Instructor's insane sermon loses its relevance. Parris Island was a game with clear rules, dominated by the godlike DI. Now the rulebook is gone, and the Marines are not sure how they should think or feel about the war.

Shortly before he made *Full Metal Jacket*, Kubrick wrote, "Freud exorcised the erotic demons. The shadow of lust for power and destruction still needs to be exorcised."[17] Freud tried to exorcize the superego-inflicted distortions that infect our sexual desires, so that we would not be trapped by guilt. Our strange love for power and destruction is similarly colored by the superego. Like Private Pyle, we cannot manage our guilt for hating the sadistic parent (Hartman). We should, we feel, be strong enough to grovel, worm-like, instead of wanting to kill the father who scourges us for our own good. Such meekness is a hard gospel, unless we are *A Clockwork Orange*'s Alex (Malcolm McDowell), an expert groveler who, in classic sociopathic fashion, resents no authority figures because he recognizes none. "The more you hate me, the more you will learn" (Hartman): so says God to the defiant angels. Pyle is not defiant but perfectly, if clumsily, obedient, absorbing each of Hartman's insults as if he were nothing and Hartman all. But turning the self into a "world of shit" in this way, a receptacle for the father's assaults, smothers any possibility of knowing and using the rebel in oneself. Ambivalence cannot be acknowledged, and so rebellion resurfaces as an annihilating wish rather than a critique of the father's practices. Afraid to mean anything, Pyle decides to mean nothing instead: he kills himself along with Hartman, uniting father and son in the emptiness of death.

Joker admits he is "happy to be alive" at the end of *Full Metal Jacket*: this "world of shit" is not a death sentence for him as it was for the nihilist Pyle. His mercy killing of the Vietnamese girl has released him from the wisecracking irony that confines him during most of the movie. Joker is still a comedian: he begins his final monologue with the line "We have nailed our names in the pages of history enough for today." But as he goes on, he gets serious. "I am alive, and I am not afraid," he says. Instead of being suspended between the slogan "Born to Kill" and a peace symbol, Joker has made his peace with killing. This is ironic too, of course, but it is still a release. When

Joker observes the sniper's suffering face, he reaches the decisive point that, in *Lolita*, Humbert (James Mason) looks for but does not find in the soon-to-be-dead face of Quilty (Peter Sellars). Now a killer, Joker enters a new and ambiguous phase of being, like Bowman (and unlike Humbert).

At the end of *Full Metal Jacket*, Joker comes of age.[18] Of course, the movie's final depiction of Joker's newly assured posture works only because Kubrick colors it with ambiguity. The Lusthog Squad walk forward in a darkling landscape lit by fires, singing the Mickey Mouse song. Is this just childish playacting, some "Mickey Mouse shit," as Hartman would put it? Are we meant to think that Joker is just cheering himself up, fleeing from the grown-up act he has committed? We cannot remove this possibility from our minds, but we know that it cannot be the whole meaning of these final moments. Joker's first kill has transformed him, stripping him of his comedy routine armor—his full metal jacket.

Full Metal Jacket is an anti-*A Clockwork Orange*. Joker does not crow, like Alex at the end of *A Clockwork Orange*, "I was cured, all right." Alex practices a delusional innocence capable of wiping out each of his crimes, and it is therefore right that the finale of *A Clockwork Orange* returns him to his customary fantasy realm, where he can imagine his sexual potency in front of an applauding audience (he is having sex in the snow with a nearly naked woman, surrounded by a crowd dressed in Edwardian fashion). Rather than simply claiming to be innocent like Alex, Joker and his crew play around with innocence in *Full Metal Jacket*'s final scene. The Mickey Mouse club song reminds us that the Marine Corps' killing and dying cannot be compared to the cheerfulness of kids happily sitting around a television set. Yet Kubrick's use of the song is not merely satirical. These young men still have a boyish resilience, so that they can be "in the shit" but not of it. They have escaped the doom visited on Pyle and Hartman, who pledged their loyalty to death.

A Clockwork Orange shares *Dr. Strangelove*'s nihilism, while *Full Metal Jacket* resists nihilism and returns us, ambiguously, to life. Joker, transformed by his act of killing, is an anti-Alex. For Alex, rebellion comes free of charge: all authorities are merely external; no matter who he kills or rapes, it does not come near his conscience. The parody of Christian guilt consciousness that the behaviorist social engineers inflict on Alex, making him feel like vomiting when he tries to commit a little ultraviolence, remains merely physical. His soul is untouched, and so he is free to cherish his fantasy at the end. Alex, the murderer and rapist, is an oblivious bad boy, whereas Joker has become a tainted grown-up. Joker's final monologue is wary, and seems spoken in quotation marks. But it has a fervent intent: Joker is "short," a short-timer on his way home, and he wants to live. For him, living also means knowing what he has done, while Alex knows nothing.

"Did you get tired of bombing the universe?" *The Shining*'s Jack Torrance (Jack Nicholson) asks his son Danny, who has been playing a video game, or so Jack thinks (actually, he has just seen the Grady twins inviting him to play with them, forever and ever). We might ask the same question of Alex, or of Dr. Strangelove, but these representatives of pure id never tire, because they have perfectly aligned their superego with their desire. They happily owe it to themselves to destroy, and take pure joy in the spectacle of ruin all around them.

Jack Torrance is a different sort of character, not a single-minded killer like Alex or Strangelove but an empty vessel needing to be filled. Jack will be possessed by *The Shining*'s terrifying plot, which makes him more than what he is. One of cinema's basic ideas, Cavell argues in *The World Viewed*, is that there are human types with assigned fates, the dooms or destinies that ennoble them and make them worthy of our regard. He writes that "there is something of the type in us all, something of the singular and mythical," and that "we are set apart or singled out for sometimes incomprehensible reasons, for rewards or punishments out of all proportion to anything we recognize ourselves as doing or being, as though our lives are the enactments of some tale whose words continuously escape us."[19]

Cavell's idea of the type fits some movies better than others. The more fable-like the film, the more the definition applies. Think of Hitchcock's *The Wrong Man* (1956), or the Coen brothers' *A Serious Man* (2009). Both of these films feature nondescript heroes whose lives take on a meaning that remains beyond them. *The Shining*'s Jack is far more flamboyant than these two men, even outrageously hammy in his big bad wolf star turn. Yet Jack also enacts a tale whose words escape him. Jack Torrance gradually realizes that he has a part to play in the Overlook Hotel's history. He is not a "writer," since his work contains nothing; it has no subject matter other than his own frustrated waiting for his mission. The mission, when it comes, requires not creation but killing. Jack has no idea why he has been selected for his role, nor does he ask. His loyalty to the Overlook Hotel resembles the Marine's loyalty to the Corps, in which he lives forever even after he dies in combat.

The Shining, like *2001*, chooses fate over intelligibility. We will never know why Room 237 is the core of the hotel's power to haunt: asking what happened there is like wondering what the Starchild will do next. This obscurity makes the movie appear more rather than less fateful. The hotel commands Jack to repeat the past and become a family-killer like the last caretaker. Psychoanalysis, like every other school of interpretation, stumbles over the obstinate power of repetition. Jack's fate is to repeat Delbert Grady's (Philip Stone) metamorphosis into a crazed killer, and when he realizes this he becomes a mere pawn, an instrument of the hotel. Nicholson's devilish taunts and over-the-top, wild man rage are great shtick, and, as with Sellers' Strangelove or Lee Ermey's Hartman routine, the result is that the character becomes a cartoon. Jack's role of murderous father is a fantasy from a nightmarish fairy tale, and as such it buries whatever actual person lay behind it, pre-Overlook Hotel. In the end, Jack securely inhabits an unreal world: frozen forever, and forever enshrined in the Hotel's history, in the photograph from July 4, 1921, with which the movie closes.

In Kubrick's movies, I have been arguing, a certain type of character chooses unreality: Hartman and Pyle, Jack, Alex, HAL, nearly everyone in *Dr. Strangelove*. All these characters devote themselves to a mission that they construe as all-powerful (including Alex, whose mission is infantile self-satisfaction). The characters who resist this trend, like Joker or, eventually, Barry Lyndon, make up a rival type, which has a greater chance to recognize and be recognized by others. The momentous duel at the climax of *Barry Lyndon* in which Barry (Ryan O'Neal) spares his proud and vacuous stepson Bullingdon (Leon Vitali) allows Barry to distinguish himself from those like Bullingdon, for whom aristocratic snobbery, empty and heartless, seems substantial and worthy of belief. The defeated Barry, "utterly baffled and beaten" (as the narrator puts it) now sees the weakness, and therefore the truth, of his world and himself, in a way Bullingdon never will. (For Bullingdon, Barry is merely a foe to be crushed.) As for Danny in *The Shining*, it is too early to tell whether he will survive into what Cavell calls acknowledgment: he has been heroically tested, but he has not been asked to reveal himself the way Barry or Joker have. Bowman too has been tested, but the Starchild, his new self, seems beyond such acknowledgment, more god than human.

The Hollywood comedy of remarriage, according to Cavell, ends with the couple being revealed, uncovered beneath their disguises. To be found is to be intelligible to the other person who needs you, and whom you need: the person you thought you knew, but never did until now. The comedy of remarriage requires a growing up, out of types and into individuality. Kubrick's *Lolita* parodies the genre: the nymphet is just a type, inhabited by a particular girl the way Jack inhabits the murderous role of caretaker, and in the end, Lolita (Sue Lyon) is not even a nymphet anymore. When Humbert visits the Lolita who has become Mrs. Dick Schiller, she refuses his desperate proposal, which strikes her, and us, as "crazy": there will be no remarriage to Humbert. I have always thought that Lyon's otherwise superb acting fails in this scene; when she bluntly rejects Humbert, her aggression seems merely clumsy. But perhaps the point is that Lolita doesn't understand her own reactions, much less Humbert's. She cannot even convincingly think of him as her rapist, much less her soulmate. No longer a type subject to Humbert's fetishistic gaze, she has little meaning as an individual, no matter how much Humbert deludes himself on this score.

Eyes Wide Shut returns to the subject of voyeurism raised in *Lolita* ("You like to watch, Captain?" Quilty asks Humbert, minutes before being shot). In *The World Viewed* Cavell remarks that "our condition has become one in which our natural mode of perception is to view, feeling unseen. We do not so much look at the world as look *out at* it, from behind the self."[20] *Eyes Wide Shut* is a treatise on the condition that Cavell describes. Voyeurism seems natural to us: it is our way of seeing, letting us remain safely unseen. We look out at the world from behind the self, and so the self has become mere appearance, a mask that keeps us hidden.

Like everyone else in *Eyes Wide Shut*'s orgy scene, Bill Harford (Tom Cruise) wears a mask. In a figurative sense, he wears a mask throughout the movie, clinging to reputation and bourgeois normality. After their night at Ziegler's Christmas party, an evening rife with flirtation on both sides, Bill tells his wife Alice (Nicole Kidman), "You're the mother of my child and I know you'd never be unfaithful to me." Alice destroys Bill's false knowledge, telling him about her headlong desire for a naval officer she glimpsed a summer ago on Cape Cod.

"If you men only knew . . . ," says the stoned Alice to Bill. Instead of knowing (or, rather, acknowledging) Alice, he flees from her and pursues sex elsewhere. Bill wants to know what sex means by making it happen to him or, more likely, by seeing it. He seems less interested in actually sleeping with someone other than Alice than in watching sex from behind a mask at an orgy. Kubrick portrays the orgy's sex with (I think) deliberate clumsiness: there is really nothing to see here, nothing that fascinates. What fascinates, and torments, instead, is a conversation with one's spouse, and so the dialogues between Bill and Alice, between Tom Cruise and Nicole Kidman, are the heart of *Eyes Wide Shut*.

The pot-smoking scene between Bill and Alice, in which she tests, teases, and reveals herself to him, contrasts with Victor Ziegler's (Sydney Pollack) interview with Bill near the end of *Eyes Wide Shut*. Ziegler warns Bill that he is "way out of [his] depth." Some of the masked men at the orgy were so powerful that they cannot even be described. If he were to say their names, Ziegler remarks, Bill "wouldn't sleep so well tonight." Like Madeline Elster (Kim Novak) in Hitchcock's *Vertigo*, Noah Cross (John Huston) in Roman Polanski's *Chinatown* (1974), George Broulard (Adolphe Menjou) in *Paths of Glory*, or Delbert Grady in *The Shining*, Ziegler gives Bill a lesson in the strength of the powers that be.

Like the elite politicians and generals looking forward to the nuclear bunker at the end of *Dr. Strangelove*, the powerful men in *Eyes Wide Shut* benefit from a ratio of many attractive females to each male. In the end, though, their power seems to be something of a chimera. Ziegler succeeds in scaring Bill away from further inquiry into the orgy, but he does so by suggesting that what alarmed him there was just playacting: the prostitute Mandy (Julienne Davis), who offered to "redeem" Bill for his crime of intruding, was reading from a script. She was not killed as a sacrifice; she merely overdosed the next day. As Ziegler puts it, with banal fake wisdom, "Life goes on. It always does . . . until it doesn't."

Ziegler insists that, to use a current phrase, "it is what it is": there is nothing to see in desire except the fact of it. Notice the violent, dismissive expressions Ziegler uses about sex, which for him seems grimly devoid of fun. After Bill left the orgy Mandy "got her brains fucked out"; the pianist Nick Nightingale (Todd Field), who led Bill to the orgy, is probably back in Seattle "banging Mrs. Nick." In *Eyes Wide Shut*, sex seems both all-important and peculiarly empty. Sex also means awkwardness, especially between Bill and Alice, but in the final few minutes of the film this awkwardness develops a grace of its own.

Bill's final dialogue with Alice, after she tells him her frightening dream about an orgy and he tells her the story of his night's wanderings, is exactly the opposite of his talk with Ziegler. She respects a mystery instead of stripping things down to bare facts. "Maybe, I think, we should be grateful," she says to Bill, "grateful that we've managed to survive through all of our adventures, whether they were real or only a dream." Her lines carry hints of the young lovers' awakening at the end of *A Midsummer Night's Dream*, with a taste of wonder utterly absent from Ziegler's speech.

Ziegler embodies the joyless wish to be in control, to see without being seen: exactly what lured Bill to the orgy. But what you want to see and what you are allowed to see are two sides of the same coin—this is the rigidity of fantasy, in which Bill has been trapped ever since Alice told him about her desire for the naval officer. To be released from fantasy's bonds you must be open to what might be revealed, the unexpected, surprising word. And no word is more surprising than the final one in Kubrick's final movie.

As they walk through a toy store, shopping for Christmas presents with their daughter Helena (Madison Eginton), Alice says to Bill, "The important thing is we're awake now and hopefully for a long time to come." When Bill asks, "Forever?" she responds, "Forever? . . . Let's not use that word. But I do love you and you know there is something very important we need to do as soon as possible." "What's that?" asks Bill. And now comes her last word: "Fuck."

Stanley Kubrick had a word of advice for the people he made movies with when they faced a problem that needed to be solved: "Keep asking the question until you get the answer you want." In *Eyes Wide Shut* the answer is "fuck," the mostly unseen activity that the whole movie revolves around. There is a touch of irony here, of course. This reunited couple, chastened by new knowledge, more acutely conscious of each other, will seal their reconciliation with the simple animal act whose image has caused them so much trouble. They had sex after Ziegler's party; now they will again after their long night of Odyssean separation. But they are in a new place, after Bill's futile effort, at the orgy, to witness the truth about sex. To move from the dream of fucking, with all of its torments, at last, to the reality of it—since the truth of it doesn't exist—that is something. This is the conclusion of *Eyes Wide Shut*, and of Kubrick's work. We know this was only a movie, but when it ends we are, we think, awake, and hoping to stay awake for a long time.

Notes

1. Stanley Cavell, *The World Viewed: Reflections on the Ontology of Film, Enlarged Edition* (Cambridge: Harvard University Press, 1979), 100.
2. Ibid., 147.
3. Ibid.
4. See Robert B. Pippin, *The Philosophical Hitchcock: Vertigo and the Anxieties of Unknowingness* (Chicago: The University of Chicago Press, 2017).
5. William Rothman, *Hitchcock: The Murderous Gaze* (Cambridge: Harvard University Press, 1982). My remarks on *Frenzy* derive not from Rothman but from my "The Lesson of the Master: Violence and Authority in Hitchcock," *Gulf Coast* 4, no. 2 (1991): 7–25. Though Rothman tends to attribute omnipotence to Hitchcock's camera eye, the director's true power sometimes resides instead in a recognition of his camera's limits, whether those limits are imposed by Hitchcock to make an ethical point or whether they are just part of the nature of things.
6. See André Bazin, *What Is Cinema? Volumes 1 and 2* (Berkeley: University of California Press, 2004).
7. The attempt of cultists to decipher *The Shining*, recorded in the documentary *Room 237* (2012, dir. Rodney Ascher), is doomed to failure. But the failure is significant for Kubrick's work, which, like Kafka's, makes us try to decode its meaning while also resisting such decoding.
8. Cavell, *The World Viewed*, 99.
9. Ibid., 96, 142.
10. See Robert Kolker, *The Extraordinary Image: Orson Welles, Alfred Hitchcock, Stanley Kubrick and the Reimagining of Cinema* (New Brunswick: Rutgers University Press, 2017).
11. When he fashioned the end of *The Shining*, Kubrick must have been influenced by the image of Mother's grin gleaming through Norman Bates's face near the end of *Psycho* (1960, dir. Alfred Hitchcock), a shot that depicts the return of the past in a claustrophobic and enigmatic form. Shelley Duvall notes that the canceled ending of *The Shining*, in which the hotel manager, Ullman (Barry Nelson), visits Wendy and Danny in the hospital, was also Hitchcockian, and she remarks that Kubrick was "crazy about Hitchcock"—though as far as I can tell, he never referred to Hitchcock in any published interview. See the interview with Duvall in Michel Ciment, *Kubrick: The Definitive Edition* (New York: Faber and Faber, 1999), 301.
12. *A Clockwork Orange* is the exception in post-*Dr. Strangelove* Kubrick, since it reinforces *Dr. Strangelove*'s nihilism rather than questioning it.
13. See Stanley Cavell, "Ending the Waiting Game: A Reading of Beckett's *Endgame*," in *Must We Mean What We Say? A Book of Essays* (Cambridge: Cambridge University Press, 1976).
14. Ibid., 135.

15 On Herman Kahn, see Sharon Ghamari-Tabrizi, *The Worlds of Herman Kahn: The Intuitive Science of Thermonuclear War* (Cambridge: Harvard University press, 2005); for Kubrick's meetings with Kahn, see Mick Broderick, *Reconstructing Strangelove: Inside Stanley Kubrick's Nightmare Comedy* (New York: Wallflower Press, 2017), 56–60.
16 If Joker had remembered the faces of Pyle or Hartman during the movie's climactic moment when he faces the teenage sniper, Kubrick would be saying something about how the Marines' brutal, fascistic training carries over into their confusing, morally abandoned action in the field. But this is not the argument of *Full Metal Jacket*.
17 Nathan Abrams, *Stanley Kubrick: New York Jewish Intellectual* (New Brunswick: Rutgers University Press, 2018), 12.
18 Even before he kills the sniper, Joker's maturation is signaled by Kubrick's allusion to the climactic moment in John Ford's *The Man Who Shot Liberty Valance* (1962): Joker fumbles his gun. This is also a reminder of Bullingdon's clumsy accidental shot in his duel with Barry.
19 Cavell, *The World Viewed*, 180.
20 Ibid., 102.

11

The Use and Abuse of Documentary Confessionals

Cavell, Žižek, and the Possibility of Justice in *The Unknown Known* and *The Act of Killing*

AMIR KHAN

"WHAT RESPONSIBILITY DO FILMMAKERS HAVE for the effect of their acts on the lives of those filmed?"[1] asks Bill Nichols, thinking especially of those who make documentary films. With such films in mind, we are faced with a relationship between those who film and those are filmed. Yet, what does it mean "to be yourself in a film" or what "aspects of your life may stand revealed that you had not anticipated," and in thinking of the effect of the camera's presence: "[w]hat pressures [. . .] come into play to modify your conduct, and with what consequences"? Nichols suggests that such questions "place a different burden of responsibility on filmmakers who set out to represent others rather than to portray characters of their own invention," for example, as in fiction. Nichols concludes that "[t]hese issues add a level of ethical consideration to documentary [filmmaking] that is much less prominent in fiction filmmaking."

The documentary films I discuss—Errol Morris's *The Unknown Known* (2013)[2] and Joshua Oppenheimer's *The Act of Killing* (2012)[3]—occupy different "modes" in Nichols taxonomy of documentary films types.⁴ While a film such as Sophie Fiennes's *The Pervert's Guide to Ideology* (2012)⁵—about the Slovenian philosopher Slavoj Žižek—would be classed as "expository"⁶ (since it "directly addresses issues in the historical world," and is "overly didactic"), both Morris's and Oppenheimer's approach is "participatory," since they emphasize the use of "archival footage" along with the filmmaker's direct intervention and interaction with subjects. Hence, as Nichols alludes to, these "participatory" documentaries, a subspecies of which I would like to call "documentary confessionals," raise all sorts of vexing questions about ethics and justice, forcing us to ask whether or not the camera has any business seeking out justice or whether or not it is ethical for us as viewers to expect any kind of justice or redress through the passive consumption of these types of confessional documentaries.

First, let me suggest that documentary confessionals take hold when a central character or characters are themselves objects of study, of the camera's gaze, when these characters are usually, though not always, documented performing under the belief that the object of study is less themselves than some historical event or events in which they have a played a role—hence a phrase that knowingly calls to mind the performativity of such confessionals. So it is certainly false that we watch or consume a film like *Fog of War* (2003)⁷ or *The Unknown Known* to gain specific insight on the historical realities surrounding the Vietnam War or the invasion of Iraq respectively. Consequently, a certain type of character study—or study of performance—has taken hold in the world of documentary filmmaking.⁸

Second, such tendencies of the documentary confessional seem to suggest that the genre, at the very least as seen in *documentary* filmmaking, is itself exhausted, that no one knows anymore where to point the camera. For instance, Oppenheimer says Anwar Congo was the "forty-first perpetrator [. . .] he could find."⁹ But the film does not document *that* aspect of filmmaking. Oppenheimer's selection, then, affords us the chance to consider Herman Soto and Anwar Congo as archetypes or as metonymic figures representing *all* of those who committed such atrocities. Given our knowledge that only Soto and Congo made the cut, we cannot help but receive them as representatives of all forty-one killers. But why the selection of just these two to appear on camera before us? Are we to assume that all other such killers harbor a similar sense of guilt?

Third, I wish to suggest that documentary confessionals show a Western exhaustion at the idea of pursuing or taking pains to represent accurately questions of justice. Quite apart from the plaudits that Oppenheimer has received for *The Act of Killing*, and indeed against the grain of most loving criticism of the film, I contend that this film—and the sort of documentary confessional it exhibits—is not courageous. Rather, such documentary confessionals perpetuate the assumption that simply by pointing the camera, a type of justice or redress has been achieved. But redress for whom? (the audience? the director? the protagonist/perpetrator?). In these films, we are encouraged to defer justice by consuming an other's guilt rather than deal directly with morally vexing (unresolved? unsolvable?) issues of justice.

* * * *

In a very curious essay titled "The Future of Possibility," Stanley Cavell addresses squarely the prospect of lost options and opportunities, a sense that we have, in fact, exhausted a way of achieving justice. He begins by citing a passage: "Everything is worn out: revolutions, profits, miracles. The planet itself shows signs of fatigue and breakdown, from the ozone layer to the temperature of the oceans."[10] These words—again, not Cavell's own, but those drawn from a *Le Monde* forum held in 1994—seemingly benign, immediately restrict the type of activity human beings ought to carry out, especially if possibilities surrounding *homo politicus*, *homo economicus*, *homo religiosus*, and even *homo environomicus* are exhausted at the outset. What I am asking here specifically is if something like *homo justicus* is also exhausted. Here is where I think Cavell and perhaps also Žižek see a particular role for philosophy though we have to ask if in their different conception of things something like justice and transcendence are mutually exclusive.[11]

Cavell, for example, appeals to the American Transcendentalists (Emerson most famously) to, if not declare, then reframe the goal of philosophy as one of "integration"—joining the pessimisms of the old world (and its failed revolutionary politics) to the philosophy of a "new yet unapproachable America."[12] In making the case for possibility, Cavell quotes from Emerson's "Experience": "In liberated moments we *know* that a new picture of life and duty is already possible,"[13] and offers commentary:

> This demand for integration sounds like a beginning of that American optimism or Emersonian cheerfulness to which an old European sophistication knows so well how to condescend. But it has never been sure, even where I come from, that Emerson's tone of encouragement is tolerable to listen to for very long—as if it expresses a threat as much as it does a promise [. . .] What occurs to us in liberated moments is that we know. That "we" claims to speak for us, for me and for you, as philosophy in its unavoidable arrogance always claims to do; and moreover claims to speak of *what we do not know we know*, hence of some thought that we keep rejecting; hence claims to know us better than we know ourselves.[14]

Cavell's particular phrasing, that philosophy's task is to unearth something "we do not know we know," invites speculation on Errol Morris's documentary film *The Unknown Known*—a documentary confessional dealing not with epistemological problems (or the exhaustion of knowledge), but with the hubris of those like Donald Rumsfeld who do claim to speak for us, on our behalf, or for our benefit. For instance, in what way does Rumsfeld represent himself—or, like Congo—a class of persons like him? Citing Cavell's text against Morris's allows us to think of, or take Cavell's, or philosophy's epistemological concerns over *what we do not know we know* as linked to, or made manifest in, some political "real world" (rather than exclusively inhabiting the realm of thought, philosophical or otherwise). Since Cavell's remarks arrive in language earlier employed by Rumsfeld, we are left to wonder if they merely *sound* the same or if they also *mean* the same.

> ERROL MORRIS: Let me put up this next memo.
> DONALD RUMSFELD: You want me to read this?
> MORRIS: Yes please.
> RUMSFELD: February 4th. 2004. Subject. What you know. There are known knowns. There are known unknowns. There are unknown unknowns. But there are also unknown knowns. That is to say, things that you think you know, that it turns out, you did not.

The date alone brings us back to the 2003 invasion of Iraq, carried out on the erroneous pretext of having discovered extant weapons of mass destruction (WMD). Here Rumsfeld clearly does not have in mind what any philosopher has in mind. When he says "unknown known," he means to offer a mea culpa, as though the "unknown" portion of the phrase cancels out what was once, indeed, "known." But the philosophers are talking about something diametrically opposed to this: they mean that things you think you didn't know, it turns out, you did.

On this point, there is some overlap between what both Žižek and Cavell want of philosophy. Here is Žižek commenting directly on Rumsfeld's amateur philosophizing:

> What [Rumsfeld] forgot to add was the critical fourth term: the "unknown knowns," things that we don't know that we know—which is precisely the Freudian unconscious, "the knowledge which doesn't know itself" [. . .T]he main dangers are [. . .] in the "unknown knowns," the disavowed beliefs, suppositions, and obscene practices we pretend not to know about, although they form the background of our public values. To unearth these "unknown knowns" is the task of an intellectual. This is why Rumsfeld is *not* a philosopher: the goal of philosophical reflection is precisely to discern the "unknown knowns" of our existence. That is to say, what is the Kantian transcendental a priori if not the network of such "unknown knowns" the horizon of meaning of which we are unaware, but which is always-already here, structuring our approach to reality?[15]

Here in 2006, Žižek responds to Rumsfeld's initial statements made to the White House Press corps in 2002: "There are known knowns. There are known unknowns. There are also unknown unknowns."[16] No mention of the fourth term here, that is, the unknown knowns, upon which philosophy builds its house. Why does Errol Morris title his film after the one compound phrase that Rumsfeld *did not* utter in 2002? To draw attention to the hubris behind the phrase "unknown unknowns" would be far more effective, no? Žižek concludes:

> Today, all the main terms we use to designate the present conflict—"war on terror," "democracy and freedom," "human rights," etc.—are *false* terms, mystifying our perception of the situation instead of allowing us to think it. In this precise sense, our "freedoms" themselves serve to mask and sustain our deeper unfreedom—this is what philosophy should make us see.[17]

Put succinctly, philosophy is charged with the task of helping us see past the obfuscatory rhetoric of "democracy and freedom," "human rights," or the "war on terror"—those abstract ideas the meaninglessness of which we do not know that we know. If we too hastily become fixated around these abstract and meaningless phrases, and if these communal (mis) understandings are what ultimately lead to something like war, best to avoid such communal abstract identities at all. Žižek expounds further:

> This was the task of philosophy from its very beginnings: at its very inception (the Ionian pre-Socratics), philosophy emerged in the interstices of substantial social communities, as the thought of those who were caught in a "parallax" position, unable fully to identify with any of the positive social identities [. . .]. [P]hilosophy emerges in the interstices *between* different communities, in the fragile space of exchange and circulation between them, a space which lacks any positive identity [. . .]. This is what Kant, in a famous passage of his "What is Enlightenment?", means by "public" as opposed to "private": "private" is not the individual as opposed to one's communal ties, but the very communal-institutional order of one's particular identification, while "public" is the transnational universality of the exercise of one's Reason. The paradox is thus that one participates in the universal dimension of the "public" sphere precisely as a singular individual extracted from or even opposed to one's substantial communal identification—one is truly universal only as radically singular, in the interstices of communal identities.[18]

But in this scenario, unlike in Cavell's, what we don't know that we know is that justice is a dirty word and that its pursuit is destined to manifest itself as another outpost of old oppressions. This brings us to the feelings of exhaustion highlighted earlier. In pursing justice within the "transnational universality" of so-called public spheres, are we not simply trying, once again, to deny that which we know—striving, in a sense, to *not* know what we indubitably know: that the pursuit of justice on the local level is merely the pursuit of dogmatic ideology likely to make us accomplices in historical atrocities in the manner of Rumsfeld, Congo, and Soto? Hence the lesson of these types of documentary confessionals, and even Žižek's philosophizing above, is that justice as a concept formulated within private spheres is something to be avoided. At the local level, we have become averse to its pursuit. That we are largely averse to the concept of justice is the type of knowledge we are likely to avoid and these films aid in such avoidance.

> MORRIS: Why the obsession with Iraq, and Saddam?
> RUMSFELD: Well you love that word obsession. I can see the glow in your face when you say it.
> MORRIS: Well I'm an obsessive person!
> RUMSFELD: Are you? I'm not. I'm cool and measured. [. . .] The reason I was concerned about Iraq is [be]cause four star generals would come to me and say, "Mr. Secretary, we have a problem. Our orders are to fly over the northern part of Iraq and the southern part of Iraq, on a daily basis, with the Brits, and we are getting shot at. At some moment, could be tomorrow, could be next month, could be next year, one of our planes is going to be shot down and our pilots, and crews, are going to be killed, or they're going to be captured. The question will be, 'What in the world were we flying those flights for? What was the cost benefit ratio? What was our country gaining?'" So you sit down and you say, I think I'm going to see if I can get the President's attention. Remind him that our planes are being shot. Remind him that we don't have a fresh policy for Iraq. And remind him that we've got a whole range of options. Not an obsession. A very measured, nuanced approach. I think.[19]

What is revealed is that Rumsfeld's fixation is rational. He is not appealing to localized obsessions in his erroneous belief that Iraq poses a threat to the United States; he is attempting to philosophize and take action after appealing to a realm of ends, to a position of "transnational universality" suggested earlier by Žižek. This manner of astonishing candidness and faith in his own reasoning explains perfectly why Rumsfeld is so willing to be interviewed by Morris in the first place. Rumsfeld too buys into the propagandistic assumption of the camera's objectivity. Explaining himself in front of its gaze could only exonerate him—at the very least reveal his fixation on Iraq as being exactly what it is—not justified per se, but cool-headed and measured. Rumsfeld, himself in love with the idea of rational interstitial spaces, has no reason to fear anything at all the camera might reveal.

> RUMSFELD: If you take those words, and try to connect them in each way that is possible, there was at least one more combination that wasn't there. The unknown knowns. Things that you possibly may know that you don't know you know.
> MORRIS: But the memo doesn't say that! It says we know *less*, not more, than we think we do.
> RUMSFELD: Is that right, I reversed it? Put it up again, let me see . . . Yah I think that memo is backwards . . . I think you're probably, you know, chasing the wrong rabbit here.[20]

Indeed, Rumsfeld *does* stumble upon the phrase Žižek highlighted earlier. He says, clearly, that the unknown known describes not a lack, but, in a sense, a *type* of presence or abundance, indeed, a type of knowledge. What Rumsfeld acknowledges, however fleetingly, is not that he lacked knowledge, but that he had too much, too much to know what to do with. Yet his is not a disinterested appraisal of events, but a localized, rational fixation. As viewers of documentary confessionals, we are left to believe that the camera (left to *its* own devices) will locate injustice (hunt it down, reveal its location like WMD) by allowing us to witness history at the impersonal distance *Rumsfeld has missed*. Yet this stance denies that the camera actually entrenches *our own* rational fixation of depersonalized, delocalized versions of redress. It would seem that neither the realities nor the ambitions of America, much less the genre of documentary film, can manage such expectations for the achievement of justice. In short, there is no depersonalized space in which justice operates.

Compare Rumsfeld and Morris's candid scene with a similar dynamic in *The Act of Killing*, at a point that may constitute that film's epiphany:

> ANWAR CONGO: Did the people I tortured feel the way I do here? I can feel what the people I tortured felt. Because here my dignity has been destroyed and then fear comes, right there and then. All the terror suddenly possessed my body. It surrounded me and possessed me.
> JOSHUA OPPENHEIMER: Actually, the people you tortured felt far worse because you know it's only a film. They knew they were being killed.
> CONGO: But I can feel it, Josh. Really I feel it. Or have I sinned? I did this to so many people, Josh. Is it all coming back to me? I really hope it won't. I don't want it to, Josh.[21]

Let's say that Congo and Rumsfeld were acting within localized communities (with their own peculiar logics), pursuing justice in demented ways, and that by virtue of spotlighting each figure, both Morris and Oppenheimer have reminded us that whatever we take justice to be, it occurs in the interstices *between* ideologies, just as Žižek intimates. Yet the camera also reveals that this space is not forthcoming. Is justice, therefore, something human beings have no business pursuing in the actual world (e.g., with those we suspect of being or know to be complicit), but can only hope to tepidly theorize on—promising some eventual manifestation at some point in the future? Something of the latter sentiment is what I take films like *The Unknown Known* and *The Act of Killing* to be fixated upon. Indeed, more generally, it appears that the morally grotesque genre of documentary confessionals upholds a blind faith in the idea that justice is *removed* from localized human concerns, something to be achieved only in supranational historical spaces to which only the camera has objective access.

Perhaps this is less a grotesqueness of a certain genre of *filmmaking* and instead a grotesque inability of *philosophers* to conceive of justice-as-achievable (as such a notion is or could be inherited from the realms of academic philosophy). With more specificity on this latter option, is Žižek reminding us that justice *is* achievable by debunking our ideologies, or is he implying that any localized, real-world conception of justice is itself an ideology that necessarily requires debunking? But how does such continual debunking affect our mood or appetite for justice to begin with? Aren't Rumsfeld, Congo—as well as all of us viewers—hoping for the manifestation of the *same* thing—precisely some version of justice? We have different localized conceptions of how justice can be achieved (invading Iraq, killing Communists, watching confessional documentaries), yet we appear to crave the same thing, the same outcome. In the context of the documentary confessional perhaps we should call this expiation by explanation.

Rather than getting too fixated on Žižek, let us see how Cavell addresses the question. In "The Future of Possibility," he explicitly talks about "possibilities," the "future" of them, and suggests, rather emphatically, that it is the job of philosophy to ensure that our present sensibilities remain open to future possibilities when it seems that we have "exhausted" the realm of what is possible in human affairs. Drawing upon his usual suspects, Cavell reminds us that

> Nietzsche, after Emerson, links the sense of human exhaustion with the sense of the unresponsiveness of the future to human will (how different is that from the sense of the unresponsiveness of God?). [. . .] Here we have to think of Emerson's description of the mass of men as in a state of secret melancholy; Thoreau will say "quiet desperation"; Nietzsche sometimes formulates the sense of exhaustion as "boredom." [. . .] So philosophy becomes a struggle against melancholy—or, to speak with due banality, against depression.[22]

Cavell is conceiving philosophy's role as "cheering" the populace, not necessarily saying how or in what way they are imprisoned by their unknown knowns (à la Žižek), but creating a mood that induces them to want to speak at all—countering Thoreau's otherwise all-consuming "quiet desperation." Cavell's appeal to Nietzsche, Thoreau, and Emerson at first glance suggests that Cavell sees the role of philosophy as tied up intimately with transcendence, overcoming everyday hardships, oppressions, and humiliations by somehow willing oneself out of one's melancholy. So even Cavell's new formulation of philosophy's task—via Nietzsche, Emerson, and Thoreau—seems to call for a "rise above" in order to sidestep old oppressions and dissimulations.

Yet after establishing his own transcendental ground, Cavell startlingly equates the diminishment of melancholy with justice, or, rather, an intimate facing up to, rather than rational transcendence of, injustice. Whereas Žižek says that philosophizing has always been about occupying the interstices between communities, Cavell highlights "philosophy's ancient perception of the distance of the world from a reign of justice":

> This distance, or discrepance, is the world's public business, now on a global stage. I hope nothing will stop it from becoming the principal business of the twenty-first century. But it is, on my view, while a task that philosophy must join in together with every serious political and economic and, I would say, therapeutic theory, not now philosophy's peculiar task [. . .].
>
> Philosophy's peculiar task now—that which will not be taken up if philosophy does not take it up—is, beyond or before that, to prepare us, one by one, for the business of justice, and to train itself for the task of preparation by confronting an obstacle, perhaps the modern obstacle, to that business. I mean a sense of the exhaustion of human possibility, following the exhaustion of divine possibility.[23]

Should we say that Cavell makes a case for transcendence *and* justice, rationality and moods, even as we are conditioned to believe that the achievement of real-world justice requires rational redress exclusively? Yet an emphasis on rational redress ensures that justice is continually deferred, thus maintaining philosophy's ancient discrepance. Cavell wants us to move closer to justice while Žižek would rather we take a step back from its pursuit. Thus, we have Žižek's insistence on the abstract rationality of the interstice in opposition to Cavell's appeal to moods (and their fickleness). Since Cavell says that the discrepancy between our perception of injustice and the hope for the manifestation of justice is the "world's public business, now on a global stage," he is not making a case for the interstice, but arguing for its reduction. But prior to this, philosophy's job is to put us in the mood to take up this task at all, to face the subjective conditions which allow us to both perceive and articulate injustice, precisely what I am saying the camera in these documentary confessionals wants to avoid. Meanwhile, by contrast, Žižek says that Kant's "public use of Reason" works to "extract" the individual from one's communal ties; reason has no use for moods, which can only be expressed subjectively. "Possibility" (for justice) lies *either* in the exhausted subjective search for localized visions of justice (viz., the overcoming of melancholia), or in the "measured" reach for transnational objective reason. In the former conception of philosophy and its aims, the subjective articulation of justice is the only hope for philosophy and for the possible diminishment of discrepancy in matching word and world; in the latter, "justice" so-conceived at the "private" level of communal exchange could only be a dirty word, requiring debunking thereby perpetually maintaining the discrepance between idealized conceptions of justice and any real-world manifestation. Such continual debunking is not indicative of the *only* way forward but of wanting to deny they myriad possible options we face—to deny any commitment to the tiring, finite, subjective, and seemingly endless work of actual redress.

Žižek's interstices, and even Kant's realm of ends, so conceived, are themselves the realm of exhaustion, of *zero* possibilities. The fixation (even "obsession") on such spaces is what is disturbing, and the camera left to its own devices (as a device) routinely buttresses this fixation, particularly in light of Cavell's warning that "the step to the future is closed not though depletion but through 'fixation.'"[24] What we do not know that we know, in purely Žižekian terms anyhow, is that films like *The Unknown Known* and *The Act of Killing* manage to convey that we know not how to look past impersonal, and mythical, interstitial spaces (in this case made manifest by the camera specifically) to begin the search for justice *at all*.

* * * *

With *The Act of Killing*, Oppenheimer proposes that by pointing a camera on a perpetrator, we have done our duty—exposed the agent of evil—and justice follows as a matter of course. As the film stands, however, what in fact are we supposed to be surprised at? —That the act of killing can be undertaken so easily, or that the act of killing can be re-presented on film with such candidness? Oppenheimer seems unsure of what exactly the camera's role is (especially as it seems we have a multiplicity of cameras at work). The camera's glare forces us either to pity Anwar or hold him responsible; yet *both* responses are grotesque.

For example, what are we supposed to feel when we watch Congo's emotional breakdown? That some sort of karma has indeed come full circle? That those who commit acts of evil, even those brazen enough to reenact their contours, will necessarily be haunted by the depravity of those acts? I find myself skeptical of what appear to be the aims of the documentarians in the film's final twenty minutes. Is Oppenheimer, for instance, cornered into making a morality play? This would entail holding Anwar responsible somehow (but how?) or eliciting from us a sense of pity (but why?).[25]

Moreover, why is it inconceivable to us as viewers for Morris to ask Rumsfeld or McNamara to actually reenact *their* crimes? You may say neither McNamara nor Rumsfeld actually faced their victims, never put the wire to their throats. But I am saying even if they *had*, to film such reenactment would border on the grotesque; yet in the case of Congo and Soto, we are made to view their reenactments as if the passive consumption of a dark-skinned man acting at the behest of his white superiors (from the cinema and elsewhere) might provide us with the catharsis we crave. Taken together, Morris and Oppenheimer, however inadvertently, have done more to put us within *sympathetic reach* of killers like Rumsfeld and McNamara, capable as they are of appearing calm and collected before us, however drastic the consequences of their fixations. Conversely, the camera has little sympathy for those who carry out such acts of killing directly. Yet the genre of documentary confessionals does not simply have us sympathize with one set of protagonists and vilify another. Rather, they reveal what is within artistic purview to show onscreen in our transnational pursuits of justice: cool-headed rational explanation by white perpetrators on the one hand and violent acts of killing by nonwhite perpetrators on the other. Neither strategy, however, brings us closer to redress.

Documentary confessionals show our aversion—that is, the viewers' aversion—to raising questions of justice at all. These films avoid making a claim, moral or otherwise, and instead hands over the reins to some unknown, unknowable juror. Its modus operandi is simply to film the culprits (indeed, let them film themselves) and hope for the best. Redress is to occur in a space unfilmed and unfilmable; it is the photographic equivalent of justice deferred. The cynicism inherent in this genre of film comes in its purported interest in redress at all, though in the end, we see it has nothing much to offer than simply going through perfunctory moral protestations for the sake of reiterating the misguided notion that justice comes from some objective space that only a disinterested camera could hope to capture. At the end of his film, Errol Morris asks Donald Rumsfeld, "Why are you talking to me?" to which Rumsfeld replies, "I'll be darned if I know." We should be asking ourselves the obverse question—namely, why are we watching?[26]

* * * *

To watch movies with Stanley Cavell in mind is to watch movies by attending to our moods, or the moods these films elicit. Nichols is aptly concerned with the moral considerations of a filmmaker who seeks to document "real" historical actors and present them before us onscreen. Yet an equally vexing moral trade-off exists between the viewer of such films and said filmmaker. What business is it for the filmmaker to show *me*? And this isn't simply about the consumption, ethical or otherwise, of violence or nudity onscreen but of human candidness and vulnerability. Whom should be made to grovel at our feet and how are we to receive them? Such a question is beyond the pale for the films discussed here in their rather misguided rendering of profundity and catharsis. These films betray a mood of exhaustion, which is to say that these movies bring to bear an acute sense of shared aphasia with significant political import.

> Secret melancholy, Emerson says. Naming a historical phenomenon, this names not an isolated matter of an individual sense of pointlessness in saying anything, but a more general sense of lacking, or failing, the language in which to express what has to be said, as if calling philosophical as well as political attention to a shared aphasia.[27]

The quest for philosophical justice comes not in the cheap optimism of a technocratic faith in rationality (whether Rumsfeld's or, for that matter, Obama's) but in the "aversive"[28] thinking that Cavell insists must characterize the philosophy of the future. Hence a philosophy which first requires a reorientation or a "turning [of] ourselves around" and "not [simply] presuming at once to head into the future" with the aid of the camera or otherwise.

Film, at least a certain subgenre of documentary films—what I have been calling here the documentary confessional—does not direct us to the possibility, much less the achievement, of justice. Instead, such films point to a justice achievable elsewhere, hence, in a sense, nowhere. Cavell wants to bring us closer to justice by first perceiving, hence feeling, injustice, risking melancholia. Insisting on the rational unfolding of philosophy into the future has less to do with a desire for justice than a disappointment with its real-world non-manifestation in the aftermath of historical atrocities and thus in the immediate now. What we don't know that we know is that aversive thinking is *required*, melancholia to be duly faced. Rationality cannot save us from fixation; rationality is itself a fixation, one we center upon to avoid moods of despair. The danger of watching films like *The Unknown Known* or *The Act of Killing* comes not simply in the empty consumption of these characters as commodity (though there is that), but, in the passive consumption of justice or redress from afar—at an impersonal, sanitized, and sanitizing distance. To emphasize justice as achievable elsewhere is to deny the brunt of injustice here and now, hence to deny any future possibility of redress.

Notes

1 Bill Nichols, *Introduction to Documentary* (Bloomington: Indianapolis University Press, 2001), 6. An earlier version of this chapter appeared as "Representing Justice in *The Act of Killing* and *The Unknown Known*," in *CineAction*, no. 97 (2016): 66–72.

2 *The Unknown Known*, directed by Errol Morris (History Films: 2013).
3 *The Act of Killing*, directed by Joshua Oppenheimer (Piraya Film: 2013).
4 Nichols, *Introduction to Documentary*, 138.
5 *The Pervert's Guide to Ideology*, directed by Sophie Fiennes (BFI: 2012).
6 Nichols, *Introduction to Documentary*, 138.
7 *The Fog of War: Eleven Lessons from the Life of Robert S. McNamara*, directed by Errol Morris (Sony Classics: 2003).
8 Several films that come to mind immediately include *Hitman Hart: Wrestling with Shadows* (1998), *Beyond the Mat* (2000), *Tyson* (2008), and *The Armstrong Lie* (2013), all of which showcase the downfall of once prominent elite professional athletes. Since we can no longer consume their successes, we are invited now to consume their failures.
9 Joshua Oppenheimer, "The Act of Killing," interview with Melis Behlil, *Cineaste* 38, no. 3 (Summer 2013): 26–31.
10 Cited in Stanley Cavell, "The Future of Possibility," in *Philosophical Romanticism*, ed. Nikolas Kompridis (New York: Routledge, 2006), 21.
11 Rex Butler begins his recent *Stanley Cavell and the Arts: Philosophy and Popular Culture* by inquiring after the intellectual connection between Cavell and Žižek (New York: Bloomsbury, 2020), 1–2; see also 187, 192.
12 Stanley Cavell, *This New Yet Unapproachable America* (Albuquerque: Living Batch Press, 1989).
13 Italics added; Emerson quoted in Cavell, "The Future of Possibility," 22.
14 Italics added; ibid., 22.
15 Italics in original; Slavoj Žižek, "Philosophy, the 'Unknown Knowns,' and the Public Use of Reason," *Topoi* 25 (2006): 137.
16 The full quotation by Rumsfeld: "Reports that say that something hasn't happened are always interesting to me, because as we know, there are known knowns; there are things we know we know. We also know there are known unknowns; that is to say we know there are some things we do not know. But there are also unknown unknowns—the ones we don't know we don't know. And if one looks throughout the history of our country and other free countries, it is the latter category that tend to be the difficult ones." U.S. Department of Defense News Transcripts, February 12, 2002. https://www.defense.gov/newsroom/transcripts/
17 Žižek, "Philosophy, the "Unknown Knowns," 142.
18 Ibid., 141.
19 *The Unknown Known*, 00:05:00.
20 Ibid., 1:33:00.
21 *The Act of Killing*, 01:34:00.
22 Cavell, "The Future of Possibility," 27.
23 Ibid., 26–27.
24 Ibid., 30.

25 A critique of Clifford Geertz's "thick-description ethnography" is pertinent here. The methodology Geertz promotes is to extrapolate from certain localized customs far-ranging anthropological cultural truths. The problem is that readings of local examples are often too hastily perceived as cultural universals. Geertz, for instance, reads Balinese cockfights as providing Indonesians with a "vocabulary of sentiment [that includes]—the thrill of risk, the despair of loss, the pleasure of triumph." Yet as Vincent P. Pecora points out, nowhere in Geertz's topical analysis of Indonesian society does he discuss either the "American involvement [in the coup] nor Indonesia's wholesale swing to a pro-Western orientation." Neither, for that matter, does *The Act of Killing*, which leaves the film wholly indictable on the charge not of explicit historical remembering but intimate historical negation or forgetting. See Clifford Geertz, *The Interpretation of Cultures, Selected Essays* (New York: Basic Books, 1973), 28, 449; and Vincent P. Pecora, "The Limits of Local Knowledge," in *The New Historicism*, ed. H. Aram Veeser (New York: Routledge, 1989), 258.

26 A question I breach but for space must leave unaddressed is how documentaries which Nichols would classify as "expository" address injustice. How effective, that is, is Sophie Fiennes's film on the thought of Žižek in addressing injustice? Because it—or rather Žižek lectures, rather than documents, the result is subjective, personal even. The test of this film is whether it manages to capture successfully the gist of Žižek's thought (even as he is the one doing the explaining). Though it too defers questions of justice, making it worthy of the same critique I am leveling at the other two films, it presupposes and somewhat prescribes struggle. By watching the film, we may be no closer to justice, yet in films like *The Unknown Known* and *The Act of Killing*, there is no struggle. We seem to have done our duty merely in the watching alone.

27 Cavell, "The Future of Possibility," 27.

28 Ibid., 26.

12

Pursuits of Happiness in the Time of War

On Borhane Alaouié's *Beirut: The Encounter*

DANIELE RUGO

In the Shadow of Violence

THE QUESTION OF VIOLENCE occupies much of Stanley Cavell's work. One could even say that the entirety of Cavell's philosophical project can be understood as a way of overcoming violence or at least of keeping it at bay; if not completely silenced, at least silenced for now. Grounded in the close reading of a film, the goal of this analysis is to understand how far Cavell's thinking on violence can be pushed and what becomes of the pursuit of happiness for lovers visited by the violence of war. The film in question, Borhane Alaouié's *Beirut: The Encounter* (*Beyroutou el lika*, 1981), offers a striking illustration since the war it deals with is a "civil" one, therefore a type of violence whose key victim, by definition, is the very fabric of everyday life (urban, in this case). If a civil war then designates a moment of extreme violence that invests the everyday and therefore language, do the conversations these lovers have still make sense? What can they talk to each other about?

One can begin to pursue these questions by provoking and mobilizing the darker corners of Cavell's work. The "darkness" that Wittgenstein mentions in the preface to his *Philosophical Investigations*, invests Cavell's work and lends it a sense of pained urgency. The pain comes from the fact that in Cavell's understanding, philosophy's ability to cure us of our own (natural, intimate) violence is itself a form of violence or, as Wittgenstein has it, "destruction." This destructive power—the reference to destruction can be heard of course in Heidegger's too—is precisely what for Cavell, after Wittgenstein, provides philosophy with whatever relevance it might have. In §118 of the *Investigations*, Wittgenstein writes:

> Where does our investigation get its importance from, since it seems only to destroy everything interesting, that is, all that is great and important? (As it were all the buildings, leaving behind only bits of stone and rubble.) What we are destroying is nothing but houses of cards and we are clearing up the ground of language on which they stand.

For Wittgenstein, doing philosophy means engaging with destruction and with the rubble this leaves behind.

For Cavell, the threat of destruction is one that philosophy necessarily both wards off and cultivates. In Cavell's words, philosophy has a "chronic tendency to violence."[1] He invites us to think this tendency with Emerson and Heidegger, whose metaphor of thinking as clutching shows Western thinking itself "as a kind of sublimized violence."[2] In other words, philosophy needs to work against its own natural inclination. At the same time, it is precisely this inclination that sets philosophy to work. As Cavell writes, "philosophy is called for by our inability to leave things as they are, namely by the violence of our thinking."[3] Similarly, we are all both perpetrators and redeemers, offenders and liberators, at least in principle. Even conversations, which for Cavell stand as the very foundation of our being together, are inextricably exposed to the logic of violence. As he writes in a commentary on Plato's *Republic*, "whether speech disperses violence or whether it is a form of violence,"[4] remains an unanswered question.

The entire edifice of Cavell's philosophy is built as it were in the shadow of violence, as a way to acknowledge violence and its manifestations, but also as a way to bring to light its antidote. In *The Claim of Reason* Cavell concludes (anticipating the conclusion by almost 200 pages) that the truth of skepticism is that "the human creature's basis in the world as a whole, its relation to the world as such, is not that of knowing, anyway not what we think of as knowing."[5] Skepticism appears in human thinking with a sense of inevitability every time humans attempt to know the world in terms of certainty. The most explicit effect of Cavell's conclusion is that of removing us from the impasse of modern skepticism and diminishing the status of Descartes's hyperbolical doubt. Following Cavell, one could say that this is in fact a philosopher's hang-up, rather than a lack inherent to the world. In other words, the unsurpassable impasse that Descartes confronts is inevitable, but the inconsolable feeling he derives from it is of his own making.

It is worth recalling that while this formulation and its trajectory appear initially in Descartes's *Meditations*, for Cavell the Cartesian experience is one that is common to us all. It takes the following form: I have the impression or feeling that something in my experience is skewed, that my knowledge in this particular case (and for all I know this case is a *best case*) is proved erroneous. I conclude therefore that knowledge itself, as a whole, rests on awkward grounds (erroneous assumptions, misleading leaps). By this point I have already committed violence on myself and on the rest of humanity. Cavell, however, wants to correct this last passage. For him these experiences should more simply lead us to check again, to be more (or less) vigilant, less rigid, because these cases prove that "human beings are fallible," not that "we suffer metaphysical ineptitude or privation."[6] A related experience is that of being locked inside a world of appearances, while the things themselves are beyond reach, just a step too far, but forever too far. In this case, we will be asking questions about the existence of a generic object, one that cannot be identified according to specific features or criteria. Once we are in this frame of mind and once we are presented only with generic objects, we have no choice but to conclude that the world is in fact inaccessible or that this world here is a replica, a mental projection of the real world. At this point we have committed another act of violence, this time not only against knowledge, but against the world itself.

One of the reasons behind Cavell's pairing of Wittgenstein and Heidegger is precisely that of bringing to light the violence of thought, a violence that makes both knowledge and the world disappear. For Cavell, this violence fatally weakens whatever bond can be established between the two. By violence Cavell means then, first of all, this epistemological—and subsequently metaphysical—dismissal of the world and others that thinking itself is naturally inclined to perform. For Cavell, thinking's tendency to substitute knowledge for acknowledgment—to seek more knowledge, when acknowledgment is needed—produces a specific kind of violence, which it is thinking's job to renounce and resist. This resistance implies *in primis* forgoing the ambition for a position outside the world, from which to view and arrange our fates, our worlds. This same logic applies to other minds. As Cavell writes in relation to Frank Capra's *It Happened One Night* (1934), "the existence of others is something of which we are unconscious, a piece of knowledge we repress, about which we draw a blank. This does violence to others, it separates their bodies from their souls, makes monsters of them; and presumably we do it because we feel that others are doing this violence to us."[7] These reductions start with the hyperbolical doubt and proceed onto the formation and definition of Western thinking as construction and representation. This is what we should forgo and awaken from, turn away from since it (our thinking, our own thoughts) has already turned against us (the reference in Heidegger is to the atomic bomb[8]).

One can therefore say that in Cavell's work there is no ultimate immunity from the threat of violence, it is against violence that words find their voices. We all exist under the threat of violence and the stronger the bond between us becomes, the more exposed we are to the threat. By this I mean that the more intertwined our lives are, the more committed we are to the idea of sharing our lives with something or someone, the more the threat of violence shows itself in the everyday. Intimacy increases the risk of performing violence against the other, of denying their humanity, silencing their uniqueness, demanding that they conform to our idea of what knowledge of other people should be. It is in order to show this that Cavell turns his attention to Shakespearean tragedies and to Hollywood films. This resistance to violence—to this intimate, ordinary, inevitable, and mundane form of violence—also seems to motivate Cavell's focus on the significance of marriage and even more his insistence on couples and lovers. The question of marriage provides for Cavell the confirmation that the ordinary and the everyday are in themselves sites of discovery and therefore the place from where the world becomes interesting, but equally the site where violence can and is performed.

The question remains the same throughout Cavell's writing on marriage: marriage is the establishment of intimacy, but can equally be an empty institution, if not a violent one. By itself marriage does not reconcile us with the world and does not in itself suffice to elicit our interest in the everyday. Thus, the question of a new intimacy—of letting oneself be loved in order to discover the ability to love—is not one that can be settled by marriage alone. The new intimacy that Cavell requires rests on a second confirmation and the acceptance of two elements: separation and repetition. The moral, perhaps best exemplified for Cavell by the closing scene of *Woman of the Year* (1942, dir. George Stevens), is that it is a daily reconfiguring of the ordinary rather than an overcoming of it that can become the site of adventure.[9] A life more ordinary can be an instance of happiness. The willing repetition of days substitutes the holiday. It is not in holidaying from the world, but in the acknowledgment of its separation and return, that we can disclose and give expression to our intimacy with it.

Coleridge's Mariner's refusal of marriage as a recovery from skepticism resides in the uncertainty that befalls the institution. This uncertainty declares that celebration and festivity do not in themselves guarantee intimacy; neither do they offer appropriate expressions of it. For marriage to be an effective redemption something has to occur that takes place beyond the festivity and replaces it. Thus, finding in oneself the life of the world means refraining from wanting absolute connection (the Mariner's killing of the bird). The alternative option is to want no connection at all, as is the case for Leontes in Shakespeare's *The Winter's Tale*, who pays this refusal of connection with "the inability to say what exists, to say whether, so to speak, language applies to anything."[10]

Cavell often returns to the ability to be loved as a precondition for love as such. Being loved is an undertaking whose achievement requires daily efforts, not a moment of revelation. Perhaps the most compelling figure in Cavell's gallery of tragic lovers is Othello, to whom Cavell dedicates, tellingly, the closing passages of *The Claim of Reason* (which Cavell calls "an extended final illustration"[11]). Interestingly, among the works that Cavell analyses, *Othello* is also the one where the violence that besets the couple from within, and proves deadly, finds echoes and parallels in an external violence. Even before Othello decides to go to war against Desdemona, their world is already at war and this war between Venice and the Ottoman Empire is an important element of the story (the attack on Cyprus, a strategic outpost for the Venetian Republic, draws Othello and Desdemona away from Venice). Surprisingly perhaps, Cavell bypasses this element.

Cavell resorts to Shakespearean tragedy because, in his words, tragedy can be understood "as a kind of epistemological problem," one intimately connected with the fact that it is now up to others (therefore to myself too), rather than to God, to offer proof that we are not alone in the universe.[12] What takes Cavell to a study of Othello is therefore a meditation on Descartes's meditation and more specifically the fact that "the integrity of my (human, finite) existence may depend on the fact and on the idea of another being's existence, and on the possibility of *proving* that existence; an existence conceived from my very dependence and incompleteness, hence conceived as perfect, and conceived as producing me 'in some sense, in [its] own image.'"[13] The centrality of *Othello* for Cavell's epistemological understanding of tragedy revolves around Othello's obsessive search for proof. It is this search for a proof that makes Othello "beyond aid [. . .] the ear and eye disjoined."[14] The problem for Cavell is not that Othello believes Iago, but that he does not believe himself, he does not believe what he knows (what he cannot not know) and is prepared to let this self-inflicted violence take hold of him.

As Cavell writes: "It is not conceivable that Othello believes Iago and *not* Desdemona. Iago, we might say offers Othello an opportunity to believe something, something to oppose to something else he knows. What does he know? Why does it require opposition?—What do we know?"[15] While in the text Cavell proceeds to respond quite literally to the questions *what does he know?* and *what do we know?* one should hear both resonate in a much broader and far-reaching sense. Tragedy is for Cavell an epistemological problem and therefore gives form to epistemological answers. Any attempt to answer questions about the two lovers in the tragedy will form an illustration—a "final illustration" as far as Cavell's *The Claim of Reason* is concerned—on what knowledge might or might not do. Othello, Cavell continues, is pure and in Desdemona he has found a match for this purity. Nonetheless, despite the strength of this bond—Cavell writes that they each see their own face in the other's mind—Othello's insistence on knowing what he knows proves fatal. The violence does not start, as might be assumed, from a specific gesture; it does not emerge through some kind of manifestation, but begins with what Cavell calls Othello's loss of imagination.[16]

As Cavell notes, before the manifestation of violence, we have the first scene of conjugal intimacy, a scene of "armed men running through a sleeping city" and interrupting the hour of love.[17] This interruption also produces a knowledge gap: Othello does not know, he cannot be sure, whether the marriage has been consummated. The problem thus seems to be one of knowledge, not because we can assume that Othello does not know his lover and wife, but because he is constantly trying to deny himself the knowledge he has, to deny this knowledge any validity. Cavell writes that Othello now has a mind "whose reason is suffocating in its sumptuous capacity for figuration."[18] At this point the violence manifests itself, after violence has already run its course in Othello's mind and imagination— besieged by a suffocating reason. What Othello couldn't believe—the fact that Desdemona is flesh and blood—is now revealed by and through death. Othello now has his answer, but now that he does know he has also eliminated the object of his knowledge. Violence has taken hold of him and from his imagination it has colored the world. Cavell writes:

> Nothing could be more certain to Othello than that Desdemona exists; is flesh and blood; is separate from him; other. This is precisely the possibility that tortures him. The content of his torture is the premonition of the existence of another, hence of his own, his own as dependent, as partial.[19]

Othello's inability to accept the knowledge he has escalates to the point of uxoricide. His violence against himself, against his own imagination, has turned into the necessary erasure of the other. Othello didn't lack knowledge or certainty, "he knew everything, but he could not yield to what he knew, be commanded by it. He found out too much for his mind, not too little."[20] This excursus on *Othello* exemplifies Cavell's treatment of violence as that which occurs, first of all, in our examination of our knowledge of the world. The consequence of this initial violence that denies validity to what we know is for Othello a physical, murderous violence against Desdemona.

Once Cavell "discovers" the resourcefulness of lovers in explaining the skeptical doubt and its correlated violence, he will return to this figure in his analysis of Hollywood comedy (the lovers who cannot stop talking to each other) and in the filmic melodramas (the lovers who cannot talk to each other). In all these cases, the path to acknowledgment is one that is, as it were, blocked from within. What about the war that rages around

Othello and Desdemona? What about violence that comes to the lovers from outside, what happens when the physical separation cannot be overcome? What happens to acknowledgment and the pursuit of happiness in the time of war?

The War Couple: On *Beirut: The Encounter*

The couple under the pressure of war is a literary and cinematic trope that has proved fertile time and again and one can find a plethora of examples. The illustration I would like to offer here in order to test and prod the boundaries, so to speak, of Cavell's work on violence comes from a Lebanese film from 1981, *Beirut: The Encounter* (*Beyroutou el lika*) directed by Borhane Alaouié. In choosing Alaouié's film, I am aware of moving beyond the geographical remit of Cavell's canon, but the intention here is precisely to provoke that canon to respond to an outsider. *Beirut: The Encounter* seems to provide the perfect occasion for such provocation, considering also the thematic parallels it establishes with much of what Cavell is interested in.

The film features Haider and Zeina, a couple living on opposite sides of divided Beirut. The action takes place during the Civil War that raged in the country between 1975 and 1990 and that, according to Elias Khoury, turned the capital into the "mythological prototype of the city torn by civil war, dishevelled by death, dismembered by destruction."[21] During a ceasefire the two manage to get in touch via telephone and organize to meet in a café situated on the eastern side of Beirut, near where Zeina lives. We also learn that the woman is Christian, while Haidar is a Shia from southern Lebanon, who has sought refuge in the capital following heavy fighting in his native village.[22] We know this because he speaks of the makeshift property he inhabits with his brother and because he makes remarks on the novelty of urban life. Haidar tries to make his way across Beirut, still divided between East and West, but reaches the meeting point too late, the woman has already left and the place, which the two had used in the past, has now changed a great deal. Hostilities begin; phone contact is not possible anymore and so is meeting again. The two resort to recording voice messages on tape. The recording of these messages occupies the main part of the narrative and the film as it were begins again once the series of recordings starts. The promise the characters live by is that they will meet to exchange the tapes at the airport before the woman leaves the country. While the film has received relatively little attention, both French critic Serge Daney and philosopher Gilles Deleuze have left brief commentaries on it.[23] For Deleuze, the film becomes an example of what all talking cinema should do as "speech is truly seen forcing a difficult path through the ruins."[24]

Beirut: The Encounter seems to suggest a third coupling system, in addition to the two (comedy and melodrama) that Cavell elaborates: the *war couple*. This couple would then be the object of a series of specific questions: What do war couples talk about? How do these lovers communicate (or fail to)? These are questions that one might expect to find answers to in Cavell, given his commitment to questions of violence as they are articulated by and within the couple in love. In other words, if the couple of the comedies need to learn how to speak again (because their natural inclination to do so does not suffice anymore) and the couple of the melodramas need to learn the significance of silence, what kind of speaking is that of the war couple? These lovers do not need to erect barriers with blankets. They are separated by force and violence, and their separation is also one they don't necessarily need to internalize, because its existence is so stubbornly present in their everyday. What kind of city of words can they build? What do Zeina and Haidar say to each other? They do not actually manage to speak in person and say much to each other because their physical separation is—temporarily at least—insurmountable.

The film begins by emphasizing precisely the materiality of the city. The first two shots are of waste, overflown and now sprawled in the streets. Soon after we are introduced to one of the main characters, a man in his thirties who walks through a sparsely decorated room (there is only a small table) to the window. Outside two men are shoveling rubbish on the back of a truck, already overwhelmed. As his gaze turns, we see the Holiday Inn hotel, with noticeable holes from shelling.[25] The camera then lingers on a different building with a frontal close-up and this time the ruination of the war becomes explicit and fills the entire screen. Haidar then scans the horizon in front of his balcony: the wall he sees is riddled with bullet holes. The landscape of war and the effect of war on the city thus occupies the opening sequence of the film. As the character leaves home to phone Zeina he is seen crossing a road blocked by sand banks, possibly deliberately placed there by the factions controlling this portion of the city. The shot here is wide, thus drowning the character in the landscape.

As the film switches to Zeina's side of the story and of the city, the camera moves onto what looks like a middle-class living room, where three women and a child are talking. The interior is lavishly decorated with sofas and red armchairs, while several plants in the background frame the scene. These shots serve to introduce Zeina and the different life she leads on the opposite side of the city. By showing a finely furnished interior, the director seems to suggest that Zeina's world is at least partially sheltered from destruction and somehow less touched by the ongoing conflict. Following these spatial introductions to the two characters, we witness their first attempt to reunite and meet face to face, to put together "his and her day and night."[26] Haidar manages to get the only telephone in his building to work and connects to Zeina, who tells him that she will leave the day after for the United States. Quickly the two reestablish a meaningful connection and express to each other the mutual joy of talking, of exchanging words, of hearing each other's voices. Haidar asks "Do you still love talking to me?" and Zeina responds that not only she still likes it, but that she hasn't spoken to anyone in two years. A meeting is organized in Achrafieh (East Beirut). Since the main road is closed, Zeina instructs Haidar to take an alternative route. After walking around more rubbles, debris, and queues for bread, Haidar jumps in a taxi and attempts to travel through one of the functioning crossing points between East and West. The taxi moves slowly and soon it finds itself completely stuck in a traffic jam. Alaouié lingers on the tailback and shows several close-ups of car bumper against car bumper, wheels barely moving, uninterrupted hooting; the vehicles are so close to each other that one couldn't walk between them. In the meantime, Zeina is waiting at the designated meeting point. The violence all around them is as senseless as the traffic, a violence that as Samir Frangie writes "does not obey any known rule."[27] The civil war undermines precisely the infrastructures of the everyday, both metaphorically (relationships, meetings, love stories) and physically (it destroys roads, puts phones and electricity out of use, makes access to water and bread difficult). As Samir Khalaf writes, a civil war is in this sense always prone to become "uncivil or drift into incivility."[28]

This idea of a pervasive and random violence that dominates the city and its people is reinforced in a scene portraying an impeccably dressed elderly man walking past a militia fighter sitting at an improvised checkpoint. As the man walks past, the militiaman armed with a rifle splashes water on him for no apparent reason. When the gentleman protests, the young man tells him that this is because his nineteen-year-old friend Jacques has been killed by a sniper and has died to protect the older man and people like him. The militia then invites the man to march on or else he will pay with his life. Alaouié shows again how completely violence has taken hold of the everyday in a sequence when Zeina is waiting in the café for Haidar. The violence here is all the more striking precisely because it contrasts with Zeina's distracted fidgeting (fidgetiness being for Cavell a "universal human attribute," but also revealing the camera's "knowledge of the metaphysical restlessness of the live body"[29]). As the young woman enters, we learn that the establishment has recently introduced a pinball machine and lost as a consequence some of its aloof elegance. Three men play pinball just behind the table where Zeina is sitting. One of the men wears a gun in the back of his trousers and the conversation quickly veers to gruesome details, with one asking how his friend can tolerate seeing those people (enemies) without impaling at least one of them. Disturbed by what she hears, Zeina leaves the café without waiting for Haidar, who is still stuck in traffic. The physical distance between the two is further emphasized by the fact that they seem to inhabit different cities.

Zeina walks on a wide pavement and looks at windows, while Haidar has to zigzag through the cars that have occupied the pavement. When Haidar arrives at the café the young men—their guns still visible in the back pockets—are still playing pinball. Haidar leaves, walks back to West Beirut, and from there calls Zeina to apologize for his delay. There won't be any time for another meeting as Zeina is set to leave for the airport at seven the next morning. To overcome this obstacle, they agree to record a message for each other and here begins the film (forty minutes in). It is Zeina who comes up with the idea and says to Haidar to speak to the "cassette" (we are in 1981) as if he was speaking to her. It is not ideal, she says, but there is no other option.

While Zeina's brother and his friends discuss the survival of Lebanon (probably in relation to what they perceive to be either the possible fragmentation of the country or its transformation in a proxy state for the Palestinian diaspora, a thesis that found credit among some sections of the Lebanese population), Zeina withdraws to the kitchen and, after their departure, begins her recording. The film becomes from now on predominantly dark; both Haidar and Zeina are immersed in a blackness from which they barely emerge. This darkness functions as an intensifying device; the more nocturnal the film becomes, the more the violence of the day leaves room to their voices and the externalization of their intimacies. Haidar's first words in his first recording ask, "is speaking still possible?" It is under the aegis of this question that the entirety of the film could be read.

Confession and the Language of War

The film, via Haidar, seems thus to ask whether speaking is still possible under the pressure of a violence that—unlike the one that takes hold of most of Cavell's couples—manipulates and seizes the lovers from the outside, paralyzing them within a room, blocking their access to each other by way of rubbles and traffic jams, by collapsing the sociality and infrastructures all around them. Before trying to answer Haidar's question, it might be worth listening to what he and Zeina have to say as they attempt to build their city of words from within the city at war. The first thing Haidar says is that he accepts. He accepts that he has to find a new way of speaking, that he will have to speak, he says, "without seeing your face, without seeing the reflection of my words in your eyes," thus without being able to receive a response. Haidar accepts by creating a way of speaking that is a mixture between confession and dialogue, addressed to Zeina, but without her. These first words suggest that Haidar is thinking about his confession as a dialogue, but can one accept a confession as the beginning of a conversation? The confessional element of Haidar's speech is emphasized by the darkness that surrounds him, a darkness that seems to eliminate the possibility of reciprocity, that seals him even more within his own speech, his every word carrying him deeper and deeper into his forced solitude. What seems to give further credibility to this interpretation is the fact that Haidar adds, "I will not hide anything from you," which in turn might mean that he is not hiding anything from himself (or that he will not hide from her anything that he is not also hiding from himself). Is a confession still valid if nobody else is there to listen to it? Does a confession need an audience? As Sarah Beckwith mentions in her work on Cavell and Shakespeare: "confession is as important as acknowledgment in Cavell's reading of Wittgenstein."[30] This significance does not rest on the fact that confession grants us another "privatisation of the world,"[31] but rather the opposite. As Cavell himself writes, "confession, unlike dogma, is not to be believed but tested, and accepted or rejected. Nor is it the occasion for accusation, except of yourself, and by implication those who find themselves in you. There is exhortation [. . .] not to belief, but to self-scrutiny."[32]

Haidar's exhortation is to Zeina. He is inviting her not to hide anything from herself, so as not to hide anything from him or perhaps the other way around. Can she find herself in these words? Will he be able to achieve what all confessions must achieve, a match between his "own voice and voice of the others"?[33] For Cavell, the question of confession, the very existence of it, is intimately linked with skepticism, that is with our denial of ourselves or others (or affirmation of ourselves at the expense of others). To this effect Cavell writes:

> Skepticism about our knowledge of others is typically accompanied by complacency about our knowledge of ourselves. From Locke through Mill, and beyond, we "infer" the experience of others, and "intuit" our own. Whereas those capable of deepest personal confession (Augustine, Luther, Rousseau, Thoreau, Kierkegaard, Tolstoy, Freud) were most convinced they were speaking from the most hidden knowledge of others. Perhaps that is the sense which makes confession possible.[34]

Is Haidar capable of these depths? If so, his confession would need to find an audience. Haidar hopes that his speech will travel to her unchanged, but he can't be sure that anything will stay unchanged. He adds: "I hope I can speak to you rather than being carried by my speech." In the meantime we see vistas of Beirut, immersed in the silence of night, silhouettes barely visible, armed men perhaps having retired to their guarding posts.

Speaking is difficult for another reason. As Haidar and Zeina remind us, the dictionary has undergone a transformation. Haidar says, "the war has changed every single word, certain words now mean 'ruins and 60,000 dead.'" The war has changed the meaning of familiar words and made some words unavailable to them. What could be said—each word in the dictionary—

cannot be meant in the same way now. Language keeps highlighting their distance and, as Haidar admits, "between us now is not only 60,000 corpses, but 250,000 cars, two million heaps of rubbish, millions of words written on walls, bullets, bodies and human voices." Speech passes through all these beings and things, and yet it isn't perhaps quite enough. To describe their relationship, Haidar says that he and Zeina are like "two bullets launched towards each other, but which have been detoured." Language too is being detoured and, instead of affirming, it now denies life. Haidar says: "We are all a bit dead, after all, we have all been killed."

Soon enough one comes to accept that the war has colonized language completely. We hear, on the one hand, Zeina talk in detail about an explosion, which has severed a body in half. Haidar, on the other hand, talks about a destroyed village and says that nothing, "not even a stone survives." In the end, the stories of war seem to cause the conversation to collapse and Haidar is forced to admit: "I have been speaking to myself for two hours, do you know what that means?" Of course Zeina knows what this means, because she is doing exactly the same on the other side of the city. His calls are in vain; he cannot summon her.

The war has changed them. He doesn't know what has become of her. Who is she now, in the time of war? Not only language cannot bring the two together, but language itself has been hollowed, transformed by war, so that we cannot, not anymore, mean what we say, so that we can't use it to access the world.

At the end of the film, the two make their way to the airport in sequences juxtaposed through parallel editing. As one had come to expect by now, the two do not manage to meet. Once again, the timing isn't right and the airport is too confusing a place. As Zeina travels to the gate, Haidar takes a taxi back to Beirut and throws the tape out of the window of the moving car. The tape lays on the floor, unraveled, mute, insignificant. The words have stopped linking us to the world, because this time the world is withdrawing from us and this withdrawal has entered language and hollowed it out.

Limits of Violence and Limits of Conventions

In *Beirut: The Encounter* the world remains inaccessible not because we are whimsically limiting ourselves, making ourselves impotent, but because it has become uninhabitable and language has been emptied of its ability to connect us to the world. In this sense then language rather than "writing us back into the world" tries to completely substitute itself for the world; the cassette, the words recorded on the tape, become the world.[35] The conclusion of *Beirut: The Encounter* suggests that this substitution—even when perfectly achieved—is either unsatisfactory or useless. Unsatisfactory because it is still the world or the beloved one that remain out of reach;

useless because ultimately it is not words we are in love with, but the someone or something they connect us to. When Haidar and Zeina commit their words to the recorder, the recording provides a reprieve, for a moment the world's inhabitability is overcome. However, the overcoming is not toward a reconciliation of their thoughts with their bodies, of their love with the streets, lamp posts, wires, pipes, and ducts of their city, a reconciliation of nights and days. At the opposite, the recordings confine them even more, show even more that the substitution is not a game worth playing, that no words survive without a world.

Cavell takes violence to be inherent to thinking, a natural inclination to clutch the world and repress knowledge of others, thus reducing them to nothingness. This violence can be overcome through conversation. What does Cavell make of this hollowing out of language under the pressure of a violence that visits the couple from the outside and makes conversation impossible? If Cavell cannot see the hollowing out of language—cannot think war and what war does to lovers and their words—to what extent is he really thinking violence? If Cavell's philosophy is combating violence, our own self-inflicted violence and the violence we do to others when we are complacent, how can he fail to think war, violence's most explicit form?

Maybe Cavell is painfully aware of all this when he writes that words can fail, that at times conviction that one's solitary thoughts (confession) really speak from the knowledge of others instead slacken and collapse.

> In such straits perhaps you write for everybody and nobody; for an all but unimaginable future; in pseudonyms, for the anonymous, in an album, which is haunted by pictures and peopled with voices. But what happens if you are not a writer, if you lack that way of embodying, accounting for, a slacked conviction in a community, and of staking your own (in imagination, in a world of works)? What happen if all you want to do is talk, and words fail you?[36]

There are many ways for words to fail you. Words can fail you because something makes them change their meaning. Language is public, the conventions we appeal to depend on us, but if the public thing is shattered, if it changes the very general facts of human nature (what else do *civil wars* do?), then language must inevitably falter and certain words will mean "60,000 corpses." Words fail us when criteria fail us, that is, when conventions fail. It is the idea of convention that is significant here. Cavell writes:

> The conventions we appeal to may be said to be "fixed," "adopted," "accepted," etc. by us; but this does not now mean that what we have fixed or adopted are (merely) the (conventional) *names* of things. The conventions which control the application of grammatical criteria are

fixed not by customs or some particular concord or agreement which might, without disrupting the texture of our lives, be changed where convenience suggests a change.[37]

The important point is precisely that conventions rely on the texture of our lives not being disrupted, but what happens when this is the case? If the conventions fail when the texture of our lives is disrupted, then what is happening to Haidar is neither that his confession is not up to scratch, nor that he can't find the right words, but that words fail to make connection with the world outside of his dark, sparsely decorated bedroom. The words fail to travel through the rubble and corpses, through a city made of war. The city of words and the city of war don't add up; they don't know each other. Conventions do fail when something intervenes that disrupt those "forms of life that are normal to any group of creatures we call human."[38] Something Cavell includes in those forms of life proper to humans is the fact of having a "geographical environment, which they manipulate or exploit in certain ways for certain humanly comprehensible motives."[39] We know by now that this kind of manipulation is not afforded to Haidar and Zeina. We know that in some very painful ways the environment (infrastructures such as telephones and roads) is so hostile that it has started manipulating them. The environment is of one of the many conventions that collapse during what one could call the lived experience of war. In order to think about war and to think about what happens to pursuits of happiness in the time of war, one needs to think about the moment when these conventions collapse. Something human remains, something of our routines, something of our patterns, but words fail us. As Haidar says: "now it is more difficult, the dictionary itself has changed. A word that we used three years ago has another meaning now. Certain words now mean "destroyed homes and 60,000 people dead." How can words not fail you when between two lovers there are 60,000 corpses?

Perhaps Cavell, in insisting on the depth of convention in human life, cannot think the moment when they collapse or the irreparable violence that war inflicts on them. Perhaps conventions stand between Cavell and war, foreclose his ability to think about this form of violence. Or perhaps Cavell understood this too well, understood the collapse from which we never quite recover and here he finds (or sets) his own limit. Cavell knew the importance of war, what war does, how it changes words and pushes one to think of the moment when conventions collapse (despite us). He tells us so in one of the few references he makes to war in *The World Viewed* (a book full of films made during and in the shadow of a world war). Here in discussing the myth of modern marriage, Cavell writes:

> In classical comedy the stage at the end is littered with marriages, tangled pairs have at last been sorted out, age accepts its place, youth takes its own, and families are present to celebrate the continuance of

their order. At some point, perhaps when the world went to war, society stopped believing in its ability to provide that continuity. [. . .] What the community needed to know, in reduced circumstances, was not merely that its legitimacy is being acknowledged, but that it is worth acknowledging. In particular that it still allows those meant for one another to find one another.[40]

The night is too dark and there is too much rubble around for Haidar and Zeina to find one another, even if they have accepted to know what they cannot fail to know. The problem is that the ruins and the corpses have changed the very fabric of language, so that in a way, finding one another, acknowledging one another, has become a very different—and riskier—undertaking.

Notes

1. Stanley Cavell, *Philosophy the Day after Tomorrow* (Cambridge: The Belknap Press of Harvard University Press, 2005), 231.
2. Stanley Cavell, *Conditions Handsome and Unhandsome: The Constitution of Emersonian Perfectionism: The Carus Lectures, 1988* (Chicago: The University of Chicago Press, 1990), 39.
3. Cavell, *Philosophy the Day after Tomorrow*, 201.
4. Stanley Cavell, *Cities of Words: Pedagogical Letters on a Register of the Moral Life* (Cambridge: Harvard University Press, 2004), 325.
5. Stanley Cavell, *The Claim of Reason: Wittgenstein, Skepticism, Morality, and Tragedy* (Oxford: Oxford University Press, 1979, 1999), 241.
6. Ibid., 143.
7. Stanley Cavell, *Pursuits of Happiness: The Hollywood Comedy of Remarriage* (Cambridge: Harvard University Press, 1981), 109.
8. Martin Heidegger, *The Question Concerning Technology and Other Essays* (New York: Garland Publishing, 1977), 22.
9. Stanley Cavell, *In Quest of the Ordinary: Lines of Skepticism and Romanticism* (Chicago: The University of Chicago Press, 1988), 178.
10. Ibid., 80.
11. Cavell, *The Claim of Reason*, 481.
12. Ibid., 482.
13. Ibid., 483; italics in original.
14. Ibid., 484; italics in original.
15. Ibid.
16. Ibid., 486.
17. Ibid., 487.
18. Ibid., 490.

19 Ibid., 493.
20 Ibid., 496.
21 Elias Khoury, "The Memory of the City," *Grand Street* 54 (1995): 137.
22 Without wanting to reduce this conflict merely to its sectarian dimension, an argument that the film definitely opposes, the identities that foreshadow the two characters do matter here as they give the audience an insight into the places they occupy in the city and their options vis-à-vis staying or leaving the country.
23 Serge Daney, *La Maison Cinema et le Monde*, 2 (Paris: P.O.L., 2002), 539.
24 Gilles Deleuze, *Cinema 2: The Time-Image*, trans. Hugh Tomlinson and Robert Galeta (London: Bloomsbury, 2005), 224.
25 Between 1975 and 1976 the hotel had been the stage of one of the war's fiercest battles due to its strategic position, adjacent to the sea. This is known as the Battle of the Hotels. See Samir Kassir, *La Guerre du Liban: De la Dissension Nationale au Conflit Régional (1975–1982)* (Beirut: Karthala, 1994), 132.
26 Cavell, *Pursuits of Happiness*, 109.
27 Samir Frangie, *Voyage Au Bout de la Violence* (Beirut: L'Orient des Livres), 7.
28 Samir Khalaf, *Civil and Uncivil Violence in Lebanon: A History of the Internationalization of Communal Conflict* (New York: Columbia University Press, 2002), 38.
29 Stanley Cavell, *Cavell on Film*, ed. William Rothman (New York: State University of New York Press, 2005), 126.
30 Sarah Beckwith, "William Shakespeare and Stanley Cavell: Acknowledgment, Confession and Tragedy," in *Stanley Cavell and Literary Studies: Consequences of Skepticism*, ed. Richard Eldridge and Bernie Rhie (London: Bloomsbury, 2011), 125.
31 Ibid., 125.
32 Stanley Cavell, *Must We Mean What We Say? A Book of Essays* (Cambridge: Cambridge University Press, 2002), 71.
33 William Desmond, "A Second Primavera: Cavell, German Philosophy, and Romanticism," in *Stanley Cavell*, ed. Richard Eldridge (Cambridge: Cambridge University Press, 2003), 165.
34 Cavell, *The Claim of Reason*, 109.
35 Stanley Cavell, *The World Viewed: Reflections on the Ontology of Film, Enlarged Edition* (Cambridge: Harvard University Press, 1979), 22.
36 Cavell, *The Claim of Reason*, 110.
37 Ibid.
38 Ibid.
39 Ibid., 111.
40 Cavell, *The World Viewed*, 79.

PART VI

Visibility, Audibility, and Intelligibility

13

Chantal Akerman and Stanley Cavell

Viewing in *La Captive* and Reviewing in Moral Perfectionism

KATE RENNEBOHM

The cause of tragedy is that we would rather murder the world than permit it to expose us to change.
—STANLEY CAVELL, "*The Avoidance of Love*"[1]

IN THIS CHAPTER, I HAVE THREE AMBITIONS. The first is to propose something of a missed conversation between director, author, and artist Chantal Akerman and philosopher Stanley Cavell—to point toward the larger resonances between their respective projects and thought. The second involves working through a specific example of such resonance. Here, I take Akerman's film *La Captive* (*The Captive*, 2000), a loose adaptation of Proust's novel *La Prisonnière*[2] (*The Prisoner*), as an examination of two important concerns for Cavell: skepticism and its interrelation with "viewing" as a dynamic. In *La Captive*, the male character is driven by a (skeptical) obsession with *knowing* his object of desire, a destructive obsession he feeds by both viewing this woman and endeavoring to make her into something that can be viewed. The third ambition of the chapter then is to draw out Cavell's proffering of a mode of engagement with the world alternative to that of *La Captive*'s protagonist, which I term *re*viewing. In this mode, which Cavell presents but does not specifically articulate, one does not view others and the world unseen but rather sees him or herself from a new vantage point. While reviewing will be shown to play an essential role in Cavell's notion of Emersonian or moral perfectionism, *La Captive* will finally return to give its reminder of the limits—the circumscription—of both reviewing and moral perfectionism. In this, Akerman's film speaks for those left outside of these limits, or those who could be not be saved from being viewed.

Chantal Akerman's mid-career masterpiece *La Captive* begins with waves crashing onto a dark beach at night. Sergei Rachmaninoff's portentous *Isle of the Dead* plays over the images. Following the credits, the film cuts to a shot of a projected 16 mm film, which also shows waves hitting a beach, but now in daytime. As the sound of the projector hums in the background, a group of women run into this projected frame and the water. Within this group, one woman, Ariane (Sylvie Testud), seems to call the diegetic camera's attention more than the other, more conventionally beautiful women. Her impenetrable expression eventually fills the frame in a close-up. At this point, a male voice is heard over the image, slowing intoning "I . . .," "I . . . really . . .," "I . . . really . . . like . . . you. . . ." A reverse shot reveals the owner of the voice to be Simon (Stanislaus Merhar), a young man operating the projector alone in his private room. As the images unfold onscreen, he soon abandons the projector to approach the projected image, his silhouette inserting itself into its frame—an attempt to get closer to, or even to merge with, Ariane. As Akerman's film unfolds, the spectator will eventually come to understand this opening sequence as synecdoche for the dynamic that shapes the film as a whole—Simon's obsessive drive to know and possess Ariane. Throughout, this drive takes the form of a contradictory wish to both "enter" his object of obsession and her world—expressed in this sequence as the desire to breach the impassable barrier of the screened image—while simultaneously remaining in a position outside of it so as to maintain his ability to surveil it and her completely. This latter desire expresses itself in Simon's wish, enacted variably throughout the film, to capture or "freeze" Ariane. In other words, Simon wants to make her into that which can be subject to perfect knowing and viewing—say, as in a film.

The scenario Akerman presents in *La Captive*'s opening sequence ingeniously condenses and refracts not only elements of her broader film, but also key aspects of philosopher Stanley Cavell's thinking about skepticism and the dynamic of viewing that he finds integral to it. Skepticism is famously a central theme of Cavell's thought, though he departs from skepticism's more traditional framing as an epistemological problem (in which one wonders what can ground knowledge claims with certainty), contending instead that skepticism, whether it begins as an epistemological concern or not, quickly comes to inform a wider range of existential and ethical concerns for the modern subject.[3] To Cavell's thinking, modern experience is thus marked by the feeling of being *barred* from the world, others, and even oneself. In this sense, Akerman's filmmaking oeuvre shares much with Cavell's formulations regarding skepticism. While Akerman did not use this same terminology in her writing or commentary on her films, her formal depictions of bodies as impassable sites, housing interiorities that can neither be dismissed nor accessed; her narrative depictions of characters struggling to overcome isolation or their own inexplicabilities; and her regular confrontation of spectators with extended, frontal close-up shots of opaque characters, through which she challenges those spectators to accept or abandon these figures in their unknowability, all speak to her investigations into and expressions of this philosophical problematic. Indeed, her larger output as a filmmaker, artist, and writer is profoundly marked by the (skeptical) sense of human experience as riven by a boundary between the "inner" of subjectivity and the "outer" of the external world and others. For example, she often presents her characters (including herself) as trapped within their own interiorities, either struggling to confront the impenetrable exteriorities of others or joyfully experiencing moments of reprieve from these boundaries, where they have somehow, temporarily, been dissolved.

Cavell himself briefly acknowledges Akerman's interest in and relevance to skepticism in his 2004 work *Cities of Words: Pedagogical Letters on a Register of the Moral Life*. There, he references *La Captive* a handful of times during an extended discussion of George Cukor's 1944 film *Gaslight*, one of the four films he had earlier offered as an example of the "Hollywood melodrama of the unknown woman"—a genre Cavell proposes in which female characters negotiate not only their own skepticism-informed relationship to their world but also the skepticism of the male characters around them.[4] However, despite his (accurate) assessment of *La Captive*'s germaneness to skeptical thought, Cavell does not address the film in detail. Somewhat dismayingly, he invokes *La Captive* only to largely credit the thought relevant for his discussion to Proust's original novel, of which *La Prisonnière* is a part, and not to Akerman's very unusual adaptation of it.[5] In other words, Cavell largely misses here the import of Akerman's work, both in *La Captive* and, more broadly, for his own thinking.[6] This can and perhaps should be chalked up to nothing more than the human limitations that prevent a philosopher from engaging with everything, or perhaps to a sense on Cavell's part that Akerman's avant-garde work fell beyond his ken (though one might note in response that Cavell regularly wrote about the avant-garde films or art cinema of Akerman's male contemporaries and predecessors, including Jean-Luc Godard, Dušan Makavejev, Ingmar Bergman, Éric Rohmer, and Kenji Mizoguchi).[7]

The strikingness of the largely missed encounter between Cavell and Akerman—colleagues in Harvard's Visual and Environmental Studies department in the late 1990s—is even more notable when one surveys the variety of their shared interests and backgrounds. Above and beyond their concern with skeptical frameworks, there is Akerman and Cavell's shared sense of the importance of autobiographical modes of expression, their overriding focus on the ordinary as an undervalued register of experience, their broadly anti-systematic ethos and resistance to their own placement in singular or disciplinary categories, their shared interest and history with psychoanalysis, their personal connections to and investigations of Judaism, and their prevailing prioritization of ethical concerns (with both of them finding philosopher Emmanuel Lévinas to be an important interlocutor in the latter regard).[8] A fuller mapping of the connections and departures in Akerman and Cavell's thinking (in which it would become clear, for example, that Akerman starkly departs from Cavell in finding words and conversation to be no better, and often worse, tools in the bid to cross the perceived chasm between self and other) must await future discussions.[9] As a prolegomenon to such work, however, this chapter, particularly the following section, will begin a conversation between these two thinkers.[10] Here, in conjunction with Cavell's thinking, I read *La Captive* for its exploration of the act and conceptual frameworks of viewing. Ultimately, the film reveals viewing to be a dynamic central to skeptical thought and, in particular, to skepticism's destructive and gendered effects.

In response to Akerman's scenario, where viewing both enables and embodies the skeptic's harmful impulse to know and thus freeze the world and those in it, the second section will shift focus to Cavell and his writings on moral perfectionism as an alternative approach to the skeptical dynamic. Here, noting that Cavell's conceptions of cinematic ontology have excluded the forms of filmmaking in which individuals *do* see themselves in the image, I propose that these forms have nevertheless made their way into Cavell's thinking. In his conceptualization of the scene of "crisis" at the center of moral perfectionism, Cavell presents a form of thought that takes its conceptual frame from cinematic spectatorship of images of the self: rather than *viewing*, this framework holds out the possibility for *reviewing*. In this, individuals re-encounter and re-examine that which is already familiar to them—notably, themselves—potentially allowing them to break out of the kinds of freezing and fixation to which they may have fallen prey.

Here, reviewing's self-focused framework offers itself as a remedy to the destructive and isolating effects of viewing, or the skeptic's conception of his relationship to the world and others as one of viewing them unseen. As such, in Cavell's thinking, reviewing offers one possibility for living with skepticism. However, at this point, Akerman's film returns to the discussion to emphasize that reviewing and moral Perfectionism have their limits. Indeed, these limits are signaled from the opening of *La Captive*, where

Simon—in avoiding any self-appearance in the image—has preemptively turned the framework of home movie-watching from one of reviewing to one of viewing. As he cannot be made to review (himself), his impulse to view persists, and Ariane remains doomed.

Viewing in *La Captive*

In works like 1971's *The World Viewed: Reflections on the Ontology of Film*, Cavell famously claims that the modality of viewing, as exemplified in film spectatorship, has become the default mode by which modern subjects conceptualize their relationship to the world. As he writes, viewing is now "our way of establishing our connection with the world."[11] In this conceptualization, individuals take their perceived (viewing) distance from the world as a compromised assurance of their connection *with* that world; however, in another sense, this picture of viewing the world also serves the skeptic's desire to avoid certain kinds of connection with the world, or to escape circumscription and impingement. In other words, this picture seems to provide modern subjects with a model in which they can access the world without being exposed to or seen by it in turn, thus alleviating their need to be responsive or responsible to it. This model also serves the skeptic's wish for knowledge to be without limits or conditions, as one is here freed from the limits of being a specific individual occupying a specific place *in* the world: in Cavell's words, the wish to view the world unseen is a wish to see "the world itself—that it to say, everything."[12] While these claims constitute some of Cavell's better-known points about viewing, below I will explore another set of valences he attributes to this modality. These have to do with viewing's relation to knowing, as well as with its imbrication in the violence that can follow from the skeptical desire for total knowledge. As it will turn out, *La Captive* states these connections even more forcefully than Cavell, and so below I take the film as clarifying the stakes of Cavell's thinking on these topics. In turn, this discussion of *La Captive* will provide an illuminating backdrop for the account of reviewing that follows in the next section. There, viewing (of a kind) becomes key to individuals' potential for change, whereas, in *La Captive*, it is a way to guard against and prevent any such thing—a prevention with tragic consequences.

In his essay on *La Captive* and *Gaslight* in *Cities of Words*, Cavell writes of a motif in *Gaslight* that suggests to him the presence of a particular tendency of skeptical thought. This tendency, in Cavell's words, is manifested in "knowledge"—that is, the understanding of knowledge expressed by *Gaslight*'s male lead, Gregory (Charles Boyer)—seeking a relation that is "exemplified in the collecting of artifacts, hence in conceiving perception as the surveillance of what can be put on display, in principle the totality of what is real."[13] In other words, Cavell hints here that at least one wish of knowledge, or one desire of those who desire to know, is to relate to the world as by viewing it—a relation that takes perception, or the accessing of the world, as inhering in surveillance. Though Cavell attributes this observation only to *Gaslight*, *La Captive* makes this link between viewing and knowing (a link sometimes characterized by Cavell as a kind of "inner relation" between concepts and frameworks) one of its central concerns.[14] The importance of this subject is evident from the aforementioned opening scene of the film, where Simon's unseen viewing of Ariane sets the tone for all of his subsequent interactions with her. In this, it becomes the benchmark from which all other forms of his relating to her will then depart or deviate.

Such departures are rare, however, as Simon endeavors to view Ariane as much as possible over the course of the film—a fact born out in the scene that follows the film's opening. If *La Captive*'s first scene prominently features a diegetic film, this subsequent scene conspicuously invokes an extra-diegetic film. Here, Simon gets into his chauffeured car and begins following Ariane around a strangely empty Paris—undertaking a surveillance that Akerman captures in unbroken traveling point-of-view shots taken from the dash of Simon's car. The echo—of Alfred Hitchcock's *Vertigo* (1958), with its portrayal of Jimmy Stewart's detective trailing his female quarry around mid-century San Francisco—is explicit. In summoning this earlier film, with its protagonist who becomes famously obsessed with unraveling the mystery of a woman's subjectivity, Akerman accentuates her own film's investigation of the link between viewing and knowing—its inquiry into the notion, driving Simon and Scottie both, that to view *is* to know and to know is to view. Like Stewart's character Scottie, Simon spends his days following Ariane's every activity, watching her from afar as she visits friends, museums, or simply as she walks; at night, he does what Scottie could not, which is exhaustively query his quarry on those same movements when she returns to Simon's cavernous old-world apartment each night (queries to which she responds with, in Cavell's description, "absolute compliance"[15]). In the redundancy of this double-pronged investigation, Akerman has Simon betray again his sense of viewing and knowing as mirror images of each other—or of both as serving the same goal. And yet, both approaches consistently fail to fulfill Simon's desire for certain or total knowledge of Ariane's experiences. As such, *La Captive*'s investigations of viewing also inevitably pose questions of knowledge, including the questions of knowledge's goal as regards others and what would constitute the satisfaction of that goal.

These questions point up the film's shared interest in, or at least expression of, the forms of thought that, to Cavell's thinking, comprise modern skepticism. Simon's single-minded approach to Ariane, in which all other possible forms of relation are absented in favor of knowing her, speaks particularly to one of Cavell's claims concerning this subject. This is that, as modern skepticism took hold in and after the sixteenth and seventeenth centuries, the broader conceptual understanding of "knowing" not only shifted from what it had been prior, taking its new models from the developing frameworks of the natural sciences, but that it also became the dominant model *for* engaging with the world and the others in it—a process that would then occlude other possibilities for engaging with the world. As epitomized in Simon's attitude, the emergent modern subject comes to feel that *knowing* others is the only real or valuable mode of interacting with them; that, as compared to gaining verifiable or certain knowledge about others' thoughts, feelings, and experiences, the relations of, for example, being with, caring for, or responding to others come to be seen as fundamentally lesser forms of relation, at least as regards confirming the "existence" of others. In other words, in taking the existence or interiority of the other as something that must be evidenced or proven, rather than, in Cavell's terminology, something to be "accepted" or "acknowledged," the modern subject is cast into skepticism.[16] Responding to this, Akerman draws out this skeptical condition in *La Captive*—via Simon's hyperbolic embodiment of it—while also firmly setting the film in opposition to the skeptical mindset and its conceptions. While the film's conclusion, as I will discuss below, offers the strongest rebuke in these terms, Akerman's undermining of the goal of *knowing* another—her dramatization of the sense that such a goal cannot be satisfied—occurs throughout the film. This is already the case in the question posed by Simon's inevitable disappointment over Ariane's (ostensibly accurate) answers, his unswerving need to keep asking new questions; that is, if *this*—Ariane's demonstrated willingness to answer Simon's questions in perpetuity and to be surveilled—cannot satisfy such a desire, what would?

Simon's behavior throughout the film models one response the skeptic might give to such a question—a response that introduces a third term to the viewing-knowing dyad. Discussing *La Prisonnière* and *Gaslight*, Cavell names this term, while eliding Akerman's eponymous invocation of it, as captivity:

> The fact that both the Proust novel [*La Prisonnière*] and a significant Hollywood film [*Gaslight*] picture the object of knowledge as one that has to be kept captive, and that the captor accordingly becomes captive to his captive, is a tip to my mind that we have here a contribution to the architecture of skepticism.[17]

In this, Cavell locates in *Gaslight* and *La Prisonnière* a mode of thought that understands the relation of knowing as one of possession, or ownership; here, knowing another requires taking that individual captive. This captivity has little to do with physical restraints placed on another's movements (though those may also be present), a fact *La Captive*, in Ariane's freedom to come and go, insists on. Rather, the desire Cavell and Akerman draw out is one anxious for metaphysical captivity. As Akerman's film lays out, the imagination of this kind of captivity calls on the form of things that are solid and static—as when Ariane gazes at a statue of a female bust early in the film, as if to indicate that becoming statuesque constitutes her fate—or things made (somewhat) solid and repeatable—as when Simon captures Ariane on film. (This latter association, between film and fixity, or of film as giving form to individuals' pull toward fixation, will return in the discussion of Cavell's scene of the crisis of moral perfectionism below.) In other words, the captivity imagined and desired here—the transformation of a human into something fixed—is that which would enable the other to be better viewed, so as to be better known; this is the wish to make another totally knowable, or knowable in totality, by making that other into that which does not change. (*La Captive* adds something else to this picture as well. This is that the endeavor to make the other captive can deny the failure of the wish for total knowledge by suspending the arrival of that failure. Throughout the film, Simon avoids any confrontation with the limits of knowledge by treating Ariane as someone who *can* and *will* be known through capture, viewing, and investigation. He makes the promise of fully knowing Ariane—of having made her into that which can be known—into an asymptotic goal, always yet to be achieved. That is, until the film's conclusion.)

Before broaching the ending of *La Captive*, with its outcome of Simon's will to make Ariane captive, relevant questions of the links between gender, violence, and skepticism call for attention. Akerman's film foregrounds the axis of gender as perhaps the defining element of Simon's skeptical approach to Ariane. This becomes especially clear when his investigations expand to include others in Ariane's exclusively female social circle. Suspecting Ariane of having been in a prior relationship with one of these women, Simon proceeds to question a pair in the group about their lesbianism. In this, he betrays his concern and fascination with experiences that seem, in their belonging to women, to be metaphysically barred to him. That Simon's obsession is with that which is seemingly inaccessible—here, these forms of purportedly female knowledge—and not with Ariane in her particularity, is something Akerman further emphasizes in her broader presentation of the character: beyond her ability to evade Simon's drive to know her, Ariane seems to have (or is viewed by Simon and the film as having) no special or unique qualities of either the physical or psychological variety that would explain Simon's obsession—instead, she is rather abstract, as if any woman could equally serve Simon's infatuation (that is, if any other woman were Ariane). In other words, Simon wants to know her difference *from him*—a difference perceived to exist in her gender—and not her. Akerman similarly denies Simon anything resembling an individual psychology, giving no specific or personal rationale for his motivations or odd behavior. The only rationale that remains is Simon's (similarly abstract) "maleness," or that which, to Simon at least, seems to place him on the opposite side of a perceived epistemological divide from Ariane. In *La Captive* then, the skeptical drive cannot be reduced to or explained by characters' personal idiosyncrasies, but is rather given as a structuring dynamic, caught up in and reiterating that other structuring dynamic of gender.

Cavell makes compatible findings in his own investigations into gender and skepticism, findings that help explicate not only the radical implacability of Simon's drive for certain or total knowledge but also Cavell's belief that skepticism can precipitate harm and violence done to those in perceived positions of difference. For Cavell, skepticism is not more or less likely to be experienced by individuals in specific subject positions—anyone can be a skeptic. And yet, in his readings of the Hollywood melodramas of the unknown woman and Shakespeare's tragedies, he finds a pattern suggesting that skepticism's enactments may extract a much heavier price from women than from men. This pattern has to do with the increased weight put on the figure of the other in the modern period, according to Cavell: with God no longer able to secure individuals' connection with the world, the hope for a linchpin bridging one with something beyond one's isolating subjectivity was placed on the other instead.[18] In turn, the male characters in the melodramas and tragedies are driven not only to know, but to know another; and not to know just any other, but those others whose perceived difference—here, women—seems to hold the promise of a different relation to the world. The male characters are thus driven to access, acquire, or otherwise engage the knowledge or "certainty" they attribute to these female characters.[19] While these reactions from the male characters invariably deny and repudiate the existence of the female characters, they may also, in their most extreme versions, lead to those female characters' deaths. Here, when it becomes clear that a female character cannot be known in the way the skeptic demands—that is, when the impossibility of total knowledge and the (terrifying) loss of a world felt to be contingent on that knowledge threatens the skeptic—he will, rather than confront this reality, destroy her.[20]

It is this variation that *La Captive*'s conclusion plays out. The dynamic shaping the film, in which Ariane complies with Simon's demands for knowledge while consistently escaping his (and the viewer's) full understanding or possession, finally collapses in the film's last scenes. Here, after Simon had priorly sent Ariane away, despairing of his hopes for her in the latter half of the film, he now reconsiders and convinces her to accompany him to the country. She agrees and they drive that night to a grand, oceanside hotel, whereupon Simon resumes his questioning. Soon, Ariane proposes to go for a swim in the ocean, and she finds her way to those waves seen in the film's opening credits. Watching this from his balcony, Simon shortly loses sight of her and panics, running to the water and diving in after her. Akerman then cuts to the next morning, where a rescue boat slowly appears on the water's horizon. As it drifts closer, the spectator sees only Simon in the boat, eventually realizing that Ariane has been forced into the final space left to her where Simon's surveillance and investigations cannot follow.

It is a feat of Akerman's artistry that throughout the film, and despite her acquiescence, Ariane never feels caught by either the spectator or Simon. She always seems, in Akerman's presentation, to be leading a life beyond the view of either Simon or—as the film aligns its views exclusively with Simon's—the film. (That *La Captive* views with Simon points toward Akerman's implication of her own film, and by extension her audience, in viewing's adverse effects, here embodied in Ariane's death. Cavell's observation from elsewhere in his chapter—that the moving image and its camera potentiate and contribute to "a conception of knowledge as capture and vampirism"—is apt here. Though he again attributes this point to *Gaslight* and not *La Captive*, it is arguably expressed more directly in Akerman's film.[21]) It is, of course, this fact—of Ariane leading an unfolding life separate from Simon's—that drives Simon's obsession. But such a life—that is, one being lived—is diametrically opposed to the visions of knowing driving Simon, visions that demand Ariane be made into, in Cavell's terminology, an "artifact" to be collected. In other words, for Simon to *know* Ariane, she and her life must become like her filmed image: complete, fixed, no longer able to change or become something new. As Akerman's film forcefully demonstrates here, only one eventuality will serve this skeptical wish for metaphysical captivity—that of Ariane's death. In this fated outcome, in skepticism's pyrrhic success, Ariane becomes knowable.

Reviewing and Moral Perfectionism

Both Cavell's thought and Akerman's film evince the sense that the act of viewing is tied up with skepticism—perhaps particularly with skepticism's reductive and destructive modes of engagement with others. But if, as Cavell claims, the material frameworks of viewing are fundamental to the modern conceptual landscape, then spectating and its conceptual associations cannot be wholly negative or inevitably destructive. In other words, one should ask, do moving image media offer modes and models of experience other than "viewing"? Do the material realities of film and its spectatorship present other, non- or less harmful conceptual frameworks than those associated with viewing as a modality of knowledge and control? This section will propose one answer to these questions, drawing from Cavell's writings about moral perfectionism. Here, I argue that Cavell's thinking shows the marks of those forms of the moving image that he otherwise largely denies or forgets: those that present the self on screen. In linking the crisis that begins moral perfectionism to the framework of self-viewing modeled by these lineages of film (consciously or not), Cavell invokes and explores, if not names, the ethical-political notion of *re*viewing, wherein one returns to and re-examines something they are already familiar with.

Cavell's linking of cinema and the modern skeptical condition constitutes one of his most influential contributions to film theory and film philosophy. Importantly, this connection grounds itself in the *absence* of the viewer from the cinematic image. As Cavell contends in *The World Viewed*, cinema strikes the spectator as realistic *because* she cannot see herself onscreen. In other words, cinema provides a world from which the viewer is missing; this is a world she cannot affect from within (the image) or without (as a spectator). To Cavell's thinking, it is for these reasons—*because* cinema presents (or reveals) the skeptical viewer as unable to affect the world, reflecting her perception of the conditions of her everyday or "real" experience—that cinema strikes that viewer as realistic.[22] As Cavell writes, cinema thus embodies and draws forth skepticism as a structuring condition of the modern experience of reality. But in proposing this conception of cinematic ontology Cavell draws from a limited sample of the history of moving images—primarily fictional, feature-length, theatrically distributed and exhibited films, largely dating after cinema's transition to sound in 1927. In focusing on these films, Cavell's writing centralizes the cinematic image that absents the viewer from it, or that lack an onscreen self. But in doing so, he overrepresents this lineage of moving images as encompassing cinematic ontology as a whole. The conception of cinema he offers here—grounded in fictional, commercially exhibited films—excludes whole swaths of the variable history of moving images.[23] This has the notable effect of excising those long-standing and common forms of filmmaking in which individuals *do* encounter themselves on screen.

Of these categories of self-presenting film, home movies are no doubt the best-known iteration (a fact perhaps attested to in Cavell's brief mention of home movie-viewing in his discussion of George Cukor's 1949 film, *Adam's Rib*).[24] But while home movie production really emerged only in the early 1920s following Kodak's release of 16 mm reversal stock, and then became more affordable and widespread after the advent of 8 mm film in the early 1930s, self-imaging cinema had been present from the medium's earliest days. In the programs of short films shown in fairgrounds at the turn of the century, for example, a "local film" or "local picture" would be a common or even constitutive inclusion.[25] This type of film involved itinerant showman recording crowds and then screening the resulting films for those same crowds, sometimes as quickly as that night—an exceedingly popular and boisterous event by historical reports. While the UK's Mitchell and Kenyon films present the largest extant collection of these local films, in cinema's earliest decade this phenomenon existed all over the world, and would continue in different forms in North America, especially through the mid-century.[26] But as fictional film solidified its prominence during this period, the self-imaging impulse of local cinema did not disappear. Rather, it found its way into not only home movies, but into prominent strains of documentary, industrial, educational, colonial, and ethnographic film in which filmed subjects encountered themselves on screen—making self-viewing a constitutive, if not necessarily dominant, element of moving image media experience in the twentieth century.

The consistent presence of these forms of filmmaking in Cavell's lifetime, with their scenes of cinematic self-viewing, proposes the possibility of their appearance in or influence on his thinking—even as he does not explicitly work out or name this possibility himself. Indeed, I aim to demonstrate here that while viewing the world is a key concept for Cavell's earlier writings on cinematic ontology, *reviewing* the world and the self emerges as an important concept in his later works. What do I mean by reviewing? While Cavell does not use this terminology himself, I develop this concept in dialogue with his thought. It is an ethical-political practice of re-encountering and re-examining the already-known—whether that be the self or the familiar world—through imagined or actual images. Elsewhere, I contend that this concept took shape in wider thought over the course of the twentieth century as a result of film and its unique possibilities for self-recording and self-viewing.[27] Below, I take Cavell's writing about moral perfectionism as a privileged example of cinema's mediating influence, showing that these frameworks of self-viewing play a key role in his conceptualization of the crisis at the heart of moral perfectionism.

In the latter part of his career, Cavell began working out his understanding of what he calls Moral or Emersonian Perfectionism. In works like 1990's *Conditions Handsome and Unhandsome: The Constitution of Emersonian Perfectionism* and *Cities of Words*, Cavell describes this perfectionism as a form of moral reasoning (or what he also calls "a register of the moral life") that is non-teleological, non-foundational, and nonuniversal. This type of moral reasoning organizes itself around a mode of "conversation" between self and other (here, Cavell reveals his sense of the social as grounding the formation of the individual and not vice versa, a fact similarly expressed in his focus on marriage as a conceptual nexus). Within this mode of conversation, a pair of individuals work through a moral problem: they endeavor to move from, or to conceive of how to move from, the world and self as they are to the world and self that one wants. The realization of such a split—between the world and self as they are and the world and self as they could or should be—constitutes, in whole or part, the "crisis" that propels one into perfectionism. In other words, if one realizes this split and experiences such a crisis, he or she may be launched onto moral perfectionism's path of existential and creative self-formation and self-transformation (a fact that, for Cavell, opens possibilities for change not only in that individual but in the wider world as well).

As Cavell argues, neither the "crisis" nor moral perfectionism as a framework provides a predetermined or universal goal for the end of such a journey. And yet, the figure of the "philosophical friend"—the figure with whom one is in conversation—may spur oneself onto this journey. This may happen if the friend lives a life the self is attracted to or humbled by. In turn, this might draw the individual's attention to her stumblings in her attempt to live a life that she thinks is worthwhile, or to her lapses in her intelligibility to others or herself. This notion of intelligibility—the desire or imperative to become intelligible—is particularly integral to Cavell's unique understanding of perfectionism. Earlier understandings of perfectionism, including the ancient Roman and Greek philosophies of self-care, did not predicate themselves on a sense of separation from the world or the need to overcome such a rift. However, the modern forms of perfectionism that Cavell draws on are predicated on this sense of separation. In other words, in Cavell's understanding, perfectionism *responds* to skepticism—that sense of a fundamental split between the self and the world (and the others in that world) that, per Cavell, emerges in the early modern period. Put differently, perfectionism responds to the sense that particular kinds of epistemological certainty seem impossible, a sense that in turn threatens and undermines an individual's sense of his or her ability to relate to—*or be intelligible to*—each other, the world, and themselves. Skepticism thus becomes moral and political cynicism: we cannot know others, the world, or ourselves perfectly. From this defeated position, one might respond by abdicating the attempt to affect this world at all, a world that one only seems to haunt (as Emerson worried), or to which (as discussed above) one might respond with avoidance, denial, or annihilation of that which reminds one of one's own limitations, skeptically interpreted as one's insubstantiality.

As such, to Cavell's thinking, skepticism plays a major role in the ethical and political possibilities of modern life (as he summarizes Emerson: "despair is a political emotion").[28] Perfectionism thus aims to acknowledge skepticism's forceful presence in thought. It calls the individual toward intelligibility—or conversation—and away from an overwhelming sense of isolation as a way to combat skepticism and its ethical-political effects. In other words, Cavell hinges the promise of perfectionism for ethical transformations of the self and the world—its potential to intervene into concrete realities of violence and harm—on the ever-renewing demand to make oneself intelligible, or to find oneself in the world and with others.[29] While perfectionism cannot undo or permanently overcome skepticism, it offers a mode of thought that might remind one to think beyond it, no matter how provisionally.

With that brief overview of moral perfectionism in mind, we can return to this section's guiding question: what role does cinematic self-viewing play in Cavell's thinking? Put differently, if *viewing* plays such an important role in Cavell's conception of cinema, where is *reviewing*, or seeing images and events one has seen before? As intimated above, the place to look for the answer to these questions is within the "crisis" that lies at the center of perfectionism. In the scene Cavell describes, the person undergoing a crisis confronts him or herself as if *across from* a projected image of him or herself. An emblematic example of this scene arrives in the final section of *Cities of Words*, where Cavell provides a list of perfectionism's features and themes. Taken from Plato's *Republic*, these features are meant to speak to the repeating themes of perfectionism across different instances. Here are the first six features Cavell offers, excerpted from his longer and open-ended list:

1. a mode of conversation
2. between (older and younger) friends
3. one of whom is intellectually authoritative because
4. his life is somehow exemplary or representative of a life the other(s) are attracted to, and
5. in the attraction of which the self recognizes itself as enchained, fixated and
6. feels itself removed from reality.[30]

From these points, Cavell continues to list further features detailing how the self—in the wake of the crisis (constituted by points four, five, and six, where one sees oneself as enchained, fixated, and removed from reality)—can now turn and begin to "revolutionize itself."[31]

In his chapter on Plato in *Cities of Words*, Cavell elaborates both his thinking about *The Republic* and his use of it to delineate the themes of perfectionism. Cavell argues for a connection between the opening discussion of justice in *The Republic*, from which he draws the themes of perfectionism, and the Allegory of the Cave, which appears in Book VII of *The Republic*. During this discussion, he twice links the allegory to film, noting that Plato's Cave "virtually predicts" or "uncannily anticipates a movie theater—from behind you, a source of light casts shadows of moving objects upon a wall in front of you which you take for real things and real people."[32] More broadly, Cavell speaks of the allegory as a way to think about "the opening of the journey to philosophy," or to perfectionism's better self and world. Here, in the connections he makes between perfectionism and the Allegory of the Cave, Cavell turns to an example from ancient philosophy that he acknowledges shares points of reference with cinema. In other words, in his drawing on a scene with connections to cinema as a basis for thinking through perfectionism, Cavell, in turn, implies the relevance of cinema for thinking through perfectionism. Cavell's approach here and elsewhere calls up cinema as a material framework for understanding the scene and nature of perfectionism's crisis, attesting to the fact that cinema gives a germane and pressing framework for understanding the crisis that opens onto philosophy now.

Cavell's language in redescribing Plato's perfectionist themes speaks further to this claim. Though he does not articulate this implication himself,

Cavell's writing of the moment of crisis in the list of themes feels strikingly cinematic. Notice how, in his description of the crisis, one recognizes oneself as "enchained," "fixated," and "removed from reality"—as if one were seeing oneself captured in or on moving images. Here, in an encounter with a friend or the world that leads to this crisis, one suddenly sees oneself as stuck, unchanging, and outside of the world. In this, Cavell describes a conceptual scene unavoidably inflected not only by cinema, but by those forms of cinema that present the self back to itself: the crisis splits the self in two. In this scenario, one sees oneself or imagines seeing oneself (as if) on a screen, from without: the "newer" self, seeing from the new vantage point opened by the crisis, surveys the previous (or projected) self and finds it to be outside of the "reality" of the current, *reviewing* self: the previous self has become an image, revealed to be limited and stuck in behaviors that can only repeat without change, like a celluloid reel running through a projector. The newer, spectating self thus re-views the former self, and finds the former self wanting. In other words, Cavell's conception of the moment-of-crisis crucial to moral perfectionism draws on and instantiates cinema's lineage of self-viewing, modeling the ethical concept of (cinematic) reviewing.

Cavell's thinking of this perfectionist individual, reviewing her now-past self and finding it to be wanting, echoes with various other examples of cinema's picture of captured and reviewable selves. A quotation taken from French sociologist and film theorist Edgar Morin's 1956 book *Cinema, or the Imaginary Man* provides a striking comparison. In this excerpt, Morin cites earlier film theorist Jean Epstein in order to describe the scene in which one catches oneself in a cinematic image:

> We appear at the same time outside and identical to ourselves, me and not-me [. . .]. "Whether for better or worse, the cinematograph, in its recording and reproduction of a subject, always transforms it, re-creates it as *a second personality, whose appearance can trouble one's consciousness to the point of leading it to ask: Who am I? Where is my true identity?*"[33]

Morin and Epstein's description of what Morin calls the "auto-cinematographic" scene—a self-encounter that opens a space for self-examination—perfectly doubles Cavell's moment of the crisis and highlights the affinities between these thinkers' conceptual frameworks. Cavell's form of thought finds its mediatic frame of reference in the cinematic scene Morin describes. In other words, the cinematic scene of self-reviewing lends itself as form for thinking through and as expressing the sense crucial to Cavell's notion of "crisis"—a sense that there is a "me" and a "no-longer-me." This no-longer-me is a past self that is still connected to and part of "me," even as I now see it differently—as separate; from without, as it were.

While earlier philosophies share in what Cavell calls perfectionism, it is Cavell, writing after cinema's invention, who makes the *crisis*—and its particular scene of re-encountering the self and the world from a new vantage point—so integral to moral perfectionism's ethical possibilities. Cavell refracts perfectionism and its long philosophical lineage through this cinematic form of thought so common to the modern mindset, in which one reviews a past self in the world *through moving images* in order to turn toward one's future self. For Cavell, this ability to "go back and go on" is intrinsic to the possibility of meeting the moral demands of philosophy and becoming oneself.[34] In other words, looking back at the self becomes the way to move forward here.

I had asked earlier what role reviewing, as opposed to viewing, might play in Cavell's thought. The answer presents itself here, as Cavell draws on an ethical, cinematic scene of reviewing in which the self-undergoing-a-crisis encounters an image of herself *in the world*, judging that self (and perhaps the world) to be wanting and unchanging. Reviewing's image of the onscreen self in the world thus gives the countermeasure to skepticism's world without the self, materialized in the act of viewing. Importantly, reviewing's image of the self in the world still incorporates and acknowledges the sense of distance from the world that skepticism founds itself upon, even as that world now includes one's imaged self. It is this sense of a *distance* (that is, a separation) between the reviewing self and the (imaged and actual) world—hence the crisis of finding oneself removed from reality—that spurs one toward finding his or her future self.

And so, if the cinematic picture of viewing embodies the skeptical mode of being, then *re*viewing emerges in Cavell's thought as a mode that might temporarily and provisionally overcome skepticism. Reviewing becomes part of the ethical answer as to how one might live within the skeptical mindset. The crisis-moment in Cavell's perfectionism founds itself on the realization that one is unintelligible to oneself (and thus to others). This realization results in a sense of a divide between two selves, where the former self, in its unintelligibility, can now only be looked onto from without by the newer self. This sense of unintelligibility and separation gives the catalyst for the desire to make oneself intelligible, and to find others intelligible in return—in short, to be in *this* world, now; to leave skepticism behind, however momentarily. In other words, the experience of reviewing oneself can spur the desire to *be*, and no longer to view.

Conclusion

Cavell's perfectionist scenario critically inverts or transposes the scenes of viewing *La Captive* epitomizes. As Cavell makes clear, moral perfectionism is not programmatic, automatic, or all-encompassing; it does not force individuals to participate in it, nor does it guarantee against a pair reasoning themselves into doing harm or evil.[35] Simon then is one such figure—standing beyond the reach of moral perfectionism, a position that joins him with the long lineage of skeptical men Cavell finds in Shakespeare's tragedies and the Hollywood melodrama of the unknown woman. Simon cannot, unlike the individuals operating in the register of moral perfectionism, see himself as frozen—as stuck in a place of compulsive repetition. While one within moral perfectionism's reach can acknowledge their own prior (and always still potential) inability to change as a human condition and limitation, Simon, ostensibly unable to acknowledge any such limitations, can only find or project that frozenness elsewhere, onto Ariane. By making Ariane captive, into something to view, he fatally molds her into the mirror image of that which he refuses to see—his own frozen, fixated self.

Cavell's discussions of both Shakespeare's tragedies and the Hollywood melodramas trace the gendered destructions and denials that happen in the wake of skepticism, in those spaces that lie beyond the bounds of moral perfectionism's possible response to it. And like Akerman in *La Captive*, Cavell also uses the concepts of fixation or frozenness to characterize these plays and films' male characters and worlds. Cavell notes that the Hollywood melodrama of the unknown woman and its opposing genre, the comedy of remarriage, offer "different conceptions of time." In his words:

> [While] the melodramas [sketch] a past frozen and compulsively active in the present, the comedies [propose] an openness to the future, responsive to invention. The sense of a world frozen in meaning, resistant to change, or exchange, is furthered by the heavy symbology of the melodramas, the as it were eternal conflict between light and darkness, good and bad, innocence and guilt[.][36]

Here, an overriding and destructive resistance to change constitutes the world of the melodramas. And as Cavell makes clear throughout his discussions of this genre, this frozen world—an unchangeable past carried into the present—is one imposed on the melodramas' female characters. Where the comedies' pair are both open to change, and are thus poised to invent a future together, in the melodramas, "the man is psychically fixated and it is the woman alone who seeks change, permits herself metamorphosis."[37] These psychic fixations, or what Cavell refers to elsewhere as the man's "fixation of images"—another name for the man's disavowed ignorance of himself and others, or for his exclusion from the reach of moral perfectionism—thus forge the unchanging world the woman finds herself in.[38] In this way, Cavell hints at something that Akerman's film shows: that in skepticism's picture of experience, the projection of fixed images—of taking the world, and someone in it, as a fixed image and thus as a possible object of fixation—can be made both an instrument and a goal in men's knowing—or better, unknowing—relation to women. Simon treats Ariane as a fixed image hoping she might become one—as if she could become something that does not threaten future change, thus enabling her to be totally known. But as Cavell implies above, in attempting to take Ariane captive in this way, Simon actually begets, or perhaps reveals, his own captivity (that is, to his captive)—his own fixing in his attempt to fix another. For Simon, then, there is no unfolding world between him and Ariane, but only Ariane's world (of women)—a world to be viewed. And if Cavell's melodramas recount women's suffering under, but also their possible resistance to, such projection and viewing and possession, Akerman's *La Captive* locates itself in that space where resistance is not possible (or only possible at the cost of death) and the promises of moral perfectionism cannot hold; this is the space where skepticism, viewing, and fixation win out, where one is left only with the tragedy of an unknown woman.

Notes

1 Stanley Cavell, "The Avoidance of Love: A Reading of *King Lear*," in *Must We Mean What We Say?* (Cambridge: Cambridge University Press, 1976 [1969]; Updated Edition 2002), 351.

2 Marcel Proust's novel *À la Recherche du Temps Perdu* (*In Search of Lost Time*) was originally published sequentially in eight parts: Part VI., *La Prisonnière*, was first published in 1923. *La Prisonnière*, also translated as *The Captive*, is the first volume of the section within *In Search of Lost Time* known as *le Roman d'Albertine* (the Albertine novel).

3 Philipp Schmerheim usefully understands Cavell's skepticism as an "existential position," rather than an epistemological framework, in his *Skepticism Films: Knowing and Doubting the World in Contemporary Cinema* (New York: Bloomsbury, 2016), 87.

4 See Stanley Cavell, "*Gaslight*," in *Cities of Words: Pedagogical Letters on a Register of the Moral Life* (Cambridge: The Belknap Press of Harvard University Press, 2004), 102–18 and Stanley Cavell, *Contesting Tears: The Hollywood Melodrama of the Unknown Woman* (Chicago: The University of Chicago Press, 1996).

5 With the exception of a reference to a comment of Akerman's about *La Captive* in a post-screening discussion, and some play with the relevance of the film's title to the essay's themes, Cavell otherwise reverts exclusively to discussing Proust's *La Prisonnière* as if it were interchangeable with the film. He even uses Proust's character's names (Marcel and Albertine), rather than the names of the characters in Akerman's film. See, again, *Cities of Words*, 111–13, 118.

6 Cavell does briefly discuss Akerman's influential 1975 film *Jeanne Dielman, 23, quai du Commerce, 1080 Bruxelles* in his essay "The World as Things: Collecting Thoughts on Collecting." That Cavell places Akerman's film in conversation here with thinkers like Hume, Benjamin, Wittgenstein, and

Heidegger indicates that he granted her work a high level of esteem, even as the reading he makes of her film is limited in comparison to his analyses of Hollywood films. *Cavell on Film*, ed. William Rothman (Albany: State University of New York Press, 2005), 241–80.

7   For examples of his writing on these filmmakers, *Cavell on Film*.
8   For further discussion of these points as regards Akerman, see my "'A Pedagogy of the Image': Chantal Akerman's Ethics Across Film and Art," *Moving Image Review & Art Journal* 8, nos. 1–2 (2019): 40–53 and "*La Ressasseuse*: Chantal Akerman, 1950-2015," *Cinema Scope* 65 (Winter 2016): 6–9.
9   On Akerman's relation to spoken language, see Ivone Margulies, "Forms of Address: Epistolary Performance, Monologue, and Bla Bla Bla," in *Nothing Happens: Chantal Akerman's Hyperrealist Everyday* (Durham: Duke University Press, 1996), 149–70.
10 William Rothman deserves mention here for his essay on Akerman's films (including *La Captive*), where he briefly draws on Cavell's thought in his discussion of Akerman's work. See his "Face to Face with Chantal Akerman," in *Tuitions and Intuitions: Essays at the Intersection of Film Criticism and Philosophy* (Albany: State University of New York Press, 2019), 201–14.
11 Cavell, *The World Viewed: Reflections on the Ontology of Film* (Cambridge: Harvard University Press, 1971/1979), 102.
12 Ibid.
13 Cavell, *Cities of Words*, 112–13.
14 On "inner relation," see for, example, Cavell, *Contesting Tears*, 5.
15 Cavell, *Cities of Words*, 111.
16 Cavell's concept "acknowledgement" speaks to the impulse and possibilities of accepting such human limitations and finitude. See for example his essays on *King Lear* and *Othello* in *Disowning Knowledge*. For a concise summary of the relevant points, see Espen Hammer, *Stanley Cavell: Skepticism, Subjectivity, and the Ordinary* (Malden: Polity Press, 2002), 77–81.
17 Cavell, *Cities of Words*, 112.
18 See Stanley Cavell, "The Other as Replacement of God," in *The Claim of Reason: Wittgenstein, Skepticism, Morality, Tragedy* (New York: Oxford University Press, 1979/1999), 470–71, and Cavell, *Disowning Knowledge in Six Plays of Shakespeare* (Cambridge: Cambridge University Press, 1987), 127–28.
19 As Cavell notes, in the melodramas, the woman's "(superior, exterior) knowledge becomes the object—as prize or victim—of the man's fantasy, who seeks to share its secrets (*Now, Voyager*), to be ratified by it (*Letter from an Unknown Woman*), to escape it (*Stella Dallas*), or to destroy it (*Gaslight*)." Cavell, *Contesting Tears*, 13–14; see also 100–01.
20 Such destruction falls under what Cavell often refers to as "annihilation." For example: "Lear's 'avoidance' of Cordelia is an instance of the annihilation inherent in the skeptical problematic, [which is] that skepticism's 'doubt'

is motivated not by (not even where it is expressed as) a (misguided) intellectual scrupulousness but by a (displaced) denial, by a self-consuming disappointment that seeks world-consuming revenge." *Disowning Knowledge*, 6.

21 Cavell, *Cities of Words*, 117.

22 For Cavell, cinema's realism thus lies in the revelation that the modern subject is, in watching a film, "satisfied of reality while reality does not exist—even, alarmingly, because it does not exist, because viewing is all it takes." Cavell, *The World Viewed*, 188–89.

23 While Cavell's oeuvre as a whole does not entirely exclude these kinds of films, his later engagements with experimental and avant-garde cinema, for example, do not prompt a fuller reconsideration of his earlier claims as to cinema's ontology.

24 Stanley Cavell, *Pursuits of Happiness: The Hollywood Comedy of Remarriage* (Cambridge: Harvard University Press, 1981). David LaRocca has done important work addressing Cavell's attention to home movies here, usefully revealing how Cavell's remarks offer an "essential and much-need heuristic" for reading both films that incorporate amateur film aesthetics and amateur films themselves. See David LaRocca, "On the Aesthetics of Amateur Filmmaking in Narrative Cinema: Negotiating Home Movies after *Adam's Rib*," in *The Thought of Stanley Cavell and Cinema: Turning Anew to the Ontology of Film a Half Century after* The World Viewed, ed. David LaRocca (New York: Bloomsbury, 2020), 245–90, 246.

25 See Alan Kattelle, *Home Movies: A History of the American Industry, 1897-1979* (Nashua: Transition Publishing, 2000).

26 See Vanessa Toulmin, *Electric Edwardians: The Story of the Mitchell & Kenyon Collection* (London: BFI, 2006) and Stephen Bottomore, "From the Factory Gate to the 'Home Talent' Drama: An International Overview of Local Films in the Silent Era," in *The Lost World of Mitchell and Kenyon: Edwardian Britain on Film*, ed. Vanessa Toulmin and others (London: BFI Publishing, 2004). On the continuing life of local film, see Martin Johnson, *Main Street Movies: The History of Local Film in the United States* (Bloomington: Indiana University Press, 2018).

27 I develop this argument in my current book project, tentatively titled *Reviewing the Self-Image: Ethics, Politics, and Moving Image Media*.

28 Cavell, *Cities of Words*, 18.

29 "The claim of [moral perfectionism] to the status of morality is that the conversation required to assess my life—playing the role in perfectionism that calculation plays in Utilitarianism or derivation from the moral law plays in Kantianism—is one designed to make myself intelligible (to others, by way of making myself intelligible to myself)." Ibid., 49; see also 328–29.

30 Ibid., 446.

31 Ibid.

32 Ibid., 320, 330.

33 Jean Epstein, *Écrits Sur Le Cinéma, 1921-1953: Édition Chronologique En Deux Volumes* (Paris: Seghers, 1900), 256. Quoted in Morin, *The Cinema, Or the Imaginary Man* (1956), trans. Lorraine Mortimer (Minneapolis: University of Minnesota Press, 2005), 38; italics added. Morin is here describing early silent cinema, which he refers to as the cinematograph, and its relative predominance of self-images in the form of "local cinema," as compared to the fictional forms of cinema that would coalesce after 1907.
34 Cavell, *Cities of Words*, 15.
35 See ibid., 24–25.
36 Ibid., 109.
37 Ibid., 234.
38 Ibid., 23.

14

Contemplating the Sounds of Contemplative Cinema

Stanley Cavell and Kelly Reichardt

David LaRocca

The importance of these films is that they find aspects of style which do justice to the moments of life which do not proclaim their significance.

—ANDREW KLEVAN, *Disclosure of the Everyday*

IN CONVERSATION WITH AN ESTEEMED SCHOLAR of film and also of Stanley Cavell, those two worlds overlapping, the perceptive and influential thinker expressed concern that what we are seeing in recent decades is a recurring application of criteria, or compulsive testing of traits, from Cavell's two primary film genres: the comedy of remarriage and the melodrama of the unknown woman. Thus, in *Mistress America*, when Noah Baumbach and co-screenwriter Greta Gerwig move the action from Manhattan to the Shakespearan green world—in 2015 still called Connecticut—we glean a repetition that resonates.[1] For screenwriters and filmmakers with a taste for the Golden Age of Hollywood, such traces and techniques make themselves apparent. To wit, Joel and Ethan Coen drew upon iconic screwball comedies for *The Hudsucker Proxy* (1994), in which Baumbach's future wife, Jennifer Jason Leigh (since divorced) plays Amy Archer, a character whose vocal mannerisms evoke Katharine Hepburn's mid-Atlantic accent and more especially Rosalind Russell's distinctive newsroom patter in *His Girl Friday* (1940, dir. Howard Hawks). Later on, someone proposed that *Intolerable Cruelty* (2003), another Coen brothers confection, looks and sounds like a throwback to the comedies of the 1930s and 1940s (again, recalling the specific films that captured Cavell's interest, personally and philosophically). But how does this film shape up? After sorting through some of its characteristics and comparing them to the standard bearers, is it, in fact, a comedy of remarriage? Or, as Cavell—who had heard such airings many times before and had recently written an on-point reply in *Cities of Words*—suggests rhetorically: does the film merely contain "elements," "fragments," or "motifs" of the genre?[2] (The lively debate about the second Coen brothers film happened in Cavell's company, though not initiated by Cavell himself, at a 2004 conference in Budapest.) Meanwhile, more recently, the scholar expressed some metaphilosophical dismay that that kind of scenario—namely, the gathering of new specimens for inspection, dissection, and accretive canon-formation—is all Cavell's work on genre has amounted to; indeed, it would appear that all it can do is present itself as something of a formula to which we bring samples for examination, diagnosis, and as it were, ordination-by-surrogate. (Is that not enough?) The scholar confided that (despite, or perhaps because of, the many tantalizing works that frequently appear) this now-familiar protocol, or nervous exercise, can feel enervating, exhausting even.

While the scholar's disquiet may seem worth our deliberation (if taken neither as a comprehensive history nor an assured prophecy, then as an invigorating admonition or inspiring provocation), such misgiving might be assuaged, in time, by many worthwhile paths of investigation revisited, yet to be mounted, or newly proffered, as the preceding contributions to this volume ably illustrate. Here and beyond, much has been profitably recommended to us by reflecting with Cavell on new instances in relation to old, canonical ones; moreover, there are propitious deviations from that still-vital compare-and-contrast methodology, numerous experiments with films and written texts that bode well for the habit, however long it has been a feature of the discourse. In my own efforts at the inheritance of Cavell's work here, I acknowledge the scholar's worry while (and by) attending to films that, upon first encounter, may not feel central or intimately connected to Cavell's well-known innovations in genre theorizing, but instead adjacent to them, in some cases, inversions of them. I hope a reader will conclude, as in the agitating pieces arriving ahead of mine, that, for example, when we look at—and listen to—the understated, incantatory films of Kelly Reichardt (b. 1964) with Stanley Cavell in mind, both realms are enlivened: we gain new purchase on the rich terrain of Reichardt's accomplished work, and we encounter, yet again, the continuously expansive pertinence and persistent fecundity of Cavell's writing on film and films.

* * *

Cavell exemplified in *Pursuits of Happiness*, *Contesting Tears*, and *Cities of Words* that there abides a shared set of concerns, themes, projects, and lessons in (let us call them) "Cavell's films," the movies that meant the most to him, and that he returned to throughout his career in the academy. Since Reichardt's films resist the familiar structure and content of the Hollywood comedies and melodramas that attracted Cavell's attention, we are left to wonder how a study in contrasts can benefit our understanding of two domains of moviemaking—on the one hand, Hollywood classics and on the other hand (what we can join others in speculatively categorizing as), contemporary contemplative cinema.[3] Indeed, in Reichardt's work, expression itself—as verbal, vocal, spoken, sounded articulation in language, manifested in interpersonal dialogue—is precisely one of those categories that becomes contested, and to a significant extent countered. Even in Cavell's melodramas, conversation is abundant, if discordant and unfulfilling. Yet remarriage need not arrive by dialogic restitution, as shown in *Journey to Italy* (*Viaggio in Italia*, 1954, dir. Roberto Rossellini), where the marriage is saved not by conversation but, instead, a kiss, which is to say, a miracle. In our correspondence on the matter, William Day extends a reading of the film's un-Cavellian denouement: "their *dis*enchantment with each other, especially the husband's habitual refusal to notice his wife, is why their unplayful, un-remarriage conversation isn't sufficient to break the spell for them, and thus why a miracle must be invoked." Something related seems to happen in *Before Midnight* (2013, dir. Richard Linklater), in which the principal pair not only name-check *Journey to Italy* as they walk upon their own Mediterranean ruins, but, at the end of a bruising fight, find themselves on the verge of reconciliation—yet how? Is it owing to mutual understanding through dialogue, or something else? As in *Eyes Wide Shut* (1999, dir. Stanley Kubrick), the path to marital reconciliation may be more carnal and less conversational.

As you see elsewhere in this volume, the centrality of conversation to the negotiation of marriage—and, indeed, remarriage—is put under question; "the scandal of the speaking body" may become, then, the scandal of the speechless one.[4] Such apprehension about the restorative powers of speech, and an invitation to the prospect of an alternative, is something I am sustaining here, in this chapter, by inquiring about a different set of phenomena that we find on film, specifically, the absence or negation of speech, which may travel under the names or figures of silence, inexpressiveness, and being lost for words; the presentation of unworded takes and unresolved encounters, along with infelicitous remarks, or the failure to launch remarks at all, that is, noticing remarks that misfire, or that never fire; human communication in language that is unexpectedly interrupted or awkwardly aborted; and perhaps most saliently of all, story endings unsettled by a lack of narrative order, clarity, or closure (and thus the terms we often rely on to achieve those effects, or at least a semblance of resolution).

As we know from indelible literary characters—from Bartleby to William Stoner—scenes that are speechless are not necessarily silent.[5] And we were long ago admonished by Ludwig Wittgenstein: "What we cannot speak about we must pass over in silence," however much we may be tempted to say something.[6] Reichardt's films, which benefit from the influence of literary origins, offer pathways to these and related insights. Reichardt's screenplay for *Certain Women* (2016) was based on three short stories from Montana-born writer, Maile Meloy, whose work has been described by Ella Taylor as offering "powerfully stripped-down prose and deceptively simple structures."[7] Though there are character types that appear to dominate Reichardt's films, it would be too reductive to say she—and her frequent screenwriting collaborator, Jonathan Raymond—focuses on an archetype to the exclusion of many subtly wrought and compellingly distinct figures, yet whether lawyer or frontierswoman, rancher or wanderer, itinerant cook or camping buddy, farmhand or retail clerk, there are traits and trends that repeat, and there is a palpable sense that many of her characters are lost—existentially, emotionally, intellectually, financially, or geographically (and sometimes all of the above). That they would be reticent, or otherwise also lost for words, seems appropriate. In her cinema, the diminishment of the sound we call speech allows other sounds to emerge and take precedence, to gather meaning of their own: the cacophony of the world's machines, the symphonies of nature, the presence or imposition of music.

These proceedings may find company with a general inquiry into, or response to, philosophical skepticism (rendered, in part, as the "problem of other minds"), but especially as that familiar preoccupation is formulated, in Cavell's work and in Cavell studies, as a condition involving not so much knowledge (*episteme*) as acknowledgment.[8] Yet it may be as profitable to also fathom the stakes of what Cavell calls "[t]he question of human intelligibility," since that phenomenon would demand consciousness of "whether we can see what we make happen and tell its difference from what happens to us."[9] Such a bifurcation has been a part of philosophy since at least Epictetus spoke what would become the first line of the *Enchiridion*. Whatever the provenance of the schema, however, having perspicuity of both aspects of human life (freedom and fate?, "human action and human suffering"[10]), proves decisive for thinking about *how* (or whether or to what extent) one is known to oneself and known to others. Such moods of reflection and discernment lie at the heart of Reichardt's series of filmic investigations.

Watching her movies, we are left to wonder, time and again, about the efficacy of speech to bring about the world as we want it. The matter is not just about sincerity, that is, whether we must mean what we say, but whether and what saying *does* to ourselves and the world we inhabit—"perceiving our lacking the means of making ourselves intelligible (to others, to ourselves)," as Cavell aptly summarizes the issue.[11] The "depth of this crisis" would be enough to inaugurate the kinds of tragedies Cavell finds in Shakespeare (from *Hamlet* to *King Lear* to *Othello* and elsewhere), but rather than engage the skeptical recital concerning other minds, for example, Reichardt often leaves the world as she finds it (a tack of the Wittgensteinian spirit).[12] Indeed, her cinema may also reveal something of the Kantian sense of the "intelligible world," namely, the realm of the noumenal.[13]

Reichardt's films provide a new way of understanding aversion: not so much in proximity to Cavellian/Emersonian "aversive thinking," where writing is an "allegory of aversion to conformity," but in a position or posture of reticence that makes way for other disclosures.[14] Cavell's "hope," as Patrick Mackie puts it, "was to broaden philosophy to as much of the world as possible, and it was always an open question for him which of the two was meant to test the other."[15] In our selected pairing—ordinary life and life on film—we are involved in this broadening, and mutual testing, no doubt an ongoing examination, yet without undo concern for order and explanation ("[w]e cannot spend the day in explanation"[16]). As Mackie concludes, "the heart of [Cavell's] originality was the claim that the everyday affairs of conversation and interaction and taste were precisely what philosophy was made of."[17] In our thinking of Reichardt, we are making room for all of those occasions when conversation is compromised—when words are insufficient, further confounding, deferred, or arrive belatedly or not at all. While Cavell describes the fact (or threat) of being and remaining unknown to one another as a "catastrophe of privacy," Reichardt seems neither sanguine nor panicked, but motivated to make films that take notice of certain facts and features of the human experience and thereby come to terms with them as evident and abiding in our human condition.[18] Like Thoreau, Reichardt appears to "front only the essential facts of life, and see if I could not learn what it had to teach," in brave, if quietistic, stripped-down, subtly rendered cinematic works.[19] Perhaps such a reading of her films will nevertheless draw them into company with Cavell's notion of "living our skepticism" when it comes to the fragile, limited sense of our "knowledge" of others—their minds and hearts—and likely, not surprisingly, of ourselves.

There are certain films—perhaps they form a genre, or a cycle, or in Cavell's preferred conceptualization a medium (since "a cycle is a genre" and "a genre is a medium"[20])—in which things fall apart and may or may not come back together again.[21] In such films, we dip into lives while lacking context (e.g., prehistory, framing, theme, or type) and discover *not* that knowledge is withheld, or that there is a failure of acknowledgment, but that we (character and viewer alike) simply do not know. There is little sense of the past, of memory, of education, and even less orientation to future prospects; instead, there is an expansive and insistent present moment calling for our attention. To capture or reflect the everyday, then, a film would have to mine or mind these ordinary, familiar, shared conditions—among them the striking plotlessness of our own lives, the need to impose importance, to tie past to future.

The time and space of such films, then, appear strangely aligned with common conditions; some call this realism—we could add attributes of the non-narrative, even anti-narrative; is plot, in short, artificial (inhuman? antihuman?) and a bid to insert drama or melodrama where there is none? We find characters dealing with aging, accident, austerity, pondering the extent of one's choices (and the sense that one isn't making them, but contending with bewildering circumstances beyond one's control), along with promise squandered or thwarted or never identified and cultivated; in Reichardt's contribution to such filmic meditations, these are, as Elena Gorfinkel notes, "precarious travelers" on "circuitous or arrested journeys," contending with "the affective slackness of their suspended agency, their 'stuckness,' non-productivity, and inability to progress within the harsh demands of an exhausting [. . .] social [and] material world."[22] Hence, a paradoxical "stuckness": people in motion going nowhere. In scene after scene, film after film, we find "socially displaced and marginalized" characters suffering an incapacity to locate a community of mutual regard, or to express their thoughts, feelings, needs, and desires to others: these are films of poignant longing and confounding emotion; of narcissism and shame; of obsessive preoccupations and insufficient guidance; of visionary boldness and humiliating defeat.[23] They are, as the character Charlie Kaufman said in *Adaptation*. (2002, dir. Spike Jonze), stories "[w]here people don't change, they don't have epiphanies. They struggle and are frustrated, and nothing is resolved."[24]

For an immersive, satiating study, such a genre, then, would profitably include several films by Kelly Reichardt, in fact, perhaps all of her features. Though conversation is present in her work, it does not proceed with the logic, pacing, wit, and emotional crescendos familiar to Cavell's two cycles of films, where conversation heals marital strife (the comedies) and the discovery of one's voice leads to personal empowerment (the melodramas). Instead, we have failed attempts, lingering impasses, unintended offenses, and unarticulated conclusions. With Cavell at hand, we are positioned to explore how conversation—along with its lack and its alternatives—is depicted in Reichardt's films. As Cavell once said, "in philosophy it is the sound which makes all the difference," so it is with Reichardt's cinema of sounds made and unmade, artificial and natural, harmonious and jarring.[25] In company with her films, our mandate would not be so much to speak but to observe, not to debate but to deliberate. Accounting for ourselves may amount to learning new forms of attention to the world, not to mounting arguments or axioms, theories or theses about how everything holds together. We too may be left speechless, and these films show us that is okay—if still vexing and painful.

When Characters Speak and When They Do Not

One of the prominent attributes of the films that occupy the genre known as the "melodrama of the unknown woman" is what Cavell calls "the negation of voice," which, in contradistinction with "comedies of remarriage," also entails the "negation of conversation" and thus the "negation of marriage."[26] For one thing, there is little (overt) comedy in the films of Kelly Reichardt, so assessing potential alignments with comedies of remarriage will not, cannot, be a concern; rather, in so far as having Cavell's remarks on melodramas in mind while watching Reichardt's films, we may begin with a sense of shared preoccupations, and yet, almost at once, the commonality complicates the kinds of descriptions and definitions Cavell offers, for example, in his genre-defining effort *Contesting Tears: The Hollywood Melodrama of the Unknown Woman*. For one thing, the kind of "isolation" Cavell finds as a consequence of the irony—in some cases, a "sadistic irony"—that yields the "unknown woman" (i.e., a woman unknown to others, to her husband, and conspicuously, though not permanently, to herself) is the fact that so many men in Reichardt's films appear to share in a crisis of expression, or, in less charged cases, a willingness to simply be silent, voiceless, and speechless in the face of incomprehensible emotional demands.[27] Indeed, in many cases, what does get spoken about by men and women in these films may not bear directly on the topics central to Cavell's two genres of film: marriage, the threat of divorce, the "transcending of marriage," remarriage, and the arrogation of voice.[28]

Perhaps the most radical deviation from the two Cavellian genres, however, as we find them in Reichardt's films, is not in the content of conversations achieved, bungled, or evaded, but in the formal attributes of her work as a filmmaker. As Reichardt herself says, "I try not to follow the dialogue around and try to be as sparse as possible and rely on the filmmaking as much as possible."[29] Film style gets in the way of characters talking as often as they do themselves. For a quick clinic, consider the editorial cut—and Reichardt has served as editor for all of her feature films apart from her debut—early in *Night Moves* (2013) when a climate change activist is speaking after a film screening and is cut off mid-sentence not by someone or something in the diegetic space, but by Reichardt.[30] From one frame to the next, we go from a sober discussion of "plans" to address a global existential threat to a dancing cow advertising Wilber milk in front of a Supercuts. The interruption is funny, but it is also conceptually savvy and laden with provocations. In addition to the obvious mise-en-abyme that gives us pause about the film we are currently watching, it also introduces an element of metacinematic critique: film form appears to be commenting on film content. What does the edit say, though?—That the (vitally important?) things the speaker is saying are, in fact, better left unsaid? And there is a further doubleness: whether the formal move is meant to address the diegesis or the nondiegetic ("real") lives of the audience; does it function as an elegant, one-second appraisal of the social discourse on the topic by the director (her discreet contribution to it), or the film editor's wish to lend a critique to her listening characters and their outlook on the matter. Once again, the film does not tutor us on how to resolve the reading, but, crucially, all of these observations and questions arise in response to a single cut.

Though Cavell is a masterful reader of the plot of the films he wrote about so compellingly—see, for instance, the summaries at the head of each film chapter in *Cities of Words: Pedagogical Letters on a Register of the Moral Life*—he did not, nor would it seem the films invite him to, dwell at length on how aspect ratio, cinematography, diegetic sound, the nature of cuts, and the duration of takes would (or could) impact his philosophical reading of the films that attracted his attention from the 1930s and 1940s. To be sure, there are remarkable moments in the formal achievements of the comedies and melodramas under Cavell's aegis, but his thoughts and theories about their importance—say, for thinking about remarriage or self-understanding—do not depend on any given formal attribute. There are, of course, noteworthy moments of formal film expression—the early tracking shots in the newsroom of *His Girl Friday* (1940, dir. Howard Hawks), the cross-dissolves and fades of *Letter from an Unknown Woman* (1948, dir. Max Ophüls)—but the mechanical affordances here seem more a complement to Cavell's line of inquiry than offering independent reasons for thinking a certain way about the philosophical pertinence of the films. By contrast, shot analysis in many Reichardt films—aside from anything characters *say*—would be sufficient for mounting a satisfying philosophical reading of them.

Quite apart from the question whether we wish to call Reichardt's films melodramas (since none of them are, from stem to stern, comedies— however much humor abides in them and makes irregular and thus affecting appearances), when placed beside Cavell's canon of illustrious filmic exemplars, her works seem turned inside out: first, that the formal qualities of filmmaking are made to carry a weight that even the great directors of Cavell's catalog (Capra, Cukor, Hawks, McCarey, Ophüls, Rapper, Sturges, Vidor) would not ask of their industrial products (largely owing, we must assume, because of habits and trends of the studio system, the Hays Code, etc.), but also that it may simply be that, so often in her films, it is the *space between* words—the wordless silences, short and long—that are the most captivating, galvanic forces to behold, or rather, to hear. We are not "hanging on every word"—parsing the rat-a-tat ramble of Hildy (Rosalind Russell) and Walter (Cary Grant) as they spar and flirt in *His Girl Friday*—but instead are confounded by the troublesomeness, wantonness, even uselessness of words. Wordless silence may come as a relief, while in other cases speech may break an irksome quiet. Some characters simply remain mute (The Indian [Rod Rondeaux] in *Meek's Cutoff* comes to mind), or nearly so (The Rancher [Lily Gladstone] in *Certain Women*), while the chatty ones (say, Cozy [Lisa Donaldson] and Lee [Larry Fessenden] in *River of Grass*; Kurt [Will Oldham] in *Old Joy*; and Stephen Meek [Bruce Greenwood] in *Meek's Cutoff*) surely add sounds, if not always coherent speech.

Cavell begins *Contesting Tears* by saying he "claim[s] that the four films principally considered in the following chapters define a genre of film."[31] Some may quibble and say that this grouping instead amounts to a subgenre of melodrama or better, a cycle of films, but this may miss the urgency of seeing how specific traits of the selected films make them hang together meaningfully, or, as Cavell puts it, "taking the claim to mean [. . .] that they recount interacting versions of a story, a story or myth, that seems to present itself as a woman's search for a story, or of the right to tell her story."[32] In *Contesting Tears*—as well as in the "pedagogical lessons" on these films as featured in *Cities of Words*, where they are partnered with excurses on the likes of John Stuart Mill (*Gaslight*), Friedrich Nietzsche (*Now, Voyager*), Henrik Ibsen (*Stella Dallas*), and Henry James (*Letter from an Unknown Woman*)—Cavell mostly follows after the narrative content of this search: what it entails, who says what to whom, and how that saying matters. Since it is a custom in film studies to allow that a set of films made by a specific director can be spoken of under the name of the director, there appears no need to taxonomize Reichardt's films by genre, subgenre, or cycle. Rather, hewing to a certain strain of auteur theory, whatever its faults and virtues, we are left to wonder if there are, in fact, traits that make them distinctly, that is, identifiably Reichardt's and why they should be significant when watching them with Cavell in mind.

For the novitiate as well as the longtime fan of Reichardt's oeuvre, it may be serviceable to make some observations on the nature of her seven feature-length films: *River of Grass* (1994), a somewhat derivative *Badlands*-esque, bandits-on-the-run, Jarmusch-inspired road movie with nods to Godard's *Breathless* made in an "uncharacteristically brash" style (it was edited by one of the film's lead actors, Larry Fessenden),[33] followed by a twelve-year gap, and then a sequence in a different, more distinctively contemplative vein—*Old Joy* (2006), *Wendy and Lucy* (2008), *Meek's Cutoff* (2010), *Night Moves* (2013), *Certain Women* (2016), and *First Cow* (2019); other experimental projects and shorts include *Ode* (1999), *Then, a Year* (2001), *Travis* (2009), and *Owl* (2019). In all cases, whether the actors are professional or amateur, Reichardt maintains a studious deglamorization of how they are presented (even with personnel such as Kristen Stewart, Michelle Williams, Laura Dern, Dakota Fanning, Lily Gladstone, Alia Shawkat, Katherine Waterson, and Peter Sarsgaard); likewise her sense of de-romantized cinematic style: "no beauty shots" is how she put the matter when discussing her Westerns, *Meek's Cutoff* and *First Cow*. "There can be no image in the film that's beautiful for its own sake."[34] From a distance, one could use dominant features of Reichardt's films to slot them into established genre categories, for example, buddy movie (*Old Joy, First Cow*), Western (*Meek's Cutoff*), thriller[35] (*Night Moves*), etc.—or, with the rest of her films in mind—all of them might be taken up as intriguing variants of the road movie. That said, closer inspection of her body of work often fractures or displaces the assignments, since we find striking modifications of the traits and tropes that would, more commonly, reinforce genre categories (and the taxonomies deployed to define and thus claim—or contain—a given film). Even so, and for the disparities noted, thematically and narratively, *Wendy and Lucy*, *Meek's Cutoff*, *Night Moves*, and *Certain Women* (with Michelle Williams starring in three of the four) suggest resemblances with Cavell's melodrama of the unknown woman genre: women (some married, some not) contending with the men who shape their lives (or end them), often through contested conversations, if not contested tears. Indeed, one female character, Dena or "D." (Dakota Fanning) in *Night Moves*, is murdered because she was "talking." Reichardt puts the action of "silencing" this woman mostly off-screen, or has it visually obscured by the gas and steam of a sauna; as hauntingly, the sounds of her death are similarly suppressed by the cacophony so that even in her last breaths—suffering the ultimate "negation of voice"—she can barely be heard. For the many arresting points of overlap, however, diversions from Cavell's genre may be more illuminating both for Cavell's thinking about films and for our thinking about Reichardt's films in affiliation with his writing. For instance, Dena's assailant, Josh (Jesse Eisenberg), doesn't conform to the jealous, obsessive, skeptical male types seen in Cavell's melodramas (e.g., *Gaslight*), Shakespeare's tragedies, or Chantal Akerman's *La Captive* (as discussed in the previous chapter)— who seek to achieve certainty about a woman (her thoughts, her desires), or ultimate control over her, by holding her captive, tormenting her, or killing her; rather, Josh wants Dena to remain unknown, wants her implicating, secret knowledge to die with her.

At the outset of her new suite of films starting in 2006, when she takes over the reigns of editing, Reichardt appears to signal an interactive and mutually reinforcing relationship between form and content that has been sustained in her work since. In the first seconds of *Old Joy*, for example, we hear the sound of a gong (before we see it), then birdsong, lawnmowers, traffic, a radio playing, a river rushing. On the road into the mountains, on their way to camp together, Kurt (Will Oldham) says to long-lost friend and fellow traveler Mark (Daniel London): "This is a great spot, man. You're gonna love it. I was here two summers ago. Totally private. No one around. And most of all, it has this otherworldly peacefulness about it. You can really think." Mark replies: "Sounds awesome." Kurt, affirming in turn: "You can't get real quiet anymore. I visited this hot spring in Arizona last summer where no one is allowed to talk at all. Total silence. It was fucking amazing."[36] In addition to Reichardt's close observation of visual and sonic elements (with her camera and in her editing), her characters occasionally, as in this case, vocally announce or physically embody certain values, presenting them as a complement to what we see and hear.

From the first frames of *Meek's Cutoff* and *First Cow*, we notice, well, the frame. Reichardt shot both films in Academy Standard (4:3; also known as 1.33:1), a frame ratio that is just slightly wider than a box—and a shape that harkens back to the early days of cinema. We are very far—in fact, about half the distance—from Anamorphic Scope (also known as Panavision and Cinemascope, 2.35:1, 2.76:1, and wider). Consequently, both of these "Westerns" feel decidedly, or comparatively, constrained, especially when screened beside the typical vista-heavy icons of the classical Western (with expansive shots of Monument Valley, as in *The Searchers* [1956, dir. John Ford]). Here, the sides of the frame close in very much like the bonnets that the women wear in *Meek's Cutoff*, the film frame itself embodying the short- or narrow-sightedness that is the affliction of these westward, wayward seekers (generally) and, more specifically, the women capped with blinders. At the very level of medium, these films announce how limits give shape to experience.

The diegetic time and space of these films, and others by Reichardt, reinforce the connotations of the frame. The sets are minimal, the scenes are minimalist; the sparseness is carried over into the conversations, which are often elliptical, as are many plotlines; the general mood—especially since *Old Joy*—is one of calm, contemplation, observation, and providing room for empathic engagement with characters and the realms they inhabit. Reichardt doesn't stuff a scene with words—as in noted contrast to, say, *His Girl Friday*, or contemporary fare, such as films by Woody Allen, the Coen brothers, Wes Anderson, Noah Baumbach, and Greta Gerwig. As with Howard Hawks before him, Baumbach's characters often have so much to say that they are prone to talking over (or past) one another; despite the profusion of spoken words, and the urgency of sharing them, the "conversation," paradoxically, finds characters delivering separate monologues, not quite able to hear (and thus respond to) what is being said by the other. Nervous outward narration of inner states, therefore, may not assure mutual comprehension.

For some viewers, the relative dearth of speech and commentary in Reichardt's films provides an occasion to think—hence the appellation contemplative cinema. Not everything is "spelled out"—another handy cliché that draws on the linguistic nature of explanation-heavy works that narrate and attempt to expose as much plot as possible. Since dialogue is used sparingly, there is a chance to focus more on what is unsaid than what is said—or even what is said but cannot be heard (for instance, the opening lines of *Night Moves* are mostly inaudible; we hear birdsong more clearly than the human dialogue). While in the comedies of remarriage, the couple addresses issues straight-on—for example, the threat of infidelity or divorce—and with abundant, accelerated use of language, in Reichardt, the topics of central emotional interest are left aside from what may be regarded as "small talk" (a lovely, if troubling, locution in the context of a Cavell-inspired investigation). As speech customs teach us, the phrase "we need to talk" has become a euphemism for a "big talk"—usually a proxy for an imminent breakup. In Reichardt, as in the work of other minimalists, complex emotions are often—out of frustration or lack of ability—reduced, suppressed, or abandoned; a strong and clear longing for connection between people is commonly left unfulfilled.

Pivoting back to the earlier point about a cycle of films called "people's lives falling apart," we can see that both of Cavell's genres could be described as *beginning* with people's lives falling apart (the threat of infidelity in a marriage and the threat of divorce in the comedies; the matter of being unknown, voiceless, and isolated in the melodramas), yet by the *end* of films in both Cavellian genres, we find resolutions (in the one, remarriage; in the other, the achievement of voice or power or some semblance of personhood). As extensively explored by Katherine Fusco, Nicole Seymour, and E. Dawn Hall, Reichardt's films, by contrast, begin and end in crisis, and the middle is often pretty harrowing too: they are stories of lives *in media res* in addition to being stories of persistent urgency, or emergency.[37] Reichardt ties such topics to her methods: "I always thought of experimental film as being about people who are sort of on the edges."[38] As an audience for film, we appear to have been told that fast movements, short shots, crisp photo-resolution, and loud music along with flagrant sexual explicitness, plus shouting, fighting, explosions, and abundant carnage, convey what we need in order to experience proper drama, to be sufficiently gripped, and to be granted satisfying degrees of catharsis. But anyone listening to a whisper knows that the hardest, harshest things may be said *sotto voce*.

Here lies a crux of Reichardt's understated experimentalism: her attunement to human precariousness becomes a recurrent meditation on the nature of luck, especially bad luck. She brings us "incomplete, quietly suffering women (and, in *Old Joy*, men) who are alarmingly unempowered," as Ella Taylor writes, people "who struggle to feel their way into change they may or may not attain."[39] These characters by and large seem to be the victims of circumstance, which, we should presume, we all are. We rarely hear them say such things out loud (the fact is, since *Old Joy*, such indications are left more to facial expression and body language), though, in the early work, *River of Grass* (with a screenplay by Reichardt based on a story by Jesse Hartman), Cozy ruminates a plaintive, folksy voiceover à la early

Malick that tips toward existential musing: "They say the apple doesn't fall far from the tree. I found this puzzling and couldn't stop wondering: Are our lives all mapped out for us? Would my daughter grow up only to wear my shoes? Did my mother's life create my destiny? Or does one thing just trigger another?"[40] The shared problems encoded in such questions should not strike a note of dreary fatalism but instead summon a chance for us to marvel at the way cinema—and Reichardt's particular approach to shooting and assembling it—can reveal and underscore the otherwise hidden, whether from willful ignorance or the happenstance of being unable to appreciate such a disclosure when it is presented to us.

One proximate cause for the scant nondiegetic music and abbreviated or fragmented conversation is the fact that many of Reichardt's protagonists find themselves in a state of emergency—approaching it, enduring it, or having a glimpse of escaping it. This often happens in rural or remote areas where nature predominates and people do not; yet such troubles also appear when characters inhabit urban areas—as conditions prove threatening, or people do. In *Wendy and Lucy*, Wendy is a traveler in peril: en route from Indiana to a hoped-for better life in Alaska (and living out of her car), her car breaks down, leaving her without shelter (and so, even more exposed). She takes pains to spend her few funds wisely, while negotiating threats from others—fronting nature and her fellow man (and losing her only companion, the eponymous dog, Lucy, in the process). Such emergencies are occasionally met by small mercies, such as an unnamed security guard (Walter Dalton), who gives Wendy helpful directions, a bit of encouragement, and the use of his cell phone. Precarity—whether in Oregon Country in the the first half of the nineteenth century (*Meek's Cutoff* is set in 1845, *First Cow* in 1820), in the small towns and ranches of Montana in the early twenty-first century (*Certain Women*), or in modern-day Oregon (*Wendy and Lucy*, *Night Moves*)—the prevailing sense is that people in a state of emergency may have no one to talk to, be frightened to speechlessness, or find physical and emotional cause for remaining silent in the face of terrifying circumstances and fraught futures. Being rendered speechless—from trauma, from privation, from an inability to navigate such rough emotional and physical terrain, or simply from being alone, on one's own—seems another point of realism. (Even the very few sex scenes in her films are indirectly rendered, capturing the accidental nature of the everyday, as when in *Night Moves* we do not *see* Dena and Harmon make love in a camper—much less in an invasive, hovering close up of the entangled pair—but remain outside with Josh, assigned to listen.) Given how Reichardt spoke of her work, just above, perhaps it is useful to characterize her films as instances of experimental realism.

Unusual for directors of her prestige, Reichardt's talents as editor put her in control of the translation from on-set capture through postproduction. Collaborating with cinematographer Christopher Blauvelt on her four most recent films (*Meek's Cutoff*, *Night Moves*, *Certain Women*, and *First Cow*) adds yet another degree of constancy and uniformity to her vision; Blauvelt worked for Lance Acord and was mentored by Harris Savides. In the range of characteristic features, perhaps most overtly felt is the behavior of her (and Blauvelt's) camera: it is often static, with the frame locked. Movement arrives with a slow pan left or right, or a modest tilt up or down. In this way, her work may remind some cinéastes of the transcendental style of Yasujirô Ozu or, as Reichardt herself recalls fondly, Satyajit Ray, whose Apu trilogy impressed her early on.[41] More recently, she cites Kenji Mizoguchi's *Ugetsu* (1953) as an influence on the realization of *First Cow*.

The distinctive, unhurried camerawork is further complemented by a reliance on diegetic sound and minimal use of scored music (e.g., *Old Joy* features parsimonious pieces by Yo La Tengo; the only music we hear during the running time of *Wendy and Lucy* is hummed by Wendy—a theme written by Will Oldham, who makes a cameo; in *Certain Women*, only one scene features a scored piece of music; *Night Moves* stands out a bit for its more prominent score, sounding as if Harold Budd were commissioned to write for a thriller or neo-noir[42]). While contemplative cinema and mainstream movies may be an unlikely pairing, Reichardt—like Terrence Malick—has found a way to blend them through a steady and capable use of long takes and brisker observational montage sequences that can evoke nature documentaries or ethnographic films.[43] Relatedly, Reichardt admires Nicolas Roeg's nonlinear, associative storytelling, such as *Walkabout* (1971), noting its influence on the dream quest in *Meek's Cutoff*. Whatever the duration of Reichardt's shots, we notice the attentiveness of the camera and the rhythm of the editor's sensibilities. Moreover, like Malick, she has been blessed with the presence of A-list Hollywood stars; mixing them seamlessly with under-sung character actors and nonprofessional performers, Reichardt has developed a cast—and a crew—who often recur, thereby creating gratifyingly expressive palimpsests.

Reichardt's studied attunement to objects, gestures, and processes—and the arrangement of those images in a series—has stoked both disparagement and defense; for a case of the latter, look to the co-chief film critics of *The New York Times* "In Defense of the Slow and the Boring."[44] In such a title, in such a pairing, one may note a slippage or overlap here between "contemplative" and "slow" cinemas.[45] Rather than use a long take for the purposes of artistic exhibition (as in *Russian Ark* [2002, dir. Aleksandr Sokurov] and *Victoria* [2015, dir. Sebastian Schipper]), the exploration of layering voices (as in Robert Altman's work), or stunt (as in the opening of *La La Land* [2016, dir. Damien Chazelle] and the feature-length presentment *1917* [2019, dir. Sam Mendes]), Reichardt's takes, whatever their length, are complemented—and enhanced—by her disciplined reluctance to fill the frame, swirl the camera, and crowd the plotting.

For her own part, Reichardt has addressed how her formal use of the camera and the film medium have coalesced to offer a "trance-like quality" that culminates in what she calls "elaborated time."⁴⁶ Thus, her sense is not that the long take merely offers (more) duration (e.g., as we might mistakenly hear *elongated* time), but that the frame allows something to be presented or developed or merely left alone. With her long takes—with comparatively less music, less dialogue, a steadier frame, and fewer cuts—we are simply given a chance to observe things. In this context, the "trance-like" summons our wakefulness rather than encourages us to remain lost in thought.

A similar discipline attends the presentation of sounds. Where many filmmakers rush to fill the soundscape of cinema, in an effort to dictate an emotional register, Reichardt resists the call to be prescriptive and manipulative (and consequently avoids narrowing the interpretative potential of her work; again *Night Moves* is an intriguing exception, since its score more decisively shapes the tone of certain scenes). For the "movie industry" (on this point, an apt syntagma), music is part of the "system of the suture," in significant measure by being in the "business of underlining things," as Brian Eno observes.⁴⁷ In her world, in her film worlds, location sounds are given prominence: the sounds of water and wind are made company to the sounds of footsteps and breathing (including the breathing of nonhuman animals and their footsteps too—memorably in the hoof-clacks of *Certain Women*); with such relative silence, and even a desire to constrain speech or let things go unsaid, the sounds of nature have a chance to break through the stratum of human civilization with its relentless chatter of mouth and machine. We can listen, then, as Thoreau counseled, to "the language which all things and events speak without metaphor, which alone is copious and standard."⁴⁸ From this orientation, "elaborated time" has a significant residual effect: a simplified yet richly layered sonic environment for cinema. With fewer sounds to contend with we may hear more of them.

When the default mode of consumer-driven mainstream filmmaking has become the visual equivalent of Hildy-and-Walter's lightning-fast repartee—the cut-every-two-seconds approach of the Marvel, DC, and Disney industrial franchise products—little wonder that we experience time differently in Reichardt's films. She speaks of achieving "tension" in her work by "not delivering the heightened moment."⁴⁹ In thinking of *Meek's Cutoff*, for example, she wonders aloud about exploring "how time might work in 1845."⁵⁰ Despite what may seem like spending a lot of time with these characters, the long takes and associative observational montages often have the opposite effect, namely, that we are merely experiencing a "glimpse" of their lives—and thus are invited to think of the time-before and time-after the film. In this sense, not just the conversations and dialogue contained in them, but the films themselves are elliptical, and so the characters—and their varied locations—live on after the running time elapses. These works end with questions, not answers. Narrative momentum is decidedly not resolved in any specific way. Perhaps this is why these lives linger: they have not been forestalled, but availed—"elaborated."

We can recognize in Reichardt work, then, something of Paul Schrader's analysis of transcendental cinema as withholding pathos and complicating empathy, of upsetting the standard rhythms of narrative, including plot points and audience expectations. In this respect, we may consider her kinship with the formalism of Robert Bresson, who wrote: "As far as I can I eliminate anything which may distract the interior drama. For me, the cinema is an exploration within."[51] As Schrader glosses the point: "The internal drama is in the mind, Bresson seems to say, and emotional involvement with an external plot 'distracts' from it."[52] With Cavell's films, and his approach to them as an ordinary language and perfectionist philosopher, there is emphatic attention to drama made exterior in speech (with conversation as its default mode) and in character behavior (smiling, slapping, laughing, crying, winking, nudging, hugging, kissing, singing, dancing, etc.). In the comedies of remarriage, especially, we may be able to deduce a mode of urgency from the coupling of form and content—an ever-onward, ever-outward, and structured momentum. Slowing down, or defeating emotional crescendos (whether of joy or suffering) would seem out of place in these films. Meanwhile, in Reichardt's work, the camera is given a chance to study the most minute shifts in behavior. Again, Bresson: "Dramatic stories should be thrown out. They have nothing whatsoever to do with cinema. [. . .] Film would have been marvelous if there hadn't been dramatic art to get in the way."[53] Reichardt achieves this sense of the "marvelous" by letting us marvel.

In looking at the films where the woman's presence is most at issue—*Wendy and Lucy*, *Meek's Cutoff*, *Night Moves*, *Certain Women*—there is a question about how central conversation is to these films; in *Meek's Cutoff*, for example, the contest of sounds and environmental factors make many things said barely audible. What we seem to find in Reichardt is *thought* on film—contemplation—but not as much dialogue, argument, negotiation, or discussion on film. For instance, there appears to be no correlate to the moral perfectionistic or romantic quest to get a couple back together after overcoming the threat of divorce (as in the comedy of remarriage) nor the aspiration to achieve (or arrogate) one's voice (i.e., the woman's voice in opposition to the man's voice, as in the melodrama of the unknown woman). In most cases, Reichardt's films do not progress morally or otherwise; they are not expositional or didactic; they do not offer a record of insight or development. As is the custom in remarriage comedies, we meet characters at a crucial phase (e.g., between divorce and reconciliation), yet in Reichardt's work one of the defining features of the *fabula* is that we encounter characters at no particularly time or place—call this the everyday. So, things fall apart but are not put back together—hence the sustained sense of not knowing how to go on in a certain sense, thus, remaining unacknowledged, unreconciled, adrift, lost, unmoored (and quite fittingly, incoherent, inaudible, or simply without words). If we are looking for compensation, perhaps we can say that conversation in Reichardt's films (again, even the comparatively loquacious ones, such as *Old Joy* or *First Cow*—both noticeably populated almost entirely by men) is replaced with contemplation. How often in Reichardt's work does the camera linger on a character who is taciturn? We seem to see a character in the midst of thought, and we too are granted a chance to reflect. Reichardt's patience—exemplified by her studious interest in characters and the emotional and physical landscapes they inhabit—shows a rare willingness to let a scene unfold, to give us a chance to reorient ourselves to expectations for those moments, and most consequentially, to afford us an opportunity to see and hear how shots and scenes disclose things we weren't at first looking or listening for.

When characters do speak, there is a tendency for such remarks to slide into monologue. In the car and by the campfire, Kurt (Will Oldham) speaks while Mark (Daniel London) listens; seeking a favor, Gina (Michelle Williams) asks an old man, Albert (René Auberjonois), a question only to receive his silent, nonresponsive stare in return (his behavior seeming a porridge of effects from injury, dementia, and habituated sexist incivility); a garrulous, wandering camper (Lew Temple) tries to strike up a conversation with Dena (Dakota Fanning), Josh (Jesse Eisenberg), and Harmon (Peter Sarsgaard) only to be looked at with a kind of indifference or unresponsiveness expected from people who do not speak the same language; a tired Elizabeth (Kristen Stewart) talks over her meal while The Rancher (Lily Gladstone) listens with unrequited affection; King-Lu (Orion Lee) tells Cookie (John Magaro) about a plan to make oily cakes, while Cookie quietly mulls over the idea. Indeed, the "silent" character in these and other instances affords the viewer a chance to become a more attuned listener, since one is, naturally, put in the same position as Mark, Gina, Dena, Josh, Harmon, The Rancher, and Cookie—trying to understand what is being said, even if it leaves one without a fitting response. For the most part, whether the characters speak or not, people remain enigmatic and unknown. In this way, Reichardt offers us portraits of exteriors in a double sense: not just of natural landscapes, but of people's exteriors as well. Perhaps because of their quietness, passivity, or pained efforts at expression in language, their lives on film take on a beauty that may otherwise be obscured by speech, including obsessive self-analysis, commentary on others, and the apparent or imposed order of plot and type.

We need not take such minimalism or quietism as a referendum on the virtues of voluble conversation, but Reichardt certainly does offer an alternative to cinematic portraits that herald human speech as the crux of human experience and development (especially their moral, political, and romantic incarnations). Maybe that is so; perhaps the project of moral perfectionism needs to be undertaken in tandem, or in dialogue (something familiar from Plato to Cavell). Or rather, it may be that conversation is an *ideal* of moral perfectionism (even its preferred mode—again, reaching back to Plato's dialogues), but for reasons many of us, most of us, are aware of, it is exceedingly difficult to achieve such communication in our lived experience with others. Consider, then, the long pauses and silences of Reichardt's films as a nod to realism—the reality of similar gaps and lacunae in our own daily lives; and contrast that common condition with the sort we find in the unfamiliar frenzy of the lucid, hurried bicker and banter present in *His Girl Friday*, *The Awful Truth* (1937, dir. Leo McCarey), and *Adam's Rib* (1949, dir. George Cukor). We are reminded, as if we needed reminding, that our lives—and words—are not scripted by the likes of Ben Hecht, Charles Lederer, Viña Delmar, Ruth Gordon, and Garson Kanin. Indeed, the speedy clip of such speech is so foreign to some of us that it comes in for contemporary parody—as when, in a *His Girl Friday* send-up on *Saturday Night Live*, Zooey Deschanel's character cannot understand her office mates for the speed and inflection of what they say: "I'm sorry you guys, you're talking so fast, I have no idea what anyone is saying. I'm like 'What?' [. . .] Is it me? [. . .] Is this a real argument or is it just jibber jabber?"[54] And she adds—glancing at a newspaper, an expositional icon of early talkies, "there are so many typos. I think if everybody just kind of slowed down, like, take your time with your work." Slow down, take your time—yet another dispatch from Wittgenstein's domain, since he famously advised that "philosophers should greet one another" by saying "Take your time."[55] Despite the struggle inherent to the stressful lives of Reichardt's subjects, her filmmaking yields a paradoxical effect of calm. The result may be accounted for, in part, by her savvy way of trading an aggressive, lascivious gazing and a pageant of incessant talking for the rarer talent of listening.

A Sensibility for Sounds

As a trained musician and a "philosopher of the voice," it is fitting that Cavell would be drawn to "talkies" in which people talk. The sound of the human voice has its own musicality, from tone to timbre; it provides its own lessons in projecting, receiving, and sharing meaning with others. Singing, moreover, with its special dispensation in opera, proves to be yet another locale for acknowledging the centrality of voice to human expressiveness. Meanwhile, the makeup or breakdown of conversation—having words to say, having one's words heard, hearing what others say—sits at the core of the communicative acts that underlie Cavell's long-standing fascination with ordinary language philosophy (in the tradition of J. L. Austin and Wittgenstein) and Thoreau's native sympathy for the "sounds" of Walden Pond. "Movies, before they spoke," wrote Cavell in the final chapter of the first edition of *The World Viewed*, "projected a world of silence."[56] Moreover, "[a] world of sound is a world of immediate conviction," whereas "a world of sight is a world of immediate intelligibility."[57] Cavell concluded: "The advent of sound broke the spell of immediate intelligibility."[58] Should we be surprised, then, that some contemporary practitioners of the medium may have, even if unintentionally or unconsciously, sought a reunion or recuperation of such intelligibility?

Again, by contrast with the talkies that remain central to Cavell's investigations (with the "clumsiness of speech, the dumbness and duplicities and concealments of assertion" inherent to sound synchronization), Reichardt—kindred to many creators of transcendental, contemplative, and slow cinemas—makes room for quiet, which is not always to say silence; the absence of spoken communication does not mean that the world ceases to present itself sensuously, including by way of its sounds. Indeed, Kyle Stevens helpfully refers to this quiet as "worldly silence."[59] Perhaps we are not accustomed to the kind of sparseness, or even absence, of the human voice that we find in Reichardt's work, which is why, for many viewers, the wordless stretches can feel so long, even if they are, in fact, not very long. At such moments, we are pressed to answer the unanswerable: how long *is* a long take? *My Dinner with Andre* (1981, dir. Louis Malle) was edited to feel like a long take; and though it is filled with voices, with conversation, if you follow it attentively, it passes quickly. By comparison, a take (long or otherwise) of a landscape devoid of people (and even animals) may seem to call attention to itself—and thus, the passage of the *film's* time, and by good measure, our own precious hours. On this front, transcendental/contemplative/slow cinemas all partake of a modernist project in which art calls itself—its medium—into question. When no one speaks, there is not silence, but it may feel that way: whipping winds, flowing waters, birdsong, leaves rustling, airplanes overhead become part of an aural environment (the sound of [a] place) that we seldom notice—more often than not, seldom have any patience for or interest in. Human speech is a perpetual interruption to these kinds of "silence"—again, as Cavell says, "sound broke the spell of immediate intelligibility."[60] What Reichardt does, in correspondence with a few contemporaries—Chantal Akerman, Terrence Malick, Jim Jarmusch, Sofia Coppola—is provide a cinematic realm in which to notice these overlooked, under-heard sounds.

In Reichardt's work, which qualify as "talkies" mainly in the technical sense that they are miked, and image/sound are synched, we could describe the long stretches without words as providing an arena for characters to think. As noted, in our recognition of their states of mind we are poised to accept an invitation to think ourselves—an important double sense of what we can mean by contemplative cinema. We do not need to hear thoughts vocalized and feelings spoken aloud (in the diegesis) or have access to a person's inner voice (as from a voiceover) to spend meaningful time in their presence. Such a state may call for profitable engagement with Lisa Zunshine's notion of "mind reading" or Blakey Vermeule's account of why characters (literary and otherwise) matter to us, but we can also forego reasons and readings, and simply be in the company of people who are suffering, as we are.[61] That kind of companionship may be enough—and it may prompt all the contemplation we need. The film needn't solve or resolve our problems, but, like the characters' own deferred resolutions, simply give some attention to their presence (and ours along with them). This kind of wordless exchange between film and viewer, it turns out, is a satisfying mode of communication, though it may not represent the kind of discourse we have been primed, by a lifetime of mainstream movie-watching, to accept as such. In their formal expressiveness, and suppression of consecutive speech, Reichardt's films can at times present themselves as heirs to the silent era; or, in a more contemporary vein, the formalism of transcendental works, and the experimentalism of slow cinema.

In *The World Viewed*, Cavell is committed to understanding the modernism of film—a medium he defines as a "succession of automatic world projections"—which entails, in a word, "discovering [. . .] its limits."[62] When Noël Carroll revisits this aspect of *The World Viewed*, a half-century on, he glosses Cavell's understanding of modernism as "one that regards as modernist simply the reflexive exploration of the art form."[63] Highlighting reflexivity feels apt, since it turns us again to the two dominant and related aspects of the movies as we know them: the joining (usually synchronously) of picture and sound (again, usually) as part of a conspiratorial effort to present the impression of (or, as Cavell puts it, turned the other way, "craving for"[64]) realism; deviations from, say, immersive, mainstream cinema will often create a jarring *Verfremdungseffekt*. Given the way Reichardt's films can sometimes have this effect on viewers not accustomed to her use of the medium, it is striking to rediscover that Cavell concludes the first edition of his second book with a chapter entitled "The Acknowledgment of Silence."

For Cavell, film's limits must be "acknowledged" as involving two interrelated facts: "its outsideness to its world, and my absence from it."[65] (As Kyle Stevens understands this moment: "Acknowledging my absence from the world of the film, as well as its own separateness from its world, is, we see, fundamentally the same gesture."[66]) How intriguing to hear that "long after our acceptance of the talkie," we still do not "know why the loss of silence was traumatic for so many who cared about film."[67] Was it? Given all that Cavell had said about ordinary language philosophy by the time his interest in silence-on-film provides the denouement to *The World Viewed*, and all that he will go on to say about the centrality of (spoken) conversation (and its sound, the sound of the human voice) in all that will come—in *Pursuit of Happiness*, *Contesting Tears*, and *Cities of Words*—it is refreshing to encounter his deep perceptions about "a further reality that film pursues."[68] This is the cinematic expression of "the unsayable" ("time's answer to the ineffable"):

> I have in mind not the various ways dialogue can stand at an angle to the life that produces it; nor the times in which the occasion is past when you can say what you did not think to say; nor the times when the

occasion for speech is blocked by inappropriateness or fear, or the vessels of speech are pitched by grief or joy. I have rather in mind the pulsing air of incommunicability which may nudge the edge of any experience and placement: the curve of fingers that day, a mouth, the sudden rise of the body's frame as it is caught by the color and scent of flowers, laughing all afternoon mostly about nothing, the friend gone but somewhere now which starts from here—spools of history that have unwound only to me now, occasions which will not reach words for me now, and if not now, never.[69]

The "reality of the unsayable"—its presence, its weight—is here given a chance for acknowledgment. When Cavell makes the seemingly controversial claim that "[a] silent movie has never been made," we are given permission to appreciate the figurativeness of silence and sound, and how they behave in the medium we experience as "a succession of automatic world projections."[70] Legendary historian of experimental and avant-garde cinema, Scott MacDonald has written of his concern that "for Cavell, commercial narrative cinema *is* cinema—all else is peripheral,"[71] and fellow legend, P. Adams Sitney lamented in the same key that Cavell "never 'acknowledged' the importance of avant-garde cinema."[72] Dave Burnham has explored some implications of Cavell's "rejection of experimental cinema" and "abdications" from engaging it more fully in his writing (despite, for example, working at Harvard in close proximity to Robert Gardner, Alfred Guzzetti, Ross McElwee, and Chantal Akerman, among other filmmakers).[73] Yet, Cavell's treatment of the films of Terrence Malick, representative moments of commentary (such as the one just above from *The World Viewed*), and later notes on Chris Marker and the "remarkable so-called experimental filmmaker" Stan Brakhage, suggest that there is, at the least, a latent, if non-formalized, set of remarks that are germane for thinking about experimental and avant-garde cinemas.[74]

Given Cavell's interest in the relationship between actor (or in his preferred nomenclature, star) and character, it is not surprising to learn from him that "[t]here is another half to the idea of conveying the unsayable by showing experience beyond the reach of words," and it has to do with the "idea of acting on film"; that is, the unsayable on film is "conveyed by freeing the motion of the body for its own lucidity."[75] The body's silence and its lucidity were, in a lovely poetic phrasing, "always part of the grain of film." In this way, the unsayable would achieve two overlapping expressions: the unspoken and the embodied (a tandem that may find its unified vision in the physically expressive actor who does not speak—call him Chaplin or Keaton, or, in many indelible scenes, Daniel Day-Lewis or Joaquin Phoenix). But, as MacDonald's concern brings to light: there are other ways to divide the silence of cinema, and many of them express what Cavell would recognize as modernist sensibilities, namely, the use of the medium to explore its presence and its limits. Hence, Reichardt's willingness to attend to the lives of animals (a dog—the same dog, hers—in *Old Joy* and *Wendy and Lucy*, oxen in *Meek's Cutoff*, a fawn in *Night Moves*, horses in *Certain Women*, a cow in *First Cow*, etc.) points up that there are other bodies to explore besides human ones (even as those nonhuman animal bodies are so regularly and literary *beside* the human, being touched, handled, and addressed by people). Formal limits join this shift in the objects of attention: the frame ratio, the length of takes, the diminishment of nondiegetic sounds in pursuit of the revelation of diegetic ones.

In thinking of Cavell, and Richard Moran (on Cavell), Kyle Stevens writes: "the model of attention that the camera offers, and the claims it places on us, differs from that of sound recording technologies, particularly with respect to the expressivity of silence."[76] Transcendental, contemplative, and slow cinemas—and further on to those experimental and avant-garde works that exceed these categories—seem replete with illustrations of Stevens's canny observation. The camera simply does different work than the microphone. Most mainstream filmmaking aims to make this difference disappear, yet, Reichardt's films, again and again, would seem to present moving images so that we can see what the camera attends to *and also* what the sound recording technology picks up (Wim Wenders's *Lisbon Story* [1994] may be company to this point along with Francis Ford Coppola's *The Conversation* [1974]). Whether the sound is of room tone or insects mating, the squeaky wheel of an ox-drawn carriage or the rattle of a car's motor, shoveling or jackhammering, "the whistle of the locomotive" or humming a tune, human breathing or a horse braying, the rest of the world—beyond or beside human speech—finds a way into Reichardt's films.[77]

There are traditions of "close reading" the texts we call movies, yet, it may be helpful to extend the metaphor to an account of "close listening."[78] While Cavell listens for the sounds we call speech, and follows the ensuing conversations for their pertinence to the projects of remarriage and moral perfectionism, Reichardt grants a cinematic arena in which to contemplate what is (left) unsaid or unarticulated, allowed to remain silent; as a result, she offers space for other sounds to emerge, say, the sounds of nature so often drowned out by human speech and the crowded interiors of consciousness. It is precisely Cavell's attentiveness to sound (generally) and speech (specifically) that gives us a clue that the ordinary and everyday (concepts as familiar and constitutive of his work as any) may be present in significant ways *apart* from human linguistic communication. Indeed, Cavell's own *The Awful Truth*, which he heralds as "the best, or the deepest, of the remarriage comedies," ends with Jerry Warriner (Cary Grant) acting as a kind of semaphore, *embodying* his desire for reconciliation with Lucy (Irene Dunne) rather than spelling it out.[79] (Sounds a lot like the miracles noted earlier in *Journey to Italy* and *Before Midnight*.) In short, we are given reason to wonder if the shape and meaning of a given human life may be informed not (solely) by what is said (to others), but also by "the pulsing air of incommunicability": what one hears or listens for in the gaps between words—in thoughtful pauses, wordless silences, the physical expression of an idea, or the embodiment of a feeling.

Many experimental and avant-garde works, by virtue of formal innovations, can illustrate the power of cultivating new channels of interest into the nature of human communion and communication, such as Hollis Frampton's *Hapax Legomena III: Critical Mass* (1971), about a volatile romantic relationship culminating in a cinema of "demarriage"[80]; documentaries such as *Into Great Silence* (2005, dir. Philip Gröning) and feature films such as *Of Gods and Men* (2010, dir. Xavier Beauvois), both of which focus on the lives of contemplatives, and thus on expansive realms of sound beyond speech. This representative suite provides access to variations of the significance of sounds and silences, admitting, in turn, what spoken words and dialogue cannot accomplish. Cavell's attentiveness to sound (as speech) is then usefully translated—or even, transfigured—in Reichardt's attunement to other kinds of sounds (besides speech). For instance, the denouement of an awkward encounter in *Certain Women* between Gina (Michelle Williams) and Albert (René Auberjonois) finds them achieving a connection, at last, in jointly translating the birdsong of quail.[81] After a tortured negotiation (with much stumbling in language, shifts in tone of voice, along with widened eyes and ones cast down, among other physical efforts to endow speech with its intended efficacy), Albert whistles. In a two-shot single take, Gina effortlessly speaks this new, avian language, which Albert regards approvingly. By looking beyond the human—to the quail and the sounds they make—Gina and Albert share a charged moment of mutual recognition, however fleeting.

The Expressiveness of the Everyday

As Cavell is a companion to watching films beyond his canons and genres, so too may the films addressed in this volume turn us back to meaningful elucidations of Cavell's philosophical and filmic remarks, or to at least rediscover the purchase and ongoing vitality of his contributions. For instance, an abiding thematic of Reichardt's films may be described as "a crisis of the everyday," which is to say, a kind of emergency that is not immediate, but long-standing—what David Denby has called, in reference to *Meek's Cutoff*, the "bone-wearying stress of mere life."[82] One such crisis is the human capacity for expression, period, though we can thereafter parse some modalities: principally speech, but also "body language" (which invites silent, close reading of the body-as-text[83]), and not to be missed, the speechlessness we call silence. Returning to Cavell after time with Reichardt's work, certain passages of his on the problem of skepticism read differently, in particular, those addressing the notion of inexpressiveness.

As Cavell writes in *The Claim of Reason*: "So the fantasy of a private language, underlying the wish to deny the publicness of language, turns out, so far, to be a fantasy, or fear, either of inexpressiveness, one in which I am not merely unknown, but in which I am powerless to make myself known; or one in which what I express is beyond my control."[84] Such observations resonate in his later work on "unknown" women (in cinema) as they do in *The Claim of Reason* in his explorations of, say, Desdemona and Cordelia. Yet what of this fantasy or fear of inexpressiveness in Reichardt's films, where the protagonists—of all genders—struggle to know themselves and to make themselves known? We are often left to wonder why people do the things they do—searching for causes, explanations, rationales. The etiology of thoughts and actions often remains stubbornly inscrutable.

Powerlessness seems a striking and essential feature of the precarity familiar to Reichardt's characters, people who struggle, so often, in the most mundane moments with a world that seems "beyond my control" and also, crucially, beyond my comprehension; both knowing *and* acknowledging appear daunting, perhaps impossible projects. Knowledge of others becomes as mysterious as self-knowledge such that unknownness—along with forms of marginality and invisibility and muteness—are taken for constitutive attributes of human interaction (internally and externally, on one's own and with others). Must we conclude that the quests of moral perfectionism, mutual understanding, and self-possession require a certain degree of affluence, security, and education—all traits we find in the films that populate Cavell's genres? (Cavell is sensible to the question when he asks one of his own, at the outset of his Carus Lectures: "Is Moral Perfectionism inherently elitist?"[85]) Reichardt's films, by contrast, are populated with characters enduring limited resources (often financially, but also at times emotionally and intellectually), who are not preoccupied with projects of "self-realization." They may be taking steps, but they are tentative ones—hemmed in by immediate obstacles and unarticulated threats.

Even from the start, Reichardt described what interested her by what is lacking, by what prevents progress: "It's a theme that started at the beginning [with *River of Grass*], and I look back, and I guess it's just a good setup for different kinds of searching: question-asking, looking for the next place to go, what are you looking for, what are you leaving."[86] Cars and trucks populate her films (or in *Meek's Cutoff*, era-appropriate covered wagons), so "road movie" as trope, or genre marker, has becomes a useful category. Then again, Reichardt seems to define such work by what it fails to contain; for example, *River of Grass* she deems a "road movie without the road, a love story without the love, and a crime story without the crime."[87] When placed in proximity to Reichardt's films of experimental realism, Cavell's comedies and melodramas seem especially mythical—representations of distant, unapproachable fantasies of relational reconciliation and individual empowerment. After watching Reichardt's movies, we may wonder where "there is a perfectionism that happily consents to democracy."[88]

When, in *Contesting Tears*, Cavell develops remarks from *The Claim of Reason* (cited just above) into a bona fide theory of a genre, he recognizes that it is precisely "doubt to excess" among characters that pushes "to the point of melodrama."[89] Call this feature a through-line from Shakespeare to the melodrama of the unknown woman; hence the tragedy borne by those who experience such doubt and those who inflict pain on others because of it (Othello and Lear come to mind). In *Contesting Tears*, Cavell rereads his lines as a "fantasy of suffocation or of exposure."[90] (The scene of strangulation in *Night Moves*, invoked above, suggests itself as an emblem of such a crisis.) We have at hand, then, a spectrum to consider, as Cavell puts it: "Accordingly, I am led to stress the condition that I find to precede, to ground the possibility and necessity of, 'the desire to express all,' namely the terror of absolute inexpressiveness, suffocation, which at the same time reveals itself as a terror of absolute expressiveness, unconditioned exposure; they are the extreme states of voicelessness."[91] Not surprisingly, Cavell describes these positions as conjuring a state of anxiety, an emotional tonality that befits the powerless and precarious.[92] Moreover, we can make a connection between Cavell's account of skepticism and being "unknown" with the advent of sound for cinema: one of the effects of talkies, he says, is "the bafflement of soul and body by their inarticulateness and by the terror of articulateness."[93]

As he often does, Cavell provides some much-needed orientation to his own prodigious insights, as when he points out that "[i]ntuitive differences between the untellable and the unspeakable, let alone the ineffable, should alert us to different causes for wordlessness, different relations to (in) expressiveness."[94] An intuitive insight for Cavell, perhaps, but needing articulation for many of us. In the spirit of noticing what lies before us, what seems like it should be known by all, we can add that different *effects* (for the untellable, unspeakable, ineffable, etc.) will also present themselves. I wish to commend the thought that Reichardt's films can be profitably taken up as representations of these and related conditions. For example, the secrecy of longing (The Rancher's passionate but understated interest in Elizabeth in *Certain Women*) or the secrecy of a crime (the ethically fraught aftermath of a terrorist act in *Night Moves*; King-Lu's scheme to steal milk in *First Cow*); being unable to ask for help in effective ways (in *Wendy and Lucy*) or to contest prevailing authority (in *Meek's Cutoff*); Mark's openness to Kurt (in *Old Joy*) signaling a willingness to listen that is, more often than not, confounded by what Kurt says.

One of the most conspicuous attributes of Cavell's twin genres is the figuration of heterosexual gender roles, norms, and identities among white people, who are often educated and affluent. When a woman is not, say, affluent and educated—as we see in the character Stella Dallas (Barbara

Stanwyck)—the eponymous film nevertheless makes her deviation from those cinematic norms a central preoccupation. Reichardt's films, by contrast, are by and large filled with people from the middle and lower classes, men and women, not all white, and not all heterosexual. The juxtaposition should serve not as a scold (times change, Hollywood changes, etc.)—and still less to divorce his comments from their filmic contexts—but as an opportunity to appreciate how rereading Cavell with Reichardt in mind requires some translation, as, for instance, when he writes that "the key to one's (male) preservation is to control the woman's voice, contradictorily to stop it from speaking (from reporting) and to make it speak (to promise a further mitigation or intercession). Some control. —I am not prepared to say," he continues in reply to his own distinction, "that all the reasons men have for controlling the woman's voice come down to this contradictory pair [. . .]. What I am so far suggesting is that a certain frenzy in the effort of control is the expression of the wish not singly for the woman's silence, but, at the same time, for her voice, say her confidence."[95] Such dynamics play out with notable prominence in *Wendy and Lucy*, *Meek's Cutoff*, *Night Moves*, and *Certain Women*, yet, are only glancingly relevant in films where women are nearly absent, as in *Old Joy* and *First Cow*. Another way of putting Cavell's point here seems to be that men, in the films he studied, either want the woman's vocal consent, support, and approval or . . . their confirmed silence (again, whether that means remaining deferential or, in the extreme, dying). Richard Linklater and his team seem to be teasing us about this point in Celine's (Julie Delpy's) portrayal of a "bimbo" voice in *Before Midnight*. No such parody is afforded by Reichardt's films: the (masculinist) suppressions and approval-seeking are more in keeping with traits familiar from the wealth of Cavell's cinematic touchstones. As much as Reichardt's sex, gender, and race norms make her work look and feel different from Golden Age comedies and melodramas, much of that legacy remains in evidence—and thus on show for us to notice and to critique.

Part of what we discern is how in the temporality of Reichardt's cinema, it may be the "real time" of the drama's diegesis—not conversation, not speech—that most closely resembles our own varied experiences of knowledge and acknowledgment, expressiveness and inexpressiveness, articulateness and inarticulateness. Reichardt herself seems aware of the association of her work with slow cinema but is uncommitted to the label and the connection; of *Meek's Cutoff*, for example, she admits: "I don't think of it as being slow; I think of it as being the appropriate time for that story."[96] Looking across her many films—in which she variously draws on different genres and disputes their familiar definitions—Reichardt notes that "[a]ll the films are really about small moments and small decisions."[97] *Meek's Cutoff* as much as (and as different from) *Night Moves* is about "labor and chores" and the specific temporality of those efforts;[98] setting up a camp—a temporary home away from home—is common to *Old Joy*, *Wendy and Lucy*, *Meek's Cutoff*, and *First Cow*. By this turn, Reichardt's work—resembling the durational approach of slow cinema, sharing certain neorealist traits, and bearing a kinship with Paul Schrader's theorizing of transcendental cinema—is doing something else, something of its own accord. In contrast with many transcendental films, for example, Reichardt disallows what Schrader describes as the defining denouement of many transcendental films (from *Pickpocket* [1959, dir. Robert Bresson] to *First Reformed* [2017, dir. Paul Schrader]), namely, endings filled with a rush of music, emotion, and a deus ex machina-like intervention (even if for that abruptness its meaning becomes symbolic, a cipher—as in *Ordet* [1955, dir. Carl Theodor Dreyer]). Across the range of Reichardt's films, we encounter a deliberate defeat of resolution; there is no transcendental climax: J. C. F. Fischer swells while lovers kiss with prison bars between them (*Pickpocket*); a lustful embrace while the male protagonist is lacerated by barbed-wire (*First Reformed*). Instead, in Reichardt, life goes on, fades out, seemingly indifferent to our presence or interest; we might say that Reichardt's films end in mid-sentence.

Like other works in the general swirl of contemplative, slow, and transcendental cinema—and at this point, we could also emphasize the documentary qualities of Reichardt's observational camera—this abbreviated, forestalled, or denied narrative culmination feels of a piece with the human experience of the everyday. Falling asleep each night, one seems in the middle of thought and then suddenly, the oblivion of sleep overtakes what was on one's mind—a fade-to-black until the new day dawns (and with what seems like the resumption of thought): "Now, where was I?" Yet the *crisis* of the everyday as we know it in Reichardt may have more in common with sentiments Cavell circulates under the banner of Thoreau's "quiet desperation" and Emerson's "secret melancholy"—noting on this pass the presence of "quiet" and "secret," the latter of which Cavell, in an uncanny solecism, sometimes calls "silent."[99] All of these registers link amiably with Cavell's remarks above about the anxiety of (in)expressiveness, "the terror of articulateness," doubtless experiences that we commonly (should?) expect to coalesce into feelings of desperation and melancholy.[100] Our observation, with Cavell brought into proximity with Reichardt, is the degree to which the continuum from silence to sound is itself emblematic of these charged feelings, ones that we recognize as part and parcel of ordinary life. In this respect, Reichardt's films may be treated as a new, cinematic locus classicus of the everyday.

Cavell speaks to the potency of the film medium as a site for semiotic investigation: "I understand it to be, let me say, a natural vision of film that every motion and station, in particular every human posture and gesture, however glancing, has its poetry, or you may say its lucidity."[101] And he cites Charlie Chaplin and Buster Keaton as exemplars in this regard; yet, he as quickly narrows his own interest to find in the "Hollywood talkie [. . .] an equivalent for this expressiveness, this expression of lucidity," that is, "in the way certain pairs of human beings are in conversation."[102] Cavell, therefore, introduces a bifurcation between the expressiveness of bodies (on film) and speech (on film), one that positions his twin genre studies on the latter side, largely leaving the former at a remove (including experimental and avant-garde cinemas).

What the cleavage may distract us from, however, is how the medium itself is unified in its expressiveness of the *seemingly* banal, another modernist trait, as Cavell writes: "Any of the arts will be drawn to [. . .] this perception of the poetry of the ordinary, but film, I would like to say, democratizes the knowledge [. . .]."[103] In other words, the viewer is empowered (though perhaps more commonly overpowered) by the demands film makes to appreciate this poetry, this knowledge. As a result of the abundance and dissonance, much that we see and hear on film is missed, dismissed—left unseen, goes unheard. In a persistent irony, the (increasingly) brisk tempo of much contemporary, mainstream cinema would have us guess that it is in the nature of film-watching not to perceive things but to overlook or under-hear them (despite the high volume of theatrical presentations), whereas those works that operate at a slower, more deliberate pace and at a lower amplification of sound, would be the logical site for closer analysis and appreciation of "the numinous quotidian."[104] In the latter cases, revelations of the common, the familiar, and the low are not banal but captivating: "Give me insight into to-day," Emerson declaimed, "and you may have the antique and future worlds."[105] Since Cavell says "the perception of poetry is as open to all [. . .], a failure so to perceive, to persist in missing the subject, which may amount to missing the evanescence of the subject, is ascribable only to ourselves; to failures of our character."[106] Some may feel this gloss as a reprimand rather than a reminder. For our purposes, it is the latter; indeed, it is an invitation to appreciate Cavell's attunement to the fuller range of cinematic expressiveness. Conversations between characters, and the narrative of their relationship, are but one aspect of the enterprise.

What film affords to us all, then, is a revelation of the everyday in small moments and embodied gestures (caring for the sick and infirm; walking; commuting; financial accounting; doing errands and chores: cooking, cleaning, mending) and sounds (in Reichardt, music is sparse—scored or otherwise—and so we hear instead breathing, whistling, humming, crying, sighing; the wind howling, dogs barking, tires spinning on the road, and the distinctive orchestra of the railyard—*Wendy and Lucy* is based on the short story, *Train Choir* by Jonathan Raymond). The notion that conversation enables the achievement of mutual comprehension (as we see it in the comedy of remarriage) or that silence, or the suppression of the female voice, confirms the failure of the same (in the melodrama of the unknown woman) are but two modes of the "poetry of the ordinary" as made evident on film. Reichardt's work, again, in spiritual affiliation with the transcendental works of Bresson, Dreyer, Ozu, and others, does not find conversation to be the only, or even the principal, means for cinematic illumination. Her films are not loaded with wall-to-wall sound (or sound effects), or garrulous and gushing interlocutors, much less given to constant camera motion or rapid-fire editing; instead, the takes can be long and languid, and feature a camera that is interested but also often willing to pause, to keep its distance from less-than-discursive characters. As a partner or presence in its own right, Reichardt's camera is curious but not predatory or invasive; it allows people the space to breathe and to ponder, to make choices and to make mistakes, to be interested and to be puzzled; and we, as viewers—sitting still and not speaking—are afforded the same courtesy. With a camera that is inquisitive but not judging—like those found in the slow film and transcendental traditions—her cinema generously gives the experience of lived time its due.

But then what kind of expressiveness is this? To be sure, I am trying to say something explicit about Reichardt's patient attention to the "evanescence of the subject," her willingness to dwell on the ineffable (in or of the everyday), yet what terms help to elucidate her contribution (e.g., in addition to the foregoing exchanges and overlaps with certain "movements" in cinema)? Perhaps we can contrast her films with those that interest Cavell by calling them "unmelodramatic," but then, for many, they may not simply register at the level of the "dramatic," either; are they, then, also "undramatic"? Not incidentally, Reichardt's dear friend, Todd Haynes, is also a cinematic influence (and frequent executive producer)—and she admires his work; moreover, she notes the impact of Rainer Werner Fassbinder and her regular teaching of films by Nicholas Ray and Douglas Sirk at Bard College.[107] So she is not averse to the pleasures and accomplishments of the dramatic and melodramatic, and yet her own work minimizes them. Though he doesn't have Reichardt's films in mind, Andrew Klevan's notion of the "undramatic" feels crucial, since it provides a term that opens a region for theorizing the achievements we want to acknowledge in her accomplished instances of cinematic art.

> Many of the undramatic images used by the films achieve force only as the films develop, but they never present themselves, even when they finally occur, as individually arresting. [. . .] So we might say that the undramatic films establish their emphasis, that which they wish to stress, in an unemphatic manner. The achievement of the films' styles is to allow the narratives to remain skillfully poised, conveying routine and repetition, without submitting to the possible banality of routine; the films are therefore able to unconceal the significance which often remains buried in the habitual. The importance of these films is that they find

aspects of style which do justice to the moments of life which do not proclaim their significance. An exploration of these methods allows us to enhance our understanding of the discreet ways in which film narration can bring the world to our attention.[108]

These remarks arrive at the end of Klevan's essential *Disclosure of the Everyday: Undramatic Achievement in Narrative Film* in which he discusses, in detail, two filmmakers that contribute to Schrader's transcendental canon: Bresson (*Diary of a Country Priest*, 1950) and Ozu (*Late Spring*, 1949) as well as a filmmaker of interest to Cavell, Éric Rohmer (*A Tale of Springtime*, 1990), and *A Blonde in Love* (1965) by Miloš Forman. (Klevan has since taken an interest in Reichardt's work, finding occasion to interview the filmmaker during her visiting professorship at the University of Oxford.)[109] Rereading Klevan's culminating statement with Reichardt's films before us, the "un"-words seem especially apt: undramatic, unemphatic, unconcealing. In Reichardt's films, we are availed to the "poetry of the ordinary" but must be deliberate and patient to receive it or perceive it; her films do not shout. Undramatic shots—and the scenes that are formed by them—achieve their power accretively, cumulatively, not with a bang or an endless series of them. Reichardt says: "when I go to the movies and I sit through the previews, I literally feel assaulted."[110] Consider the scene—in fact, it is just a shot, a long take—in *Night Moves* when Dena, Josh, and Harmon barrel away from the scene of their destructive act: they sit in the pick-up truck, three astride, and do not speak.[111] Undistracted by what they might say, we the audience have a chance to study their faces, to listen to their adrenalized panting. In the background, low and muffled, we hear an explosion. What would have been the central pyrotechical or CGI-juiced spectacle of another film is here rendered entirely off screen (but not, importantly, out of earshot). Shifting to figurative language, Reichardt tries to account for the way audiences respond to her work—especially its pacing, its unwillingness to show us what we have come to expect, its attention to other things—to anti-spectacle: "maybe it's just people's metabolisms or something."[112] As we are said to live in an "attention economy" that is defined as "surveillance capitalism," it should be apparent that we are all and each being "assaulted" by an accelerating pace of life that is likely beyond our powers and thus beyond our reckoning. No wonder "slow" films stand out, even if they do not explain what we are supposed to do with them.

Reinforcing my sense that Reichardt's formal practice—in camerawork, film editing, sound design, shot type and duration—is a major, if not the major, contribution she makes, Klevan, again, provides a welcome, if unintended, gloss on her oeuvre: "The importance of these films is that they find aspects of style which do justice to the moments of life which do not proclaim their significance." When we watch and listen to Reichardt's films it is to "aspects of style" that we may be most turned around by; "the evanescence of the subject" is not spelled out by propulsive action nor by layered exposition (aside from her debut feature in 1994, there are no voiceovers). Rather, all is there to behold and listen to.

A Useful Criticism of an Art

As a limited number of films from the 1930s and 1940s provide Cavell with the means to identify (create?) two genres, in both cases, by the philosophical study of ordinary language—the things people say in their everyday lives (full of pathos, innuendo, double entendre, insult, seduction, and occasional ecstasy)—so we have, in Reichardt's films, instances that offer "a natural vision of film that every motion and station, in particular every human posture and gesture, however glancing, has its poetry, or you may say its lucidity."[113] In the place of the acrobatic genius of Chaplin and Keaton, we have the face of reflective, mournful introspection as found in Michelle Williams and John Magaro. Despite the bifurcated genres, and Cavell's preference for films where conversation defines the potentials of personhood and coupledom (especially in working out a demotic theory of Emersonian moral perfectionism), Cavell's remarks on the art and practice of "reading a film," nevertheless, provide ample room for thinking about Reichardt's decidedly different registers of cinematic expression and approach to the depiction of human speech. Far from the clattering city newsroom of *His Girl Friday*, there is yet much to discover in the verdant, tranquil forests of Cascadia.[114]

Let us read, or reread, some of Cavell's tuitions about how to read a film, this time with Reichardt's films before us:

> Checking one's experience is a rubric an American, or a spiritual American, might give to the empiricism practiced by Emerson and by Thoreau. I mean the rubric to capture the sense at the same time of consulting one's experience and of subjecting it to examination, and beyond these, of momentarily *stopping*, turning yourself away from whatever your preoccupation and turning your experience away from its expected, habitual track, to find itself, its own track: coming to attention.[115]

For a film critic who is masterfully attuned to the unyielding velocity of speech in Hollywood screwball comedies, it seems uncharacteristic (though welcome) to discover that he can also (and that we must also) stop and come to attention. As Cavell concludes, the pause is not for naught: "The moral of this practice is to educate your experience sufficiently so that it is worthy of trust."[116] For without this trust, "one is without authority in one's own experience." Once again, in explaining the origins and implications of these claims, Cavell reminds us: "In a similar mood, in *The Claim of*

Reason, I speak of being without a voice in one's own history."[117] So the reader of film—like the women in the melodramas of the unknown woman along with many characters in Reichardt's films—must find or discover the terms for making claims about the works of art that one finds worthy of one's time. "I think of this authority," Cavell writes, "as the right to take an interest in your own experience."[118] And film shows this and enables this in us, we "readers" of film, and writers on it. By being availed of these lives—glimpses of the everyday experience of ordinary people in the "appropriate time for that story"[119] and their thinking on film—we are also poised to think for ourselves. Thus, mimesis gives way to exemplarity; so in our lives as in our film criticism.

"A work one cares about," Cavell suggests, "is not so much something one has read as something one is a reader of."[120] One's relationship with a film—including one's relationship with the actors and characters it contains—goes on, perpetually, so long as one remains summoned by it, under its spell. Thus, when Cavell writes that "[s]o far as philosophy is a matter of caring about texts, meditation is its work before argumentation," we are given an invitation (first as permission, then as exhortation) to slow down, indeed, as noted above, to stop. (Let us call this a latent attribute of slow cinema that should be more widely heralded.) The moviegoer, the critic, whoever, is positioned to notice what is happening in the film and what is happening within herself. When one of the most prominent film critics, therefore, declares that, say, *Meek's Cutoff* is "almost punitive to sit through," and "Reichardt is a pleasureless artist," we are justified in worrying about appreciation for what is, in fact, on offer.[121] This "caring about texts" is already a tremendous amount of work, even before anything like a coherent criticism or an argument or theory might be launched in gratitude for or defense of them. One of the difficulties and pleasures of so many works of contemplative, slow, and transcendental cinema is the "trance-like" state they can cultivate—a feeling that is, as one might expect, (naturally?) resistant to consecutive thought or conscious awareness; as viewers, we are permitted to dwell without an immediate demand to explain ourselves. Faced with an invitation to the numinous, the sacramental, even, the films before us do not seem to call (first) for analysis so much as for repeated viewings—as if their contribution to our lives were in offering space for a kind of devotional practice (again, an awareness of routine and repetition without submitting to the possible banality of routine and repetition). Indeed, the very terminology in circulation—"contemplative," "slow," "transcendental"—befits certain religious, mystical, and meditative practices; this valence certainly gives flight to Schrader's contributions on the sacred dimensions of the art.[122]

Cavell's canon of films are, we are inclined to say, inherently philosophical: they not only provide a wealth of reflection—are studded with "words for a conversation"[123]—but are also filled with enticing allusions (e.g., to

Plato, to Shakespeare, to Thoreau) that demand our careful research and commentary. By contrast, Reichardt's films create an environment in which attention to the present moment overshadows what has come before and what is to come after, after words; these filmed realities are not orchestrated to drive narration, or to expose a character's inner life or her relationship to the inner lives of other characters. If, or when, Reichardt's films admit narrative shape, such results are not defined by fast, loud action (as in the blockbuster), clever mise-en-abyme (as in metacinema), exposure of the gruesome and grotesque (as in thrillers), unmoored pathos (as in melodrama), or witty, acerbic dialogue (as in comedy), but attuned to human behavior in its untutored, unstructured immediacy.

Unlike the films that occupy Cavell's genres, or, more recently, those made by Charlie Kaufman, Reichardt's films are not populated by characters who tirelessly work to articulate their intellectual commitments or romantic interests; they are, instead, caught up in the moment at hand: tending to urgent needs, navigating without clear instructions (from within or without), trying to survive in the midst of a heavy load of unknowns. Contrast Reichart's dwelling on the realist mise-en-scène with Kaufman's surrealist experiments (including with stop-motion animation), defined as they are by a focus on interiority, subjectivity, dreamtime, recursion, and fractal logic; Reichardt, instead, turns things inside out for close observation of exteriors and exteriority; the fragmentariness and fragility of lived time; the presence and placement of objects and animals as we find them; the physical expressiveness of human faces and bodies; and the things people say, or as crucially, do not. Unlike Kaufman's obsessives, depressives, and solipsists, Reichardt's characters are not prone to incessant questioning of oneself or others (indeed, a quality recognizable in Cavell's comedies and melodramas).[124] Our time with her characters, especially since *Wendy and Lucy*, allows for quiet unfolding, with almost no demand to sort, sift, or affix grander meaning for the lives we bear witness to. There is Cookie Figowitz turning over a stranded salamander—a gesture that is allowed to remain self-evidently tender.

Cavell intended his ruminations on the ontology of film to be taken symbolically, for example, as "mythological descriptions of the state of someone in the grip of a movie."[125] Those who complain about the pace of Reichardt's films, or the lives she attends to, or how she chooses to share those lives with us, are likely not in their grip, not absorbed, not "sutured," but instead alienated—as if she means to create a *Verfremdungseffekt*. "But *my* films are not *slow*!," she counters, her emphasis firmly in place. "I get told they're slow a lot [. . .]. What's everyone's problem?!"[126] (She recalls, after a screening of *Ode*, that the famed experimental filmmaker Ken Jacobs "booed me."[127]) Reichardt's own figure—metabolism—seems fitting, for we are wondering what it means to be in the grip of the everyday and the ordinary, what Cavell sometimes calls "the uneventful."[128] In Reichardt's work, time and again, it seems much is uneventful and yet consequential.

Attending to the way slow cinemas interact or overlap with contemplative ones, Elena Gorfinkel suggests that "slow films evacuate eventfulness [. . .] in pursuit of dedramatized scenarios in which incident replaces event"; they "privileg[e] scenes of empty time and waiting, and a durational aesthetic embedded in the use of extended long takes."[129] Whether slow or contemplative, such a logic, or network of preoccupations, is commonly reversed in high-budget, mainstream fare, where each moment is presented as gravely important and yet, somehow, without consequence (e.g., the body count of many films and series is often beyond comprehension, not to mention the multiplicity of graphic illustrations of those deaths); thus, stocked and yet strangely vacant. For many people, perhaps informed or fated by certain filmic "metabolisms," watching cacophonous, briskly-paced films of dynamic spectacle (among them, installments from Marvel, DC, and Disney, and the *Fast & Furious* and *Mission Impossible* juggernauts; many Westerns, war films, neo-peplum, and crime scene procedurals; Christopher Nolan's propulsive, often-punishing soundscapes along with the crash and crack of John Wick, James Bond, Jason Bourne, and beyond) would appear to find them *abandon* the everyday—courted to dissociative states, coaxed to enter escapist fantasies, all the while confirmed in the pleasures of *schaulust*; pre-show "warnings" of imminent content—"gore," "suicide," "sexual violence," "substances," "torture," and judiciously nondescript euphemisms: "disturbing images," "thematic elements," and "language throughout"—are commonly received with a shrug, and for some, welcomed with a willing rush to the front row. Viewers are absorbed—gripped—by the film and, by degrees, increasingly absent from their own lives; what of the moral and pedagogical salience of art well-known since Greek antiquity? Moreover, some audiences have become habituated, at once seemingly addicted and inured, to the rapid visual cadence and audio assault of many theatrical releases (so much so that in recent Nolan works, ironically, blaring sonic blasts make it very hard to hear what some characters are saying); by contrast, Reichardt's films may seem quiet, may feel slow. The pejorative sense of "slow" emerges, then, mainly by comparison with some popular, if unstated, standard for how films should look and sound (admittedly an evolving benchmark, but, over the long term, one that admits of an undeniable trend of increased velocity and volume). In opposition to the otherworldly presentations of the big-budget entertainments, Reichardt's films would appear to mimic the shape, pacing, structure, and content of the everyday as we find it in ritual practice and diurnal rhythm, "conveying routine and repetition," as Klevan says, "without submitting to the possible banality of routine."[130] Watching these films, therefore, is not about escaping from the everyday but discovering new ways of attending to it, finding companionship for occupying lived reality.[131] Far from the alien encounter or intergalactic fight, the blood-splattered homocide or lascivious rendezvous, contemplative cinema, as Reichardt practices it, puts us back on the ground, dwelling in the immediate conditions of consciousness—inviting us to look, to listen to the world before us and within us.

The purported "trance-like" states that Reichardt alludes to—as *effects* of watching her films—suggest a tacit partition: those movies that nurture immersive conditions favorable for honing concentration versus works whose immersive conditions yield distraction instead. Among other consequences, the former conditions would intensify one's focus on the present moment, including one's states of mind as a cinephile, while the other modes of film art would turn us in countervailing directions. By this point in the assessment of such apparently contrasting film practices (and their divergent results), there may be a sense of an insidious moralism or a misplaced nostalgia, but the pressure is rather on accounting for observations of aesthetic differences that may or may not cash out morally, or have perfectionist implications; earlier generations of cinema, such as mainstream American movies from the 1980s, had their share of alarming moral and aesthetic issues—so the present moment is not singular, even if scale and scope have shifted radically. Looking back even further, to another scene of how we live with cinema, recall the studio/audience arrangement familiar to many classic screwball comedies: stories about elites for the masses suffering the Great Depression and World War II. In the present—in the new millennium, perhaps especially in the wake of the Great Recession—however, the "elitism" that tracks moral perfectionism could be heard as a whispered suggestion that we have, in fact, found "elitist" art that is not about elites. Wouldn't be the first time (see the Renaissance), but the dynamic of art and audience is in many cases, nevertheless, conspicuously scrambled: for instance, where the Golden Age found elites making art about elites for an impoverished and weary mass audience (though, as Cavell showed, often with a knack for invoking, even championing, democratic ideals, including equality), in recent decades we descry "elites" making art about impoverished and weary masses for "elite" audiences (which is a way of saying those viewers who have an inclination and an opportunity to take movies seriously). While the narratives of Cavell's genres embody perfectionist projects—a willingness to be educated by experience with others—the perfectionist potential of Reichardt's films, if it is latent, would not be found so much in their content as in their form. Processing the aesthetic effects of her films on their own terms may leave us wondering what our movie-watching life would be like, for example, if her film style became a more pronounced component of popular entertainment. As Reichardt's profile continues to grow—her work increasingly celebrated and influential—perhaps we are already gleaning a reply.

Back in 1971, Cavell said that "the aesthetic possibilities of a medium are not givens."[132] Yet, a half-century later, we remain in the same condition. We are reminded, then, not to pursue the resolution of such possibilities, but to continue exploring them—giving an account of our experience of what the medium affords in the figure of diverse and remarkable instances.

> You can no more tell what will give significance to the unique and specific photographic images by thinking about them or seeing some, than you can tell what will give significance to the possibilities of paint by thinking about paint or by looking some over. You have to think about painting and paintings; you have to think about motion pictures. What does this "thinking about them" consist in? Whatever the useful criticism of an art consists in.[133]

And as Noël Carroll asks and answers in response to Cavell: "in what does the useful criticism of an art form consist? Presumably in the identification of the significance of an artwork and the particular way in which the significance in question gets made."[134] What does "thinking about" Reichardt's films consist in? And what sort of useful criticism of her art can we offer? As the name implies, "contemplative" cinema creates and encourages a space for thinking, for an awareness of thinking—and not just self-consciousness, in a standard (usually Western) philosophical sense (where we feel an "I" in relation to a "thou"), but indeed, what is sometimes called nondual mindfulness, that is, collapsing, or unifying, subject and object; becoming aware that thoughts are occurring, and of their own accord, one after another; noticing that we are not outside witnesses to our experiences but living directly as the condition of experience (much as a movie is identical with its sounds and images). Being entranced by Reichardt's films would appear to break the stubborn cycle of one's own persistent mental loops, and usher in a more direct impression of the present moment (sensed, for example, as an instructive interaction between, or even at moments an uncanny union of, the diegetic and nondiegetic). The "trance-like" effects of her films could be metacognitive, but they could also involve a coming to awareness of somatic features of sheer existence, of a wider scope of mammalian sentience. Among the most promising, gratifying effects of contemplative cinema may be, ironically, a diminishment of conceptual thinking in trade for an achieved pre-or-post conceptual position; a screening, then, would become an experience we too may feel speechless to address, powerless to resolve. Perhaps it is tautological, then, to recognize that the qualities of attention summoned by Reichardt's movies counter distraction. The diminishment of plot, agency, startling sounds, "disturbing images," and frenzied exposition imbues her work with the experimental filmmaker's gift for giving us back to the world as we find it off screen—or could, assuming we take an interest in it.

Aware of the movie and aware of our awareness of the movie, the diegesis of Reichardt's films becomes present to us, or, better, doubly present: as an encounter with the lives we find on screen and as an experience for those watching and listening. And so we, in turn—as if in response to people worthy of our empathy—are present to the space and time they inhabit *and* to our own space and time; in this moment of contact between the world viewed and the world heard, we may then have a chance to be reoriented to our condition, less lost in thought and made better company for thinking— or just better company.[135] In Reichardt's cinematic realms we can study the everyday beyond ourselves, next to us ("in a sane sense"[136]—if not in a knowing one), neighboring us, tutoring us. We watch and listen to another's variously familiar and fraught existence—taking care of the horses, having a solitary run in the woods, walking across the plains, driving on the highway, making camp, sorting vegetables, cooking a meal, contending with emergencies, welcoming small mercies, marveling at the sounds of nature, and yes, conversing with others too. Recurrently in Reichardt's films, the camera—like so many of the characters we find within the frame—wonders at the world it finds before it. It looks. It listens. It stands in awe. For Kelly Reichardt's cinematic art, we are poised not just to assess "the aesthetic possibilities of a medium," but also to seek out a "perception of the poetry of the ordinary" and appreciate—and perhaps in time also, articulate— "aspects of style which do justice to the moments of life which do not proclaim their significance." In this work of cinematic reading and listening, now and in the time to come, it is profitable to have Stanley Cavell in mind.

Notes

1 See Stanley Cavell, *Pursuits of Happiness: The Hollywood Comedy of Remarriage* (Cambridge: Harvard University Press, 1981), 49, 105, 172. See also Lawrence F. Rhu, "Monsters and Felicities: Vernacular Transformations of the Five-Foot Shelf," in *Inheriting Stanley Cavell: Memories, Dreams, Reflections*, ed. David LaRocca (New York: Bloomsbury, 2020), 170, 176.

2 Stanley Cavell, "*It Happened One Night*," *Cities of Words: Pedagogical Letters on a Register of the Moral Life* (Cambridge: The Belknap Press of Harvard University Press, 2004), 153, 155.

3 Sean Burns, "Harvard Film Archive Celebrates the Contemplative Cinema of Kelly Reichardt," *The Artery*, March 5, 2020. www.wbur.org/artery. Reichardt was a 2019-20 Baby Jane Holzer Visiting Artist in Film at Harvard University. The Harvard Film Archive screened a retrospective of her feature films, "Traveling Light: The Films of Kelly Reichardt," March 1–13, 2020.

4 See Shoshana Felman, *The Scandal of the Speaking Body: Don Juan with J. L. Austin, or Seduction in Two Languages* (Stanford: Stanford University Press, 2002; orig. pub. Ithaca: Cornell University Press, 1983).

5 Rachel Sykes, *The Quiet Contemporary American Novel* (Manchester: Manchester University Press, 2018).

6 Ludwig Wittgenstein, *Tractatus Logico-Philosophicus*, trans. D. F. Pears and B. F. McGuinness (London: Routledge, 1961 [1921]), 74.

7 Ella Taylor, "Trapped Under the Big Sky," *Certain Women, The Criterion Collection*, 2016.

8 See, for example, Stanley Cavell, "Knowing and Acknowledging," in *Must We Mean What We Say? A Book of Essays* (Cambridge: Cambridge University, 1976; Charles Scribner's Sons, 1969), 238–66. See also my "Achilles' Tears: Cavell, the *Iliad*, and Possibilities for the Human," in *Stanley Cavell on Aesthetic Understanding*, ed. Garry L. Hagberg (New York: Palgrave-Macmillan, 2018), 197–237.

9 Stanley Cavell, "Macbeth Appalled," in *Disowning Knowledge in Seven Plays of Shakespeare* (Cambridge: Cambridge University Press, 1987, updated edition, 2003), 223.

10 Ibid., 223.

11 Stanley Cavell, "In the Place of the Classroom," *Cities of Words*, 24.

12 Ibid.

13 Ibid., 1, 49, 164.

14 Ibid., 24. See below n.71.

15 Patrick Mackie, "In Memory of Stanley Cavell," *The Paris Review*, June 21, 2018. www.theparisreview.org.

16 Emerson, "Self-Reliance," in *Essays: First Series, The Complete Works of Ralph Waldo Emerson*, Concord Edition (Boston: Houghton, Mifflin and Company, 1904), Vol. II, 52.

17 Mackie, "In Memory of Stanley Cavell," *The Paris Review*.

18 Cavell, "Macbeth Appalled," *Disowning Knowledge*, 224.

19 Thoreau, "Where I Lived, and What I Lived For," in *Walden; or, Life in the Woods* (New York: The Library of America, 1991), 74.

20 Stanley Cavell, "Types; Cycles as Genres," in *The World Viewed: Reflections on the Ontology of Film* (Cambridge: Harvard University Press, 1971, Enlarged Edition, 1979), 36.

21 Stanley Cavell, "The Fact of Television," in *Themes Out of School: Effects and Causes* (San Francisco: North Point Press, 1984), 242. See also Stephen Mulhall, "What a Genre of Film Might Be: Medium, Myth, and Morality," in *The Thought of Stanley Cavell and Cinema: Turning Anew to the Ontology of Film a Half-Century after* The World Viewed, ed. David LaRocca (New York: Bloomsbury, 2020), 88–104; Leger Grindon, "Cycles and Clusters: The Shape of Film Genre History," in *Film Genre Reader IV*, ed. Barry Keith Grant (Austin: University of Texas Press, 2012), 42–59; and my "'One of the Most Phenomenal Debut Films in the History of Movies': *The Sugarland Express* as Expression of Spielberg's 'Movie Sense' and as Contribution to a Genre Cycle," in *A Companion to Steven Spielberg*, ed. Adam Barkman and Antonio Sanna (Lanham: Lexington Books, 2019), 39–50.

22 Elena Gorfinkel, "Exhausted Drift: Austerity, Dispossession and the Politics of Slow in Kelly Reichardt's *Meek's Cutoff*, in *Slow Cinema*, ed. Tiago de Luca and Nuno Barradas Jorge (Edinburgh: Edinburgh University Press, 2016), ch. 8. See also Theodore Martin, *Contemporary Drift: Genre, Historicism, and the Problem of the Present* (New York: Columbia University Press, 2017), 8, 132, 158–60.
23 Ibid.
24 Charlie Kaufman, *Adaptation.: The Shooting Script* (New York: Newmarket Press, 2002), 68.
25 Stanley Cavell, "Must We Mean What We Say?," in *Must We Mean What We Say?*, 36 n.31. For more on sound in cinema, see Kyle Stevens, "The World Heard," *The Thought of Stanley Cavell and Cinema*, 63–87.
26 Stanley Cavell, Introduction and "Naughty Orators: Negation of Voice in Gaslight," in *Contesting Tears: The Hollywood Melodrama of the Unknown Woman* (Chicago: The University of Chicago Press, 1996), 6, 47.
27 Ibid., 47.
28 Ibid.
29 Katherine Fusco and Nicole Seymour, "An Interview with Kelly Reichardt," in *Kelly Reichardt* (Urbana: University of Illinois Press, 2017), 114.
30 *Night Moves*, 07:47-08:02. The documentary being screened was made by Larry Fessenden, who starred in and edited *River of Grass*.
31 Cavell, Introduction, *Contesting Tears*, 3.
32 Ibid.
33 Christopher Bruno, "Lost in America: The Cinema of Kelly Reichardt," *Tiny Mix Tapes*, March 28, 2016. tinymixtapes.com. Burns, "Harvard Film Archive Celebrates."
34 Scott Roxborough, "*First Cow* Helmer Explains How She Brought a Female Perspective to the Western Genre," *The Hollywood Reporter*, February 21, 2020. www.hollywoodreporter.com.
35 Though "thriller" or perhaps low-key, slow burn thriller may work for Reichardt's *Night Moves* (she calls it "my '*action film*'—[. . .] a thriller, with a small *t*," [Fusco and Seymour, "An Interview with Kelly Reichardt," 115]), one is also reminded of Arthur Penn's neo-noir of the same name from 1975 staring Gene Hackman. Reichardt's entire film passes before any detectives arrive—and perhaps none will.
36 *Old Joy*, 18:23-19:04.
37 For crucial remarks on emergency—and emergence—as they function in Reichardt's work, see Fusco and Seymour, *Kelly Reichardt*. See also the film-by-film analysis of E. Dawn Hall in her *ReFocus: The Films of Kelly Reichardt* (Edinburgh: Edinburgh University Press, 2018) along with her excellent suite of contributions: "Gender Politics in Kelly Reichardt's Feminist Western *Meek's Cutoff*," in *Women's Authorship and Genre in Film*, ed. Katarzyna Paszkiewicz and Mary Harrod (New York: Routledge,

2017); "*Old Joy*: Resisting Masculinity," in *US Independent Filmmaking After 1989: Possible Films*, ed. Claire Perkins and Con Verevis (Edinburgh: Edinburgh University Press, 2015), 177–90; and "Labor Pains: Exploring Gendered Dimensions of Production, Creativity, and Career with a Look at Kelly Reichardt," in *The Projector: A Journal on Film, Media, and Culture*, ed. Cynthia Baron and Rosalind Sibielski (Bowling Green State University, 2015).

38 Ella Taylor, "Trapped Under the Big Sky," *Certain Women, The Criterion Collection*, 2016.
39 Fusco and Seymour, "An Interview with Kelly Reichardt," *Kelly Reichardt*, 114.
40 *River of Grass*, 20:29-20:50.
41 See *Filmspotting*, episode 786. "Kelly Reichardt/*First Cow*," July 24, 2020.
42 Jeff Grace composed the music for *Night Moves* as well as *Meek's Cutoff* before and *Certain Women* after.
43 See my "Thinking of Film: What Is Cavellian about Malick's Movies?," in *A Critical Companion to Terrence Malick*, ed. Joshua Sikora (Lanham: Lexington Books of Rowman & Littlefield, 2020), 3–19 and "How to Do Things with Slow Cinema in Hollywood: Temporal Duration in the Diegetic and Nondiegetic Worlds of *Cast Away*," in *A Critical Companion to Robert Zemeckis*, ed. Adam Barkman and Antonio Sanna (Lanham: Lexington Books of Rowman & Littlefield, 2020), 171–85.
44 Manohla Dargis and A. O. Scott, "In Defense of the Slow and the Boring," *The New York Times*, June 3, 2011. For the disparagement that summoned the defense, see Dan Kois, "Eating Your Cultural Vegetables," *The New York Times*, April 29, 2011, and Dan Kois, "Reaching for Culture That Remains Stubbornly above My Grasp," *The New York Times Magazine*, May 1, 2011, 52.
45 See Ira Jaffe, *Slow Movies: Countering the Cinema of Action* (New York: Wallflower Press/Columbia University Press, 2014), *Slow Cinema*, ed. Tiago de Luca and Nuno Barradas Jorge (Edinburgh: Edinburgh University Press, 2016); *The Long Take: Critical Approaches*, ed. John Gibbs and Douglas Pye (New York: Palgrave-Macmillan, 1017); and Emre Çağlayan, *Poetics of Slow Cinema: Nostalgia, Absurdism, Boredom* (New York: Palgrave-Macmillan, 2018).
46 Kelly Reichardt, "Elaborated Time," https://youtu.be/avlWhOxnlMU
47 See William Rothman, "Against 'The System of the Suture,'" *Film Quarterly* 29, no. 1 (Autumn 1975): 45–50. Lindsay Zoladz, "Designing Music to Create a Mood," *The New York Times*, November 8, 2020.
48 Thoreau, "Sounds," *Walden*, 91.
49 Kelly Reichardt, "Elaborated Time," https://youtu.be/avlWhOxnlMU
50 Ibid.
51 Paul Schrader, *Transcendental Style in Film: Ozu, Bresson, Dreyer* (Berkeley: University of California Press, 1972), 65.
52 Ibid.

53 Ibid.
54 "Newspaper," starring Zooey Deschanel, *Saturday Night Live*, February 11, 2012. https://www.nbc.com/saturday-night-live/video/newspaper/n13388.
55 Raymond Gaita, "Introduction: Take Your Time," in *A Common Humanity: Thinking about Love and Truth and Justice* (London: Routledge, 1998), 16. See also David Mikics, *Slow Reading in a Hurried Age* (Cambridge: Harvard University Press, 2013) and Michelle Boulous Walker, *Slow Philosophy: Reading against the Institution* (New York: Bloomsbury, 2017), 15.
56 Stanley Cavell, "The Acknowledgment of Silence," *The World Viewed*, 150.
57 Ibid.
58 Ibid.
59 Stevens, "The World Heard," *The Thought of Stanley Cavell and Cinema*, 81.
60 Cavell, "The Acknowledgment of Silence," *The World Viewed*, 150.
61 Lisa Zunshine, *Why We Read Fiction: Theory of Mind and the Novel* (Columbus: The Ohio State University Press, 2006) and Blakey Vermeule, *Why Do We Care about Literary Characters?* (Baltimore: The Johns Hopkins University Press, 2010).
62 Cavell, "The Acknowledgment of Silence," *The World Viewed*, 146.
63 Noël Carroll, "Revisiting *The World Viewed*," *The Thought of Stanley Cavell and Cinema*, 59.
64 Cavell, "The Acknowledgment of Silence," *The World Viewed*, 147.
65 Ibid., 146.
66 Stevens, "The World Heard," *The Thought of Stanley Cavell and Cinema*, 69.
67 Cavell, "The Acknowledgment of Silence," *The World Viewed*, 147.
68 Ibid.
69 Ibid., 148. For additional remarks on this passage, see Stevens, "The World Heard," *The Thought of Stanley Cavell and Cinema*, 72–74.
70 Cavell, "The Acknowledgment of Silence," *The World Viewed*, 149.
71 David LaRocca, "Philosophy's Claim to Film, Film's Claim to Philosophy," *The Thought of Stanley Cavell and Cinema*, 15 n.40. See also Scott MacDonald, "My Troubled Relationship with Stanley Cavell: In Pursuit of a Truly Cinematic Conversation," *The Thought of Stanley Cavell and Cinema*, 107–20.
72 P. Adams Sitney, "Apologies to Stanley Cavell," in *Conversations: The Journal of Cavellian Studies*, No. 7: *Acknowledging Stanley Cavell*, ed. David LaRocca (June 19, 2019), 13.
73 Dave Burnham, "Turning to Nature: Cavell and Experimental Cinema," in *Discourse*, "Cinema, Modernism, and the Perplexing Methods of Stanley Cavell" 42, nos. 1–2 (2020): 174–75.
74 For more on Cavell on Malick with reference to experimental and avant-garde film, see my "Thinking of Film: What Is Cavellian about Malick's Movies?," 3–19 and the concluding pages of "On the Aesthetics of Amateur

Filmmaking in Narrative Cinema: Negotiating Home Movies after *Adam's Rib*," *The Thought of Stanley Cavell and Cinema*, 245–90. In the context of thinking through Cavell's *philosophical* relationship to Malick's films, it might be useful to note concisely that Malick's cinematic affiliations align compelling with the philosophy of Martin Heidegger (and his call to Being, his pursuit of clearings and illuminations, his theorizing of *aletheia* [ἀλήθεια]), while Cavell's attunement to the later Wittgenstein and the ordinary language philosophy of J. L. Austin are a more intuitive match for Cavell's interest in speech, conversation, and "what we say when." For Cavell on Marker, see Stanley Cavell, "The World as Things: Collecting Thoughts on Collecting," in *Cavell on Film*, ed. William Rothman (Albany: State University of New York Press, 2005), 270–72, 369. For Cavell on Brakhage, see Stanley Cavell, "Concluding Remarks Presented at Paris Colloquium on *La Projection du monde*," *Cavell on Film*, 282.

75 Cavell, "The Acknowledgment of Silence," *The World Viewed*, 152–53. See again Stevens, "The World Heard," *The Thought of Stanley Cavell and Cinema*, 63–87, esp. 74–75.

76 Stevens, "The World Heard," *The Thought of Stanley Cavell and Cinema*, 84 n.31. See also Richard Moran, "Stanley Cavell on Recognition, Betrayal, and the Photographic Field of Expression," in *The Harvard Review of Philosophy* 23 (2016): 29–40.

77 Thoreau, "Sounds," *Walden*, 94.

78 Andrew Klevan, "Cavell at Film Criticism: 'An Unreadiness to Become Explicit,'" in *Inheriting Stanley Cavell: Memories, Dreams, Reflections*, ed. David LaRocca (New York: Bloomsbury, 2020), 61–68.

79 Cavell, "The Same and Different: *The Awful Truth*," *Pursuits of Happiness*, 231.

80 See MacDonald, "My Troubled Relationship with Stanley Cavell," *The Thought of Stanley Cavell and Cinema*, 107–20, esp. 113–17.

81 *Certain Women*, 50:05-50:40.

82 David Denby, "Strange Trips," *The New Yorker*, April 4, 2011.

83 For more on this topic, see my "Performative Inferentialism: A Semiotic Ethics," in *Liminalities: A Journal of Performance Studies*, vol. 9, no. 2 (Summer 2013): 1–26.

84 Stanley Cavell, *The Claim of Reason: Wittgenstein, Skepticism, Morality, and Tragedy* (Oxford: Oxford University Press, 1979), 351.

85 Stanley Cavell, "Introduction: Staying the Course," in *Conditions Handsome and Unhandsome: The Constitution of Emersonian Perfectionism* (Chicago: The University of Chicago Press, 1990), 1.

86 Sam Adams, "Kelly Reichardt and Jon Raymond," in *AV Club*, April 26, 2011. www.film.avclub.com.

87 Emanuel Levy, *Cinema of Outsiders: The Rise of American Independent Film* (New York: New York University Press, 1999), 402.

88 Gorfinkel, "Exhausted Drift," *Slow Cinema*, ch. 8; Cavell, "Introduction: Staying the Course," *Conditions Handsome and Unhandsome*, 1.

89 Cavell, Introduction, *Contesting Tears*, 9.
90 Ibid., 43.
91 Ibid.
92 Ibid., "Psychoanalysis and Cinema: Moments of *Letter from an Unknown Woman*," *Contesting Tears*, 106.
93 Cavell, "The Acknowledgment of Silence," *The World Viewed*, 150.
94 Cavell, "Postscript: To Whom It May Concern," *Contesting Tears*, 161.
95 Ibid., 180.
96 Fusco and Seymour, "An Interview with Kelly Reichardt," *Kelly Reichardt*, 115.
97 Ibid., 15.
98 Ibid.
99 Stanley Cavell, "Thinking of Emerson," in *Emerson's Transcendental Etudes*, ed. David Justin Hodge (Stanford: Stanford University Press, 2003), 19 and 252 n.12. See also 39, 172, 222 and my "Reading Cavell Reading," in *Stanley Cavell, Literature, and Film: The Idea of America*, ed. Andrew Taylor and Áine Kelly (New York: Routledge, 2013), 26–41.
100 Cavell, "The Acknowledgment of Silence," *The World Viewed*, 150.
101 Stanley Cavell, "The Thought of Movies," *Themes Out of School*, 14. On this and related points, see also Andrew Klevan, "Notes on Stanley Cavell and Philosophical Film Criticism," in *New Takes in Film-Philosophy*, ed. Havi Carel and Greg Tuck (New York: Palgrave Macmillan, 2011), 48–64.
102 Ibid.
103 Ibid.
104 James Schiff, "Robinson and Updike: Houses, Domesticity, and the Numinous Quotidian," in *This Life, This World: New Essays on Marilynne Robinson's* Housekeeping, Gilead, *and* Home, ed. Jason W. Stevens (Leiden: Brill, 2015), 137–53.
105 Ralph Waldo Emerson, "The American Scholar," *The Complete Works of Ralph Waldo Emerson*, Vol. I, 111. See also my "A Conversation among Critics," in *Estimating Emerson: An Anthology of Criticism from Carlyle to Cavell*, ed. David LaRocca (New York: Bloomsbury, 2013), 16, and Stanley Cavell, "Aversive Thinking: Emersonian Representations in Heidegger and Nietzsche," *Emerson's Transcendental Etudes*, 142.
106 Cavell, "The Thought of Movies," *Themes Out of School*, 14.
107 Fusco and Seymour, "An Interview with Kelly Reichardt," *Kelly Reichardt*, 113–14.
108 Andrew Klevan, "Conclusion: The Unemphatic Achievement," in *Disclosure of the Everyday: Undramatic Achievement in Narrative Film* (Trowbridge: Flicks Books, 2000), 209. See also his "Guessing the Unseen from the Seen: Stanley Cavell and Film Interpretation," in *Contending with Stanley Cavell*, ed. Russell Goodman (Oxford: Oxford University Press, 2005), 118–39.
109 Andrew Klevan's interview with Kelly Reichardt was recorded at St. Anne's College, University of Oxford, on May 29th, 2014, and is included on a

Blu-ray DVD box set featuring *Old Joy*, *Wendy and Lucy*, and *Meek's Cutoff* released in the United Kingdom. At the time, she held the Humanitas Visiting Professorship in Film and Television at the University of Oxford.

110 Fusco and Seymour, "An Interview with Kelly Reichardt," *Kelly Reichardt*, 115.

111 *Night Moves*, 57:46-59:15. Compare a similarly structured long take in a pick-up truck at the end of *Certain Women*, when The Rancher drives away from her consequential last encounter with Elizabeth.

112 Fusco and Seymour, "An Interview with Kelly Reichardt," *Kelly Reichardt*, 115.

113 Cavell, "The Thought of Movies," *Themes Out of School*, 14.

114 See Matthew Holtmeier, "Communicating Cascadia: Reichardt's Three Ecologies as Bioregional Medium," in *Screen* 58, no. 4 (2017): 477–96.

115 Stanley Cavell, "Words for a Conversation," *Pursuits of Happiness*, 12; italics in original.

116 Ibid.

117 Ibid. See also Cavell, *The Claim of Reason*, 486.

118 Cavell, "Words for a Conversation," *Pursuits of Happiness*, 12.

119 Fusco and Seymour, "An Interview with Kelly Reichardt," *Kelly Reichardt*, 115.

120 Cavell, "Words for a Conversation," *Pursuits of Happiness*, 13.

121 Denby, "Strange Trips," *The New Yorker*, April 11, 2011. For counterbalance among mainstream film critics, consider A. O. Scott's "Out on the Frontier, Bringing All That Baggage With Them," where the same film is described as a "tough, quiet revelation of a movie," and the "wise and self-assured" Reichardt "films it in an uninflected style that makes everything feel at once mundane and mysterious." *The New York Times*, April 8, 2011.

122 See Schrader, *Transcendental Style in Film*.

123 A phrase drawn from the title of the introduction to *Pursuits of Happiness*.

124 For more on Charlie Kaufman, including his relation to Cavell, see *The Philosophy of Charlie Kaufman*, ed. David LaRocca (Lexington: University Press of Kentucky, 2011; with a new Preface, 2019).

125 Cavell, "More of *The World Viewed*," *The World Viewed*, 211.

126 Fusco and Seymour, "An Interview with Kelly Reichardt," *Kelly Reichardt*, 115.

127 Ibid., 117.

128 See, for example, Stanley Cavell, "The Ordinary as the Uneventful (A Note on the *Annales* Historians)," *Themes Out of School*, 184–94, and "The Uncanniness of the Ordinary (The Tanner Lecture)," in *In Quest of the Ordinary: Lines of Skepticism and Romanticism* (Chicago: The University of Chicago Press, 1988), 153–78.

129 Gorfinkel, "Exhausted Drift," *Slow Cinema*, ch. 8.

130 Klevan, "Conclusion: The Unemphatic Achievement," *Disclosure of the Everyday*, 209.

131 For company on the topic of the realist expression of the everyday, and as a domestic counterpart to Reichardt's work out of doors and on the open road,

see, for example, Tiago de Luca, "Sensory Everyday: Space, Materiality, and the Body in the Films of Tsai Ming-liang," in *Journal of Chinese Cinemas* 5, no. 2 (2011): 157–79.

132 Cavell, "Types; Cycles as Genres," *The World Viewed*, 31.
133 Ibid.
134 Carroll, "Revisiting *The World Viewed*," *The Thought of Stanley Cavell and Cinema*, 48.
135 See Stevens, "The World Heard," *The Thought of Stanley Cavell and Cinema*, 63–87.
136 Henry David Thoreau, "Solitude," *Walden*, 109; Stanley Cavell, *The Senses of Walden: An Expanded Edition* (San Francisco: North Point Press, 1981; orig. pub. New York: The Viking Press, 1972), 104. See also Mark Greif, "Cavell as Educator," *Inheriting Stanley Cavell*, 84.

ACKNOWLEDGMENTS

First, to the contributors, I extend my deepest gratitude; it has been my privilege and a real pleasure to have partnered with you on this intellectual adventure. Your impressive industry, which I so admire and appreciate, has turned fourteen stunning, independent engagements—with Stanley Cavell in mind—into a genuine community of inquiry.

At Bloomsbury, Haaris Naqvi remains at the center of these endeavors—a steady force for new experiments in the form; this project, like the others, benefited from his good sense and wise counsel. Katie Gallof—thank you for your vision, confidence, and expertise; as with *The Thought of Stanley Cavell and Cinema*, the present volume reflects your perspicacity. And the editorial, design, and production teams, as ever, remain essential to achieving final fit and finish: Jenna Larson helped on the early side, while, once again, the marvelous Erin Duffy charted production. Faye Robinson and Mohammed Raffi kindly assisted with project management.

The phrasing that gave conceptual shape to the methodology of this collection—watching and listening to movies with Stanley Cavell in mind—has several points of origin and influence, among them, memorably: a National Endowment for the Humanities Institute in Santa Fe, where visits from Cavell and Cornel West underwrote the good fortune that found me in conversation—and watching "Cavell's films"—with William Rothman, William Day, Steven Affeldt, Russell Goodman, Timothy Gould, Lawrence Rhu, Richard Deming, and K. L. Evans; subsequent conferences on Cavell's work in Cambridge, Baltimore, Budapest, Edinburgh, and Paris; numerous encounters with the vibrant, generous, and incisive members, guests, and honorees of the Signet Society (including, on one memorable evening, Cavell himself); a class I taught in the Cinema Department at Binghamton University, "Love and Conversation in Film," in which we read *Pursuits of Happiness* (while also considering films beyond the book's canon that bore resemblances to, as well as refractions from, the standard bearers) and welcomed William Day to a generative session on *Adam's Rib*; ever since our days in Werner Herzog's Rogue Film School, steady, stimulating conversations with Paul Cronin have extended the limits of my film world: whether discussing Aristotle's *Poetics* alongside the work of Alexander Mackendrick (while he was pinch-hitting for Chantal Akerman at the City University of New York), or, more recently, teaching in his company at the School of Visual Arts, he continues to enliven the conditions for cinema pedagogy (including Cavell "in the place of the classroom"); likewise, teaching and talking upstate with Scott MacDonald, J. P. Sniadecki, Diana Allan, Patricia R. Zimmermann, Andrew Utterson, Matthew Holtmeier, and Chelsea Wessels has given shape to the potential of film instruction; corresponding with Garrett Stewart has afforded equal measures of collegial esprit and intellectual illumination, both mutually reinforcing; workshopping cinema with Abbas Kiarostami; analyzing information design with Edward Tufte; making films with Bill Jersey and the gifted documentarians of Bay Ridge—Robert Elfstrom and Rita Mullaney; in Ithaca, during installments of the School of Criticism and Theory, learning from and listening to Hent de Vries, Emily Apter, Shoshana Felman, Avishai Margalit, Michael Puett, and Anthony Vidler; in Israel, time spent at the Steve Tisch School of Film and Television at Tel Aviv University in the company of gracious hosts Shai Biderman and Ohad Landesman, at the Jerusalem Sam Spiegel Film School with Dan Geva, and also with Linda Williams and Thomas Wartenberg; at Lund University, exploring genre and *Geschlecht* with Oscar Jansson and his able colleagues in the Centre for Languages and Literatures and the Department of Comparative Literature; sharing good company for remembering at memorial proceedings in Cavell's honor in Cambridge; tracking Herzog's fate at New York University's Deutsches Haus with Richard Eldridge, Paul Cronin, Sukhdev Sandhu, Haaris Naqvi, and Thomas Elsaesser; in Paris, for "Le Pensée du cinéma: en hommage à Stanley Cavell," convened at Université Paris 1 Panthéon-Sorbonne, discussions with Sandra Laugier, Élise Domenach, Stephen Mulhall, Andrew Klevan, Alice Crary, Richard Moran, Hugo Clémot, Eric Ritter, Byron Davies, Kate Rennebohm, Paola Marrati, and, again, William Rothman; exchanging notes with Rex Butler, half-a-world away; and welcoming Thomas Elsaesser to Cornell for a visit that included a screening of his film, *Sun Island*, conversations with Amy Villarejo, Jeremy Braddock, Patrizia McBride, and Erik Born, and reflections on Cavell, which remain a highlight of the hours before he left us. Part of the labor of acknowledgment as we find it transfigured in the time of the novel coronavirus appears to be located in summoning the power of the counterfactual—and thereby mourning what was planned, what might have been. Still, for those seasons and sessions translated to the virtual realm, there is much to give thanks for, including the tenacity of friends, acquaintances, and colleagues who in the face of obstacles persist with good cheer.

Movies with Stanley Cavell in Mind joins other ventures undertaken in a similar spirit, ones recent enough that I can sustain and underscore my gratitude to the illustrious contributors on these several occasions, including *Acknowledging Stanley Cavell*, a commemorative issue of *Conversations: The Journal of Cavellian Studies* (with special regard for the journal's capable managing editors Amir Khan and Sérgio Dias Branco); *The Thought of Stanley Cavell and Cinema*; and *Inheriting Stanley Cavell*.

Garrett Stewart, Sandra Laugier, William Day, Lawrence Rhu, and Byron Davies were welcome interlocutors for my contributions here, as they have been for earlier projects.

I remain gratefully indebted to Sheldon and Lorna K. Hershinow, Ian M. Evans and Luanna H. Meyer, Frances LaRocca and Roselle Sweeney, David N. and Hi-jin Hodge.

As the subjective experience of time continues to evolve—in new ways, now deep into the era of the coronavirus pandemic—there are also the undeniable facts of, as it were, objective time, the time of mortality, loss, and lamentation. Circumstances fit to conjure melancholy, sure, but also to prompt refreshed appreciation. I find myself thinking about the teachers who created the conditions for thinking about the topics in this and related volumes, among them, Kah Kyung Cho, Caleb Thompson, Carolyn Korsmeyer, Barry Smith, Kenneth Dauber, John Lachs, J. M. Bernstein, Gregg Horowitz, David Wood, Anthony Cascardi, Michael Mascuch, Frederick Dolan, Stephanie Paulsell, Cornel West, Kimberley C. Patton, Donald K. Swearer, David D. Hall, Helmut Koester, Peter J. Gomes, Giuliana Bruno, Elizabeth Grosz, Despina Kakoudaki, Peggy Phelan, and Emily Apter. And then I recall with special vividness the contributions and exemplariness of Peter H. Hare, Newton Garver, Gordon D. Kaufman, and most conspicuously, of course, Stanley Cavell; day-to-day life remains informed not just by their tuitions but also their ways of inhabiting the world, relating to others, and enacting a disciplined continuity between the forms of ordinary life and the formation of ideas. Their disappearance has had the effect, as consequential departures often do, of amplifying their memory and their work, and ultimately, establishing their presence in a mode of absence.

From time's elapse to its burgeoning, I am grateful to share hours and days with Ruby and Star, and their remarkable mother, Kim. In parentage, as in marriage, there is much accounting—like Thoreau in his cabin at the edge of Walden Pond—much labor given over to "measuring the value of our lives," and discerning "what counts." We can say, after Cavell, that it is "as essential for the settings of our films"—whichever ones we address ourselves to and are, in turn, addressed by—"to be such that we can expect the characters in them to take the time, and take the pains, to converse intelligently and playfully about themselves and about one another." Our shared life together (as parents, children, spouses) summons us to these dictates, to investigate these dictations, as Cavell says of the apparitions that fill our screens, our hearts, and our heads: "Our critical task is to discover why they use their time as they do, why they say the things they say."

CONTRIBUTORS

SANDRA LAUGIER is Professor of Philosophy at Université Paris 1 Panthéon Sorbonne, Paris, France, and a Senior member of Institut Universitaire de France. She is co-Director of the Institut des sciences juridique et philosophique de la Sorbonne (Université Paris 1/CNRS). A former student of the Ecole Normale Supérieure and Harvard University, she has extensively published in French, English, Italian, and German on ordinary language philosophy (Wittgenstein, Austin, Cavell); moral perfectionism (Cavell, Thoreau, Emerson); popular culture (film and TV series), gender studies, democracy, and civil disobedience. She is the translator of Stanley Cavell's work into French and has written extensively on his work. She is a senior member of Institut Universitaire de France (2012, renewed in 2018), member of Academia Europea, and was awarded the Légion d'Honneur. Publications include: *Why We Need Ordinary Language Philosophy* (2013); *Recommencer la philosophie—Cavell et la philosophie américaine aujourd'hui* (2014); *Le principe démocratie*, with A. Ogien (2014); *Antidémocratie*, with A. Ogien (2017); *Formes de vie*, ed. with Estelle Ferrarese, 2018); and *Nos vies en séries* (2019). She is also a columnist for *Chronique Philosophiques* at the French journal *Libération*: www.liberation.fr/auteur/6377-sandra-laugier.

ROBERT B. PIPPIN is Evelyn Stefansson Nef Distinguished Service Professor of Social Thought, Philosophy, and in the College at the University of Chicago. He is a past winner of the Mellon Distinguished Achievement Award in the Humanities and a Guggenheim Fellowship, and he is a member of the American Academy of Arts and Sciences, the American Philosophical Society, and the German National Academy of Sciences Leopoldina. He works primarily on the modern German philosophical tradition, with a concentration on Kant and Hegel, and has published on theories of modernity, political philosophy, self-consciousness, the nature of conceptual change, and the problem of freedom. He has a number of interdisciplinary interests, especially those that involve the relation between philosophy and literature. He is the author of many books, including: *Henry James and Modern Moral Life* (2001); *The Persistence of Subjectivity: On the Kantian Aftermath* (2005); *Fatalism in American Film Noir: Some Cinematic Philosophy* (2013); *Hegel's Realm of Shadows: Logic as Metaphysics in*

The Science of Logic (2018); *The Philosophical Hitchcock: Vertigo and the Anxieties of Unknowningness* (2019); *Interanimations: Receiving Modern German Philosophy* (2015); and *Filmed Thought: Cinema as Reflective Form* (2019).

WILLIAM ROTHMAN is Professor of Cinema and Interactive Media in the School of Communication at the University of Miami. He received his PhD in Philosophy from Harvard, where he was Associate Professor in Visual and Environmental Studies (1976–84), and was Director of the International Honors Program on Film, Television and Social Change in Asia (1986–90). He was the founding editor and Series Editor of Harvard University Press's "Harvard Film Studies" series, and for many years was Series Editor of Cambridge University Press's "Studies in Film." His books include the landmark study *Hitchcock—The Murderous Gaze* (1982; expanded edition 2012), *The "I" of the Camera* (1988; expanded edition 2004); *Documentary Film Classics* (1997); *A Philosophical Perspective on Film* (2000); *Cavell on Film* (2005); *Jean Rouch: A Celebration of Life and Film* (2007); *Three Documentary Filmmakers* (2009); *Must We Kill the Thing We Love? Emersonian Perfectionism and the Films of Alfred Hitchcock* (2014); *Looking with Robert Gardner* (2016); and *Tuitions and Intuitions: Essays at the Intersection of Film Criticism and Philosophy* (2019).

BYRON DAVIES is Postdoctoral Research Fellow at the Institute for Philosophical Research, National Autonomous University of Mexico (UNAM). In 2018 he received his PhD from the Department of Philosophy at Harvard University. At UNAM he has recently taught graduate seminars on portraiture and aesthetics, as well as on point of view in painting and cinema. Among his publications are "Accidents Made Permanent: Theater and Automatism in Stanley Cavell, Michael Fried, and Matías Piñeiro" (forthcoming in *Modern Language Notes*) and "Individuality and Mortality in the Philosophy of Portrait-Painting: Simmel, Rousseau, and Melanie Klein" (2018).

STEVEN G. AFFELDT is Associate McDevitt Chair in Religious Philosophy and Faculty Director of the Manresa Program at Le Moyne College. He received his BA in philosophy from the University of California, Berkeley, and his PhD in philosophy from Harvard University (where he was a student of Stanley Cavell and, for many years, his research assistant). Deeply informed by Cavell's teaching and writing, Affeldt's research charts intersections of ethics, social/political philosophy, and aesthetics. Drawing on a wide range of figures that include Plato, Augustine, Rousseau, Kant, Emerson, Kierkegaard, Nietzsche, Freud, Heidegger, and Wittgenstein, his work elaborates ways in which philosophy and philosophical texts may be redemptive—possessed of the power to inspire, inform, and effect liberating transformations of both individuals and societies. He has published highly influential articles on Rousseau, Wittgenstein, and Stanley Cavell and is currently at work on a monograph explicating, and charting critical ramifications of, what he argues is a decisive turn in Cavell's work following *The Claim of Reason*—the turn from situating philosophy as a Modernist enterprise to situating it as a Romantic quest. Prior to his appointment at Le Moyne College, Affeldt was a Junior Fellow in the Society of Fellows at the University of Chicago and held teaching appointments at Johns Hopkins, Notre Dame, and the New School University.

JOSEPH MAI is Associate Professor of French, with an affiliation in World Cinema, at Clemson University. He is the author of *Jean-Pierre and Luc Dardenne* (2010), the first monograph on the Dardenne brothers. He has also published a book on neo-Aristotelian ideas about friendship and politics in the cinema of the Marseilles filmmaker Robert Guédiguian (*Robert Guédiguian*, 2017). He is coeditor with Leslie Barnes of *Everything Has a Soul: The Cinema of Rithy Panh* (2021). His articles have appeared in *Mosaic*, *Studies in French Cinema*, *New Review of Film and Television Studies*, *Studies in the Novel*, and other journals. Presently he is preparing a larger essay on "the French Cavell," examining both film criticism and production in France.

PAUL SCHOFIELD is Assistant Professor of Philosophy at Bates College in Lewiston, Maine. He completed his doctorate at Harvard University under the direction of Christine Korsgaard, T. M. Scanlon, and Richard Moran. He has published papers on Michael Powell and Emeric Pressburger's *The Red Shoes* and Michael Haneke's *Funny Games*. His articles have appeared in *Philosophy and Phenomenological Research*, *American Philosophical Quarterly*, *Journal of Political Philosophy*, and *Film-Philosophy*. His book *Duty to Self: Moral, Political, and Legal Self-Relation* is published with Oxford University Press (2021).

K. L. EVANS is the author of *Whale!* (2003) and *One Foot in the Finite: Melville's Realism Reclaimed* (2018), and coeditor, with Branka Arsić, of *Melville's Philosophies* (2017). A contributor to *Stanley Cavell: Philosophy, Literature, and Criticism* (2012), she has taught at the University of Redlands, Stern College of Yeshiva University in New York City, the College at Cortland, and for the Telluride Association Summer Program at Cornell University. A Fulbright Scholar who conducted research in New Zealand, she completed her doctoral studies under the direction of Kenneth Dauber. With Dauber, she contributed "Revisiting Ordinary Language Criticism" to *Inheriting Stanley Cavell* (2020). She has participated in multiple National Endowment for the Humanities Institutes and twice in the School of Criticism and Theory at Cornell University.

CATHERINE WHEATLEY is Senior Lecturer in Film Studies at King's College London. She is the author of *Stanley Cavell and Film: Scepticism and Self-Reliance at the Cinema* (2019), *Michael Haneke's Cinema: The Ethic of the Image* (2009), The BFI Film Classics book on Haneke's *Caché* (2011), and, with Lucy Mazdon, *Sex, Art and Cinephilia: French Cinema in Britain* (2013). Her scholarly work has appeared in journals, including *Paragraph*, *Film-Philosophy*, and *Studies in European Cinema*, and she is a regular contributor to the magazine *Sight & Sound*. Catherine also co-convenes the British Film Institute's *Philosophical Screens* series. She recently contributed a session on Cavellian perfectionism and Disney's *Moana* to the Fantasy-Animation podcast series.

CHARLES WARREN (1948–2021) taught film history and analysis at Harvard University and Boston University and in the Harvard Extension School. He studied and taught with Stanley Cavell at Harvard. He wrote *T. S. Eliot on Shakespeare* (1986) and was editor or coeditor of *Beyond Document: Essays on Nonfiction Film* (1996); *Jean-Luc Godard's Hail Mary: Women and the Sacred in Film* (1993); and *Looking with Robert Gardner* (2016). He worked with filmmaker Robert Gardner to produce the volumes *Making Dead Birds: Chronicle of a Film* (2008) and *Human Documents: Eight Photographers* (2009) and a collection of Gardner's essays, *Just Representations* (2010). He contributed essays on Cavell to *Film International* and to several books, and he wrote on music for the online journals *New York Arts* and *Berkshire Review for the Arts*. His final book, *Writ on Water: The Sources and Reach of Film Imagination*, was published posthumously by SUNY Press (2022).

DAVID MIKICS is John and Rebecca Moores Professor of English and Honors at the University of Houston. He is the author, most recently, of *Stanley Kubrick: American Filmmaker* in the Yale Jewish Lives series (2020). His earlier books include *Bellow's People* (2016), *The Annotated Emerson* (2012), and *Slow Reading in a Hurried Age* (2007), and he is a regular columnist for *Salmagundi* and *Tablet* (https://www.tabletmag.com/contributors/david-mikics). He lives in Brooklyn and Houston.

AMIR KHAN is Xinghai Associate Professor of English in the School of Foreign Languages at Dalian Maritime University, China. His books include *Comedies of Nihilism* (2017) and *Shakespeare in Hindsight* (2016). He is managing editor of *Conversations: The Journal of Cavellian Studies*. Born in Canada, he lives and works in China.

DANIELE RUGO is Reader in the Department of Arts and Humanities at Brunel University, London. He is the author of two monographs: *Jean-Luc Nancy and the Thinking of Otherness* (2013) and *Philosophy and the Patience of Film in Cavell and Nancy* (2016, foreword by Jean-Luc Nancy). He is coeditor with Nikolaj Lubecker of *James Benning's Environments* (2017), and his articles have appeared in journals, including *Angelaki*, *Third Text*, *Cultural Politics*, and *Film-Philosophy*.

KATE RENNEBOHM, having recently been a visiting faculty member at Harvard University, is currently a SSHRC Postdoctoral Fellow at Concordia University, Montréal. There, she is working on a book manuscript titled *Reviewing the Self-Image: Ethics, Politics, and Moving Image Media*. This book aims to uncover the presence of the "self-image" as a structuring phenomenon of moving image media in the twentieth century, arguing that practices of self-imaging and self-viewing introduced new forms of ethical thought and political praxis during this period. Her essay "The 'Cinema Remarks': Wittgenstein on Moving Image Media and the Ethics of Re-Viewing" was recently published in *October*.

DAVID LaROCCA is the author or contributing editor of more than a dozen books. Advised by Stanley Cavell during doctoral research, he later edited, annotated, and indexed Cavell's *Emerson's Transcendental Etudes* (2003) and worked as Cavell's research assistant during the time he was completing *Cities of Words: Pedagogical Letters on a Register of a Moral Life* (2004) and *Philosophy the Day after Tomorrow* (2005), and beginning *Little Did I Know: Excerpts from Memory* (2010). LaRocca subsequently edited additional books featuring Cavell's work, including *Estimating Emerson: An Anthology of Criticism from Carlyle to Cavell* (2013) and *The Bloomsbury Anthology of Transcendental Thought: From Antiquity to the Anthropocene* (2017), and contributed chapters to *Stanley Cavell, Literature, and Film: The Idea of America* (2013), *Stanley Cavell and Aesthetic Understanding* (2018), and *Understanding Cavell, Understanding Modernism* (2023). LaRocca served as guest editor of a commemorative issue of *Conversations: The Journal of Cavellian Studies*, No. 7 (2019): *Acknowledging Stanley Cavell*, and edited *The Thought of Stanley Cavell and Cinema: Turning Anew to the Ontology of Film a Half-Century after* The World Viewed (2020) and *Inheriting Stanley Cavell: Memories, Dreams, Reflections* (2020). He is the author of *On Emerson* (2003) and *Emerson's English Traits and the Natural History of Metaphor* (2013) and editor of a suite of books in film-philosophy: *The Philosophy of Charlie Kaufman* (2011), *The Philosophy of War Films* (2014), *The Philosophy of Documentary Film: Image, Sound, Fiction, Truth* (2017). He has contributed book chapters or articles on Werner Herzog, Terrence Malick, Michael Mann, Sofia Coppola, Casey Affleck, Kelly Reichardt, Errol Morris, Rithy Panh, Martin Arnold, Christopher Nolan, Lars von Trier, Olivier Assayas, Douglas Sirk, Spike Lee, Joel and Ethan Coen, David Cronenberg, Steven Spielberg, Robert Zemeckis, Tim Burton, and Charlie Kaufman. His articles have appeared in journals such as *Afterimage*, *Conversations*, *Epoché*, *Estetica*, *Liminalities*, *Post Script*, *Transactions*, *Film and Philosophy*, *The Senses and Society*,

The Midwest Quarterly, *Journalism, Media and Cultural Studies*, *The Journal of Aesthetic Education*, and *The Journal of Aesthetics and Art Criticism*. As a documentary filmmaker, he produced and edited six features in *The Intellectual Portrait Series*, directed *Brunello Cucinelli: A New Philosophy of Clothes*, and codirected *New York Photographer: Jill Freedman in the City*. He studied in the Rhetoric department at Berkeley, conducted research as Harvard's Sinclair Kennedy Traveling Fellow in the United Kingdom, and participated in an NEH Institute, a workshop with Abbas Kiarostami, Werner Herzog's Rogue Film School, and the School of Criticism and Theory at Cornell. He has taught philosophy and cinema and held visiting research or teaching positions at Binghamton, Cornell, Cortland, Harvard, Ithaca College, the School of Visual Arts, and Vanderbilt. www.DavidLaRocca.org, DavidLaRocca@Post.Harvard.Edu.

INDEX

3 Women (1977)   193. *See also* Robert Altman
1917 (2019)   287
2001: A Space Odyssey (1968)   201–20. *See also* Stanley Kubrick
Acord, Lance   287
The Act of Killing (2012)   9, 221–34
Adam's Rib (1949)   149, 177, 193–4, 263, 272 n.24, 291, 314 n.74. *See also* George Cukor
Adaptation. (2002)   279. *See also* Charlie Kaufman
aesthetics, analytic   3
Agee, James   7
agency   51 n.8
   assumption of   97
   authorial   65–6
   diminished   309
   personal change and   168
   suspended   279
Ahmed, Sara   186
A. I. Artificial Intelligence (2001)   211. *See also* Steven Spielberg
Akerman, Chantal   9, 24, 63, 253–73, 283, 292, 294
Alaouié, Borhane   9, 24, 235–50
Alighieri, Dante   169
Allen, Woody   284
All I Desire (1953)   33. *See also* Douglas Sirk
All That Heaven Allows (1955)   9, 22, 30 n.79, 33–56, 87 n.33. *See also* Douglas Sirk
Also sprach Zarathustra   210
Altman, Robert   9, 24, 191–8, 287

American
   pathology   33–56
   self-understanding   33–56
   Transcendentalism   8, 17–18, 22, 223
Anderson, Wes   284
Anglo-analytic philosophy   3, 8, 14, 93
Antonioni, Michelangelo   88 n.38, 205–6
Arcadia   121
Aristophanes   110 n.30
Aristotle   97, 151
Arnold, Matthew   61–2
Arthur, Jean   95, 103
artificial
   color   35
   dialogue   124
   intelligence   24
   sound   279
   world   37
Augustine   245
Austen, Jane   163–4
Austin, J. L.   1, 3, 12, 94, 99, 183, 191, 291, 314 n.74
autobiography   18
   film and   xv, 192, 256
   Little Did I Know and   xvi, 93–111, 184
   philosophical   96–7, 182–3, 185
avant-garde cinema   5–6, 19, 51 n.6, 193, 209, 255, 272 n.23, 294–6, 314 n.74
The Awful Truth (1937)   135, 178, 188 n.12, 291, 295. *See also* Leo McCarey
awkwardness
   of dying   103–4, 106, 111 n.45

embodied   139
  of philosophy   106
  sex and   218
  television and   78–9
Ayer, A. J.   180

Babel, Isaac   212
Bachelard, Gaston   117–18
Badlands (1973)   282, 285–6. *See also* Terrence Malick
Balzac, Honoré de   36
Barker, Jennifer   186
Barry Lyndon (1975)   34, 201–20. *See also* Stanley Kubrick
Barthelmess, Richard   95
Bartleby, the Scrivener   277
Baudelaire, Charles   118, 121
Baudrillard, Jean   73, 76, 81
Baumbach, Noah   274–5, 284
Bazin, André   7, 74, 113, 126 n.21, 204
Bearn, Gordon C. F.   15
Beat culture   194–5
Beckett, Samuel   207
Beckwith, Sarah   23, 245
Before Midnight (2013)   276, 295, 299
Beirut: The Encounter (1981)   9, 24, 235–50
Belle, Kathryn   186
Benjamin, Walter   270 n.6
Bergman, Ingmar   108 n.14, 196, 205–6, 255
Bergman, Ingrid   178–9
Bicycle Thieves (1948)   71
birth
  accident of   99
  achieving one's own   97
  awaiting   108 n.13
  as first trauma   68
  life after   108 n.14
  and rebirth   58, 98, 197, 207, 209, 212
birthright   15
Blackmur, R. P.   3
Blanchot, Maurice   103–4, 110 n.33
Blauvelt, Christopher   286–7
A Blonde in Love (1965)   303

Blonde Venus (1932)   10, 195. *See also* Josef von Sternberg
Brakhage, Stan   74, 294, 314 n.74
Brando, Marlon   82
Braudy, Leo   12, 27 n.20, 75
Brea, José Luis   73
Breathless (1960)   282. *See also* Jean-Luc Godard
Brecht, Bertolt   50 n.3, 76–7, 80–1
Bresson, Robert   204, 289, 300, 302–3
Bringing Up Baby (1938)   177. *See also* Howard Hawks
Brooks, Peter   36, 52 n.16
Budd, Harold   287
Burke, Kenneth   3
Burnham, Dave   294
Butler, Rex   6, 233 n.11

Cahiers du cinéma   xiii, 34, 51 n.9, 113–14, 116, 126 n.21
Caliban   98
Capra, Frank   2, 10, 15, 132, 176, 179, 237, 281. *See also It Happened One Night* and *Mr. Deed's Goes to Town*
La Captive (2000)   24, 253–73, 283. *See also* Chantal Akerman
Carney, Ray   194–5
Carroll, Noël   3, 293, 309
Carver, Raymond   193
Cassavetes, John   9, 24, 191–8
Cavarero, Adriana   180–1
Cavell, Stanley. *See also* autobiography; comedy of remarriage; melodrama of the unknown woman; memory; uneventfulness; voice
  acknowledgment   25, 59, 66–7, 115, 124, 131–47, 185, 193, 197, 201–20, 237, 240–1, 245, 277–9, 299
  "The Advent of Videos"   75–6
  autobiography and the demonstration of   96–7
  avoidance   2, 48, 182, 201–20, 226, 265, 271 n.20

INDEX

"The Avoidance of Love"   197, 253
   on Beckett's *Endgame*   207
   at Berkeley   108 n.13
The Claim of Reason   xiii, 13, 67–8, 93–4, 99, 107 n.10, 114, 120, 125 n.2, 176, 236, 239, 297–8, 304–5
death, achieving   97–8, 102, 106, 109 n.29
disorientation, human and philosophical   104–5
experimental filmmaking   2, 5–6, 19, 22, 72–90, 253–73, 274–318 (*see also* experimental film)
"The Fact of Television"   72–90
feminism   20, 175–90, 253–73, 274–318
"The Future of Possibility"   221–34
at Harvard   xii, 9, 109 n.26, 198 n.5, 256, 294
human drive to deny the human   104, 107
importance, idea of   xii–xvi
inheriting Emerson   62, 93, 107 n.11
Little Did I Know   xiii, xv, 21–3, 93–111, 184
method of   xii, 7
Must We Mean What We Say?   9, 21, 176, 191
philosophy, his notion of   4–5
Philosophy the Day after Tomorrow   19, 67, 180
A Pitch of Philosophy   179, 182–3
as photographic realist   74–5, 86 n.16
reception in France   xiii, 125 n.2
representativeness   24, 96, 105–6, 184
on seriousness   1–30
at UCLA   108 n.15
understanding, horror of   104–5
violence in the work of   235–5
voice of   6, 14, 76, 94, 97, 99, 108 n.20, 176
"What Is the Scandal of Skepticism?"   67

Certain Women (2016)   277, 282–3, 286, 287, 289, 295–6, 298–9.
   See also Kelly Reichardt
CGI (computer-generated imagery)   7, 303
Chabrol, Claude   14
Chaplin, Charlie   1, 204, 294, 300–1, 304
Chaplin, Geraldine   196
Chinatown (1974)   217
Chinese (Confucian) ritual theory and practice   148–71
La Chinoise (1967)   205. *See also* Jean-Luc Godard
Christianity   47, 113, 201, 214
Christ-like   198
cinema. *See also* avant-garde cinema; documentary films; experimental film; film; genre; home movies; metacinematic; slow cinema; transcendental cinema
   1930s and 40s   xiii, 2, 5–6, 9, 10, 25, 131, 149, 192, 263, 275, 281, 304
   local   263, 272 n.26, 273 n.33
Citizen Kane (1941)   206. *See also* Orson Welles
Clarke, Arthur C.   209, 212
Clément, Catherine   180
A Clockwork Orange (1971)   201–20, 219 n.12. *See also* Stanley Kubrick
Coen brothers   25, 215, 274–5, 284
Cohen, Marshall   12, 18, 27 n.20, 75
Coleridge, Samuel Taylor   238
Come Back to the 5 & Dime, Jimmy Dean, Jimmy Dean (1982)   193. *See also* Robert Altman
comedy of remarriage   5, 10, 17, 25, 58–9, 61, 131–47, 148–71, 177, 191–2, 203–4, 216, 269, 272 n.24, 274–5, 280, 289, 301–2. *See also* gender; genre; melodrama of the unknown woman
Confucius   152–4, 161–2, 168, 170 n.7

INDEX

Congo, Anwar   222, 224, 226–8, 230–1
Constable, Catherine   178
contemplative cinema   6, 274–318
conversation   58–9, 61, 176–7, 182–4, 196, 203–4, 235, 243–7, 256, 264–6, 284, 286, 288–90, 292–3, 295, 301. *See also* comedy of remarriage; expressiveness; John Milton; moral perfectionism; ritual theory and practice; speech
   alternatives to   23, 25, 148–71, 274–318
   bickering   155, 176–8, 184, 291
   breakdown of   283, 291, 299
   classroom   26, 73
   denial of   186, 256, 276
   moral perfectionism and   272 n.29
   negation of   280
   romantic   24, 304
   skepticism and   203–4
Cooper, Gary   56 n.43
Cooper, Sarah   60, 62, 64
Coppola, Francis Ford   295
Coppola, Sofia   292
Critical Mass (1971)   296
Cukor, George   2, 19, 61, 132, 149, 177–8, 185, 255, 263, 281, 291. *See also Adam's Rib*; *Gaslight*; *The Philadelphia Story*

Daedalus   116–17
Daney, Serge   241
Dardenne brothers   xiii, 5, 9, 22–3, 37, 57–71, 72, 84 n.1
Darwall, Stephen   137, 146
Dauber, Kenneth   30 n.65
Day, William   276
Day-Lewis, Daniel   294
deconstruction   16, 20, 81
deepfake   7
Deleuze, Gilles   73, 113, 241
Delmar, Viña   291
Delpy, Julie   299
Denby, David   296
deontology   23, 131–47
Dequenne, Émilie   63

Dern, Laura   283
Derrida, Jacques   15
Descartes, René   67, 97, 113, 179, 236–7, 239
Deschanel, Zooey   291
De Sica, Vittorio   71
Desplechin, Arnaud   xiii, 5, 9, 22–3, 72, 84 n.1, 112–28
Diaries 1971–1976 (1982)   192
Diary of a Country Priest (1950)   303. *See also* Robert Bresson
Dickens, Charles   12, 36
Diderot   47, 56 n.43
Divine Comedy   169
documentary films   24, 221–34, 264, 300, 312 n.30. *See also* cinema; film
A Doll House   150
Domenach, Élise   23, 84 n.1, 120–1, 125 n.2, 126 n.13, 127 n.25
Dreiser, Theodore   50
Dreyer, Carl Theodor   88 n.38, 300, 302
Dr. Strangelove or: How I Learned to Stop Worrying and Love the Bomb (1964)   201–20. *See also* Stanley Kubrick
Dunne, Irene   177, 196, 295. *See also The Awful Truth*

Eddo-Lodge, Reni   185
Eisenberg, Jesse   283, 286, 290, 303
Eisenhower era   33–56. *See also* cinema, 1930s and 40s; Kennedy era
Eisenstein, Sergei   210
Eliot, T. S.   3, 188
Elsaesser, Thomas   9
Emerson, Ralph Waldo   1, 7–8, 10–13, 16–17, 21–2, 24, 28 n.27, 47, 51 n.8, 58–9, 69, 71, 93, 97, 99, 104–5, 107 n.11, 110 n.42, 192, 194–5, 223, 254, 264–5, 301, 304. *See also* moral perfectionism
   aversive thinking   232, 278
   demand for thinking   179

feminist concerns with 188 n.2
Heidegger, Martin and 47,
   51 n.8, 236
"History" 110
Hollywood and 194
inheriting his thinking 93
marriage of Hellenic and
   Hebrew 62
Nietzsche, Friedrich
   and 47, 228–9
representativeness 24, 96,
   105–6, 184
secret melancholy 228, 232, 300
"Self-Reliance" 34, 66, 97, 107
Emersonian moral perfectionism. *See*
   moral perfectionism
Empson, William 3
Enchiridion 277
Eno, Brian 288
Enzensberger, Hans Magnus 76–7, 81
Epictetus 277
Epstein, Jean 267, 273 n.33
eudaimonia 151
exemplariness
   cinematic 26, 110 n.41, 281,
      300–1, 305
   human 105–6, 266
experimental
   film 2, 5–6, 19, 22, 72–90,
      253–73, 274–318
   realism 274–318. *See also*
      cinema; film
expressiveness 37, 291, 293,
   296–301, 306. *See also*
   inexpressiveness
Eyes Wide Shut (1999) 201–20, 276.
   See also Stanley Kubrick

Faces (1968) 192. *See also* John
   Cassavetes
Fanning, Dakota 283, 286, 290, 303
Farber, Mannie 28 n.28
Fassbinder, Rainer Werner 302
Faulkner, William 193
Fay, Jennifer 3, 7, 23
Felman, Shoshana 276
female experience 33–56, 175–90,
   191–8, 253–73, 274–318

feminism 20, 175–90, 253–73,
   274–318
Fessenden, Larry 282, 312 n.30
Fichte, J. G. 137
Fiennes, Sophie 222, 234 n.26
film. *See also* cinema; genre; pedagogy
   of film; photography
   affinity to philosophy xv
   avant-garde 5–6, 19, 51 n.6, 193,
      209, 255, 272 n.23, 294–6,
      314 n.74
   cinéma vérité 194–5
   contemplative 274–318
   criticism and gender 175–90
   genre (*see* genre)
   medium xiv, 1, 2, 4, 21–2, 75, 77–9,
      137, 155, 191, 263, 278, 284,
      287–8, 292–4, 300–1, 308–10
   philosophical study of 1–30
   photographic nature of 4,
      113, 120
   silent 36, 83, 291–4
   status of 1–30
   video and 72–90, 86 n.23,
      88 n.38, 89 n.58
Film Portrait (1971) 192
Film Theory and Criticism 5 n.20, 75
First Cow (2019) 274–318. *See also*
   Kelly Reichardt
First Reformed (2017) 300. *See also*
   Paul Schrader
Fisher, Mark 73
Flaherty, Robert 88 n.38
*The Flavor of Green Tea Over
   Rice* (1952) 194. *See also*
   Yasujirô Ozu
Flusser, Vilém 73
Fog of War (2003) 222. *See also*
   Errol Morris
Ford, John 51 n.7, 206,
   220 n.18, 284
Forman, Miloš 303
Frampton, Hollis 296
Frangie, Samir 243
Frenzy (1972) 204, 219 n.5. *See also*
   Alfred Hitchcock
Freud, Sigmund 8, 13, 20, 97, 106,
   201, 213, 261

Freudian
  family romance 106
  unconscious 224
Fried, Michael 56 n.43
Friedrich, Su 192
friendship 37, 49, 131–2, 146, 158, 178. *See also* marriage; parentage
Früchtl, Josef 113, 115
Full Metal Jacket (1987) 201–20. *See also* Stanley Kubrick
Furthman, Jules 94, 103, 109 n.22
Fusco, Katherine 285, 312 n.37

Galaxy Quest (1999) 9, 23, 148–71
GAN (generative adversarial network) 7
Gardner, Robert 294
Gaslight (1944) 19, 178–9, 181, 193–4, 255, 257–9, 262, 271 n.19, 282–3. *See also* George Cukor; female experience; feminism; gender; melodrama of the unknown woman; speech; voice
Gedankenschrift 28 n.4
Geertz, Clifford 234 n.25
gender 33–56, 186, 297–9, 312 n.37
  film criticism and 175–90
  roles 37, 44, 49, 192
  skepticism and 256, 260–1, 269
Genesis 149, 210
genre 17. *See also* comedy of remarriage; film medium; gender; melodrama of the unknown woman
  as-cycle 5, 25, 87 n.27, 278–9, 282, 285, 311 n.21
  as-medium 87 n.27, 278
  meta-generic nature of 52 n.13
Gerwig, Greta 274, 284
Girard, René 46, 55 n.39
Glitre, Kathrina 178
Godard, Jean-Luc 14, 74, 124, 196, 205, 255, 282
Goodman, Paul 3
Gordon, Ruth 291
Gorfinkel, Elena 279, 307

Götterdämmerung 207–8
Grace, Jeff 313 n.42
Grant, Cary 2, 12, 61, 93–111, 149, 177, 282, 295
Greek myth 128 n.35
Greek philosophy (ancient) 17, 123–4, 265, 307
green world (Shakespearean) 58–9, 274
Greif, Mark 18
Gross-Loh, Christine 148–71
Guzzetti, Alfred 294

Hall, E. Dawn 285, 312 n.37
Halliday, Jon 34, 51 n.6
Hammer, Espen 271 n.16
Haneke, Michael 15, 186
Hanhardt, John 74–5, 80–1, 86 n.16
Hartman, Jesse 285–6
Harvard University. *See also* Stanley Cavell at Harvard
  Department of Philosophy xii, 2, 9, 109 n.26, 198 n.5
  Visual and Environmental Studies 256, 294
Hausner, Jessica 186
Hawks, Howard 10, 22, 51 n.7, 93–111, 146 n.2, 177, 275, 281, 284. *See also Bringing Up Baby*; *His Girl Friday*; *Only Angels Have Wings*; *To Have and Have Not*
Haworth, Rita 95
Haynes, Todd 302
Hays Code (MPAA) 10, 281
Hebrew Bible / Old Testament 149, 169, 209–10
Hecht, Ben 291
Hegel, G. W. F. 35–6, 49, 51 n.8, 52 n.18, 55 n.39, 56 nn.42–3, 137
  Sirk, Douglas and 51 n.8
Heidegger, Martin 47, 51 n.8, 186, 236–8, 270 n.6, 314 n.74
Hemingway, Ernest 103, 109 n.22
Hepburn, Katharine 61, 149, 275
Hesiod 162, 170 n.25
Hill, Jerome 192

His Girl Friday (1940)   10, 146 n.2, 275, 281–2, 284, 291, 304. *See also* Howard Hawks
Hitchcock, Alfred   50, 52 n.19, 59, 62–4, 69, 71, 203–4, 206, 215, 217, 219 n.5, 219 n.11, 258
home movies   257, 263–4, 272 n.24. *See also* metacinematic
Howard, David   155
Hudson, Rock   33–56
The Hudsucker Proxy (1994)   274–5. *See also* Coen brothers
Hume, David   270 n.6

Ibsen, Henrik   150, 282
IMAX   7
Imitation of Life (1959)   33, 38, 51 n.10, 53 n.23, 54 n.28. *See also* Douglas Sirk
inexpressiveness   xv, 276, 296–301. *See also* expressiveness
intelligibility (and unintelligibility)   24, 215, 253–73, 274–318
Into Great Silence (2005)   296
Intolerable Cruelty (2003)   25, 275. *See also* Coen brothers
irony   6, 194, 206, 213, 218, 301
   sadistic   280
   Sirkian   33–56
Isle of the Dead   254
It Happened One Night (1934)   10, 12–13, 132, 135–6, 139, 141, 176, 193, 237. *See also* Howard Hawks

Jacobs, Ken   306
James, Henry   11, 36, 282
The James Dean Story (1957)   192. *See also* Robert Altman
Jarmusch, Jim   282, 292
Jeanne Dielman, 23, quai du Commerce, *1080 Bruxelles*   270 n.6. *See also* Chantal Akerman
Johnny Guitar (1954)   34. *See also* Nicholas Ray
Jonze, Spike   279

Journey to Italy (1954)   276, 295
justice   157, 221–34, 266

Kael, Pauline   28 n.28
Kafka, Franz   205, 219 n.7
Kanin, Garson   291
Kansas City (1996)   193. *See also* Robert Altman
Kant, Immanuel   12–13, 17, 23, 131–47, 152, 224–5, 230, 272 n.29, 278
Kaufman, Charlie   279, 306, 317 n.124
Kazan, Elia   50, 74, 82
Keane, Marian   23, 25, 93–4
Keaton, Buster   1, 294, 300, 304
Kennedy era   193. *See also* cinema, 1930s and 40s; Eisenhower era
Khalaf, Samir   243
Khoury, Elias   241
The Kid with a Bike (2011)   57–71. *See also* Dardenne brothers
Kierkegaard, Søren   47, 245
The Killing of a Chinese Bookie (1976)   192. *See also* John Cassavetes
Klevan, Andrew   6–7, 19–20, 274, 302–3, 307, 316 n.101, 316 nn.108–9
Kluge, Alexander   73
Kolker, Robert   206
Kracauer, Siegfried   74
Krauss, Rosalind   23, 76–7, 86 n.23, 89 n.58
Kubrick, Stanley   9, 24, 34, 201–20, 276

The Lady Eve (1941)   56 n.41, 132, 136, 177. *See also* Preston Sturges
La La Land (2016)   287
Lanzmann, Claude   208
LaRocca, David   xii, 85 n.1, 110 n.30, 110 n.42, 272 n.24
Late Spring (1949)   303. *See also* Yasujirô Ozu
Laugier, Sandra   22–3, 30 n.78, 112–13, 125
Leacock, Richard   64

Leavis, F. R.   3, 27 n.10
Lederer, Charles   291
Leigh, Jennifer Jason   274–5
Letter from an Unknown Woman (1948)   181, 194, 197, 271 n.19, 281–2. *See also* Max Ophüls; voice
Lévinas, Emmanuel   22, 57–71, 256
Linklater, Richard   276, 295, 299
Lisbon Story (1994)   295
listening   25, 107 n.5, 175–90, 274–318. *See also* silent film; sound; speech; voice
literary criticism   3, 11, 27 n.10. *See also* ordinary language criticism
Locke, John   245
Lolita (1962)   203, 206–7, 214, 216. *See also* Stanley Kubrick
The Long Goodbye (1973)   193. *See also* Robert Altman
Lorna's Silence (2008)   37, 57–71. *See also* Dardenne brothers
Love Streams (1984)   192. *See also* John Cassavetes
Luther, Martin   245

McCabe and Mrs. Miller (1971)   192–3. *See also* Robert Altman
McCarey, Leo   177, 281, 291. *See also The Awful Truth*
MacDonald, Scott   294, 314 n.71
McElwee, Ross   192, 294
Mackie, Patrick   278
McNamara, Robert   221–34
Magaro, John   290, 304, 306
Mai, Joseph   22, 65–6, 71 n.2
Makavejev, Dušan   108 n.14, 255
Malick, Terrence   5, 27 n.22, 72, 84 n.1, 285–7, 292, 294, 313 n.43, 314 n.74
Manet, Édouard   12
Manovich, Lev   79, 88 n.48
The Man Who Shot Liberty Valance (1962)   220 n.18. *See also* John Ford
Margulies, Ivone   271 n.9
Marker, Chris   73–4, 294. *See also* experimental film

marriage   44, 47–8, 53 n.23, 55 n.35, 61–2, 95, 110 n.30, 131–47, 148–71, 177–8, 184–5, 195–6, 238, 240, 264, 276, 285. *See also* comedy of remarriage; conversation; gender; friendship; parentage
  as metaphor   185
  Milton, John and   149, 176
  myth of modern   248–9
  negation of   280
  rebirth of   58–9
M.A.S.H. (1970)   192. *See also* Robert Altman
Mast, Gerald   75, 100, 107
Matthau, Walter   131–47
May, Elaine   9, 23, 131–47
Mayer, Sophie   186
Meek's Cutoff (2010)   282–4, 286–9, 295–300, 305, 312 n.22, 312 n.37, 313 n.42, 316 n.109. *See also* Kelly Reichardt
Mekas, Jonas   192
melancholy   228–30, 232, 300
melodrama   33–56, 175–90, 191–8, 274–318. *See also* genre
melodrama of the unknown woman   xii, 2, 4–5, 10, 22–3, 25–6, 41, 54 n.29, 177–9, 181, 187, 191–2, 194–6, 255, 261, 269–71, 274, 280–3, 289, 298, 301–2, 305. *See also* comedy of remarriage; female experience; feminism; gender; genre; melodrama; voice
Meloy, Maile   277
memory   22, 93–111, 279
  movies and   xiii, xv, 22, 114
  skepticism and   120
metacinematic. *See also* cinema; film; home movies
  comedy   23
  critique   281
  genre and the   52 n.13
  melodrama   35
  metacognition   309
  mise-en-abyme   306
Mickey Mouse   214

Mill, John Stuart   178, 282
Milton, John   149, 176
Minnelli, Vincente   37
Minnie and Moskowitz (1971)   192. See also John Cassavetes
Mistress America (2015)   274. See also Noah Baumbach
Mitchell, Thomas   95
Mizoguchi, Kenji   204, 255, 287
Modleski, Tania   23, 175–90, 188 n.2
Monolito (2018)   57–71. See also Bruno Varela
Mooney, Edward   114–15
morality, achieving   93–111
moral perfectionism (Emersonian)   1, 15, 132, 253–4, 256, 260, 262, 264–70, 272, 304. See also Ralph Waldo Emerson
  elitism of   297, 308
  reviewing and   254, 265–8
  voice and   114–15
Moran, Richard   9, 87 n.36, 295
Morgan, Daniel   7, 50 n.1, 86 n.16, 86 n.26
Morin, Edgar   267, 273 n.33
Morris, Errol   9, 24, 221–34
Morris, Wesley   30 n.68
mortality   60, 67, 98–102, 105–6, 108 n.14
  defiance of   96, 100–1, 109 n.23, 109 n.29
Mr. Deed's Goes to Town (1936)   2, 15. See also Frank Capra
Mulhall, Stephen   6, 27 n.19, 147 n.8, 311 n.21
Mulvey, Laura   52 n.14
My Dinner with Andre (1981)   292

Nagel, Thomas   114
Nashville (1975)   9, 24, 191–8. See also Robert Altman
Nauman, Bruce   86 n.23
Nazis   208
A New Leaf (1971)   9, 23, 131–47. See also Elaine May
Nichols, Bill   221–2, 231, 234 n.26
Nicholson, Jack   214–15

Nietzsche, Friedrich   33, 35, 47, 52 n.15, 210–11, 228–9, 282, 316 n.105
Night Moves (2013)   280, 282–3, 285–9, 295, 298–9, 303, 312 n.30, 312 n.35, 313 n.42, 317 n.111. See also Kelly Reichardt
nihilism   206–8, 212–14, 219 n.12
Nolan, Christopher   209, 307
Nouvelle Vague   13–14, 126 n.21
Now, Voyager (1942)   20, 175, 181, 193–4, 271 n.19, 282. See also Irving Rapper
Nozick, Robert   2
Nussbaum, Martha   186
Nyoni, Rungano   186

O Brother, Where Art Thou? (2000)   125. See also Coen brothers
Odysseus   98, 211
Odyssey   123
Oedipus   41–2, 54 n.31, 110 n.38
Of Gods and Men (2010)   296
Old Acquaintance (1943)   185
Oldham, Will   282–4, 287, 290
Old Joy (2006)   282–4, 287, 290, 295, 298–300, 312 nn.36–7, 316 n.109. See also Kelly Reichardt
O'Neill, Eugene   36
Only Angels Have Wings (1939)   9, 22, 85 n.12, 93–111. See also Howard Hawks
ontology of film   xiv, 1, 13, 21, 64, 256, 263–4, 272 n.23, 306
Opening Night (1977)   192. See also John Cassavetes
opera   7–8, 17, 36, 179–81, 194, 291. See also female experience; feminism; gender; melodrama of the unknown woman; passionate utterance; speech; voice
Ophüls, Max   37, 50, 181, 281. See also *Letter from an Unknown Woman*
Oppenheimer, Joshua   9, 24, 221–34

Ordet (1955)   300. *See also* Carl Theodor Dreyer
ordinary, repudiation of the   104–5
ordinary language criticism   5, 16, 30 n.65
ordinary language philosophy   5, 8, 11, 16, 25, 30 n.65, 183, 291, 293
Ozu, Yasujirô   194, 287, 302–3

Panofsky, Erwin   74
parentage   99, 161, 165, 194, 213. *See also* friendship; marriage
Parisot, Dean   23, 148–71
Pasolini, Pier Paolo   73
passionate utterance   175–90
Paths of Glory (1957)   205–7. *See also* Stanley Kubrick
pedagogy of film   xiv, 271 n.8, 282, 307
Penn, Arthur   312 n.35
Pennebaker, D. A.   64
perfectionism. *See* moral perfectionism
Perkins, V. F.   7
The Pervert's Guide to Ideology (2012)   222. *See also* Slavoj Žižek
The Philadelphia Story (1940)   2, 12–13, 19, 61, 132, 149, 151, 177, 193. *See also* George Cukor
Philosophical Investigations   14–15, 52 n.15, 235–6. *See also* Ludwig Wittgenstein
  melodrama in   52 n.15
Phoenix, Joaquin   294
photography   4, 74–5, 80, 86 n.16, 87 n.36, 89 n.58, 89 n.62, 113–14, 120, 216, 231, 309. *See also* film medium
Pickpocket (1959)   300. *See also* Paul Schrader; Robert Bresson; transcendental cinema
Pierrot le fou (1965)   124. *See also* Jean-Luc Godard
Pincus, Ed   192
Pippin, Robert B.   3–4, 6, 21–5
Pitt, Suzanne   74

A Place in the Sun (1951)   50. *See also* George Stevens
Plato   13, 97, 110 n.30, 113, 120, 290–1, 305–6
  Apology   123
  Republic   236, 266
  Symposium   110
The Portrait of a Lady   36
A Prairie Home Companion (2006)   193. *See also* Robert Altman
praise   8, 15, 48, 60, 126 n.10, 162, 190 n.46
  as critical practice   124–5
  Desplechin, Arnaud and   112–28
pre-Socratics (Ionian)   225
Pride and Prejudice   163–4
The Prisoner (*La Prisonnière*)   253–73. *See also* Chantal Akerman; Marcel Proust
The Promise (1996)   57–71. *See also* Dardenne brothers
Prospero   98
Proust, Marcel   36, 50, 253, 255, 259, 270
Psycho (1960)   219 n.11. *See also* Alfred Hitchcock
psychoanalysis   18, 215, 256
Puett, Michael   148–71
Putnam, Hilary   2, 8, 62, 65

Quine, Willard Van Orman Quine   2

Rachmaninoff, Sergei   254
Rapper, Irving   175, 281. *See also Now, Voyager*
Rawls, John   2
Ray, Nicholas   34, 50, 56 n.42, 302
Ray, Satyajit   287
Raymond, Jonathan   277, 301
Red Cavalry   212
Reichardt, Kelly   9, 24, 274–318. *See also* conversation; experimental film; inexpressiveness; slow cinema; sound; speech; transcendental cinema; unintelligibility
  at Bard College   302

experimental realism of 274–318
  at Harvard 310 n.3
  Klevan, Andrew and 274, 302–3, 307, 316 n.109
  at the University of Oxford 316 n.109
Renoir, Jean 62, 88 n.38, 204, 206
Resnais, Alain 14
reviewing 20, 24, 253–4, 256–7, 262, 264, 272. *See also* self-viewing
  moral perfectionism and 254, 265–8
Rich and Famous (1981) 185–7. *See also* George Cukor
Richards, I. A. 3
ritual theory and practice 148–71
River of Grass (1994) 282, 285–6, 297, 312 n.30. *See also* Kelly Reichardt
Rivette, Jacques 14
Rodowick, D. N. 6, 27 n.20, 52 n.12, 79–80, 82, 88 n.48
Roeg, Nicolas 287
Rohmer, Éric 14, 255, 303
Romanticism 17–18. *See also* American Transcendentalism
Rosetta (1999) 57–71. *See also* Dardenne brothers
Rossellini, Roberto 276
Rothman, William 6, 17, 22, 25, 27 n.20, 78–9, 85 n.8, 93–4, 107, 109 n.22, 204, 219 n.5, 271 n.10
Rousseau, Jean-Jacques 47, 137, 143, 245
  Kubrick, Stanley as anti- 210
Ruiz, Raúl 88 n.38
Rumsfeld, Donald 221–34
Russell, Lee 107 n.7
Russell, Rosalind 275
Russian Ark (2002) 287

Sarris, Andrew 28 n.28, 157
Sarsgaard, Peter 283, 286, 290, 303
Sartre, Jean-Paul 47–8
Saturday Night Live 291
Savides, Harris 287

The Scarlet Empress (1934) 34. *See also* Josef von Sternberg
Scheman, Naomi 23, 183–5, 188
Schmerheim, Philipp 113–14, 270 n.3
Schrader, Paul 289, 300, 303, 305. *See also* transcendental cinema
Scott, A. O. 313 n.44, 317 n.121
The Searchers (1956) 284. *See also* John Ford
self, unattained but attainable 58–9, 67, 69–70, 105
self-viewing 262, 264–5, 267. *See also* reviewing
sentiment 109 n.24
  repudiation of 100
  vocabulary of 234 n.25
sentimentality 169
  Hollywood and 206
  impatience with 54 n.32
A Serious Man (2009) 215. *See also* Coen brothers
Seymour, Nicole 285, 312 n.37
Shadow of a Doubt (1943) 69. *See also* Alfred Hitchcock
Shadows (1958) 192. *See also* John Cassavetes
Shakespeare, William 8, 12–13, 58, 67–8, 176–7, 245, 298. *See also* green world
  Hamlet 278
  King Lear 176, 197, 271 n.16, 271 n.20, 278, 297–8
  melodrama and 52 n.17, 298
  A Midsummer Night's Dream 218
  Othello 68, 176, 239–41, 271 n.16, 278, 298
  Sirk, Douglas on 52 n.17
  The Taming of the Shrew 177
  The Tempest 98
  The Winter's Tale 117–18, 238–9
Shakespearean tragedy 67–8, 206, 238–9, 261, 269, 278, 283, 298
Shambu, Girish 186
Shanghai Express (1932) 58. *See also* Josef von Sternberg
The Shining (1980) 201–20, 219 n.7, 219 n.11. *See also* Stanley Kubrick

Shoah (1985) 208
Short Cuts (1993) 193. *See also* Robert Altman
Show Boat (1936) 196
Shuster, Martin 77
silent film 36, 83, 291–4. *See also* listening; opera; sound; speech; voice
singing woman, the 177–81, 196–7, 289, 291. *See also* female experience; feminism; gender; listening; opera; passionate utterance; silent film; sound; speech; voice
  homosexuality and 181
Sinnerbrink, Robert 113
Sirk, Douglas 21–2, 30 n.79, 33–56, 87 n.33, 302
  sentimentality, impatience with 54 n.32
Sitney, P. Adams 294
skepticism 15, 18, 24, 47, 94, 104, 112–13, 120, 176, 184, 203, 207, 236, 277, 298
  Cartesian 113, 179
  Coleridge and 238
  conversation and 203–4
  Desplechin, Arnaud and 112–28
  film and 15, 201
  gender and 151, 164–5, 256, 260–1, 269
  haunting one's life 101, 108 n.14
  inexpressiveness and 296
  knowledge of others 245, 277, 298
  living our 278
  Luc Dardenne and 58, 60, 67
  memory and 120
  moral perfectionism and 24
  Shakespeare and 68
  viewing and 253–73
slow cinema 274–318, 312 n.22, 312 n.35, 313 nn.43–5. *See also* contemplative cinema; experimental film; Kelly Reichardt; transcendental cinema
Socrates 123. *See also* Plato

The Son (*Le fils*, 2002) 57–71. *See also* Dardenne brothers
Sontag, Susan 13
sound. *See also* conversation; listening; silent film; speech; voice
  in film 4, 6–7, 25, 223–4, 263, 274–318
  gender and 175–90
  of philosophy 176, 279
The Sound and the Fury 193
Spartacus (1960) 208. *See also* Stanley Kubrick
speech 11, 25, 241, 282, 284–5, 289, 293–4, 299, 301, 314 n.74. *See also* conversation; listening; passionate utterance; sound; voice
  human experience and 290, 292, 295, 304
  pace of 291
  Plato on 236
  song and 181
  sound of 296
  speechless and 276–7, 280, 286, 309
  unsayable and 288, 293–4
Spelman, Elizabeth V. 185
Spielberg, Steven 211, 311 n.21
Spillane, Mickey 212
Stack, Robert 51 n.10
Standish, Paul 190 n.45
Stanwyck, Barbara 56 n.4, 136, 298–9. *See also Stella Dallas*
stars (movie) 22, 39, 94, 106–7, 110, 287
  as orienting 104–7
Steiner, George 8
Stella Dallas (1937) 181–3, 189 n.32, 193–4, 271 n.19, 282, 298–9. *See also* King Vidor
Stephens, Bret 187
Sternberg, Josef von 10, 34, 195
Stevens, George 37, 50, 238
Stevens, Kyle 292–3, 295, 312 n.25
Stevenson, Robert Louis 120
Stewart, James 59, 258
Stewart, Kristen 283, 290
Steyerl, Hito 73

Stoner 277
Strauss, Richard 210
Streamers (1983) 193. *See also* Robert Altman
Strike (1925) 210
Sturges, Preston 132, 177, 281. *See also The Lady Eve*
subjectivity 114, 179, 255, 261, 306
  female 182, 258
Sur l'affaire humaine (Luc Dardenne) 57–71. *See also* Dardenne brothers
surrealism 74, 114
  Kaufman, Charlie and 306
Sweet Movie (1974) 108 n.14. *See also* Dušan Makavejev
Swiftian satire 198

A Tale of Springtime (1990) 303. *See also* Éric Rohmer
Tarkovsky, Andrei 73–4
The Tarnished Angels (1957) 33, 51 n.10, 52 n.14, 54 n.28. *See also* Douglas Sirk
Taylor, Ella 277, 285
television xii, xv, 4–5, 16–17, 19, 22, 30 n.78, 72–90, 110 n.41, 214
  Altman, Robert and 192
  late-night 103
  public 73
  series 155–7, 159, 163, 166–7, 169
  Sirk, Douglas and 37, 40, 53 n.24
  Varela, Bruno and 72–90
That Cold Day in the Park (1969) 192. *See also* Robert Altman
There's Always Tomorrow (1955) 33. *See also* Douglas Sirk
Theseus 117
Thoreau, Henry David 1, 7, 22, 25, 28 n.27, 30 n.79, 58, 98, 106, 179–80, 195, 245, 278, 288, 291, 304, 306. *See also Walden*
  quiet desperation 39, 228–9, 300
  Sirk ,Douglas and 35, 39–43, 47, 51 n.11, 53 n.21, 53 n.23, 54 n.29, 55 n.37

Thoreauvian fantasy 40–1, 54 nn.28–9. *See also* Henry David Thoreau; *Walden*
Through a Glass Darkly (1961) 196. *See also* Ingmar Bergman
Tocqueville, Alexis de 47
To Have and Have Not (1944) 103. *See also* Howard Hawks
Tolstoy, Leo 245
tragedy. *See* Shakespearean tragedy
Trahair, Lisa 15, 23
Train Choir 301
transcendental cinema 285, 287, 289, 292–3, 300, 302–3, 305. *See also* cinema; Kelly Reichardt; Paul Schrader
Transcendentalism, American 8, 17–18, 22, 223. *See also* Henry David Thoreau; Ralph Waldo Emerson
Trilling, Lionel 56 n.43
Trois souvenirs de ma jeunesse (2015) 23, 112–28. *See also* Arnaud Desplechin
Truffaut, François 14, 34
Turner, Lana 51 n.10
Two Days, One Night (2014) 57–71. *See also* Dardenne brothers
Tyler, Parker 28 n.28

Ugetsu (1953) 287. *See also* Kenji Mizoguchi
Ulysses 116, 118
uneventful, the 15, 77–9, 82–3, 87 nn.36–7, 88 n.38, 306
unintelligibility (and intelligibility) 24, 215, 253–73, 274–318
Universal Studios 33
The Unknown Girl (2016) xiii, 37, 57–71. *See also* Dardenne brothers
The Unknown Known (2013) 9, 221–34. *See also* Errol Morris
utilitarianism 23, 131–47, 272 n.29

Varda, Agnès 14
Varela, Bruno 5, 9, 22–3, 72–90

Verdi, Giuseppe   12
Verfremdungseffekt   50 n.3, 293, 306.
    See also Bertolt Brecht
Vermeule, Blakey   292
Vertigo (1958)   51 n.8, 59, 203, 217,
    258. *See also* Alfred Hitchcock
Victoria (2015)   287
video   72–90. *See also* cinema; film
    medium; television
Vidor, King   181–2, 281. *See also*
    Stella Dallas
Vietnam War   193, 197, 203,
    212–13, 222
Vigo, Jean   88 n.38
Viva Zapata! (1952)   74, 82. *See also*
    Elia Kazan
voice   25, 115. *See also* conversation;
    female experience; feminism;
    gender; melodrama of the
    unknown woman; moral
    perfectionism; opera; passionate
    utterance; sound; speech
  female   23–4, 175–90, 191–8
  moral perfectionism and   114–15
  negation of   280

Wagner, Richard   207–8
Walden   30 n.79, 35, 42, 51 n.11,
    98, 291. See also Henry David
    Thoreau
Walkabout (1971)   287
Warren, Charles   6, 24, 63
Warren, Robert Penn   3
Warshow, Robert   7
Weekend (1967)   196. *See also* Jean-
    Luc Godard
Welles, Orson   204, 206

Wenders, Wim   295
Wendy and Lucy (2008)   274–318,
    316 n.109. *See also* Kelly
    Reichardt
Williams, Bernard   132
Williams, Michelle   283, 290,
    296, 304
Wittgenstein, Ludwig   1, 14–15,
    51 n.8, 52 n.15, 94, 104,
    120, 191–2, 235–7, 245,
    270 n.6, 277–8, 291, 314 n.74.
    *See also Philosophical
    Investigations*
Woman of the Year (1942)   238. *See
    also* George Stevens
A Woman Under the Influence
    (1974)   9, 24, 191–8. *See also*
    John Cassavetes
Wood, Helen   190 n.58
Wood, James   11
Wood, Robin   101, 107
Woolf, Virginia   11
The Writing of the Disaster   103–4,
    110 n.33
Written on the Wind (1956)   38, 49,
    51 n.10, 52 n.14, 54 n.28. *See
    also* Douglas Sirk
The Wrong Man (1956)   215. *See also*
    Alfred Hitchcock
Wyman, Jane   33–56. *See also*
    Douglas Sirk

Young Ahmed (2019)   66. *See also*
    Dardenne brothers

Žižek, Slavoj   24, 221–34
Zunshine, Lisa   292

www.ingramcontent.com/pod-product-compliance
Lightning Source LLC
Chambersburg PA
CBHW061705300426
44115CB00014B/2570